BEAUTY
UNLIMITED

BEAUTY
UNLIMITED

EDITED BY PEG ZEGLIN BRAND

FOREWORD BY CAROLYN KORSMEYER

INDIANA UNIVERSITY PRESS
BLOOMINGTON AND INDIANAPOLIS

Indiana University Press
601 North Morton Street
Bloomington, Indiana 47404-3797 USA

iupress.indiana.edu

Telephone orders   800-842-6796
Fax orders   812-855-7931

∞ The paper used in this publication meets the minimum
requirements of the American National Standard for Information
Sciences—Permanence of Paper for Printed Library Materials,
ANSI Z39.48-1992.

Manufactured in the United States of America

Library of Congress Cataloging-in-Publication Data

Beauty unlimited / edited by Peg Zeglin Brand ; foreword by
Carolyn Korsmeyer.
    p. cm.
  Includes index.
  ISBN 978-0-253-00642-4 (cl : alk. paper) — ISBN 978-0-253-
00649-3 (pb : alk. paper) — ISBN 978-0-253-00653-0 (eb) 1.
Beauty, Personal. 2. Human body—Social aspects. 3. Body
image. I. Brand, Peggy Zeglin.
  GT499.B43 2012
  306.4—dc23
                              2012023025

1 2 3 4 5 18 17 16 15 14 13

In memory of
my late husband,
best friend,
and fellow philosopher
who loved beauty
Myles Brand
(1942–2009)

I, too, find the flower beautiful in its outward appearance:
but a deeper beauty lies concealed within.

PIET MONDRIAN

CONTENTS

Foreword \ CAROLYN KORSMEYER xiii

Introduction \ 1

PART 1. REVISING THE CONCEPT OF BEAUTY: LAYING THE GROUNDWORK

1.
Arthur Danto and the Problem of Beauty \ NOËL CARROLL 29

2.
Savages, Wild Men, Monstrous Races: The Social Construction of Race in the Early Modern Era \ GREGORY VELAZCO Y TRIANOSKY 45

3.
Beauty's Relational Labor \ MONIQUE ROELOFS 72

4.
Queer Beauty: Winckelmann and Kant on the Vicissitudes of the Ideal \ WHITNEY DAVIS 96

5.
Worldwide Women \ ELEANOR HEARTNEY 126

PART 2. STANDARDS OF BEAUTY

6.
Jenny Saville Remakes the Female Nude: Feminist Reflections on the State of the Art \ DIANA TIETJENS MEYERS 137

7.
Indigenous Beauty \ PHOEBE M. FARRIS 162

8.
Is Medical Aesthetics Really Medical? \ MARY DEVEREAUX 175

9.
The Bronze Age Revisited: The Aesthetics of Sun Tanning \
JO ELLEN JACOBS 192

10.
¿Tienes Culo? How to Look at Vida Guerra \ KARINA L. CÉSPEDES-CORTES
AND PAUL C. TAYLOR 218

11.
Beauty between Disability and Gender: Frida Kahlo in Paper Dolls \
FEDWA MALTI-DOUGLAS 243

PART 3. THE BODY IN PERFORMANCE

12.
Beauty, Youth, and the Balinese *Legong* Dance \ STEPHEN DAVIES 259

13.
Bollywood and the Feminine: Hinduism and Images of Womanhood \
JANE DURAN 280

14.
Seductive Shift: A Review of *The Most Beautiful Woman in Gucha* \
VALERIE SULLIVAN FUCHS 293

15.
Feminist Art, Content, and Beauty \ KEITH LEHRER 297

16.
ORLAN Revisited: Disembodied Virtual Hybrid Beauty \
PEG ZEGLIN BRAND 306

PART 4. BEAUTY AND THE STATE

17.
Beauty Wars: The Struggle over Female Modesty in the Contemporary
Middle East and North Africa \
ALLEN DOUGLAS AND FEDWA MALTI-DOUGLAS 343

18.
Orientalism Inside/Out: The Art of Soody Sharifi \
CYNTHIA FREELAND 347

19.
Beauty and the State: Female Bodies as State Apparatus and Recent
Beauty Discourses in China \ EVA KIT WAH MAN 368

20.
Gendered Bodies in Contemporary Chinese Art \
MARY BITTNER WISEMAN 385

Contributors 407
Index 413

Foreword

CAROLYN KORSMEYER

The venerable problem of the One and the Many is nowhere more dramatic than with Beauty—that ultimate value, inescapable in aesthetics, contentious in art, capricious in fashion, and altogether debatable. Inviting yet resisting definition, beauty oscillates between particular and universal. It is a value applicable to objects and scenes in nature, to works of art, and to persons: this mountain pass, this song, this face. And yet what trait could a mountain share with a person? If both are beautiful, is the description univocal? Even within the realm of art, one is hard-pressed to figure out the common link between a beautiful symphony and a beautiful sculpture. Moreover, beauty is a contestable value within the artworld. Is all good art *pro tanto* beautiful? Or does beauty comprise a more limited range of artistic virtues, ceding equal standing to the grotesque, the sublime, the ugly, and the monstrous?

Plato offered a standard to stabilize the oscillation between individual beauties and the idea of beauty itself. Diotima's speech in the *Symposium* recommends that one begin by loving the beauty of a person, the individual beloved, moving from there to the beauty of all boys, then to that of all humans, and thence to the beauty of institutions and abstractions, and finally—almost—reaching Beauty itself, that Form that unites individual beauties by bestowing upon each a portion of its essence. Philosophers, following in the footsteps of Plato, have often focused on the last item in this sequence, hoping ambitiously to unify the many instances of beautiful things—objects, scenes, artworks—under a general concept. This endeavor traditionally has required that one leave behind the starting point of beauty: beautiful bodies incarnate. For only by ignoring the beauty of the human form can one escape the thrall of physical desire and enter the purer world of aesthetic pleasure. Or can one? It is the task of many of the essays in this volume to suggest that the pursuit of Beauty retains at least a trace of some originary eroticism.

To be sure, abstract, absolute beauty has sometimes been sought as a relief from physical and carnal preoccupations, as with Schopenhauer's sense that aesthetic experience is the sole occasion when the will is at rest; Santayana's observation that in beauty the soul cherishes its freedom from connection with the body; or even Iris Murdoch's claim that beauty is an occasion for "unselfing," for directing attention away from oneself to the world around. Few would argue that beauty can never perform this purifying function, although perhaps it has been pursued with disproportionate attention. It is general, universal beauty that has usually commanded the attention of philosophers, who tend to ignore the individual beauties that manifest it in imperfect and heterogeneous ways. Particularly neglected has been the human body, for beauties of the flesh provoke sensuous desires and their fulfillment, physical rather than aesthetic pleasures. And yet, as these essays make clear, the body is one of the most enduring and powerful aesthetic elements that we live with. What is more, since bodies are so frequently represented in visual art, attention to beauty in the flesh illuminates painted beauties (and their contraries) as well.

Attractions to and aversions from the human body command attention aesthetically, erotically, morally, and socially. Here, too, we find the question of common or diverse tastes manifest. How pancultural are criteria by which the human form is judged to be beautiful? Has nature itself, employing the implements of evolution, perhaps endowed our perceptual machinery with common aesthetic standards? If so, can the erotic tinge of physical beauty truly be transcended in the way that Plato willed, or are tastes molded by innate propensities to seek forms traceable to some remote impulse for sexual selection?

Alternatively, is it the case that tastes are so heavily influenced by social needs and norms that criteria for beautiful human bodies are linked to the structures of gender, social hierarchies, skin color, musculature, youth, and authority—all of which different cultures impose in strikingly variant ways? A social constructionist approach invites consideration of greater heterogeneity among physical beauties, but it is likely to be just as anchored to an erotic charge as evolution's putative common criteria. In either event, beauty wields power—insofar as the body is a site for social values, political changes, and the imposition of norms that implement these. While this approach does not necessarily signal the Many winning out over the One, it represents a radical shift of attention to the kinds of beautiful objects that possess the most immediately evident social and psychological force, and that also manifest obdurate differences among criteria for attractiveness.

In the last generation, aesthetic theorists have thoroughly questioned the notion that beauty can be purified from social influences that invade our standards of taste. In fact, it is more comfortable now to speak of beauties in the plural, without expectation that beautiful things are necessarily judged by the same gauge. Nor is it so common any longer to consider beauty and other aesthetic virtues innocent of political meaning, not only when it comes to the appearance of one's face and body but also when it comes to one's tastes in art, as Pierre Bourdieu famously insisted. The feminist influence on the revaluation of beauty has been particularly complex. On the one hand, there are challenges to restrictive models of beauty that pressure women in most cultures to mold and decorate their bodies in conformity with local norms. Probing more deeply, such challenges reveal the spread of values that they manifest—of class, ethnic type, race, lineage. Gender and racial-body type both have their standard norms and their more subtle and subversive roles to play in social aesthetics, as several of the essays here explore. On the other hand, there is also the expansion of the concept of beauty to encompass body types that by more conventional standards would be judged awkward, imperfect, ugly. In the hands of politically informed artists, individuals, and critics, beauty can be accepted and expanded, or rejected and critiqued.

Whatever approach one favors, the relationships between the most abstract and disembodied sense of beauty and the physical, erotic sense are clearly harder to sever than many philosophers have previously realized. The soul may be glad to forget its connection with the body, as Santayana put it, but that gladness indicates that the connection is there to be forgotten in the first place. And often it is not so much forgotten as reshaped and transfigured. Such transformations are explored here with excursions into the place of beauty in art; into the queering of beauty in the exemplars of beautiful artworks; into explorations of the marginal and exotic that allure while defying conventional models; into the literal carving of facial features for cosmetic and artistic purposes that both conform to and challenge norms of appearance. In such different contexts these authors dramatize the various ways that beauty can function in relation to personal desires, artistic values, and social authority. Here we can discover beauty not only as a quality and a value, but also as a project and a practice that drives our lives from both within and without—internal standards, external expectations, and ambivalence meeting in provocative disputation.

BEAUTY
UNLIMITED

Introduction

PEG ZEGLIN BRAND

We are more than a full decade into the new millennium and, inevitably, the world has become smaller, more complex, and immanent. Post-9/11, we live daily with the "war" on terror. An image of a veiled woman is fraught with political overtones, yet stunning in its starkness, simplicity, and evocation of beauty that is innocent and long gone (plate 1).

Try to ignore world events, debates over nuclear proliferation, arguments over immigration, battlegrounds of ethnic cleansing, strategies for economic recovery, and you will appear out of touch and indifferent. Assert your self, your home state, or your country as superior and someone—somewhere—will invariably challenge your claim on the grounds of economic, political, or religious principles. YouTube, 24/7 news, blogs, Twitter, and iPhones allow people across the globe to access one another, at least on a technological level, thereby making all of us Other.

Visually, we can never go back. Isolationism is naïve in an era of collapsing Twin Towers, the tortures at Abu Ghraib, and extraordinary rendition. We enjoy—or endure—a new era of representation, artistic production, and aesthetics. Images abound; we cannot escape their impact. Is it a brave new world or one of bravado and abandoned beauty? Beauty must compete with the horrors of the world as well as the images that we are not allowed to see.[1] How do we see and process world events, such as the quiet and unremarkable return of a woman to her home devastated by war (plate 2)? Is beauty relegated to the scrap heap or insistently, perhaps even unintentionally, ever-present?

Consider a comparison of two prime ways we as viewers might choose to perceive an image of such an event: as photo-documentary and as artistic vision. Plate 2, taken by photojournalist Michael Kamber, cannot help but portray a certain beauty of contrasts—the lone figure against the clutter of brick and stone, the vertical figure against the slope of a destabilizing horizon and clear blue sky—as well as an irony of reversals: the blackness of life against the whiteness of rubble and death. The photo was prominently placed on the front page of the *New York Times* on July 12, 2008, and its caption read, "Nafeeya Mohsin looked over what remained of her house last month, two days after returning to it in the village of Al Etha in Iraq."[2] Did Kamber intend to capture the haunting beauty he portrays, or is beauty far from his mind when he sets out to accurately document a moment in time? Moreover, how do we as viewers process the beauty we see: with despair? Disinterest? Or perhaps a bit of both?

Compare the image in plate 3, which is uncannily similar. Three years earlier, video artist Lida Abdul had returned home to find whiteness and ruin as well, but, in her case, within her native Afghanistan.[3] How does this portrayal of the lone dark figure amidst the whitened ruins of her former house compare? Does this work of "fine art" exhibit beauty better than the more recent journalistic photo? A sensitive observer would not presume so distinct a difference and would, I suspect, allow the artist to document and the journalist to beautify. As viewers who process and perceive beauty in the two photos, we might ask ourselves whether this beauty differs from past, traditional beauties we have come to enjoy for their pleasure(s) or their promise of happiness.[4] What sorts of pleasure or happiness can be felt, if any? How is our perception of beauty in the second image informed by our knowledge of its title, *White House*—particularly once we know that Abdul spends the full five minutes of the video whitewashing (with a brush and a bucket of paint) architectural ruins? The term is, of course, ambiguous in meaning, vacillating as it does between the residence of the U.S. president who ordered the initial bombing of the Taliban in 2002–2003 (George W. Bush) and the resulting white rubble that underlies the action of the artist who whitewashes. To whitewash is to hide the truth about something or to cover up.

Difficult questions like these can challenge the presumptions operative in our perception, (re)cognition, and interpretation of these images as examples of beauty. They are landscapes, but do not easily resemble idyllic scenes of the eighteenth century or the tempests of J. M. W. Turner. They are records of human suffering, but not abstracted like the figures in Picasso's *Guernica*. Instead, they jolt us back to the here and now in their function as "real" scenes of actual lives, i.e., as art critic Eleanor Heartney reminds us, as "bearers of truth."[5] Given that such images impugn core philosophical notions like aesthetic distance, disinterest, and simplistic notions of pleasure, beauty begs for reassessment in order to propel itself forward with intent and resolve. Some art critics fear that in this day and age, beauty has become "an infatuation" on the part of artists who seek an escape from distasteful politics and difficult art.[6] Others see, and welcome, beauty that hurts—as in the video by Lida Abdul.[7] How can beauty both evade the contentiousness of world politics and also capture a fragile vision in the maelstrom of war? Perhaps a new approach to beauty is needed . . . to reconcile the dissonance.

The essays of *Beauty Unlimited* position readers in the twenty-first century by pointing them forward and forcing them into the future, toward a more extensive and far-flung understanding of beauty. Clearly, the past cannot—and should not—be ignored; in aesthetics and the philosophy of art, revered pronouncements on beauty by standard-bearers like Plato, Burke, Hume, and Kant inevitably serve as a backdrop to any modern approach one might adopt in assessing representations of war, abuse, the environment, cultural identity, even fashion and the popular cultural icons that saturate our visual fields. The authors in this volume bring a fresh perspective to such imagery; they ask new questions and they acknowledge the overlap of scholarship on the topic of beauty from such fields as art criticism, art history, music, film, dance, feminist theory, and cultural studies, in addition to philosophy. Beauty as an interdisciplinary exercise quickly complicates simplistic assumptions underlying one's aesthetic experience and pleasurable reaction. Whether we're ready or not, it drags in the nonaesthetic in all its clumsy inclusiveness, i.e., issues of ethics, politics, gender, race, ethnicity, and class.

Our challenge is to decipher visual representations of beauty—both unfamiliar and problematic—through an integrated context of apprehension and appreciation. New images of beauty presented by authors in this volume embed layers of meaning that invite us to review past philosophical and aesthetic theories through broader cognitive and global perspectives. They propose new examples that deviate from standard examples of the past—so ably represented by the canon of ancient Greek ideals and the European "great masters"—and the paradigmatic beauty so often depicted in Western popular culture that enshrines the bloom of youth with flawless perfection, whiteness, and socially and culturally acceptable standards of femininity. The authors presented here serve as guides for scholarly adventures into new terrain, i.e., for beauty unlimited.

The Backdrop of Beauty

One reviewer, writing for a philosophy journal, listed recent titles in the ever-growing discourse on philosophical concepts of beauty: *Natural Beauty: A Theory of Aesthetics beyond the Arts*, by Ronald Moore (2007); *Six Names of Beauty*, by Crispin Sartwell (2004); *The Abuse of Beauty*, by Arthur C. Danto (2003); *Beauty*, by James Kirwan (1999); *Beauty in Context*, by Wilfried Van Damme (1996); *Beauty Restored*, by Mary Mothersill (1984); and *A New Theory of Beauty*, by Guy Sircello (1975).[8] He could have also included such notables as *Beauty: A Very Short Introduction*, by Roger Scruton (2011); *Beauty*, by Roger Scruton (2009); *The Art Instinct: Beauty, Pleasure, and Human Evolution*, by Dennis Dutton (2009); *Functional Beauty*, by Glenn Parsons and Allen Carlson (2008); *Plato and the Question of Beauty*, by Drew A. Hyland (2008); *Beauty's Appeal: Measure and Excess*, edited by Anna-Teresa Tymieniecka (2008); *Aesthetics and Material Beauty*, by Jennifer A. McMahon (2007); *Kant on Beauty and Biology*, by Rachel Zuckert (2007); *Only a Promise of Happiness: The Place of Beauty in a World of Art*, by Alexander Nehamas (2007); *Values of Beauty: Historical Essays in Aesthetics*, by Paul Guyer (2005); a reissue of George Santayana's *The Sense of Beauty* (2002); *The Metaphysics of Beauty*, by Nick Zangwill (2001); *Aesthetic Order: A Philosophy of Order, Beauty and Art*, by Ruth Lorand (2000); *Real Beauty*, by Eddy M. Zemach (1997); *What About Beauty?* by Marcia Eaton (1997); and *The Gift of Beauty: The Good as Art*, by Stephen David Ross (1996). Exhibiting an amazing array, these titles are even more astounding when we consider that, less than twenty years ago, some philosophers had, with great certainty, declared the death of beauty as an essential feature—or any feature at all—of art; James Kirwan, cited above, and Marcella Tarozzi Goldsmith, author of *The Future of Art: An Aesthetics of the New and the Sublime* (1999), are only two such examples. Few philosophers dared to disagree. But much has been written in the past decade or two, and this is just the tip of the iceberg. These philosophical texts focus on the aesthetic experience and its resulting pleasures, yet seem to bear little resemblance to other disciplinary approaches to beauty that run parallel to this inquiry within aesthetics. Books from nonphilosophical disciplines have an even wider audience than books routinely listed under "aesthetics" or "philosophy of art."

Consider, for instance, the following titles authored by writers in literature, art history, and aesthetic theory who cast their nets more widely than those of philosophical aesthetics: *Truth, Beauty and Goodness Reframed*, by

Howard Gardner (2011); *100,000 Years of Beauty*, a five-volume set edited by Elisabeth Azoulay, Angela Demian, and Dalibor Frioux (2009); *Posing Beauty: African American Images from the 1890s to the Present*, by Deborah Willis (2009); *Finding Beauty in a Broken World*, by Terry Tempest Williams (2009); *The Bureaucracy of Beauty: Design in the Age of Its Global Reproducibility*, by Arindam Dutta (2007); *In Praise of Athletic Beauty*, by Hans Ulrich Gumbrecht (2006); *Beauty and Art, 1750–2000*, by Elizabeth Prettejohn (2005); *For the Love of Beauty: Art History and the Moral Foundations of Aesthetic Judgments*, by Arthur Pontynen (2005); *History of Beauty*, by Umberto Eco (2004, and reissued multiple times); *Speaking of Beauty*, by Denis Donoghue (2003); *Extreme Beauty: Aesthetics, Politics, Death*, edited by James Swearingen and Joanne Cutting-Gray (2002); *On Beauty and Being Just*, by Elaine Scarry (1999); *Behold the Man: The Hype and Selling of Male Beauty in Media and Culture*, by Edisol Wayne Dotson (1999); *Beauty and the Contemporary Sublime*, by Jeremy Gilbert-Rolfe (1999); *Beauty and the Critic: Aesthetics in an Age of Cultural Studies*, edited by James Soderholm (1998); *Concepts of Beauty in Renaissance Art*, edited by Francis Ames-Lewis and Mary Rogers (1998); and *Beauty Is Nowhere: Ethical Issues in Art and Design*, edited by Richard Roth and Susan King Roth (1998). These authors approach the topic through disciplinary avenues that may overlap with philosophy but rely more commonly upon histories of art, artifactuality, and cultural production than their counterparts in aesthetics. Sometimes representations alone form most of the content of inquiry, as in *Rough Beauty*, by Dave Anderson (2006), a glimpse at a Texas town that kept blacks at bay by holding Ku Klux Klan marches, or *Vanishing Beauty: Indigenous Body Art and Decoration*, a documentation of primitive tribes over four continents by Bertie Winkel and Dos Winkel (2006). Moreover, what is particularly notable is by how many titles—and how far beyond its meager beginnings—the discussion of beauty has grown since the publication of my edited volume *Beauty Matters* in 2000. In the introduction to that volume, I cited only two texts as particularly influential (and controversial): *The Invisible Dragon: Four Essays on Beauty*, by Dave Hickey (1993), and *Uncontrollable Beauty: Toward a New Aesthetics*, by Bill Beckley and David Shapiro (1998).[9]

Even more different in focus and scope are titles such as *Spellbound by Beauty: Alfred Hitchcock and His Leading Ladies*, by Donald Spoto (2009); *Bathers, Bodies, Beauty: The Visceral Eye*, by Linda Nochlin (2006); *Swooning Beauty: A Memoir of Pleasure* (2006) and *Monster/Beauty: Building the Body of Love* (2001), both by Joanna Frueh; *Venus in the Dark: Blackness and Beauty in Popular Culture,* by Janell Hobson (2005); *Beauty and Misogyny: Harmful Cultural Practices in the West,* by Sheila Jeffreys (2005); *Inventing Beauty: A History of the Innovations That Have Made Us Beautiful,* by Teresa Riordan (2004); *The Beauty Industry: Gender, Culture, Pleasure,* by Paula Black (2004); *Body Work: Beauty and Self-Image in American Culture,* by Debra L. Gimlin (2002); *Venus in Exile: The Rejection of Beauty in 20th-Century Art,* by Wendy Steiner (2001); *Aching for Beauty: Footbinding in China,* by Wang Ping (2000); *Reconcilable Differences: Confronting Beauty, Pornography, and the Future of Feminism,* by Lynn S. Chancer (1999); *The Power of Beauty,* by Nancy Friday (1996); *The Symptom of Beauty,* by Francette Pacteau (1994); *Ideals of Feminine Beauty: Philosophical, Social, and Cultural Dimensions,* edited by Karen A. Callaghan (1994); *Body Outlaws,* edited by Ophira Edut (1998, with revised editions in 2000 and 2003), and, last but not least, the landmark bestseller by Naomi Wolf, *The Beauty Myth: How Images of Beauty Are Used against Women* (1991). These titles constitute a third track that runs parallel to the other two, often invoking the name of Venus—the ancient goddess of love—in ominous ways: Venus in the dark, Venus in exile. With repeated references to women, their bodies, ideals of female beauty, and their cultural creation and consumption, these studies are less about the supposedly universal and "innocent" pleasure(s) inherent in standard philosophical notions of beauty than they are about the identification of uniquely sexualized male pleasure enjoyed at the expense of women whose bodies are routinely on display and may have, incidentally, undergone considerable pain and discomfort to conform to feminine ideals. (Frueh, an exception here, also focuses on female pleasures.) Making little attempt to strive for objectivity, as philosophers would prefer they do, these authors approach the topic with unabashed subjectivity, i.e., from a feminist standpoint, routinely invoking their experiences *as women* to assess female beauty within patriarchal cultural contexts that consistently devalue women (and women's pleasure).

One particularly new and bold approach to the "disarming" of Venus and her entrenched ideals is undertaken by Ann Millett-Gallant in *The Disabled Body in Contemporary Art* (2010). I have argued elsewhere that the (self-) depiction of the disabled body for the purposes of redefining beauty—as in the case of performance artist Mary Duffy, born without arms, who poses nude as the classical statue of Venus de Milo in order to "disarm" Venus— exemplifies the agency of the artist, in unheralded autonomous defiance of the norms of feminine beauty long honored by Kenneth Clark and other revered art historians and critics.[10] My endorsement of Duffy's intentionality is neither new nor unique within her context of supporters within art history and disability studies, but serves to alert aestheticians to a growing body of work that they can no longer ignore when teaching introductory philosophy of art classes, however replete with obligatory PowerPoint images of the Greek goddess and her Renaissance revisionings. To disarm Venus is to symbolically dismember and destroy her; what remains of the original aesthetic experience when we view an armless Duffy as an armless statue? How do we describe what we now see? Moreover, is there any pleasure involved?

The "problem of beauty" as seen by some feminist theorists is not so much the conflict of its moral and aesthetic implications—namely, the question of whether beauty is good or bad for women (although writers like Wolf and Jeffreys clearly argue its dangers on moral grounds)—but is, instead, pragmatic: "how is beauty defined, deployed, defended, subordinated, marketed or manipulated, and how do these tactics intersect with gender and value?" This is the question posed by Claire Colebrook in the introduction to a 2006 special issue of the journal *Feminist Theory* on the topic of beauty. In it, she casts the context for a feminist political discussion of beauty within the following framework: "If beauty has been associated with the viewed, passive, mastered and nakedly displayed female body, it has also been associated (as in Kant's aesthetic) with a purely formal, disinterested and elevating regard." Given the latter association—and the fact that art appreciators everywhere seek the many aesthetic pleasures that beauty may bring—Colebrook argues against generalizing "a simple moral value" for our familiar concept or phenomenon of beauty, in spite of its "centrality to philosophy, everyday life, art, politics and culture."[11]

The editor of the special issue, Rita Felski, argues that new feminist perspectives on beauty will not only build upon important past feminist critiques that "expose the ugly underside of beauty," such as female subjugation, but also promote an invigorated dialectic of aesthetics and politics that does not become dominated by politics.[12] Traditional notions of aesthetic value and pleasure are prominent components of beauty, and they indeed have their place and are worth savoring; new feminist perspectives on beauty will further explore these dimensions alongside the political. If we reverse the direction of inquiry, however, it is not at all clear that traditional philosophical aesthetics is similarly interested in the political or feminist aspects. In fact, Felski argues,

> Contemporary aesthetic theory, I believe, has been led astray by its conflation of the aesthetic with the artistic and its subsequent, virtually exclusive, focus on the sphere of high art. The challenge for feminism is to rein back its

compulsion to immediately translate aesthetic surfaces into political depths; or rather, to keep both surface *and* depth in the mind's eye, teasing apart the multifarious socio-political meanings of texts while also crafting richer and thicker descriptions of aesthetic experience.[13]

The essays in *Beauty Unlimited* hope to move forward in a similarly balanced direction, that is, to motivate the evolution of such new feminist perspectives on beauty, since "all of us, women included, continue to seek out and take solace in beauty."[14] They are organized in four sections in order to maximize strengths and commonalities and to provoke thought: Part 1—"Revising the Concept of Beauty: Laying the Groundwork," Part 2—"Standards of Beauty," Part 3—"The Body in Performance," and Part 4,—"Beauty and the State." The persistence and power of beauty is on full display; aestheticians need to rise to the challenge, to push the boundaries of comfortable inquiry, and to imagine beauty anew.

Part 1. Revising the Concept of Beauty: Laying the Groundwork

Just a quick glance at the literature has shown us the diversity of writing on the topic of beauty, and yet, sadly, a closer look reveals the persistent lack of influence that parallel tracks have had on the ongoing philosophical tradition. Most philosophers have yet to acknowledge the insights and advances made by art historians and cultural critics who find issues of race, gender, class, disability, and sexuality to be essential to discussions of beauty. One exception is Arthur C. Danto, an influential philosopher who has been art critic for various publications, art exhibition catalogues, and *The Nation*. It is his work on which the first essay in this volume, by Noël Carroll, focuses. In "Arthur Danto and the Problem of Beauty," Carroll presents an overview of the intersection of Danto's theories of art and beauty, based on an important set of lectures Danto delivered in 2001 outlining "the problem" of beauty, which he published as *The Abuse of Beauty* (2003). Carroll discusses the threat that beauty poses to Danto's long-standing theory of art as a problem of containment. Narrowly construed, beauty is that which is pleasing to the eye or ear, but the requirement that art have such a discernible property was banished long ago with the advent of German expressionism, Dadaism, and, more recently in the twentieth century, Conceptual Art. Therefore, for Danto, the definition of "art" cannot rely on a discernible property like beauty unless it is a form of internal beauty, i.e., unless it serves the meaning or content of the artwork. Such beauty significantly differs from external beauty (or "dumb beauty"), recognizable as eye candy or delightfully contrived artifice.

In the second essay, "Savages, Wild Men, Monstrous Races: The Social Construction of Race in the Early Modern Era," cultural critic Gregory Velazco y Trianosky delves into the modern conception of race that initially developed in the early 1500s—both visually and textually—yielding a problematic concept of "the savage." The author draws upon Noachic legends, according to which the three peoples of the earth—the inhabitants of Africa, Asia, and Europe—each descended from one of the three sons of Noah. He argues that eighteenth- and nineteenth-century writers invoked medieval manuscript illustrations and legends of the Wild Man and monstrous races that were based, in part, on European visits to the New World, in order to craft a notion of "the savage" that is highly racialized and stubbornly pervasive. He urges aestheticians and historians of philosophy to explore these early origins of modern ideas and images of race that continue to influence us today.

A third essay further invites expansion of the concept of beauty while invoking the foundations of historical philosophical figures. In "Beauty's Relational Labor," Monique Roelofs looks at race, gender, and class in the Scottish Enlightenment (as embodied in Shaftesbury, Hutcheson, Burke, and Adam Smith) as well as historical critics of this tradition (Mandeville and Wollstonecraft) in order to bring out moral and political difficulties with the concept of beauty, especially its controversial role in supporting the allegedly adequate moral and political social order. After describing the flip side of beauty's ethical and political aspirations, Roelofs sketches a relational approach between aesthetics, race, and gender. While the essay is not specifically focused on the body, it does critically examine both Burke's reading of the body of a black woman and Wollstonecraft's challenge to the feminine focus on the body. Her discussion is framed by a close reading of a Brazilian novel by Clarice Lispector, *The Hour of the Star*, which Roelofs cites as an example of *écriture féminine*, a genre of feminine writing that philosopher Hélène Cixous promoted in her 1975 essay "Le Rire de la Meduse."[15]

The next essay, "Queer Beauty: Winckelmann and Kant on the Vicissitudes of the Ideal," offers an analysis of objects familiar to readers of Johann Joachim Winckelmann and Immanuel Kant that present us with what the author calls "a paradox." Art historian Whitney Davis cites the role of pederastic representations of youthful male beauty in order to explore how they have fed into the canonical representation of beauty in the modern

Western tradition, despite the ban on homosexuality in the modern world. The "paradox," from a strictly Kantian point of view, is that there should be no queer beauty for Kant, but, Davis argues, there clearly was. Much as Roelofs focuses on race and gender, Davis delves deeply into the assumptions beneath standard philosophical conceptualizations of beauty in order to bring hidden issues of sexuality to light, particularly as they function to reinforce standards for canonic inclusion.

Finally, "Worldwide Women," an important essay by art critic Eleanor Heartney, rounds out this section. It is reprinted from its original venue, *Art in America*, and included here to familiarize readers with a variety of works by women artists that have been canonized (with a small "c") in a well-known and highly publicized feminist exhibit: the Brooklyn Museum's 2007 "Global Feminisms: New Directions in Contemporary Art." Heartney's essay offers noteworthy scrutiny of both the range of curatorial choices made by the veteran feminist art critic Linda Nochlin and her less experienced co-curator, Maura Reilly (nearly ninety artists from fifty countries were chosen for the show), and the curators' presupposition that the term "feminism" still has a shared meaning, in spite of its evolution over time and its current unpopularity with younger women. The use of the plural, i.e., "feminisms," supplies what "feminism" lacks. But as Heartney notes, "global feminisms" inevitably reveals "the unequal march of feminism internationally," and she challenges the use in 2007 of a phrase with which Western feminists are typically more comfortable, particularly in their attempts to export or impose their views upon others. In the catalogue for the exhibition, the curators posit "a transnational network of global feminisms."[16] The array of artworks discussed in Heartney's essay will invite the reader to be more receptive to the creative innovations advanced in the next section of this book, where female artists and nonartists alike push the boundaries of the first phase of feminist art (1960–2000) and female expression into new and unchartered territory.

Repositioning the Body

Since the human body is the site of performance in a variety of ways, not the least of which includes the variations used by news agencies and mainstream media to cast worldwide *events* (like returns to homes in devastated war zones) in terms of *persons* and their personal narratives, many of the authors in this volume focus on the body in terms of agency, mode of representation, and embodied identities across cultures. Artists can act and assume agency (as in Lida Abdul's performance of whitewashing in *White House*);

they can appear to us via a particular medium or art form (as in a video or still shot of that performance); and they can present themselves through art that yields multiple meanings within a particular culture (its sociopolitical context of origin) as well as across cultures. Let us reposition the artist and the artist's body, allowing the artwork to guide the expansion of the concept of beauty and its accompanying enterprise of aesthetics.

Consider a pair of photographs by IngridMwangiRobertHutter entitled *Static Drift*, from the 2001 "Global Feminisms" show.[17] These photographs contrast regions of the world as a "bright dark continent" and "burn out country" by means of maps imposed on the artist's own female body that contrast two shades of color, indicating a "drift" that is apparently not moving but rather "static" (plate 4a and b). An artist of Kenyan origin, MwangiHutter documents the dislocation of moving between her native land and Germany, thereby renegotiating her identity in a new and other culture. Once relocated, the immigrant feels "other" not only to the natives of her new land, but also, inevitably after a time, to those left behind in her homeland. As one critic describes the constant shifting of geographic identity, self-definition becomes a process of negotiating between conflicting feelings of belonging:

> The individual becomes multiple, a mosaic of possibilities. In her videos, performances, and photo works, Ingrid Mwangi projects this fractured perception, in which we see ourselves through the eyes of others. In such a case, our own sense of identity defines the borders of a continually shifting process of self-protection, responding, for instance, to globalization.[18]

The particular case of MwangiHutter differs from those of other artists who have journeyed west, according to critic Simon Njami, particularly because she uses her own body to depict herself as two kinds of "other," i.e., to depict her "dual belonging":

> She is certainly African, her family name attests to that, but her German mother helped her avoid a trap: the comfort of the established image that can be identified and described. It was never an issue for her to acquire the language of the other, since she was at once the same and other. She spent the first fifteen years of her life in Kenya, where she was born, before leaving for Germany, where she lives and works today. Her dual belonging is not only symbolic, it is physical. It runs through her veins and is read on her body. And that richness, which makes her both from here and from there, creates a fragility in her, a prism through which she tries to see herself and see the world.[19]

The representation of MwangiHutter's body captures the multiple levels mentioned above: that of agency, mode of representation, and embodied identity within a multicultural context. She is the agent and performer of her art; she documents herself by photographing her body in the act of performing; and she questions and creates a fluid identity based on her place— as both one and the other—within the broader cultural framework of the world: across continents. Her body becomes the locus of a "mosaic of possibilities" that is documented and recorded but also functions at a higher level: as an icon or symbol within a visual language of bodies represented on a worldwide stage of news, popular culture, art galleries, etc. Horst Gerhard Haberl focuses on the use of her body as a tool that advances the potential for communication across a broadening global context:

> In the photo series *Static Drift*—as an example of a "different" readability of the world—the performer exposes her "Borderlines," having had the "Burn Out" of a Germany shadow burned into the skin of her stomach by the white sun, or the words "Bright Dark Continent" into the stencil of Africa. As a media artist she is familiar with the rhetorical power of projected pictures, signs, symbols and texts, and aware of the media characteristics of the body as a vessel of memory and remembering, a generator of energy fields, data logger and processor, both receiver and transmitter—but also as a resounding body or instrument.[20]

What does the analysis of MwangiHutter's work, alongside that of Lida Abdul, show?

First, that contemporary art is complex, nuanced, and intimately tied to—and expressive of—the world outside the narrow confines of the mainstream "artworld" of the high-profit New York and London galleries, museums, and auction houses. Political art is being made by numerous non–New York artists, who are often involved in local and international issues and, not surprisingly, in artistic and political activism. Some of the artists presented in this volume, particularly women around the world who have relocated to new lands or who routinely travel the world between (home)lands, define themselves in terms of political activism bent on abolishing injustices to women everywhere. Heartney's "Worldwide Women" probed issues of war, exile, abuse, sexuality, and identity. Beauty—in particular, of the female body—often played a role in conveying a political message. This is not news, of course, since women have often used their bodies to undermine stereotypes about beauty and its traditional role in providing pleasure within the artistic canon and the artworld. Often their intent is to disrupt their easy classification as objects of sexual longing and to subvert viewers' aesthetic pleasure; the intentionality is provocative and complete.

As exemplified by MwangiHutter's *Static Drift* photographs, there is a desire to erode comfortable dichotomies between here and there, private and public, self and other. All of the artists chosen for the "Global Feminisms" show were born after 1960, and Heartney gives a sense of what third-wave feminism is all about: *differences* among women (whereas second-wave feminists sought commonalities but were primarily white, middle-class, and hetero), the blurring of boundaries (the fluidity of cultural identity and sexuality), the move away from postmodern appropriation (particularly through images of victimhood) toward a postfeminist sense of agency and empowerment, and the political and parodic expression that some critics find too "didactic" and lacking focus on "aesthetic pleasure."[21] Even after decades of feminist art and evolving gender constructions, basic questions remain and debates continue over feminists' use of sexually explicit imagery (since such imagery may also inadvertently serve the patriarchy) and how political art may function as a viable strategy for gaining attention and recognition (given that severe gender inequities continue to persist).

Consider, for a moment, how distant MwangiHutter's (real) "self-portrait" of her nude torso is from that of the (imaginary) portrait of Olympia, as depicted by Manet's nude model, Victorine Meurent.[22] At first glance, they seem light years apart; yet they are connected as embodiments and expressions of beauty, particularly by means of the use of the meaning-laden female body. When film theorist Laura Mulvey introduced her theory of the male gaze in the 1970s, she emphasized the passivity of the female sitter who is positioned for the scopophilic gaze of the male viewer.[23] When bell hooks suggested an oppositional gaze, she called attention to the predominance of images of white women looked at by the viewer of color.[24] Yet many aesthetes continue to promote the same gaze that objectifies, sexualizes, and stultifies the female on view.[25] Alternative modes of reading have been suggested by feminist theorists over the years that reveal multiple meanings below the surface—what philosopher Carolyn Korsmeyer so aptly calls "deep gender."[26] How might we probe for deep gender, and how might we cast the difference between the approaches in perception and interpretation of artworks such as MwangiHutter's and Manet's?

The old-fashioned philosopher would look for the pleasure inherent in the work, accessible by means of a possessing gaze that reflects a dominance of male over female, clothed over naked, and privileged over powerless, all the while denying his feelings of desire and outwardly feigning disinterest.

He would tout the aesthetic properties of the composition in order to distract attention from the titillation he feels while looking upon an exotic body "under" his gaze. Alternatively, a more enlightened viewer might delve below the surface—beyond personal urges—to dig deeper, discovering gender as one key to unraveling and understanding "the problematic" of a woman's body, which is *not* necessarily on view primarily for the delectation of a(ny) male viewer. The difference hinges on the attribution of agency, and to what degree.

Most old-fashioned interpreters attribute agency to the model for Olympia because Victorine Meurent notoriously stares back at the viewer! This was considered scandalous in 1864; most sitters were prostitutes and did not presume to return the viewer's gaze. This reading of Olympia as accorded some degree of agency by her creator has prevailed for nearly one hundred and fifty years. But what degree of agency does Meurent display in comparison to MwangiHutter, who controls the entire creative process and utilizes her own body as the "canvas" or mode of representation? A reading of deep gender provides a broader framework in which female artists create and utilize beauty to a more intense degree, reclaiming female agency from the male artists who depicted women in days past. Consider some examples of this interpretive strategy as outlined by the authors in Part 2.

Part 2. Standards of Beauty

The widespread Western obsession with female beauty, perfection, cosmetic surgery, and youthfulness places female bodies in a unique position when they are scrutinized as objects that also convey political meaning and ethical embodiment. In a recent volume entitled *Too Beautiful to Picture: Zeuxis, Myth, and Mimesis,* Elizabeth C. Manfield eloquently tracks the limits of natural beauty and societal pressures that come to bear upon women by revisiting the story of the ancient painter Zeuxis, who, in his attempt to portray Helen of Troy, used five different models because each was individually inadequate.[27] Cosmetic surgery was not available in ancient Greece, Renaissance Europe, or eighteenth-century England and Scotland, the birthplaces of philosophical aesthetics. Its extensive use today can be seen as evidence that any traditional notion of "beauty" risks marginalization when the entire playing field has changed and women (and men) can drastically change their looks at will. Critics of widespread contemporary beauty practices challenge Western postmodern feminists who claim that women gain empowerment and agency through invasive procedures like body art and cosmetic surgery. Like Naomi Wolf, who wrote before cosmetic surgery became a billion-dollar annual industry,[28] Sheila Jeffreys has more recently argued in *Beauty and Misogyny: Harmful Cultural Practices in the West* that they are socially acceptable forms of self-harm that serve to perpetuate the subordination of women under patriarchy.[29] Looking at standards of beauty can be intriguing and is essential to any forward-looking discussion of beauty, and the authors in this section take up the challenge with vigor and insight.

For instance, in her essay entitled "Jenny Saville Remakes the Female Nude: Feminist Reflections on the State of the Art," Diana Tietjens Meyers explores how British artist Jenny Saville (also represented in the "Global Feminisms" exhibit of 2007) reconfigures representations of feminine body images, endowing the human body with subjectivity and agency. Having previously written on the concept of women's agency and self-knowledge,[30] Meyers extends her work in exploring the autonomy of bodies to Saville's paintings, explaining the psychocorporeal aspects of an artist's work that monumentally rejects "admired or idealized beauty." Saville's nudes are endowed with agency and power, for instance, while Victorine Meurent, depicted by Manet as Olympia, exemplifies "the defensive agency of the powerless in the presence of the powerful."

Like MwangiHutter, several other artists discussed in this volume straddle multiple worlds, exploring identities that mix together dominant and minority subcultures and, in one case, geographically distant locations. "Indigenous Beauty" is a photo essay by Phoebe Mills Farris, who artistically documents the inherent possibilities of Native American beauty, infused as it is with generational differences, tribal background, and racial mixing.[31] These photographs of women and men with roots in the tribes of the eastern coast of the United States display a physical appearance that diverges from the "typical" images familiar to the dominant white culture, namely, those of Indians of the Plains states and the American Southwest. Instead Farris highlights the cultures found on the Atlantic coast and in the Caribbean, particularly those who had early contact with Europeans, Africans, and racially mixed nonwhites. She honors their traditions of indigenous beauty by presenting a rich range of examples that emphasize skin tone, facial features, dress, and, in some instances, native regalia.

Mary Devereaux, a scholar in medical ethics as well as aesthetics, explores the parameters of cosmetic surgery in the pursuit of beauty in her essay, "Is Medical Aesthetics Really Medical?" An incredibly thorough body of scholarship now exists on the topic; consider the provocative nature of only two titles by Sander Gilman: *Making the Body Beautiful: A Cultural History of Aesthetic Surgery* (1999) and *Creating Beauty to Cure the Soul* (1998). An influential body of feminist work has been inspired by the writings of Kathy Davis: *Dubious Equalities and Embodied Differences: Cultural Studies on Cosmetic Surgery* (2003) and *Reshaping the Female Body: The Dilemma of Cosmetic Surgery* (1995). Devereaux provides a history and terminology of cosmetic surgery in order to question the commonly accepted claim that cosmetic surgery qualifies as a form of healthcare, that is, as a legitimate branch of medicine. In an age of escalating healthcare costs and urgent medical concerns, can one's (mere) beautification be categorized as a medical need?

Jo Ellen Jacobs broadens the scope of women as consumers in her essay, "The Bronze Age Revisited: The Aesthetics of Sun Tanning." Examining why skin color is part of our definition of beauty, she explores the aesthetic aspect of tanning and the skin color that is considered most beautiful in light of racial politics and media hype. Advertisements for both skin-darkening and skin-lightening products reflect the practices of different cultures and different stories about their practices, but, Jacobs argues, women with pale skin are preferred worldwide except in one "bizarre" culture: our own Caucasian-dominated European and American world.

Karina L. Céspedes-Cortes and Paul C. Taylor's essay, "¿Tienes Culo? How to Look at Vida Guerra," explains the career of Cuban-born model Vida Guerra and the persistent gap between white hegemonic masculine norms of female sex appeal, on one hand, and black and Hispanic ones on the other. Guerra's ability to cross over from black "gentlemen's magazines" to their white counterparts suggests that this gap is narrowing. The authors consider the meaning of Guerra's popularity against the backdrop of racial and sexual meanings most famously crystallized by the tragic career of the nineteenth-century South African woman publicly displayed in Europe, Sara Baartman, the so-called Hottentot Venus. Re-presented by contemporary artists like Renée Cox and Tracey Rose, the story of Baartman's removal from South Africa and subsequent display for British and French white voyeurs is one of exploitation and abuse. The legacy of this misuse—for "scientific purposes," no less—is a travesty, an enduring domination of the black female body by white privilege and superiority. No analysis of beauty and race can proceed without measuring its continuing impact on contemporary audiences.

Another instance of a woman's inability to control her reception (and perception) by the public is the marketing of a paper-doll version of the well-known—indeed, venerated—late Mexican artist Frida Kahlo. In "Beauty between Disability and Gender: Frida Kahlo in Paper Dolls," an essay located at the intersection of beauty, disability, and gender, Fedwa Malti-Douglas brings our attention to the representations of Kahlo for children's consumption in a colorful paper-doll book (with text in both English and Spanish) entitled *Aquí cuelgan mis vestidos* ("Hang My Clothes Here"). The sort of thing a little girl might typically play with, the book presents a variety of outfits for dressing the doll, all of them authentically detailed and verifiably worn by the artist in photographs and her own paintings. However, the book presents Kahlo's body as beautiful and perfect; standing in high heels, she looks like a fashion model, whereas in reality, her bout with childhood polio and a life-threatening streetcar accident at age eighteen left her disabled and physically challenged. Furthermore, her gender crossing—wearing men's suits and painting herself so outfitted—adds to the mystique of her persona and her art, and belies the ultra-feminine doll version marketed to little girls.

These ruminations give rise to the reconceptualization of the concept of beauty along new and different paths. Having repositioned the body, particularly the artist's body, at the center of increased agency of the female depicted, let us consider additional ways to defy the limits of the old concept of beauty.

Part 3. The Body in Performance

In "Beauty, Youth, and the Balinese *Legong* Dance," Stephen Davies discusses the female artist and performer who participates in "classic" Balinese dance and who presents herself to the world as the quintessence of grace, charm, and beauty while slowly discovering that age is the dislocating factor in her traversal of two worlds. Although she has full agency and control, she performs in a cultural framework that is as little under her control as is her natural process of aging. This example introduces the broader cultural framework of the performing arts, moving us beyond the static world of visual art.

Jane Duran provides a guide to problematic, conflicting images of women in Hindi-language cinema in her essay, "Bollywood and the Feminine: Hinduism and Images of Womanhood," in order to make the case that such representations are culturally complex and not susceptible to one interpretation or reading. She provides a focus for gender-related issues that draws on the region's architectural history, religious practices, and colonial influences to provide an insightful overview. The striking similarities between dance scenes in Bollywood films and Western music videos entice the reader into deeper exploration of the continuing erosion of cultural differences.

Valerie Fuchs reviews a two-screen video installation which appeared in the 2007 Venice Biennale by Yugoslavian artist Breda Beban in her essay, entitled "Seductive Shift: A Review of *The Most Beautiful Woman in Gucha.*" Filmed at a gathering of trumpet musicians in Serbia, *The Most Beautiful Woman in Gucha* captures the passionate interaction between a beautiful belly dancer, an inebriated young man, and a group of Romany musicians. Like other contemporary artworks, this film hovers between "the realness of a documentary situation and its fictionalization through subjective manipulation."[32] This challenge to filmic conventions yields two videos that invite viewers to participate and complete the narrative. In subtle ways, the viewer is invited into a context of Others, i.e., invited to become part of the story and to partake in—to deliberately not distance herself from—the activity.

Keith Lehrer's essay, "Feminist Art, Content, and Beauty," is an epistemologist's foray into the feminist forest of art that reconfigures one's sense of self through sensory experience. While exploring his feelings about the work of Judy Chicago, Carolee Schneemann, and ORLAN, he highlights the performance of each artist, arguing that their art confronts the viewer directly, and that its value—and perhaps also its beauty—lies in that confrontation. Such provocative, challenging, and disturbing experiences challenge the normally comfortable viewer to exercise her autonomy, to remake herself, and to ultimately remake the world. There is pleasure involved; tied to beauty, it offers us a new way of experiencing art, and, ironically, we can become driven to seek out feminist art, in order to study its profound and surprising effect upon us.

The next essay, my own, continues an analysis of the work of the French performance artist ORLAN, begun earlier in my edited volume *Beauty Matters* (2000). If anything, ORLAN has become more visually outrageous with her latest series of photographs, while simultaneously—to the relief of the squeamish—bringing her "aesthetic surgeries" to an end. In "ORLAN Revisited: Disembodied Virtual Hybrid Beauty," the evolution of the artist's work is scrutinized in light of her own proclamations and writings on hybridity, virtual identity, and disembodiment. She forges ahead into an imaginary world that blends together history, portraiture, and elusive identity. I challenge several feminists who call her work "monstrous," in the hope of elucidating more thoroughly the intentionality of the artist and her easily misunderstood oeuvre. She becomes hybrid, "mutant," a "nomad of identity," and never fails to provoke.

Part 4. Beauty and the State

The final section of this volume with an eye toward "repositioning the body" deals with beauty and the state. Perhaps no one was more opposed to the creation or appropriation of beauty during political turmoil than the French existentialist Simone de Beauvoir. Writing in Paris during and immediately after World War II, she routinely cast beauty as a luxury and a distraction when art should be about the business of conveying truth, regardless of difficulty. Beauvoir was talking about elite Italian aesthetes who were "occupied in caressing the marbles and bronzes of Florence" while pretending to be apolitical in a fascist state,[33] but beauty—particularly involving the female body in interactions with the state—turns us in another direction, one in which beauty can function within the state on a personal, and in some countries highly political, level. For example, American and British suffragists were routinely characterized by male critics as manly and unattractive; naturally, their critics argued, to want to vote like a man is to want to be like a man. To utilize one's body in the service of the state, or indeed in opposition to the state, can open widening pathways to exploring deep gender in the artworks of various cultures.

In order to better understand the concept of beauty within the representation of Muslim women, a short essay coauthored by Allen Douglas and Fedwa Malti-Douglas offers a glimpse into an attitude unfamiliar to Western viewers, namely, that of women who, for religious or other reasons, choose to cover their heads and often their entire bodies. "Beauty Wars: The Struggle over Female Modesty in the Contemporary Middle East and North Africa" offers a glimpse into the reasoning behind the equation of modesty with morality in a variety of cultures that prohibit the display of female nudity and in which visions of female display are competing. The past three to four decades—the height of the second wave of the women's movement in the West—have witnessed a shift from less veiling to more, prompting the authors to note, "Today, it is the unveiled woman who is the exception" on the streets of Arab cities like Cairo and Tunis. Fashion can function as a political tool for women: wearing the veil can become a touchstone of anti-immigration policy (as in France); revealing a lock of hair can function as a sign of revolt (as in Turkey); and refusing to wear a veil on a university campus can provoke attacks by young men who accuse unveiled women of behaving shamefully.[34] New fashion magazines, however, blend Western influences into the aesthetic of modesty predicated on what the authors cite Kariman Hamza, a popular Egyptian television personality, as calling the "clothing of obedience," again bringing two seemingly disparate worlds together. Hamza's magazine, *Elegance and Modesty*, blends the two in unprecedented ways. (Interestingly, its title uses a word meaning "elegance" instead of the standard one for "beauty.")

In "Orientalism Inside/Out: The Art of Soody Sharifi," Cynthia Freeland features the photographs of an Iranian-born artist who lives in Houston but returns home to document young women in her native land, while also creating hybrid photo montages that blend contemporary people with Persian miniatures. Freeland confronts head-on the issue of orientalism, a concept made famous by critic Edward Said in 1978 when he described the enterprise of scholars who attempted to explain the Orient to the West, thereby reinforcing their position of superiority while designating Orientals as "other." Freeland notes that the casting of Muslim-Americans as "other" on the basis of their physical appearance, which has greatly increased after 9/11, serves to complicate the representations of artists who, like Sharifi, present the "other" to "us" in order to enhance our understanding. With a foot in both cultures, she challenges the gap between East and West, provoking reactions from viewers who may feel discomfort, but rarely dispassion. Emotions are tapped when viewing a veiled woman photographed by Sharifi (recall plate 1), but Freeland educates us by explaining the artist's intent, which is to dispel our deeply ingrained stereotypes and expectations. Sharifi does not see an oppressed woman in a hijab, nor does she depict the Western male fantasy of an exoticized Arab.[35] Her *Women of Cover* series offers a more realistic and balanced view, serving to connect people across a cultural divide, on the various sides of which "fashion" takes on multiple meanings in a Muslim context that expects propriety. Her blending of documentary style and fictive strategy (like that of Beban's videos) once again occupies the space—and tension—between cultural conventions.

Unlike MwangiHutter in *Static Drift*, the women depicted by Sharifi are fully clothed. Modesty is a concept rare in the West, and a revisiting of beauty cannot help but expose the cultural divide between the perception of a viewer who seeks to see an Arab woman as mysterious, exotic, and "other" and the artist's vision and aesthetic intentions to the contrary. Our reading of the images of veiled women presents the most pressing challenge to a traditionally ingrained approach to beauty that presumes nude women are *naturally* objects of male (and female) pleasure. Consider the long-standing canon of art-historical "masterpieces" satirized by the Guerrilla Girls in a poster that asks, "Do women have to be naked to get into the Metropolitan Museum?"[36] Since Western art history uniformly teaches viewers to read canonic images of nude women as objects created solely for the viewer's pleasure and delight, we must process the works of Sharifi differently, thereby expanding our notion of beauty into unfamiliar terrain.

Eva Kit Wah Man examines bodies under service to the state in "Beauty and the State: Female Bodies as State Apparatus and Recent Beauty Discourses in China"—a fascinating look at China's 2008 hosting of the Olympics. Man charts the impact of the Western global economy on female beauty within the context of China's state apparatus and ever-growing consumer society. Surveying changes in beauty standards and the roles of women since 1919, the author brings us to the present day, in which Chinese women are homogenized into smiling servitors as hostesses for Olympic visitors. Recall the state's decision to present to hundreds of millions of international viewers, during the opening ceremony, nine-year-old Lynn Miaoke, who lip-synched "Ode to the Motherland" in order to conceal the real singer, seven-year-old Yang Peiyi, whose voice was better but who had imperfect—thus unbeautiful—teeth. "The audience will understand that it's in the national interest," said Chen Qigang, a member of China's Politburo and the ceremony's chief music director, in an interview with Beijing Radio. Chen asked for the last-minute change, according to one writer, because "the country's quest for perfection apparently includes its children."[37] Consider also the pending investigation into the Chinese women's gymnastics team, entered as sixteen-year-olds; one girl missing her baby teeth was suspected of being no more than fourteen.

From within the same culture but from a different perspective, Mary Bittner Wiseman examines a variety of artists in "Gendered Bodies in Contemporary Chinese Art." The nude has not been a genre in either traditional or contemporary Chinese art, as it has been in the art of the West since its introduction in classical Greece. It emerges in recent representations of the human body in China not as a female body identified or valued as an object of desire but rather as a site and possibility of the body's "flowering." Wiseman poetically describes the Chinese emphasis on the process by which artists create; this contrasts sharply with the emphasis, in Western art appreciation, on the final product. For women in China who choose to portray themselves in their art, the complexities are twofold: they defy a tradition of male artists picturing women in more demure ways, and they challenge cultural norms of women's subservience to men that go as far back as the Confucian era.[38] The times are changing in China today, and yesterday's protesters are today's stars.[39] The women who are pushing the boundaries of art and propriety may indeed acknowledge Western influences, but they pointedly seek to create their own unique forms of women's vision and embodiment.

Conclusion: Beauty Revisited; Beauty Unlimited

In the Evelyn Waugh novel *Brideshead Revisited: The Sacred and Profane Memories of Captain Charles Ryder,* the main character and narrator looks back from his vantage point in 1944 to a simpler and happier time. His life as a privileged white male at Oxford twenty years earlier—replete with an ample and steady allowance, servants to bring tea, and plenty of friends with whom to drink, carouse, and travel across Europe—had been far more pleasurable than the experience of war. Ryder reminisces about his college friend, "the 'aesthete' *par excellence*," as "a young man who seemed to me, then, fresh from the somber company of the College Essay Society, ageless as a lizard, as foreign as a Martian. . . . I found myself enjoying him voraciously, like the fine piece of cookery he was."[40]

Enjoying the company of an aesthete and reliving the beauty of the past can seem easy and comforting. But the nagging problems of growing up, searching for one's identity and purpose in life, rebutting the persistent imposition of religious ideologues, and watching a best friend succumb to alcoholism all come to impinge upon the main character's joys and freedom from care. But revisit Brideshead Charles Ryder does, and when he is encamped as a soldier in a crumbling castle where he once dined on fine wines and found diversion from more serious matters of life, he grows nostalgic and comes to understand the strengths and weaknesses of the persons who helped form him in his life: those who ultimately brought him some feeling of love and some measure of wisdom. In revisiting Brideshead, he recalls memories both sacred and profane, yet looks forward to the future with optimism and good cheer. In similarly revisiting beauty, we recall theories both lofty and mundane, and we, too, can look forward to a future of promise with fresh eyes and an open mind. The promise of beauty may not involve the nostalgic happiness of old, but its pleasures—unconventional and complicated, to be sure—may provide at least one form of escape from the world. Unlimited beauty provides a new window onto the world, through which we may both see ourselves as other, and see others as part of ourselves.

Notes

1. Images of deceased United States soldiers returning from the Iraq War were forbidden to be shown on the news during the George W. Bush era. See Michael Kamber and Tim Arango, "4000 U.S. Deaths, and a Handful of Images," *New York Times,* July 26, 2008, http://www.nytimes.com/2008/07/26/world/middleeast/26censor.html.

2. Michael Kamber's photo appears online in conjunction with an article by Alissa J. Rubin, "Iraqi Shiites Reclaim a Village Razed by Sunnis," *New York Times,* July 12, 2008, http://www.nytimes.com/2008/07/12/world/middleeast/12diyala.html.

3. Plate 3 is a still from Abdul's video *White House,* which premiered in 2005 at the 51st Venice Biennale, where Abdul was the first official representative for Afghanistan in the Biennale's hundred-year history. Lida Abdul's work has been shown internationally and she was included in the 2007 U.S. exhibit "Global Feminisms"; see the exhibit's catalogue, *Global Feminisms: New Directions in Contemporary Art,* ed. Maura Reilly and Linda Nochlin (London: Merrell; New York: Brooklyn Museum, 2007), as well as the online Feminist Art Base at the Elizabeth A. Sackler Center for Feminist Art at the Brooklyn Museum, http://www.brooklynmuseum.org/eascfa/feminist_art_base/index.php. Abdul, who works in photography, performance, and video art, currently resides in Afghanistan, where she often enlists local residents to participate in projects that explore the relationship between architecture and identity; see http://lidaabdul.com.

4. Both Arthur C. Danto and Alexander Nehamas have cited Stendahl's remark "Beauty is the promise of happiness." See Arthur C. Danto, *The Abuse of Beauty: Aesthetics and the Concept of Art* (Peru, Ill.: Carus, 2003), and Alexander Nehamas, *Only a Promise of Happiness: The Place of Beauty in a World of Art* (Princeton: Princeton University Press, 2007).

5. Eleanor Heartney, "A War and Its Images," in *Defending Complexity: Art, Politics, and the New World Order* (Lenox, Mass.: Hard Press, 2006), 13. The essay was originally published in *Art in America* (October 2004).

6. Heartney, introduction to *Defending Complexity,* i.

7. Els van der Plas, "Lida Abdul: A Beauty That Hurts," in *Lida Abdul,* ed. Renata Caragliano, Stella Cervasio, Nikos Papastergiadis, Virginia Pérez-Ratton, and Els van der Plas (Torino, Italy: hopefulmonster, 2008).

8. Dan Vaillancourt, review of *Natural Beauty: A Theory of Aesthetics beyond the Arts,* by Ronald Moore, *Journal of Aesthetics and Art Criticism* 66, no. 3 (Summer 2008): 303–305.

9. Peg Zeglin Brand, ed., *Beauty Matters* (Bloomington: Indiana University Press, 2000), still available for purchase at http://www.iupress.indiana.edu/product_info.php?products_id=63581.

10. Peg Brand, "Beauty as Pride: A Function of Agency," *APA Newsletter on Philosophy and Medicine* 10, no. 2 (Spring 2011): 5–9, http://www.apaonline.org/APAOnline/Publications/Newsletters/Past_Newsletters/Vol10/Vol_10.aspx, under "Philosophy and Medicine 1." See also three other articles in the volume, all delivered at the APA Eastern Division meeting, December 2010: Anita Silvers, "From the Crooked Timber of Humanity, Something Beautiful Should Be Made!"; Sara Goering, "Disability, Internalized Oppression, and Appearance Norms"; and Bonnie Steinbock, "Comments on Talks by Silvers, Goering, and Brand, APA December 2010." For a classic iteration of art-historical ideals of female beauty that "must reflect a peaceful or integrated frame of mind," see Kenneth Clark, *Feminine Beauty* (New York: Rizzoli, 1980), 7.

11. Claire Colebrook, "Introduction," in "The Feminine and the Beautiful," ed. Rita Felski, special issue, *Feminist Theory* 7, no. 2 (August 2006): 132.

12. Rita Felski, "'Because It Is Beautiful': New Feminist Perspectives on Beauty," in Felski, "The Feminine and the Beautiful," 273.

13. Ibid., 281.

14. Ibid.

15. Cixous' essay was translated into English by Keith Cohen and Paula Cohen and published as "The Laugh of the Medusa," *Signs* 1, no. 4 (Summer 1976): 875–93. In homage to French theorists of the feminine, Vanda Zajko and Miriam Leonard's *Laughing with Medusa* was published by Oxford University Press in 2006.

16. Maura Reilly, "Introduction: Toward Transnational Feminisms," in Reilly and Nochlin, *Global Feminisms*, 17. This show, along with a second show, "WACK! Art and the Feminist Revolution," and their accompanying catalogues, are tied to efforts to counter the erasure of women's artistic achievements since the 1970s, as outlined by the Feminist Art Project. For more discussion of this effort and its relationship to the future of philosophy, see Peg Brand, "The Feminist Art Project (TFAP) and Its Significance for Aesthetics," in *Feminist Aesthetics and Philosophy of Art: The Power of Critical Visions and Creative Engagement*, ed. Lisa Ryan Musgrave (London: Springer, 2013).

17. IngridMwangiRobertHutter is the preferred name of the collective artist(s), blending Mwangi's identity with that of her husband, Hutter; for more information on their work, see http://www.ingridmwangiroberthutter.com/.

18. N'Goné Fall, "Providing a Space of Freedom: Woman Artists from Africa," in Reilly and Nochlin, *Global Feminisms*, 75.

19. Simon Njami, "Memory in the Skin: The Work of Ingrid Mwangi," trans. Jeanine Herman, http://ingridmwangi.de/_/text__simon_njami.html. Originally written for *Looking Both Ways: Art of the Contemporary African Diaspora*, catalogue (New York: Museum for African Art; Gent: Snoeck, 2003).

20. Horst Gerhard Haberl, "Art is the Message," http://www.ingridmwangi.de/_/text_horst_gerhard_haberl-art_is_the_message.html. Originally written for Ingrid Mwangi et al., *Your Own Soul* (Heidelberg: Kehrer, 2003), 32–41.

21. Peter Schjeldahl, art critic for the *New Yorker*, as Heartney reports in "Worldwide Women," this volume.

22. For the famous painting of Olympia, see the website of the Musée d'Orsay, at http://www.musee-orsay.fr/index.php?id=851&L=1&tx_commentaire_pi1[showUid]=7087.

23. Laura Mulvey, *Visual and Other Pleasures*, 2nd ed. (New York: Palgrave Macmillan, 2009).

24. bell hooks, *Black Looks: Race and Representation* (Boston: South End Press, 1999).

25. See, for instance, Nehamas, *Only a Promise of Happiness*, and Charles Harrison, *Painting the Difference: Sex and Spectator in Modern Art* (Chicago: University of Chicago Press, 2006). See also my reviews of the former (in *The Journal of Aesthetics and Art Criticism* 65, no. 2 (Spring 2007): 244–46) and the latter (http://www.caareviews.org/reviews/1051).

26. Carolyn Korsmeyer, *Gender and Aesthetics: An Introduction* (New York: Routledge, 2004).

27. Elizabeth C. Manfield, *Too Beautiful to Picture: Zeuxis, Myth, and Mimesis* (Minneapolis: University of Minnesota Press, 2007°).

28. Alex Kuczynski, *Beauty Junkies: Inside Our $15 Billion Obsession with Cosmetic Surgery* (New York: Doubleday, 2006).

29. Sheila Jeffreys, *Beauty and Misogyny: Harmful Cultural Practices in the West* (Hove: Routledge, 2005).

30. Diana Tietjens Meyers, *Gender in the Mirror: Cultural Imagery and Women's Agency* (New York: Oxford University Press, 2002).

31. Steven Leuthold outlines the differences between Western and indigenous cultures' descriptions of aesthetic experience by arguing that the latter often emphasize arts that involve embodied, often religious experience ("Is There 'Art' in Indigenous Aesthetics?" in *Indigenous Aesthetics: Native Art, Media, and Identity* [Austin: University of Texas Press, 1998], 45–63).

32. The phrase is quoted from an advertisement for the film at the Speed Museum, Louisville, Ky.

33. Simone de Beauvoir, *The Ethics of Ambiguity* trans. Bernard Frechtman (1948; New York: Citadel, 1996), 76. See also my essays "The Aesthetic Attitude in *The Ethics of Ambiguity,*" *Simone de Beauvoir Studies* 18 (2001–2002): 31–48, and "Salon-Haunters: The Impasse Facing French Intellectuals," in *The Contradictions of Freedom: Philosophical Essays on Simone de Beauvoir's "The Mandarins,"* ed. Sally J. Scholz and Shannon M. Mussett (State University of New York Press, 2005), 211–26.

34. Recall Azar Nafisi's narrative of the veiling required on her Iranian campus: *Reading Lolita in Tehran: A Memoir in Books* (New York: Random House, 2004).

35. Consider the insightful analysis presented by Mohja Kahf, *Western Representations of the Muslim Woman: From Termagant to Odalisque* (Austin: University of Texas Press, 1999).

36. The poster is online at "16 Years Later," Guerrilla Girls, http://www.guerrillagirls.com/posters/getnakedupdate.shtml.

37. Cara Anna, "China Had 'Cute' Girl Mime Opening Ceremony after Singer Banned for Crooked Teeth," *Huffington Post*, August 12, 2008, http://www.huffingtonpost.com/2008/08/12/cute-girl-mimed-opening-c_n_118349.html.

38. See Eva Kit Wah Man, "Female Bodily Aesthetics, Politics, and Feminine Ideals of Beauty in China," in Brand, *Beauty Matters*, 169–96.

39. Zhang Yimou, the creative director of the 2008 Beijing Olympics' spectacular opening ceremony, was a former dissident who was punished by the government and then came around to working for it. See David Barboza, "Gritty Renegade Now Directs China's Close-Up," *New York Times*, August 8, 2008, http://www.nytimes.com/2008/08/08/sports/olympics/08guru.html.

40. Evelyn Waugh, *Brideshead Revisited: The Sacred and Profane Memories of Captain Charles Ryder* (1944; New York: Back Bay Books, 2008), 32–33.

PART 1.

REVISING THE
CONCEPT OF BEAUTY

LAYING THE GROUNDWORK

1. Arthur Danto and the Problem of Beauty

NOËL CARROLL

On Why Beauty in the Narrow Sense Appears to be a Problem for Danto

Arthur Danto's *The Abuse of Beauty: Aesthetics and the Concept of Art* is Danto's most recent, through-written monograph on the philosophy of art. An obvious question occasioned by its publication is: what is it intended to add to Danto's previous treatises on the philosophy of art, such as *The Transfiguration of the Commonplace* and *After the End of Art?* The simple answer, of course, is beauty. But, why, one asks, does Danto need to address beauty?[1]

I suspect that Danto has at least three motives for addressing the issue of beauty. The first is maybe the most proximate, but the least important. During the late 1990s, the artworld, where Danto presided as a leading critic, was abuzz with talk of beauty and its imminent rehabilitation. Second, the renewed respectability of beauty reminded philosophers that beauty and art had, it seemed, until the nineteenth century gone together like a horse and carriage. So, should not a complete philosophy of art have something to say about what they were doing together all that time?

But lastly, and perhaps most seriously, beauty—narrowly construed—presents a clear and present philosophical danger to the concept of art that Danto currently defends. Thus, Danto, it seems to me, needs to come to terms with beauty as a matter of theoretical damage control. Beauty, narrowly conceived, has the potential to threaten the generality of Danto's theory of art. Therefore, Danto needs, so to speak, to contain it.

How does beauty, narrowly construed, imperil Danto's system?

In order to answer this question, let us first review Danto's system. As is well known, Danto now defends the view that a candidate x is an artwork only if 1) x is about something, and 2) whatever x is about is presented or embodied in an appropriate form. The first condition here is the necessary requirement that a candidate have content—that it be about something. Danto often refers to this content as a "meaning" (or, perhaps, meanings). This content is semantic or thematic, by which Danto means subject to interpretation. This content, in turn, needs to be realized or presented—frequently, Danto says, "embodied"—in a form that is appropriate or suitable to it.

The form should fit the content—that is, advance it in a compelling or, at least, suggestive way. For example, an archway celebrating a triumph should be imposing and substantial, such as the one in Paris; arches like those of McDonald's are too flimsy to herald historic glory appropriately. One might also call the embodiment of what the artwork is about "style." On Danto's account, the style of the artwork should contribute to the expression of whatever it is about.

Although the notion of embodiment seems to demand manifestation in some physical medium, Danto does not seem to require this, since he will count as an artwork Robert Barry's untitled entry "All of the things I know but of which I am not at the moment thinking—1:36 PM, June 15, 1969." Presumably, this work's mode of presentation is ingeniously suitable to and even appositively supportive of its content, namely, that art can be anything, even something nonmanifest.

Though widely admired, Danto's concept of art has been frequently criticized. One criticism is a recurring objection to the necessity of his first condition—the content condition, the requirement that all artworks be about something, or, even more precisely, that they must bear meanings. For aren't there artworks, properly so-called, that are, so to say, beneath meaning, thematically or semantically construed? This is where beauty, in the narrow sense, enters the picture; certain beautiful artworks might be unavoidable examples of artworks that are bereft of or beneath meaning.

Beauty, narrowly construed, is a matter of that which is pleasing to the eye or the ear. It is a response-dependent property of sights and sounds—specifically of those sights and sounds that deliver pleasure to the human frame upon exposure. This is a conception that Socrates introduces—only to dismiss—in his attempt to characterize *kalon* (a word often, though I think misleadingly, translated as "beautiful" in English) in his *Hippias major*.

If by *kalon* we mean to signal the fine or the excellent, we may agree with Socrates' rejection of the definition of beauty as what is pleasant to the visual or the auditory senses.[2] Nevertheless, the suggestion that one sense of "beauty," albeit a very narrow sense, is essentially involved with pleasing the eyes and ears does seem to capture a primary usage of the concept of beauty. When we call a person or a landscape beautiful, isn't this just what we have in mind?

But, returning to Danto's concept of art and to his problem with beauty, might not something be an artwork that is simply beautiful in the narrow sense—for example, a ravishing pattern? We look at it and exclaim "Wow!" We can't take our eyes off of it. It irresistibly engages our ancient, mammalian perceptual system and caresses it pleasurably. We *like* to look at it.

Yet it is dumb beauty—a delightfully contrived artifice, although, from a semantic or symbolic or thematic perspective, it is a meaningless one. Call it eye candy; nevertheless, even if it says nothing, few will deny it is an artistic achievement. However, Danto's conception of art would seem to have no accommodation for works like this one which probably most informed art lovers, in contrast, would readily countenance as examples of the genuine article.

In other words, Danto's general theory of art requires that artworks be about something and that their mode of presentation suggest some comment or perspective upon whatever they are about, or that the form otherwise reinforce or advance the content of the work. But isn't it likely that there are artworks, properly so-called, that are made solely with the intention to delight the eye or ear—to afford visual or auditory pleasure?

Call these beautiful artworks *simpliciter*: works whose purpose is discharged exhaustively by the presentation of a design that, upon being perceived, elicits a palpable pleasure or a thrill, engendered by the act of looking or hearing, with no greater import. Think of a delightful tune or a lovely pastel abstraction. Since these artworks have no meaningful content, they would seem to be counterexamples to Danto's philosophy of art.

One response that Danto has made to criticisms like this is blunt—to wit: there are no such artworks. He challenges critics to come up with one.[3] Indeed, given any putative example, he believes that he can show that it is *really* about something. Many beautiful artworks from the past that may strike us as mere eye candy actually served ritual, or religious, or political, or other cultural purposes. If we knew more about the culture from which they emerged, we would grant this. Give him an example, and Danto boldly promises to reveal its meaning.[4]

Furthermore, with various modern works of art that may appear to be simply beautiful—say, some Minimalist abstractions—Danto will argue that, far from being meaningless, they contribute to a dialogue about the nature of art. A work by Frank Stella, for example, "says" something about the function of the edge of paintings by calling our attention to it. Thus does Danto pledge to disarm all the counterexamples—traditional and modern, beautiful or otherwise sensuously arresting—brought forth to embarrass his theory.

One hardly knows whether Danto, or even Danto assisted by an army of art historians and anthropologists, is up to the task of vanquishing all the plausible existing examples in this neighborhood. Yet it does not seem to me that Danto can banish the problem of simply beautiful artworks (a.k.a. sheer eye candy) by such feats of interpretive legerdemain. For even if every legitimate artwork so far can be assimilated in this way by Danto's theory (a proposition about which one may be reasonably skeptical), certainly it is conceivable that an artist *could* create something intended to be simply beautiful, construed narrowly, and which would in fact thrum our perceptual apparatus delightfully; informed art lovers would be disposed to regard such a design as art.

Perhaps the work abstractly deploys the sort of serenely appealing symmetries that, since the dawn of humanity, have served as positively reinforcing attractors for creatures like us.[5] Such a work would not be *about* what is appealing to humans. It would simply be appealing.

Let us imagine that the piece is the product of an artist armed with a vast understanding of the psychology of the human perceptual system, an MRI, and the technical staff to go along with it. He relentlessly probes the relation between our pleasure centers, the flow of dopamine, and the stimuli that trigger it. His project is the greatest alliance of art and science since folks tackled perspective in the Renaissance. And it is a great success. Everyone who sees the work produced as the result of this research feels joyously absorbed, as if enveloped in a pleasant embrace. If we hung a picture from this artist's series on our wall, who would deny that it is an artwork?

Danto would have to.

But then surely that is the worse for Danto's concept of art.

In order to negotiate this line of objection, Danto needs to tell us how beauty, narrowly conceived, fits into his philosophy of art in a way that either explains or explains away examples like the preceding one or, at least, renders their disenfranchisement tolerable. And that is the burden of his book *The Abuse of Beauty.*

On Why Beauty Has No Place in Danto's Concept of Art

In order to comprehend Danto's approach to the problem of beauty, one first needs to grasp his theory or definition of art. Central to that conception of art is a commitment to the view that beauty, understood narrowly, is not part of it. Danto reaches this conclusion through a philosophical argument that is buttressed by a certain confluence of historical narratives.

The philosophical argument is quite simple. The first premise is nicely captured by the slogan "art is not something that the eye can descry." You cannot tell whether or not a candidate is an artwork simply by looking. Whatever property or properties are constitutive of art status, they are not manifest.

This premise is ostensibly established by the consideration of artworks, including Marcel Duchamp's readymades (for example, his metal canine grooming comb), and Andy Warhol's *Brillo Box*, both of which are by this late date incontestably artworks while, at the same time, also being indiscernible from their real-world, non-artwork counterparts (ordinary steel combs, on the one hand, and Brillo packing cartons, on the other). Consequently, since there are genuine artworks, like these, that are indiscernible from their real-world, non-artwork counterparts, then discernible properties are not among the necessary or essentially defining properties of art.

But beauty, narrowly conceived, is, if nothing else, a discernible property. That it tickles the relevant senses is in large measure what we intend by the concept of sheer beauty. Therefore, such beauty is not among the essentially defining properties of art—or, more simply, sheer beauty is not a necessary constituent of the concept of art.

Stated in a nutshell, the argument goes like this:

1) If some property x is part of the concept of art (i.e., is a necessary or essentially defining feature of art), then it is a property that is, in principle, indiscernible (something that cannot be eyeballed, something that cannot be detected by the senses).
2) Beauty, narrowly construed, is, by definition, eminently discernible (it is what gives pleasure to the eyes and the ears).
3) Therefore, by *modus tollens*, beauty is not part of the concept of art.

The first premise of this argument is bolstered by two art-historical narratives. The first, pursued at length in Danto's *After the End of Art*, is the story of the artworld's reflexive aspiration, after the advent of photography, to define itself essentially from within the resources of art—for example, to show forth, by means of painting, what painting really is. This led to the attempted Modernist (à la Clement Greenberg) reduction of painting to such strategies as the salient foregrounding of flatness, followed by the Dada-inspired Pop Art riposte of indiscernibilia, like Warhol's *Brillo Box* and Roy Lichenstein's cartoon panels.

The latter artworks, and other pieces like them, defeated the claim that a discernible property like flatness could define the painterly artwork. However, they did not deliver a comparable definition of art. Instead, on Danto's view, they established that such a definition could not be developed in terms of discernible properties, thereby, in the process, disenfranchising beauty, that most discernible property, as a plausible defining property of art.[6] Consequently, in appreciation of this scenario, Danto's conception of art contains no mention of beauty.

But there is also a second, in some respects converging, art-historical narrative that Danto mobilizes against any consideration of beauty as an essential feature of art. It is the story of the avant-garde's often politically motivated war against beauty, the avant-garde's attempt to stamp out beauty—a dogged and intractable campaign, continued into the present day by the progeny of the likes of Dada, Surrealism, and Fluxus, which campaign Danto calls "the abuse of beauty."

Stated briefly, this story begins in an artworld that for centuries—even millennia—regarded beauty as the outward sign of the good and the true and which, for that reason, conceived of the role of art as the portrayal of a culture's conception of the good and the true in the robes of beauty. Then the plot thickens. Artists, notably in the West, came to deeply suspect their culture's conception of the good and the true due to the horrors in which these conceptions seem to be implicated—wars (like the First World War), the squalor of industrialization and urbanization, political oppression, economic exploitation, imperialism, and so on—you name it. In response, artists set out to kill the messenger—art (a.k.a. the *beaux arts*).

This is the origin of what Danto calls *kalliphobia*.[7] It explains the emergence of German Expressionism, with its pronounced figural distortions, and then Dada, and Fluxus, but also tendencies like Conceptual Art, which in many cases abjures not only any glimmering of beauty, but sensuous properties altogether. Of course, by the time that Dada, Fluxus, and Conceptual Art arrive on the scene, this story flows into the previous one. For in the passion to drive beauty from the republic of art, every discernible property is eschewed as a necessary feature of art. In an act of supreme renunciation, we might think of the intractable avant-garde as proclaiming that everything (every manifest property) must ultimately go. In some cases, even object-hood is disavowed in order to evade commodification.

The consequence of this for the philosophy of art is that, since many bona fide practitioners have exiled from their artworks discernible proper-ties like beauty, no comprehensive conception of art can rest upon discern-ible properties, including beauty, narrowly construed. That is, once again, the first premise of Danto's argument is put in place by gleaning the moral of a historical narrative. But this second narrative — the abuse of beauty nar-rative — also provides us with another reason to divorce beauty from the con-cept of art: a great many artists, representing substantial art movements, have divorced it from the practice of art. Thus, if theory reconstructs practice, then beauty, narrowly construed, cannot be part of the concept of art *sub specie aeternitatis.*

And, of course, Danto's characterization of art makes no explicit refer-ence to any discernible property; most notably, for our purposes, it makes no mention of beauty, narrowly conceived. As you may recall, x is a work of art according to Danto only if 1) x is about something, and 2) x is real-ized in a form or style appropriate to whatever it is about. Nevertheless, this leaves unexplained the perennial, seemingly intimate relation of beauty to art as well as unanswered the question of how we can in good philosophi-cal conscience cashier works of sheer beauty, as imagined previously, from the order of art.

Explaining (or Explaining Away) the Relevance of Beauty to Art Properly So-Called

Nowadays Danto likes to refer to his conception of art as a matter of embodied meanings. Artworks have meanings — semantic or thematic con-tent. That is, they are about something. And said meanings are presented, realized, expressed, or embodied in a form suitable or appropriate to them. What is the relevance of beauty to artworks? In short, beauty, narrowly con-strued, is one form of embodiment, one way of presenting whatever the art-work is about to an audience.

Moreover, in some cases, this mode of presenting whatever the work is about may be appropriate, as in the case of a positive allegorical render-ing of the virtue of charity which represents it as beauteous, perhaps even in the form of a lovely woman. In other instances, embodying a certain subject charmingly — for instance, visually prettifying what one actually intends to exemplify the horrors of war—can cause the artwork to miss its mark. When beauty is relevant to art, it is because the beauty contributes to whatever the work is about. In this regard, beauty is important for art just so far as it is an aspect of artistic meaning, namely as a contribution to the embodiment of that meaning in a manner that is suitable or subservient to, or facilitative of, whatever the work is about. In this way, Danto is able to neatly fold sensuous beauty into his otherwise rigorously cognitive theory of art.

Beauty, narrowly construed, is only one of the traditional aesthetic properties—properties, as Alexander Baumgarten would have it, of sensuous cognition—which Danto's theory of art might initially appear to neglect. But his treatment of beauty, narrowly construed, indicates how he will handle the lot of them. Aesthetic properties, like heaviness, will be relevant to artworks only insofar as they promote the content of those artworks. The heaviness of the façade of the courthouse, for example, can be pertinent to the architectural artistry of the building in that it may help to convey the feeling of the gravity of the law.

Aesthetic properties of this sort, of which beauty, narrowly construed, is a primary example, are, in a way of speaking, part of the pragmatic address of the artwork—a rhetorical feature, if you will. Such properties may move the audience in a way consonant with the theme that the artwork aspires to transmit. The faith of martyrs is portrayed beautifully in order to make it attractive—in order to inspire emulation.

This is why beauty is always on the side of the angels. Buddha is often embodied in supremely handsome figures so as to make viewers love his teachings. In other words, beauty—where it is pertinent to works of art *qua* art—has a rhetorical function within the work to perform, namely to embody whatever the work is about, or to express its meaning in a fashion that reinforces or forwards or is otherwise conducive to the assimilation or acceptance of the artwork's content. The meaning the work is supposed to advocate, where advocacy is what is in question, is what can be served by embodying it in a beautiful form—frequently, for example, in the outward form of a beautiful human body.

By the way, Danto can tell a similar story about ugliness—as a response-dependent, sensuous property—in artworks. Where ugliness, so conceived, is relevant to the art in a piece, this relevance is due to the contribution that the ugliness at issue makes to the meaning of the work. Satan is embodied in monstrous forms in order to make us shrink in revulsion from the evil ways he symbolizes. The statue of the Prince of the World at the Cathedral of St. Sebald in Nürnberg reveals the flesh on its backside to be in an advanced state of decay for the purpose of engendering in the faithful an aversion, rooted in an experience of disgust, to worldly things.

Ugliness, like beauty, can function as a rhetorical lever[8] and, thus, can count as a legitimate strategy for instantiating the embodiment clause of Danto's definition of art. It is in this way that aesthetic properties like ugliness and beauty make ontological contact with the nature of art as propounded by Danto. They are not part of the concept of art, but they are respectable, typically effective, and well-precedented ways of instancing the concept's requirement of embodiment.

Where beauty, narrowly construed, is in the service of the meaning or content of the artwork, Danto calls it "internal beauty." Although internal beauty as such is not a defining feature of art, it can be a proper part of the artwork *qua* art where it occurs, because it can be one of the (many) ways of implementing the embodiment condition of the concept of art. Another way of putting this might be to say that when beauty conspires in the appropriate embodiment of the content of the artwork, then it is *artistic* beauty, since it is beauty that functions to satisfy one of the necessary conditions of art.

This, of course, suggests that there can be beauty in an artwork that is not connected to the content or meaning of the work. Danto calls this "external beauty," and it is not a proper part of the artwork, even though it may be attached to it. Likewise, a piece of sheer eye candy belongs to the category of external beauty—beauty on the outside with nothing (no meaning, no content) on the inside. Perhaps a golden shot glass studded with glittering, eye-catching jewels, but with no purport whatsoever, is an example of external beauty, as would be any other sort of mere mute decorative design.

Danto's notion of internal beauty provides art historians with an extremely useful heuristic for addressing aesthetic properties, like beauty, where they are functioning as internal properties of the artwork. Once the art historians ascertain the meaning of the work, their next order of business is to divine the way in which the beauty of the work contributes to its meaning. Why is the value of liberty, for example, embodied as a bare-breasted woman? Yet this heuristic may serve not only the purposes of the art historian, but also those of the art critic, as Danto has shown with his explications of the function of internal beauty in individual artworks, such as Robert Motherwell's *Elegy to the Spanish Republic*, and in entire oeuvres, such as that of Robert Mapplethorpe.

Danto's heuristic with regard to internal beauty, moreover, is applicable to art forms other than painting, photography, and sculpture. Quite obviously, the practice of text setting in music is an effort to match the commitments expressed in hymns to sensuously beguiling sounds that encourage assent. And one can also find internal beauty employed in recent motion pictures. In the film *Brokeback Mountain,* certain of the homosexual interludes between the two cowboys are set within cinematically pronounced contexts of stunning natural landscapes. The horizon line is low and the screen fills up with the bluest of breathtaking skies; the cloud formations, with their strong white volumes, are equally mesmerizing. Without a doubt, the director, Ang Lee, is emphasizing the beauty of the natural vistas in these scenes in order to thematically mark these moments in the cowboys' lives as the most special, most pleasurable, most intense, most satisfying, and, yes, the most beautiful in their otherwise straitened experience.

Internal beauty is the most important philosophical discovery of Danto's *The Abuse of Beauty.* Not only is Danto's heuristic a singular contribution to art history and to the criticism of the arts in general; the idea of internal beauty also answers the theoretical question of why beauty can be important to art genuinely so called. It is not because beauty, narrowly construed, is, as the phrase *beaux arts* insinuates, a defining feature of art, but because some beauty in the narrow sense—specifically, internal beauty—is a tried and true, very humanly accessible way of appropriately embodying and/or rhetorically advancing that which the pertinent artwork is about.

Internal beauty, that is, can be a proper instance of artistic embodiment, while not being the whole of it. Thus does the proposal of internal beauty dissolve the philosophical quandary of why it is that beauty historically has stood in and, in truth, still stands in such an intimate relation to the practice of art, while also not figuring as a necessary or essential condition of the concept of art.

Furthermore, it is my hypothesis that by means of the notion of internal beauty, Danto hopes to fend off those critics of his theory who charge that it permits no room for beauty. His rejoinder is that, in fact, as just demonstrated, his philosophy of art has ample space for beauty, narrowly construed, so long as we are talking about internal beauty. Indeed, the link between Danto's concept of art and internal beauty is quite a nice one—smooth and logically unforced.

Moreover, I suspect that Danto thinks that as art historians, art lovers, and philosophers of art, we should be concerned with no other form of beauty than internal beauty. It's paintings like Raphael's *The Transfiguration* (fig. 1.1) that we care about, not pretty pinky rings. The beauty that is not internal beauty—the eye candy *simpliciter* and the external beauty attached, but not intrinsically so, to artworks—no more deserves our attention than the swaths of pleasant wallpaper at Home Depot.

Figure 1.1. Raphael (Raffaello Sanzio) (1483–1520), *The Transfiguration*. Pinacoteca, Vatican Museums, Vatican State.

This line of rebuttal, supposing it to be Danto's, of course, may be not so much a matter of explaining the relation of external beauty to the concept of art as it is an attempt at explaining its apparent relevance away. But if it is Danto's intention, as I have just interpreted it, to explain away the possibility that works of sheer beauty can be artworks, I do not think that he will be ultimately successful.

On the one hand, this approach will not square with ordinary usage. Few will deny that a pretty, pastel, abstract design is a work of art, even if it is only a trivial one. Nor, at this late date in the evolution of secular hedonism, can Danto deny that a piece such as this might be nothing more than an altogether mute pleasure machine. That is, he won't be able to talk his way out of cases like this. Moreover, shifting art forms, does Danto really intend to dispute the fact that the impressive numbers of pleasing orchestral tunes—sans titles, texts, and/or programs—are works of art?

In addition, even art historians, art lovers, and philosophers of art should be wary of quarantining experimentation in the production of sheer beauty—call it external beauty, if you want—from the practice of art, since the innovation in and discovery of what provokes sensuous pleasure, notably the beauties of sight and sound, promise to inaugurate fresh strategies for artistic embodiment. Surely the continuous interrogation by artists of beauty is scarcely a dispensable part of the process we identify as the practice of art.

Thus, I do not think that Danto has conclusively defeated the problem of artworks without meaning which was introduced in the first section of this essay. A leading possibility in this regard, as indicated, involves putative artworks of surpassing beauty in the narrow sense. By introducing the notion of internal beauty, Danto has substantially decimated the range of counterexamples to his theory which hail from the direction of the beautiful. Nevertheless, he has not, to my mind, demonstrated that an artist might successfully create a work solely intended to bring pleasure to the senses by means of abstract sights and/or sounds which the rest of us would of necessity have to refuse, on conceptual grounds, to countenance as an artwork.

However, rather than ending this section on a dour note, let me propose a friendly amendment to Danto's theory of the concept of art. Let us emend Danto's aboutness condition to read: x is an artwork only if it possesses a point or a purpose. Of course, the point or purpose of the work might be to impart some meaning or to expound some theme or to advance some content. But it also might be merely to deliver an absorbing and pleasurable experience through the manipulation of sights and/or sounds. Or the point might be to elicit some other kind of experience sans meaning. The purpose of certain

1960s flicker films, for example, was to cause afterimages in the viewer in order to alert them to neglected aspects of our perceptual apparatus.

On this reformulation, x is a work of art only if 1) x has a point or purpose 2) which it presents, embodies, realizes, or implements in an appropriate form, manner, or style. This version of the theory saves those of a Dantoesque persuasion from counterexamples that might well up from the realm of art beneath meaning.

Danto, of course, might reject this proposal, possibly on the grounds that the characterization of art just submitted is not sufficient to distinguish art from many other things, including most functional tools. Doesn't a hammer have a purpose, and isn't the form of the hammer, with its weighted head, appropriate to the purpose of driving nails?

Fair enough. But Danto's own version of the theory comprises only two necessary conditions that do not add up to sufficiency either. Thus, both Danto's official view and our suggested reformulation need more teeth. Something needs to be added.

A suggestion: Might not that something have to do with the atmosphere of theory and of the histories of art that Danto taught us about in his first essay in the philosophy of art—"The Artworld?"[9]

Arthur Danto's Concept of Art and Beauty in a Broader Sense

Thus far, this essay has examined the relation between Arthur Danto's philosophy of art and beauty, narrowly conceived. By beauty, narrowly conceived, I have been thinking of beauty as a response-dependent property of sights and sounds that give rise to pleasure. This is a notion introduced but then abandoned by Socrates in the *Hippias major,* although later endorsed by the Stoics.[10] This is the version of beauty that I think Danto has foremost in mind in his discussion of beauty—especially internal beauty—in his treatise *The Abuse of Beauty.* It is also the construal of beauty that I myself prefer, because it is the simplest and least ambiguous one available. However, it is undoubtedly not the only conception of beauty on offer. For, as remarked earlier, sometimes the notion of beauty is run together with ideas of the fine, the excellent, the good, and even the true.

Now is not the time to attempt to catalogue all of the broader senses of beauty which are still in play, since even if I had the erudition (which I do not), I do not have the space. Nevertheless, I would like to call attention to at least one of the broader notions of beauty, since by its lights Danto's concept of art is not in principle in any way remote from beauty but, ironically, is but another instance of the equation of art and beauty, where beauty has a broader sense than that encountered so far.

As I have already repeated more than once, Danto's theory of art is that x is an artwork only if 1) x has content, and 2) x presents this content in an appropriate form. However, this characterization is also historically a characterization of beauty in one of its broader senses. Danto freely and even proudly admits that the origin of his account of the concept of art derives from the philosophy of Hegel.[11] But Hegel, in turn, acknowledges that he got the idea from Hirt's consideration of the beautiful in several arts.

The formula for art that Hegel appears to proffer (and which Danto expropriates)—namely, that art has a content presented in an appropriate manner—is precisely a theory of beautiful art. For Hirt, the beautiful is the perfect, and the perfect is "that which is adequate to its aim, that which nature or art aimed at producing within the given genus or species."[12] Adequation or appropriateness here is a case of beauty in the broader sense. Thus, the theory of art from which Danto allegedly takes his marching orders, when traced back to its origin in Hirt, could be parsed as: art equals beautifully portrayed content.[13]

Nor did the pertinent understanding of beauty originate in Hirt. It is a very ancient idea. It appears in Vitruvius's *De architectura* as what has been called *décor* theory, or, more formally, the "rational theory of appropriateness," (where the Latin *décor* is a translation of the Greek *to prepon*). As expounded by Vitruvius, the leading idea of the *décor* theory is that the form of a beautiful work of architecture should be appropriate to its meaning. With respect to columns, since the Doric order is the most austere, it is to be used in temples to martial divinities like Mars, Minerva, and Hercules, while the Corinthian order, being more ornate, is most suitable for floral gods and demigods like Venus, Flora, and the nymphs.[14] Moreover, Vitruvius's theory here may have been inherited from Theophrastus's *On Style*, which, in turn, got it from Aristotle's *Rhetoric*. Indeed, to refer to the *Hippias major* once again, the idea that *kalon* is "the appropriate" is a notion that Socrates introduces only to reject it.

Where beauty in this particular broader sense is a matter of the adequation of form to content, it is conceivable that something that is not beautiful, or even ugly, narrowly construed—that is, something that is displeasing to sight or hearing—could, nevertheless, be beautiful in this second sense. This is how we get the idea of a beautiful picture of a hideous thing. The statue *The Prince of the World* is a case in point. Though literally revolting, it is a suitable (a.k.a. beautiful in the larger sense) presentation of its animating idea or meaning. Thus, anything that counts as a work of art according to Danto's theory of art thus far is also, in terms of this broader understanding of beauty, also beautiful. But in that case, there is not, as Danto assumes, any real distance between the concept of art and the domain of beauty and, therefore, no reason to ponder their subtle connects and disconnects.

Undoubtedly, Danto will want to reject this conclusion by hewing closely to what I call beauty, narrowly construed. I think that is the right way to go in philosophical discussions of beauty in general, and I would also agree that it is the narrow view of beauty that seems generally implicit in Danto's discussion. Nevertheless, the fact that his concept of art emerges historically in the context of a discussion that moves so freely between beauty and art suggests that he might revisit his sources in order to disentangle his commitments from theirs, and to articulate the differences in this vicinity with greater analytic clarity than he has so far.

Notes

This essay was previously published in *Il mondo dell'arte dopo il tempo: Prospettive sull'estetica di Arthur C. Danto*, ed. Michele di Monte (Rome: Meltemi Editore, 2008).

1. Arthur C. Danto, *The Abuse of Beauty: Aesthetics and the Concept of Art* (Chicago, Ill.: Open Court, 2003). His previous monographs on the philosophy of art are *The Transfiguration of the Commonplace* (Cambridge, Mass.: Harvard University Press, 1981); and *After the End of Art* (Princeton: Princeton University Press, 1997).

2. Though I agree that Socrates is right to abandon as an account of *kalon* (the fine) the idea that *kalon* is a matter of pleasing the pertinent senses, I don't agree with the reasons Socrates adduces for this conclusion in the text.

3. See Arthur Danto, "Art and Meaning," in *Theories of Art Today*, ed. Noël Carroll (Madison: University of Wisconsin Press, 2000), 130–40.

4. Danto might attempt to reject examples like these on the grounds that they do not really threaten his definition of art. He might argue, for example, that all his "aboutness" condition requires is that it be appropriate to attempt to interpret artworks, not that all artworks have interpretations. So long as the eye candy in question strikes reasonable people as worth exploring for possible interpretations, Danto may say, it meets his conditions, and, furthermore, this removes the troubling artworks from the board. However, I still maintain that there can be beautiful artworks that just dazzle us without inclining us to interpret them.

5. Contemporary psychology has correlated a nearly universal association of symmetry with human beauty and attempted to explain this by suggesting that such symmetry is a sign of health and, therefore, a reproductive asset from an evolutionary point of view. In this regard, the appealing and attracting pleasure that arises from symmetrical sights has its biological origins, so to speak, as an adaptive carrot. For an introduction to this view with references for further reading, see David Buss,

Evolutionary Psychology: The New Science of the Mind (Boston: Allyn and Bacon, 1999), 118–19, 141–42. Interestingly, this hypothesis was already suggested in the ancient world. Galen, commenting upon the Stoic Chrysippus, attributes to the latter a belief in a connection between health and the harmony of the parts of the body which he, Galen, illustrates by reference to the *Canon* of the sculptor Polyclitus. See J. J. Pollitt, *The Ancient View of Greek Art: Criticism, History, and Terminology* (New Haven: Yale University Press, 1974), 14–15.

6. In this way, Danto, like Plato and Hegel before him, disbars art from doing metaphysics on the grounds that its medium is bound to the senses such as vision — though I hasten to add that Danto's metaphysics are different from those of his predecessors. For more analysis of Danto's disenfranchisement of art, see Noël Carroll, "The End of Art?" in "Danto and His Critics: Art History, Historiography and *After the End of Art*," ed. David Carrier, theme issue, *History and Theory* 37, no. 4 (December 1998), 17–29.

7. Arthur Danto, "*Kalliphobia* in Contemporary Art; or, Whatever Happened to Beauty?" in *Unnatural Wonders: Essays from the Gap between Art and Life* (New York: Farrar, Strauss, and Giroux, 2005), 321–32.

8. See, for example, Noël Carroll, "Ethnicity, Race, and Monstrosity: The Rhetorics of Horror and Humor," in *Engaging the Moving Image* (New Haven: Yale University Press, 2003), 88–107.

9. Arthur Danto, "The Artworld," reprinted in *The Philosophy of Art*, ed. Alex Neill and Aaron Ridley (New York: McGraw Hill, 1995), 201–23.

10. See Wladyslaw Tatarkiewicz, *A History of Six Ideas: An Essay in Aesthetics* (The Hague: Martinus Nihoff, 1980), 122.

11. See G. W. F. Hegel, *Introductory Lectures on Aesthetics*, trans. Bernard Bosanquet (London: Penguin, 1993), chapter 2, section 31, p. 20.

12. Ibid.

13. In my essay "Beauty and the Genealogy of Art Theory," I argued that a certain conception of beauty, as derived from Kant especially, shaped the trajectory of much subsequent art theory. As indicated above, I now think that it may be the case that Hegelian versions of art theory are also indelibly marked by a background of traditional conceptions of beauty, albeit a different conception than the Kantian theory of free beauty. See Noël Carroll, "Beauty and the Genealogy of Art Theory," in *Beyond Aesthetics* (Cambridge: Cambridge University Press, 2000), 20–40.

14. Pollitt, *The Ancient View of Greek Art*, 68–69.

2. Savages, Wild Men, Monstrous Races: The Social Construction of Race in the Early Modern Era

GREGORY VELAZCO Y TRIANOSKY

The modern conception of race is often thought by philosophers to have developed during the eighteenth and nineteenth centuries in response to a unique confluence of scientific, philosophical, and imperial forces; and in recent decades some impressive work has been done to excavate the details of its construction during this period.[1] Of course philosophers generally acknowledge, if only in passing, that this late modern construction has its roots in various medieval traditions, among which are typically mentioned the medieval versions of the Noachic legend, according to which the peoples of the earth can be divided into three broad groups (African, Asian, and European), each descended from one of the sons of Noah.[2]

I will argue, however, that an analysis of the visual images created by Europeans during the first half-century after 1492 reveals that the essential elements of the late modern conception of race are put into place during that period. In brief, the tremendous social, economic, and political pressures that culminate in this comparatively brief moment yield the modern notion of "the savage." I will suggest that from its inception this notion is an inherently racialized one, and that it is the nodal point from which, in broad outline and in much of its detail, the template is drawn for the more familiar eighteenth- and nineteenth-century understandings of non-European races.

Moreover, I will argue that the modern notion of the savage is synthesized, not directly from the Noachic legends, but from images drawn, sometimes literally, on the margins of medieval understandings of humanity: powerful and deeply entrenched images of the Wild Man and the monstrous races. This synthesis is made possible, first, by the ways in which the discovery and colonization of the New World expand the boundaries of the world defined as European to include faraway places previously known only through rumors, legends, and the testimonies of medieval authorities. At the same time, the discovery and colonization realign these newly familiar and redefined boundaries with the old margins of medieval mythology. It is this transfer of old, mythologized concepts to newly discovered living peoples, virtually completed in the very moment of discovery, that is the fountain-head of late modern conceptions of race. My investigation is preliminary, and much work remains to be done, particularly on the larger historical context of the early colonization; but I hope it will be enough to convince aestheticians and historians of philosophy to venture beyond the well-worn paths of the late modern era to uncover the earlier origins of modern ideas and images of race.

It is important to place the artwork discussed here in its art-historical context. The high-art style of the sixteenth century often referred to as "mannerism" has been characterized by one art historian as showing "an insistently cultured grace and accomplishment . . . accompanied by the kindred qualities of abstraction from natural behavior and appearances, bizarre fantasy, complexity and invention."[3] The best-known images of the early colonization and conquest of the Americas, produced by the de Bry family at the end of the sixteenth century, fit this characterization well. Even a cursory review of a representative selection of Theodor de Bry's engravings, as they are published in Michael Alexander's *Discovering The New World: Based on The Works of Theodor de Bry*, for example, will confirm that author's claim that de Bry is "a mannerist in the heyday of mannerism."[4] Our attention here, however, will be on earlier images of America, produced under rather different circumstances. The history of the production of these earlier, pre–de Bry images points to artists and artisans whose work is, if not necessarily more immediate, then at least more free of the dominant mannerist conventions. Most of the images of America and American Indians discussed here are woodcuts produced by artisans trained as cabinetmakers, rather than engravings produced by artists or goldsmiths trained or supervised by artists.[5] With some well-known exceptions, the work of these artisans was not regarded as highly among patrons of the arts. Nor was it expected to conform closely to the high-art standards of the day. In many early cases it was intended only to increase the attractiveness of a book or pamphlet to a mass audience. These early pictures are often drawn hastily, in many cases by artisans whose only guide was the text, working under the commercial pressures of producing mass-market publications like the various editions of

Christopher Columbus's 1493 letter. One need not embrace a naïve realism to point out that it is characteristic of these works that they pay much less attention to fidelity to the text being illustrated (whatever one makes of the issue of its factual legitimacy) than they do to the exigencies of the printing process and, perhaps above all, to the marketability of what is produced.

The point of focusing on this earlier, artisanal work is not that, in so doing, we can catch a glimpse of what American Indian people were "really like," but rather, one might say, that in so doing we can catch a glimpse of what European people were "really like." This earlier work allows us to glimpse familiar and less polished, workaday European preconceptions about strange peoples, not so heavily influenced, perhaps, by the dominant high-art conventions of the time.

To be sure, many of the earliest drawings already display the same political and economic motivations that are often drawn to our attention in commentaries on the later, more polished work of de Bry and others. In particular, the explicit interest in colonization and subjugation is present from the very beginning. In addition to these often crudely explicit interests, many of the early drawings also reveal European attempts to understand the new and unfamiliar through old and familiar European ideas, creatively reworked, but nonetheless expressed in tropes, symbols, and metaphors that were pervasive throughout the Middle Ages and early Renaissance. This attempt, understood as itself an interested one, is all the more powerful because the viewer, as a member of a broadly shared European culture, is encouraged to respond to what is represented through the lens of the old myths, familiar, rewritten, and rendered incarnate.

Consider, for example, the long, unkempt hair of the Indians as portrayed in many of the woodcuts produced in the first five years after the initial contact, often as adjuncts to the letters of Columbus or Vespucci. While some have claimed, I think rightly, to find more subtle and attenuated references to hairiness in later sixteenth-century engravings (those of de Bry, for example), in the earliest representations that concern us here the hairiness of the Indians is explicit and highly visible. Although it is tempting to understand this early commonplace as serving a wholly metaphorical function rather than a literally descriptive one, the writers of the day appear to have understood it literally. The sixteenth-century writer André Thevet, for example, remarks with consternation and disapproval on the persistent European tendency to portray American Indians as hairy despite the near-unanimity of eyewitness reports to the contrary.[6] On the other hand, hairiness is a trope that is deployed from the times of the Babylonian empire (in the Epic of

Gilgamesh) and the Old Testament (in the story of Cain and Abel, and again in the story of Jacob and Esau) to the present-day United States (see, for example, Benicio del Toro's reprise of the title role in *The Wolfman*, [dir. Joe Johnston, 2010]) as the signature mark of the outsider, the one who is Other, or the one who is more brutish and less civilized. It is present in almost every European tradition in the form of images and stories of the Wild Man.[7] Here the point is that these portrayals have probably always served a number of interwoven functions. What was new, although not entirely unprecedented, in the early portrayals of American Indians was the European attempt to deploy the descriptive power of traits like hairiness, their symbolism, and their significance in their experience of living, breathing peoples whom Europeans encountered far from home. Similarly powerful presentations and representations of American Indians call on the tradition of the monstrous races. For example, the use of the *cynocephali*, the monstrous race of dog-headed people (described by Pliny and dozens of medieval texts that follow him), to depict the alleged cannibalism of American Indians in an illustration in Lorenz Fries's 1525 edition of Vespucci's *Carta marítima*, published in Strasbourg, instantly made it a familiar instance of the medieval trope of the horrific practices of faraway and alien peoples.[8]

The woodcut presents an outdoor scene as if at a butcher's shop, complete with chopping block and dog-headed butcher. Hung around the block are recognizably human limbs, and on the block are a human head, a hand, and a leg that the butcher is in the process of cutting, arm raised over his head. To one side another *cynocephalus* arrives riding a llama—a familiar period representation of the exotic character of New World fauna—with what appears to be an older child tied hand and foot to his saddle, ready, we may presume, for butchering. A great deal is communicated in the image by a few simple strokes of the artisan's pencil, with no annotation or explication required, and no artistic sophistication or classical knowledge on the part of the observer presupposed. The stage is thus quickly set for the ordinary Europeans (working-class people and small-business owners) who make up many of the early colonizers to see American Indians, if not literally as dog-headed, then as properly represented by the symbolism of dog-headedness: namely, as lacking in one or more of the qualities necessary for interactions governed by the *jus gentium*, or perhaps even the *lex naturalis* itself—in short, as "savages," as they quickly came to be called in a variety of sixteenth-century European languages. These two tropes—the hairy Indian and the dog-headed cannibal—thus serve as an introduction *en breve* to the transfer and transformation of mythic concepts in their application to living peoples.

This creative application of mythic concepts is encapsulated in the modern idea of "the savage." In this way the transformation of medieval myth into modern "reality" lays the groundwork for the racialized treatment of American Indians as essentially and irredeemably Other. It is to a more detailed examination of this process of transformation that we now turn.

Old Images

We may begin to understand the making of the idea of "the savage" by examining in a little more detail two strands deeply woven into the European mythology of the Middle Ages: the stories of the monstrous races and the images of the Wild Man.

Character of the Monstrous Races

The monstrous races first make their appearance in ancient Greek writings, perhaps in the work of Herodotus; but the most influential source of information about them during the Middle Ages is unquestionably the *Historia naturalis* of Pliny the Elder (23–79 CE).[9] Identical descriptions or obvious variations on Pliny's appear repeatedly and with nearly identical illustrations, from the important and widely read work of Isidorus of Seville (560–636 CE) to the margins of the Hereford *Mappa mundi* (1290), to the *Travels of Sir John Mandeville* (circa 1357), which is sometimes claimed to have been an important reference work for Columbus.[10] They continue to appear frequently in translations of Pliny and other works contemporary with Columbus's voyages: for example, in the frontispiece of Hartmann Schedel's *Das Buch der Croniken und Geschichten*, published in 1493, where *cynocephali*, Cyclopes, *blemmyae* (humanoids with no heads, whose faces are in their chests), *sciopods* (humanoids with one giant foot), and others appears as borders on either side of the text.

There are many monstrous races; but even a modest effort at cataloguing the variations shows the consistency of their descriptions across a great range of medieval sources.[11] To understand how the tradition of the monstrous races provided creative materials for the emergent notion of the savage, I propose that we divide the monstrous races into two groups: those whose phenotype is identical to that of known humans, but whose behavior or culture is represented as strange and alien to European audiences; and those whose phenotype itself is so strange and bizarre as to be beyond the range of what is regarded as familiarly human, typically signaling bizarre or outré behavior as well. In the former category one group is of particular interest for the European response to the New World, namely, the *anthropophagi*. The *anthropophagi* are cannibals who are variously described as eating their enemies, their friends, their family members, and certainly any available strangers.

Depictions of cannibalism are of course standard fare in representations of New World peoples; but the pictures published soon after 1492 are quite striking and fairly direct in their reliance on the earlier traditions. The earliest extended account of cannibalism in the New World, and the earliest of the captivity narratives that later formed a staple of Puritan literature, is the story offered by Hans von Staden, who claimed to have been kidnapped by the Tupinambá of Brazil and held captive by them for six months. A series of woodcuts depicting his experiences were executed in 1557, apparently under his direct supervision.[12] Though published a little later than the period under consideration here, one example is particularly representative. In this illustration, a bearded von Staden appears in the lower center of the image, mouth open in horror or perhaps admonition, arms extended and index fingers pointing at some of the horrors he sees: a kneeling figure about to be slaughtered by a Tupinambá's club; a headless torso being dismembered; limbs being roasted over an open fire; and a small child, under the approving eyes of his parents, carrying a severed human head. Woodcuts like this repeatedly reenact this device of the single, shocked European observer who encounters customs and cultures far removed from his own.[13] In the von Staden illustrations, as in earlier sources like Mandeville's *Travels*, this device is used to frame the depiction of cannibalism. In many early depictions New World cannibals are represented as a group, to convey that their behavior is characteristic of a certain culture; and their behavior is interwoven with scenes of family and friendship, emphasizing the "normality" of these horrific activities for this monstrous race. This is suggested, for example, by the aforementioned presence of a child carrying a severed head in the Von Staden woodcut, and also in a widely reprinted 1505 German woodcut of the Tupinambá by Johann Froschauer that accompanied a German edition of Vespucci's *Carta*, in which two children and a nursing baby are gathered at their mother's lap, directly under the head and dismembered limbs of what appears to be a hapless European, while Vespucci's ships may be seen disappearing toward the horizon.[14]

Even when the Indians are portrayed as doing horrific things, however, they are nonetheless represented at the same time as "normal" or even beautiful in appearance, as one might perhaps have expected from a monstrous race whose distinguishing feature is behavior and culture rather than phenotype.[15] For example, Columbus comments on how "well formed" and "shapely" the Tainos are, prefiguring a classicized notion of beauty that became a commonplace of the eighteenth century, but at the same time echoing a much older notion of ugliness or "monstrosity" as involving distortion or misshapenness.[16] Referring to information he claims to have garnered from his Taino informants, he says,

> In these islands I have found no human monstrosities, as many expected, but on the contrary the whole population is very well formed. . . . Thus I have found no monsters, nor had any report of any, except in an island [called] "Carib" . . . which is inhabited by people who are regarded in all the islands as very fierce and who eat flesh. . . . They are no more malformed than are the others, except that they have the custom of wearing their hair long like women.[17]

This dissonance between phenotype and behavior may appear startling at first, until one realizes that it invokes the frequently depicted contrast between two types of monstrous races adumbrated above. The Froschauer woodcut discussed above is typical in this respect.

In the second category of monstrous races—those who are phenotypically dissimilar as well as culturally or behaviorally alien—may be found the *donestre*, lion-headed people who pretend to understand the foreign languages of travelers, and then kill them, devour their bodies, and mourn over their heads, as related in an eleventh-century version of *The Marvels of the East*.

Perhaps unsurprisingly, the particular traits and behaviors represented do not always remain firmly on one side or the other of the distinction I have drawn. The pretense of linguistic familiarity, and the friendliness it is used to express, reappear in one of the most familiar and horrific vignettes offered by early European explorers of the New World and their publishers, namely Vespucci's 1501 *Carta marítima*. It represents seductive American Indian women, hardly monstrous in appearance (though with clearly exaggerated buttocks), who lured one of Vespucci's sailors onto land and into conversation, killed him, and ate him while his horrified mates looked on from aboard ship.[18]

Of even greater interest among the phenotypically alien monstrous races, because of their more frequent appearance in New World settings, are the *cynocephali*, the dog-headed people, pictured in their New World habitat in an illustration to the 1530 edition of Vespucci's *Carta marítima*. Traditionally the *cynocephali* displayed two contradictory features. On the one hand they were often described as cannibals, (e.g., in the Siena College Bestiary of 1277). On the other hand they were also often described either as Christians or as a people capable of being converted to Christianity.[19] One or the other or both of these features are, of course, often deployed in depictions and descriptions of American Indians, both earlier and later, a point to which I will return.

Geography of the Monstrous Races

Together with the distinction just discussed between two types of monstrous races, the geography of the monstrous races is key to understanding the transformation involved in the New World deployment of these stock figures of the European imaginary. Even as late as the fifteenth century, the monstrous races were typically located in "the East," a region that seems to have incorporated many of the lands east of the River Don and now settled by Slavic peoples, as well as central, southern, and eastern Asia.[20] This location is reinforced by medieval readings of the extremely popular fourth-century *Alexander Romance*, which was interpreted as describing a wall built by Alexander the Great, or sometimes a chain of mountains (often identified with the Caucasus), that blocked off the known world from the monstrous races to the east and north of Europe, the Middle East, and Asia Minor.[21]

The location of the monstrous races in the East places them on the margins, far from the center of the world as Europeans lived it, in places with which Europe has no large-scale human interaction. More precisely, they are located in places regarding which Europeans have no imperial interests. That is to say, whatever Europeans want from the East during the Middle Ages, they do not desire to occupy it; and whatever resources they draw from it are drawn primarily by trade or by travel, and not by conquest.[22]

Moreover, this lack of imperial interests is reciprocated. From the fifth-century invasions of the Huns and the seventh-century incursions of the Avars beyond the lands now occupied by various Slavic groups until the thirteenth-century invasions by the Tatars and Mongols, the residents of the areas east of the River Don, including central, southern, and eastern Asia, generally had no substantial imperial interests of their own in Europe. It is because of this mutual lack of imperial interest that these places can easily be imagined by most medieval Europeans as utterly alien and distant. And, in turn, it is because these locations are so alien that locating the monstrous races there allows them to function as a locus for imaginative European exploration and definition of the boundaries of being human. This placement allows the monstrous races to be pictured, not just as moderately different with respect to custom and phenotype (as, say, the Germans might differ from the French), but as radically different kinds of beings, who live in ways that are shockingly different and horrendous, and whose phenotype is often shaped in equally alien or monstrous ways. In short, from its beginnings, the mythology of the geographically distant monstrous races serves both literal and metaphorical functions. It is for this reason that it is beside the point to ask whether the use of portrayals of the monstrous races in describing American Indians is meant literally or not. Here, as in the more specific case of attributions of hairiness, its creative use in European understandings of the American Indians reveals the same dual function, in which geographic distance permits the encounter to be read as a form of living speculation on the humanity of those who are Other with respect to behavior, culture, and perhaps even phenotype. How this dual function provided some of the key ingredients of an alchemy in which both the understanding of the monstrous races and the understanding of American Indians were transmogrified will be addressed below.

The Wild Man

The second inhabitant of the medieval European imaginary who some-how comes to life in the encounter with the New World is the Wild Man. The Wild Man is described in some medieval sources as one of the monstrous races; but there are crucial differences. Setting aside the special case of the ordinary person who becomes wild for some period of time,[23] it is clear that there is a long tradition of seeing the Wild Man as a naturally solitary figure who is violent and lascivious, often preying upon travelers or innocent women.[24] Moreover, his geography is typically unlike that of the monstrous races, for he inhabits the woods or the mountains comparatively close to European towns and villages.[25] Indeed, it is this bestial solitude in proximity to European culture and society that is the defining feature of the Wild Man, as Mary Shelley's use of the trope in *Frankenstein* reminds us.[26]

Images of the hirsute Wild Man are very frequently taken over without significant modifications into early depictions of American Indians, where the standard medieval weapon of the Wild Man, namely, a club or tree limb, becomes the club or spear, or sometimes a bow and arrow, as in the 1505 Florentine edition of Vespucci's letter, *De novo mundo*. In the fifteenth and sixteenth centuries, pictures of Wild Families become more common; and the figure of the Wild Woman, which had always had a separate trajectory with a rather different significance, now becomes part of the family ensemble.[27] We will return to the significance of this critical and fairly late shift in the mythology of the Wild Man below.

With respect to geography the Wild Man is typically very unlike the monstrous races. The Wild Man, whether accompanied or not, lives in relatively close proximity to Europeans. Nonetheless, as with the monstrous races, the places he occupies are not the objects of imperial European interests. He lives in the mountains, or in the old-growth forests that still covered much of Europe at least until 1250 CE or so. These are, from the point of view of most Europeans, *terra incognita*, vast and largely unknown islands, right in the midst of Europe. They are therefore, like "the East," suitable sites for imaginative explorations of human nature.

To understand how figures of imagination like the Wild Man and the monstrous races, often conceived of as real but almost always beyond ordinary experience, richly symbolic and at the same time freighted with the fears, anxieties, and values of everyday Europeans, came to serve as the foundations for the understanding of American Indian peoples, we must turn now to one remaining piece of the puzzle, namely, the radical geographic changes occurring in the thirteenth through fifteenth centuries with respect to the areas previously assigned to the creatures of imagination. These changes pave the way for the fifteenth- and sixteenth-century extension from the realms of fantasy onto the realities of New World peoples.

The Transformation of Europe

Invasions from "The East"

First, during the thirteenth through fifteenth centuries Europe is repeatedly under attack by waves of invaders from the east and the southeast. In the years 1220–25 the Mongols encircled the Caspian, sacking the Genoese outpost in Crimea. They invaded Armenia and Azerbaijan, and they completed the conquest of Bulgaria and Ukraine by 1240. No sooner were the Mongol invasions over than the Ottoman Turks began their rise to military and political prominence, circa 1299. In 1389 the Ottomans defeated the Serbs at the Battle of Kosovo, thus opening routes of military expansion from the East into Europe. In 1453 Constantinople fell to the Ottomans, and by 1529 they were at the gates of Vienna. From 1423 to 1571 (the Battle of Lepanto) they were a constant threat to the merchant states of Italy, particularly to Venice.

I have suggested that, prior to the thirteenth century, at least, the Eastern location of the monstrous races ensured that encounters with them played out largely as imagined confrontations rather than as encounters with living beings. As a result of the Tatar, Mongol, and Turkish incursions, however, the Eastern lands come alive for Europeans. This is certainly not to say that

Europeans suddenly begin to believe that these lands were really there and really inhabited. Because of the trade in silk and spices, as well as the much older westward movement of religious ideas from India, Europeans were long aware of the reality of China, India, and the lands between there and Europe. But for five hundred years and more, most of the peoples of what we now think of as Europe were familiar with *gens* (peoples) east of Asia Minor primarily through travelers' tales, or perhaps through the signs and symbols of the goods and ideas that came with those tales.[28]

In short, what is new in the thirteenth through fifteenth centuries is that peoples from these places now make an undeniable and widespread appearance in Europe itself. In general it is difficult to overstate the importance of the centuries-long experience of the Ottoman presence in redefining European images and European geography of "the Orient"; but the present point is that, from the perspective of the three hundred years immediately preceding the New World encounter, the Ottomans constitute simply one more great wave of peoples from the East who forcibly present themselves in Europe.[29] Together the Mongols, the Tatars, and the Ottomans irrevocably alter European understandings of the character of those regions.

At first European observers try to place the invaders into the familiar categories. Consider, for example, this depiction of the Tatars from Matthew of Paris's *Chronica majora* for the year 1240 CE, which reflects common belief in much of the Europe of his time, and which appears in a section significantly entitled "An Irruption of the Tatars":

> In this year, that human joys might not long continue, and that the delights of this world might not last long unmixed with lamentation, an immense horde of that detestable race of Satan, the Tatars, burst forth from their mountain-bound regions, and making their way through rocks apparently impenetrable, rushed forth, like demons loosed from Tatarus (so that they are well called Tatars, as it were inhabitants of Tatarus); and overrunning the country, covering the face of the earth like locusts, they ravaged the eastern countries with lamentable destruction, spreading fire and slaughter wherever they went. Roving through the Saracen territories, they razed cities to the ground, burnt woods, pulled down castles, tore up the vine-trees, destroyed gardens, and massacred the citizens and husbandmen. . . . The men are inhuman and of the nature of beasts, rather to be called monsters than men, thirsting after and drinking blood, tearing and devouring the flesh of dogs and human beings. . . . They drink the blood which flows from their flocks, and consider it a delicacy. . . . They have no human laws, know no mercy, and are more cruel than lions or bears . . . and when they have no blood, they greedily

drink disturbed and even muddy water. . . . They know no other country's language except that of their own, and of this all other nations are ignorant. For never till this time has there been any mode of access to them, nor have they themselves come forth, so as to allow any knowledge of their customs or persons to be gained through common intercourse with other men. . . . The Saracens, therefore, desired and begged to be allowed to enter into alliance with the Christians, in order that they might, by multiplying their forces, be enabled to resist these human monsters.[30]

Similar descriptions and depictions of the Turks as a monstrous race may be found in Montaigne and Rabelais several centuries later.[31] Moreover, despite early attempts to demonize their outward appearance, the Tatars, the Mongols, and the Turks were initially understood as monstrous races of our first type, whose distinguishing characteristics are extremes of behavior—cannibalism and extreme cruelty, for example—rather than a bizarre or alien phenotype.[32]

For this very reason, however, after the invasions of the Tatars, Mongols, and Turks into European space the peoples of Asia can no longer be seen as faraway people known only in myth and travelers' tales. Instead they must be regarded as really existent, unavoidably present beings. These invasions from the East thus force a new place in the European imaginary: a place for living beings from the East, familiar if nonetheless horrifying in appearance, who leave their distant abodes and intrude into Europe itself. The humanity of these invaders may or may not continue to be in question as they are reconstructed as hordes, heathens, idolaters, barbarians. That is a question for another occasion; but they clearly are monstrous races no longer.

In short, those who are phenotypically familiar and who irrupt into the central places of Europe can no longer be constituted entirely by the imagination; and the places they come from therefore can no longer be properly regarded as the source of monstrousness. It is, after all, precisely the lack of direct observation and constant contact which permits imagination to be the definer of the monstrous races. Consequently, after the thirteenth century it becomes more and more difficult to define the East as the home of monstrous races. Thus, if the function of the monstrous races as an imaginative locus for European meditations on the limits of being human is to be maintained, the monstrous races must be relocated away from the center of European experience to some new and distantly imagined periphery from which, as before the invasions of the thirteenth and fourteenth centuries, they do not threaten the European center. The monstrous races from the East thus gradually become mythologies in need of a new location—a location which the Americas must have seemed, at least at first blush, to offer.

Deforestation of Europe

With respect to medieval ideas of the Wild Man, there is another significant set of pressures at work. Beginning in the eleventh century, but peaking in the period 1250–1500 CE, much of Europe experiences deforestation on a massive scale as a result of population growth and the widespread use of wood as fuel. Deforestation involves the destruction of many of the places in which the Wild Man abides.[33] At the same time, the urbanization of Europe is underway by 1300 CE. Indeed, "the twelfth and thirteenth centuries . . . saw the founding of more new towns than any time between the fall of Rome and the Industrial Revolution."[34] Deforestation and urbanization, taken together, remove the experience of living near and around wild places from the quotidian lives of more and more Europeans.

In sum, during the thirteenth through fifteenth centuries the old imagined places, both nearby and far away, become more and more populated. In the case of the local forests, they are now populated with familiar peoples and ways of life, as the forests shrink and the cities expand; and in the case of the lands to the East, they are populated with strange peoples who are actively and aggressively involved (as opposed to being merely imaginatively represented) in the quotidian lives of Europeans. The result is that both the Wild Men and the monstrous races are in different ways displaced. They began the thirteenth century as mythologies that were each in their own way essentially tied to certain kinds of locations; but during the period in question they become dislocated mythologies. The Wild Man's "habitat" vanishes as the nearby forest shrinks, and the monstrous races ride the roads of Europe instead of remaining far away, where they belong. Both have become mythologies in need of relocation.

The Construction of "The Savage"

The Relocation of the Monstrous Races

We can now appreciate how the New World encounter provides precisely such a relocation. Consider first the monstrous races. At first glance, at least, if they are relocated to the New World they revert to the status of strange, faraway beings who have no imperial interests in Europe. Perhaps this was why it was so natural for Columbus and other early explorers to speculate, as they did constantly, about which of the monstrous races they would find in various parts of the Americas.[35] In the New World the monstrous races appear to have been properly restored to their natural place, so to speak: far away, simultaneously setting boundaries to the human world, its geography, and the diversity of its inhabitants—boundaries that are, at least in the first decades after 1492, explored largely through the work of the European imagination.

The newly emerging logic of colonization quickly complicated this relocation, however. The Americas were not simply a substitute for the central Asian steppes or the river valleys of India. Instead Europeans came to see various parts of the New World as objects of imperial interest. The "newe landes" became, not simply places to be visited, traveled through, or traded with, but instead *colonies*, places to be acquired. The relevant use of the term "colony" in English begins in the mid-sixteenth century. In this usage, the *Oxford English Dictionary* says, a colony is "a settlement in a new country; a body of people who settle in a new locality, forming a community subject to or connected with their parent state; the community so formed, consisting of the original settlers and their descendants and successors, as long as the connexion with the parent state is kept up."[36] In the sixteenth century, then, at least in English, a colony becomes literally a place that is now claimed and settled by Europeans. Moreover, the "connexion" with the parent state is not a merely formal one. One recalls that the irresolvable conflict generated in the twentieth century by the *pied noir*'s dual loyalties to France and to Algeria was grounded in one fundamental fact, namely, that Algeria was a *départment* of France, and so, literally, French soil, a part of France. There is a way in which all colonies are like this, however, whether they are formally named as lands "subject to or connected with" the "parent state," or whether they are formally understood to be part of it, like unfortunate Algeria. This is the social and cultural significance of the elaborate disembarkation ceremonies, in which land is claimed, as Columbus put it, "in the name of the King and Queen."[37] It comes out with particular clarity in that strange and ephemeral Spanish institution, the *requerimiento*, by which Indians were informed (in Spanish or Latin) that they were subjects and their lands were possessions of the Spanish crown, and that violent resistance would result in destruction and enslavement, as constituting rebellion upon the part of "vassals" from whom loyalty was to be expected.[38] The logic was the same as the logic the Castilian monarchs might have imposed on a rebellious town in Extremadura or León.

A colony is in this way a reflection of the metropolis (literally, the "mother country") itself. The imperial interests that create the colony draw the metropolis out of its original location; and its peoples, its revenues, and its culture are adapted, and perhaps even replicated, in a new place. The new place, distant though it may be, is therefore no longer the proper possession of the Other. It is no longer "theirs," but, in the eyes of the colonizers, "ours." Seen in this way, the strange logic expressed in the *requerimiento* becomes much easier to understand.

It is therefore all but inevitable that, in the first New World encounters, American Indians are frequently portrayed as "human monsters," to use Matthew of Paris's vivid phrase quoted above, who invade the newly Europeanized spaces.[39] Like the Tatars and the Turks, they are cannibals, they easily become violent, and they lack an understanding of the mores of "civilized" peoples.[40] The paradox of seeing the original inhabitants of "the newe landes" as intruders or invaders of European space is no doubt striking to us; but the magical logic of colonial discourse makes it self-evident to the European writers and illustrators of the period.[41] Indeed, it is precisely this idea for which a familiar European argument of the sixteenth and seventeenth centuries serves as propaedeutic, namely, the argument that, as Robert Gray put it in 1609, "these Sauages have no particular proprietie in any part or parcell of that Countrey, but only a generall residencie there, as wild beasts haue in the forrest, for they range and wander up and downe the Countrey [and have no fixed habitation]"[42]

The Relocation of the Wild Man

The identification of the Indians as monstrous races is very quickly placed in tension with their very proximity to newly Europeanized space, however. Because of the alchemical logic of "the colony," they are now located in spaces that are immediately adjacent to, if not overlapping with, "our" places. Without having changed location at all, they no longer come from far away, as the Tatars and the Mongols did. They are now as close to "our" spaces as the forest at the edge of the settlement. In this respect it is tempting to think that they are better understood as Wild Men, but only insofar as "our" places have been extended to include the colony.

In any case, unlike the Wild Man himself, at least in his paradigmatic incarnations, the Indians are social beings. As the Europeans understood from the very beginning, they do not live as solitary creatures of the woods, but have their own communities, traditions, and values.[43] Nor are the Indians a fantasy like the Wild Man, known mostly through stories, festivals, and art, and only rarely through alleged sightings. They do not magically retreat as the land is deforested, or as it comes under "civilized" European control, leaving behind nothing but legends of "Little People" or "Bigfoot." Instead, they increasingly come out of the forest, into the settlement itself, bringing their raw and wild habits with them, just as Europeans always feared that the Wild Man might. In the European colonies, the fantasy in Lucas Cranach's horrific depiction of the "cannibal or werewolf," published in 1510, seems instead to have become real: a wild-eyed man on all fours, with elongated fingers and bare feet, hair askew, and clothes torn to reveal his hirsute back, emerges from the forest in the foreground to invade the homestead of a peasant couple. He carries off a small child in his mouth, while all around him are severed limbs and heads, some partially gnawed. In the background the father looks on in shock from the cowshed, while the mother, standing in the doorway of the house with arms helplessly raised over her head in horror, tries to gather her two remaining children to her side.[44]

At the same time, because it is the Europeans who have the imperial interests this time, the colonizers see the Indians in a different light, namely, in relation to the imperial resources they are seeking. The forests and untamed lands are not to be ceded to these Wild Men, for the resources of the newly accessible world constitute the explicit rationale for the early voyages of exploration, and perhaps even for many of the later ones. At first the Indians are seen as the key to this exploitation of resources, as the early entries of Columbus's log illustrate so powerfully. Then, over time, they come to be seen themselves as a natural resource that must be tamed to be utilized, as the early Spanish practices of *encomienda* and enslavement indicate. In any case, their wild behavior is a real threat to imperial interests. Thus, if they cannot be Christianized, civilized, or at least enslaved, in the final analysis they become, not a natural resource or a tool for the exploitation of natural resources, but a natural obstacle, to be "cleared away" to make way for civilized life, just as the old-growth forests of the Americas were cleared to make way for civilized spaces.[45]

Race and the Concept of the Savage

I have argued that the identity of the Indians cannot easily be fitted into the traditional categories of the European imaginary that we have discussed. The Indians are too close by to be constituted as the faraway monstrous races; and at the same time too highly social and too active in the lives of the European colonies to be classified simply as the Wild Men of old. The circumstances and the logic of colonization thus create tensions in the application of the old, displaced categories that are resolved by their transformation into new and newly localized concepts. Properly understood, the idea of "the savage" can be seen precisely as a resolution of these tensions, forged out of old materials under the pressure of new experiences. It should come as no surprise, therefore, that the term "savage," in its uses as a label for a kind of person or group of people, emerges for the first time during the sixteenth century, in English, in Spanish, and probably in other Romance languages as well.[46] The development of the idea of "the savage" thus constitutes an extraordinarily and horrifically creative transmogrification of the old categories. On the one hand, the "savage" is constituted not as a solitary individual, but as a member of a culture or "race" who is set apart from Europeans not primarily by phenotype,[47] but by symbolically extreme forms of behavior and character, including cannibalism, sexual perversion, and the propensity to violence, all of which are heavily freighted with significance in European understandings of themselves and the world. Moreover, although the savage naturally occupies lands far from the center of civilization, namely Europe itself, through the mystification of colonization he appears from the nearby forests and the hills to directly threaten European places, peoples, and interests. The features of the Wild Man and of the monstrous races are in this way creatively reordered and combined to yield a new group of people, "the savages."

The features of this *gens* in many cases literally define the expected behavior and culture of American Indians and their progeny, as sixteenth-century discussions about whether the Indians could be "civilized" should suggest.[48] But their well-worn and familiar ring also underscores the symbolism of such traits as characteristic European markers of the Other; and their ubiquity in early accounts and representations of the early encounters points to the enduring significance of such symbolism for Europeans during the colonization and conquest to follow. This can be seen more clearly if we reflect for a moment on the next important phase in the evolution of the idea of the savage, namely its seventeenth-century racialization.

The term "race" (in the usages relevant to racial ideology) emerges for the first time during the seventeenth century;[49] but in this case the concept named, i.e., that of a group originating from a particular geographical area, united by descent, and characteristically displaying certain phenotypic or characterological traits, is certainly far older.[50] Nonetheless, the power of the concept, once "named," is greatly augmented. Beginning in the seventeenth century, the term "race" can be used to draw attention to the cluster of features just mentioned in order to make them salient in explanation, understanding, and evaluation, and to tie them to other explanatory-evaluative concepts and hypotheses. Moreover, the old concept is transformed by its early modern naming. The result is what I will call the "interiorization" of race, and the image of the savage plays a crucial role in this transformation. It is to a brief discussion of this transformation that I now turn.

The imperial confrontation with the now-savage races of "the newe landes" raises a question about their humanity that is much more immediate and pressing than questions about the humanity of the monstrous races. As I have suggested, it is almost unanimously agreed from the time of the very earliest reports that American Indians are not significantly different from Europeans with respect to phenotype.[51] On the other hand, that there are vast differences in culture and behavior that distinguish them from Europeans is generally taken to be indisputable. But are these behavioral and cultural differences, symbolic and freighted though they are, superficial ones, or do they indicate some deep essential contrast between known peoples and the inhabitants of "the newe landes"?

The older version of this question is raised frequently during the Middle Ages in debates over the human status of monstrous races. On the one hand, the behavior of monstrous races like the *cynocephali* is marked by the by-now-familiar trio of habitual, even uncontrolled, violence, cannibalism, and sexual perversion. On the other hand, even the *cynocephali* can be converted to Christianity, and so redeemed. Indeed, one medieval tradition has it that St. Christopher himself was a *cynocephalus* prior to his conversion.[52] Saint Augustine says,

> Whoever is anywhere born a man, that is, a rational, mortal animal, no matter what unusual appearance he presents in color, movement, sound, nor how peculiar he is in some power, part, or quality of his nature, no Christian can doubt that he springs from that one protoplast [Adam's seed]. We can distinguish the common human nature from that which is peculiar, and therefore wonderful [i.e., surprising or worthy of remark].[53]

The status of the monstrous races as imagined groups whose function it is to allow the free play of questions about the nature of humanity ensures that their common humanity remains fundamentally contentious. In the case of the savage, however, the imperial pressures of dealing with living beings who have ideas of their own about how the Encounter should proceed mean that the question is quickly closed. The general supposition of the imperial enterprise is that Augustine is mistaken, and American Indians are, though phenotypically within the range of the familiar, radically different, and inferior, in their deeper nature.

This understanding of the savage appears most dramatically in a project that may at first seem out of place, commingled as it is with the overtly violent imperial projects of enslavement, exploitation, and extermination. This is the imperial project of what we may call mass Europeanization. It attempts a radical religious and cultural rehabilitation of savage life. Although this particular project has its precedents (for example, in the Spanish colonization of the Canary Islands in the fifteenth century), the scale of the American version is probably unequaled in European history.[54] But even supposing that the rehabilitation of "savage" behavior, language, and mores is, or can be, successful,[55] the question remains of how the relation between these outward changes and the inward nature of the savage thus rehabilitated should be understood.

In general, the view that evolves from the mid-sixteenth through the seventeenth century is that it is impossible even by Europeanization to transform, or to transform fully, the savage nature.[56] On this view, savage nature is irredeemably savage; and even changes in language use and outward behavior should not be taken to indicate that what lies beneath the rehabilitated surface has truly changed at all.[57] Here another medieval element has been incorporated into the terrible creation that is the idea of the savage: the idea of an inherited curse that cannot be altered, perhaps not even through the supernatural power of conversion and baptism.[58] Through the mediation of this notion, the idea of the savage evolves into its familiar modern form. It is not merely that their phenotypically innocent appearance belies their monstrous behavior, as in the case of old monstrous races like the *anthropophagi*. Instead their appearance, as well as their potentially Europeanized behavior and mores, all merely cloak the monstrousness they carry within.[59] The liminal status of the monstrous races, underwritten by their wholly imaginary existence, has now been transformed into the notion, shaped by imperial interests, of the fixed status of the savage in a hierarchy of human or quasi-human peoples. Their status as human or nonhuman is no longer uncertain and debatable; but their characteristic brand of humanity is fixed as inferior by something interior, something that cannot be changed.

In short, the newly minted idea of the savage, completed by the familiar idea of an ineradicably depraved inward nature, enables Europeans to relocate or reconceive the traits that mark the savage as inward when, thanks to the project of Europeanization, they may not always be observable in outward comportment. This relocation is marked by the redefinition of an old idea, race, newly named in the seventeenth century and now understood as "interiorized savagery." The term "race" functions precisely to draw attention to this understanding of the peoples of the Americas: it picks out a savage nature that is heritable and unalterable, no matter how outward behavior is changed, and that is revealed to the eye, if at all, perhaps only by an unchanging and unchangeable skin color. The savage of the New World thus becomes a Caliban indeed, the doomed offspring of the Wild Man and the monstrous races, midwifed by imperial interest, cursed, marooned in isolation from the metropolis, and permanently enslaved by his putative master through the magical invocation of "race."

NOTES

I would like to thank John Block Friedman, who many years ago first piqued my interest in the monstrous races; Monique Roelofs for her unstintingly wise and generous advice on an earlier draft of this paper; an anonymous referee for his or her helpful comments on an earlier draft; and Peg Zeglin Brand for her insight and her patient work with a dilatory author. All the images referred to in this paper, as well as others, may be found on my website: https://sites.google.com/site/gregoryvelazcoytrianosky/.

1. I have in mind particularly the important work of Robert Bernasconi. See, for example, his "Who Invented The Concept of Race? Kant's Role in the Enlightenment Construction of Race," in *Race*, Blackwell Readings in Continental Philosophy 2, ed. Robert Bernasconi (Malden, Mass.: Blackwell, 2001), 11–36. See also his magisterial *Concepts of Race in the Eighteenth Century* (New York: Thoemmes Continuum, 2001), and his edited collection *American Theories of Polygenesis*, Concepts of Race in the Nineteenth Century 1, 7 vols. (New York: Thoemmes Continuum, 2002).

2. A notable exception to this cursory philosophical treatment of the pre–eighteenth century development of the idea of race is the work of Alison Bailey. See her "Thinking about Race and White Supremacy as if Gender Mattered," paper presented to the California Roundtable on Philosophy and Race, October 5–6, 2007, at California State University, Northridge.

3. John Shearman, *Mannerism* (London: Penguin, 1967), 23. The term "mannerist" is a vexed one among art historians, however, as Linda Murray notes. She herself restricts its use to "works produced in certain parts of Italy" (Linda Murray, *The High Renaissance and Mannerism: Italy, the North, and Spain, 1500–1600* [London: Thames & Hudson, 1977], 124–25).

4. Michael Alexander, ed., *Discovering the New World: Based on the Works of Theodor de Bry* (New York: Harper and Row, 1976), 10.

5. See Alan Shestack, *Fifteenth-Century Engravings of Northern Europe from the National Gallery of Art: December 3, 1967–January 7, 1968*, with a preface by Lessing Rosenwald and an introduction by Alan Shestack (Washington, D.C.: National Gallery of Art, 1967). See also Arthur M. Hind, A *History of Engraving & Etching from the Fifteenth Century to the Year 1914* (1923; New York: Dover, 1963), 20.

6. Olive Dickason, *The Myth of the Savage* (Edmonton: University of Alberta Press, 1984), 77–80.

7. See Charles Zika, *Exorcising Our Demons: Magic, Witchcraft, and Visual Culture in Early Modern Europe*, Studies in Medieval and Reformation Thought 91 (Leiden: Brill, 2003), 433.

8. A very useful survey of the presence of the monstrous races in the New World may be found in Peter Mason, *Deconstructing America: Representations of the Other* (New York: Routledge, 1990), chapter 4. The image from the *Carta marítima* is taken from Carl Smeller's course page, http://faculty.txwes.edu/csmeller/Human-Prospect/ ProData09/EurExpansion/Fries1525CanDog308.htm, where it is attributed to Lorenz Fries, *Uslegung der Mercarthen oder Carta Marina* (Strasbourg, 1525).

9. The canonical work on the history of the monstrous races remains John Block Friedman, *The Monstrous Races in Medieval Art and Thought* (Syracuse, N.Y.: Syracuse University Press, 2000). Pliny and his Greek and Roman antecedents are discussed in chapter 1. Pliny's catalogue of the monstrous races appears in book 7 of the *Historia naturalis*. A translation of book 7 roughly contemporary to the period under discussion is in *The Historie of the World: Commonly Called the Naturall Historie of C. Plinius Secundus, Translated into English by Philemon Holland* (London: A. Islip, 1601), http://penelope.uchicago.edu/holland/pliny7.html.

10. John Mandeville, *The Travels of Sir John Mandeville: The Fantastic 14th-Century Account of a Journey to the East* (Mineola, N.Y.: Dover Publications, 2006). This edition includes a series of woodcuts from the second Augsburg edition, 1481. Mason, *Deconstructing America*, 92 n.1 discusses the evidence and concludes that it is very likely that Columbus was familiar with Mandeville. Flint confirms that Columbus read (and annotated) a 1489 Italian translation of Pliny, even if he had not read Mandeville (Valerie I. J. Flint, *The Imaginative Landscape of Christopher Columbus* [Princeton: Princeton University Press, 1992], 46, 53).

11. For one catalog, along with very interesting speculations about the underlying principles of classification, see Mason, *Deconstructing America*, chapters 5 and 6.

12. Hans von Staden, *Warhaftige Historia und Beschreibung eyner Landtschafft der wilden, nacketen, grimmigen Menschfresser-Leuthen in der Newenwelt America gelegen* (1557), available on Project Gutenberg's German site; the illustration described here is at http://gutenberg.spiegel.de/buch/5531/44. See Alexander, *Discovering the New World*, 8.

13. This device is often used in the text of Mandeville's 1357 *Travels* (though not in its accompanying illustrations, at least of the second Augsburg edition). This text, mentioned above, was widely reprinted and available during the period under discussion.

14. This image may be found in a variety of places, including William C. Sturtevant's "First Visual Images of Native America," in *First Images of America: The Impact of the New World on the Old*, ed. Fredi Chappelli (Berkeley: University of California Press, 1976), opposite 1:424, where it is identified only as "now in Munich." See http://www.antropologiavisual.cl/imagenes12/articulos/c13.jpg.

15. Compare the woodcuts of some of the monstrous races in the 1481 second Augsburg edition of Mandeville, *Travels*, who are very ordinary in appearance, such as the Lamarians, who "go all naked and they scorn when they see any strange folk going clothed.... They eat more gladly man's flesh than any other flesh.... Thither go merchants and bring with them children to sell to [the Lamarians] ... and if they

be fat they eat [these children] anon" (120), and the Tracodans, who "eat flesh of serpents, and they eat but little. And they speak nought but they hiss as serpents do" (130). On the color of the Taino as represented by Columbus, see note 59 below.

16. For a subtle and insightful discussion of this conception of monstrosity, see Nöel Carroll, "Ethnicity, Race, and Monstrosity: The Rhetorics of Horror and Humor," in the predecessor to the current volume, *Beauty Matters,* ed. Peg Zeglin Brand (Bloomington: Indiana University Press, 2000), 37–56. Because the latter regions are and always have been part of the Mediterranean world, they are to my knowledge rarely if ever described as possible locations for the monstrous races. They are too close and too intertwined with European experience to serve that function, either before or after the rise of Islam.

17. Quoted by Flint, *The Imaginative Landscape of Christopher Columbus,* 144.

18. This is another widely available image. See, for instance, Alexandre Coello de la Rosa, "'Good Indians,' 'Bad Indians,' 'What Christians?' The Dark Side of the World in Gonzalo Fernandes de Oviedo y Valdes," *Delaware Review of Latin American Studies* 3, no. 2 (August 15, 2002), http://www.udel.edu/LAS/Vo13-2Coello .html, with the caption "Johann Grüniger, *Clubbing Member of Vespucci's Crew,* by Johann Grüniger. German illustration of 1509 to Amerigo Vespucci's *Lettera* [sic] *to Piero Solderini (1504)."* The Froschauer woodcut discussed previously may well be another depiction of the same 1501 text.

19. See Friedman, *The Monstrous Races,* chapter 4.

20. See ibid., 8, 39. See Benjamin Braude, "The Sons of Noah and the Construction of Ethnic and Geographical Identities in the Medieval and Early Modern Periods," *The William and Mary Quarterly* 54, no. 1 (January 1997): 109. Both these sources point out that the monstrous races were also sometimes located in "Ethiopia," used as a general term for those parts of Africa known or imagined to be inhabited by black Africans. In this paper I concentrate on their location in the East.

21. David Gordon White says that "the Alexander Romance, or the *Pseudo-Callisthenes,* first composed in Alexandria before the fourth century, was the block-buster bestseller of the entire Middle Ages," and "the prime vehicle for the medieval lore of the monstrous races." He claims that the descriptions of "barbarian tribes" in the *Romance* were conflated with the ancient "commonplace" of barbarian races who are walled off from the civilized world by a mountain range "running from the Caucasus in the West across all of Asia to an Eastern Sea, identified with the coast of India" (David Gordon White, *Myths of the Dog-Man* [Chicago: University of Chicago Press, 1991], 52–54).

22. The Middle East and portions of Asia Minor are probably the first areas in which Europeans had imperial interests. For this reason, among others, the contrast between European relations with the East and those with the Middle East, Asia Minor, and northern Africa during the same period is dramatic. Because the latter regions are and always have been part of the Mediterranean world, they are to my knowledge rarely if ever described as possible locations for the monstrous races. They are too close and too intertwined with European experience to serve that function, either before or after the rise of Islam.

23. I have in mind here both the saints in the very early "hairy anchorite" tradition and the individuals in somewhat later medieval tales, for example Orlando in

Ariosto's *Orlando Furioso*, who go mad from being spurned in love, or for other reasons. For a useful introduction to the early thematic of the "wild hairy anchorite," see Roger Bartra, *Wild Men in the Looking Glass: The Mythic Origins of European Otherness* (Ann Arbor: University of Michigan Press, 1994), 53–54. See also Richard Bernheimer, *Wild Men in the Middle Ages: A Study in Art, Sentiment, and Demonology* (New York: Octagon Books, 1970), 8. (Bernheimer actually thinks that, in the Middle Ages, the Wild Man is understood in general to be nothing more than a human being who has suffered some kind of [reversible] degeneration or derangement.)

24. See Bartra, *Wild Men in the Looking Glass*, 100–101; and Timothy Husband, *The Wild Man: Medieval Myth and Symbolism* (New York: Metropolitan Museum of Art, 1980), 3. Bartra summarizes the character of the Wild Man neatly as, "gloomy isolation, unrestrained aggression, and perverse lasciviousness" (117).

25. See Bernheimer, *Wild Men in the Middle Ages*, 23; and Husband, *The Wild Man*, 2, 119.

26. In Shelley's novel, "the Monster" lurks alone in the woods for several years, and first speaks with his creator in the Alps. Compare Sir Walter Scott's use of the trope of the Wild Man in his story "The Black Dwarf," available through Project Gutenberg at http://www.gutenberg.org/ebooks/1460. The figure of the solitary Wild Man is powerfully persistent, as the contemporary myths of the solitary Bigfoot or Sasquatch should suggest. In fact, these creatures are often labeled "Wild Man" or "Wild Man of The Woods" in contemporary popular accounts, as even a casual search on the Web will verify.

27. See Bartra, *Wild Men in the Looking Glass*, 104, and the woodcuts and engravings following; and Husband's comments on late fifteenth- and early sixteenth-century engravings of the wild family, *The Wild Man*, 131–33. On the medieval history of the image of the wild woman, see Bernheimer, *Wild Men in the Middle Ages*, 33–40.

28. Nothing in my discussion should be taken to imply that "the East" was univocally or solely understood as the abode of the monstrous races. Thus the narrative, geographical, and sociopolitical distance I have described also sustains a variety of other images of "the Orient." In particular, the "Marvels of the East" tradition represented "the Orient" as containing fabulous wealth, exotic (but not monstrous) phenotypes, and cultures and practices recognizable as variants on familiar European ones. The Prester John tradition and the notion that the earthly paradise lay in "the East" should also be mentioned. These images of a paradisiacal Orient form the main subject of discussion in John F. Moffitt and Santiago Sebastián, *O Brave New People: The European Invention of the American Indian* (Albuquerque: University of New Mexico Press, 1998). These images are sometimes mixed and blended into the imaginary of the monstrous races in the descriptions of groups like the *brahmani* or *bragmanni*, "a race of naked wise men who spend their days in caves," discussed by Friedman, *The Monstrous Races*, 12, 164–66.

29. The alienness of the Turks—in contrast, say, with the familiarity of their Byzantine predecessors—has of course to do in large measure with their status as Muslims who, unlike the "Saracens," actually invade what is seen as a Christian world. See Robert I. Moore, *The Formation of a Persecuting Society: Power and Deviance in Western Europe, 950–1250* (London: Wiley-Blackwell, 2001), on the

L

integration of Christianity into European identity. In this respect, the rise of the Ottomans clearly appears to redefine where "the East" begins, as Asia Minor is transformed from a place of trade and quotidian interaction into a site of military conflict. But an examination of the place of Islam and the Ottoman Empire on European conceptions of the Other must await another occasion.

30. J. A. Giles, transl. and ed., *Matthew Paris's English History from the Year 1235 to 1273* (London: George Bell and Sons, 1889), 1:312–13. This vivid description is accompanied by a lurid woodcut, frequently reprinted, of Tatar cannibalism and rapine. It is available online at http://commons.wikimedia.org/wiki/File:Cannibalism_in_Maarrat_an-Numan.jpg. See also Suzanne Lewis, *The Art of Matthew Paris in the Chronica Majora* (Berkeley: University of California Press, 1987), 282–87; and Debra Higgs Strickland, *Saracens, Demons, and Jews: Making Monsters in Medieval Art* (Princeton: Princeton University Press, 2003), 192–94.

31. I am told that there are still seaside villages in Italy where small children are induced to come in from the shore with the admonition that "it's getting dark, and if you don't come in the Turks will eat you" ("Ti mangiano i turchi"). It is also claimed by some sources that Allied soldiers were told by their commanders during the Gallipoli campaign in World War I, "If the Turks catch you they will eat you" ("The Gallipoli Campaign 1915: All the King's Men and 1/5 Norfolk Regiment," http://www.canakkale.gen.tr/eng/closer/closer.html).

32. The very absence of references to phenotype in Matthew of Paris's otherwise vivid description serves as some confirmation of this.

33. See Bartra, *Wild Men in the Looking Glass*, 81, 134. At the same time, the inevitable accompaniment of deforestation during the period in question is the near-eradication of wolves, the most powerful living representatives of the wildness of the forest. This is particularly dramatic in Britain, where, notoriously, Edward I ordered in 1281 the extermination of all wolves in England. It appears that wolves did indeed become more and more scarce after this time. On the other hand, it must be said that the eradication or radical reduction in wolf populations occurred much later—indeed, sometimes not until the nineteenth century—in many other parts of Europe, including Germany, which is the source of many of the early woodcuts and drawings under discussion. See "Wolves Wander into Germany, Aiding a Resettlement Effort," *New York Times*, May 25, 2001, http://query.nytimes.com/gst/fullpage.html?res=9E0 7E6D6133AF936A15752C1A9679C8B63.

34. *Encyclopedia Britannica Ultimate Reference Suite*, CD-ROM (Chicago: Encyclopedia Britannica, 2008), s.v. "city."

35. See, for example, Mason, *Deconstructing America*, chapters 5 and 6. Flint confirms that Columbus read and annotated a copy of Pierre d'Ailly's widely distributed compilation, *Imago mundi*, published between 1480 and 1483 (*The Imaginative Landscape of Christopher Columbus*, 54). She comments that Columbus's annotations evince his particular interest in cannibalism among the monstrous races. It should be noted, however, that in his log Columbus sometimes pokes fun at those who genuinely expect to find phenotypically distinct monstrous races such as *cynocephali* and *blemmyae* among the inhabitants of the New World.

36. *Oxford English Dictionary*, 2nd ed. (hereafter *OED*), s.v. "colony." The earliest appearances of this word in this sense are dated to 1548–49 and 1555. Even

the use of the term in English descriptions of Greek or Roman settlements is documented by only one reference prior to this time.

37. See, for example, Columbus's description of his very first landfall in S. Lyman Tyler, *Two Worlds: The Indian Encounter with the European, 1492–1509* (Salt Lake City: University of Utah Press, 1988), 37–38. Compare the well-known portrayal by Jan van der Straet (Stradanus) of Vespucci discovering America, which may be found, e.g., at http://commons.wikimedia.org/wiki/File:Stradanus_America.jpg.

38. The absurdity of reading such a document to Indians who spoke neither Spanish nor Latin was too much even for the Spaniards, and the practice was abandoned before the end of the period under discussion. A Spanish-language version of the *requerimiento* may be found in Luis Lopez Nieves, "Requerimiento [Ficción jurídica: Texto completo], Monarquía Española, redactado por Juan López de Palacios," http://www.ciudadseva.com/textos/otros/requeri.htm. An English translation is given by Wikipedia: http://en.wikipedia.org/wiki/Requerimiento.

39. The visual images represent the humanity of the Indians very clearly and unambiguously, as an inspection of the images under discussion will show, even though contemporary commentators on the early encounter remain divided on the question of their humanity. Needless to say there are other, conflicting images of the Indians, for example in Columbus's and Las Casas's well-known portrayals of the Caribbean Indians as innocent and childlike. Fairly early versions of the image of the "noble savage" may also be found. I do not discuss the construction of those images of the "childlike savage" or "noble savage" here, nor their complex interweaving with the images of the "bestial savage," which strictly speaking is our main topic here.

40. Peter Hulme points out that the very act of violent resistance to the establishment of trading outposts and colonies was often regarded by early Europeans as a violation of the *jus gentium*, which required all nations to allow free entry and access to peaceful trading expeditions. Thus, by resisting European settlement, the Indians placed themselves outside the protection of the law of the peoples (Peter Hulme, *Colonial Encounters: Europe and the Native Caribbean, 1492–1797* [London: Methuen, 1986], 161–62). As Hulme intimates, this argument was made by Francisco de Vitoria, the great natural lawyer and a well-known defender of the rights of the Indians, among others. See Dickason, *The Myth of the Savage*, 130–31, for a succinct summary of de Vitoria's views on these matters. Contrast Kant's notion of the savage as the one who lives "without law" in "Perpetual Peace: A Philosophical Sketch," Second Definitive Article, on the website of Vincent Ferraro, Mount Holyoke College, http://www.mtholyoke.edu/acad/intrel/kant/kant1.htm.

41. Compare Hulme's analysis of how the 1622 massacre of Virginia colonists is understood by contemporaries as a slaughter of the natural inhabitants of the land by the Indians, who are cast as "unnatural Naturalls" (Hulme, *Colonial Encounters*, 160). Hulme seems to me to miss the point, however, since he thinks that this reversal of the roles of native people and intruding colonists is only made possible by the massacre. It seems to me, on the contrary, that it is impossible to understand the response of writers like Samuel Purchas to the massacre (quoted by Hulme) unless one posits that, prior to this event, the English already saw themselves as the true "Naturalls" or native inhabitants of the land.

42. Quoted by Hulme, *Colonial Encounters*, 158. It is worth noting that the wild man is generally conceived of as having no property or possessions.

43. Perhaps it is therefore unsurprising that most European portrayals of Wild Families postdate the 1492 encounter and the widespread circulation of Columbus's 1493 letter. Building on top of the occasional earlier idea of the Wild Men as a sort of monstrous race, this "socialization" of the Wild Man, so to speak, makes possible the portrayal of whole ethnic groups as "wild," as we will see shortly.

44. Cranach's woodcut can be found at http://en.wikipedia.org/wiki/File:Werwolf. png. See Husband's brief discussion of this image and the relation between the wild man and the werewolf in *The Wild Man*, 110.

45. Compare Patrick Brantlinger's brilliant analysis of a later European under-standing of the logic of extermination in his *Dark Vanishings: Discourse on the Extinction of Primitive Races, 1800–1930* (Ithaca: Cornell University Press, 2003).

46. The *OED*, 2nd. ed., s.v. "savage," records 1588 as the first time the term is used as a noun in this way, contemporaneous with its first use as an adjective to describe "uncivilized" persons. Other related uses in reference to persons, character, or behav-ior are either contemporaneous as well, or later. It may also be worth mentioning that the word Kant uses which is translated as "savage" appears to be "wilde" or "wilder." See Robert Hanna, "Kant and Nonconceptual Content," on Hanna's website at the University of Colorado, Boulder, http://spot.colorado.edu/~rhanna/kant_and_content .htm. Compare von Staden's use of "wilden," which is sometimes translated as "savage."

47. But recall our opening discussion on the place of hairiness in early descrip-tions of American Indians, and the persistence of such descriptions well into the sev-enteenth century.

48. The *locus classicus* here is the work of Lewis Hanke. See his *The First Social Experiments in America: A Study in the Development of Spanish Indian Policy in the Sixteenth Century*, Harvard Historical Monographs (1935; Gloucester, Mass.: Peter Smith, 1964); *Aristotle and the Indians: A Study in Race Prejudice in the Modern World* (1959; Bloomington: Indiana University Press, 1970); and *All Mankind Is One: A Study of the Disputation between Bartolomé de las Casas and Juan Ginés de Sepulveda in 1550* (1974; DeKalb: Northern Illinois University Press, 1994).

49. OED, s.v. "race (*sb.*)²." Ivan Hannaford provides detailed examples of the use of the term as it evolves from older meanings in the sixteenth and seventeenth centu-ries in *Race: The History of an Idea in the West* (Baltimore: Johns Hopkins University Press, 1996), 175–82.

50. See, for example, the evidence cited in Hannaford, *Race*, chapters 1–5. Hannaford himself claims that the idea arises in the early modern period, but he appears to conflate the question of when the concept originated with the question of when the relevant usage of the term began. I suspect that this is a common error among philosophers of race.

51. For example, Columbus says of the people of Hispaniola, "Both sexes were handsomer than any they had hitherto seen, their color light, and, if clothed and guarded from the sun and air, would be nearly as fair as the inhabitants of Spain" (Tyler, *Two Worlds*, 75). See also note 59 below.

52. Friedman, *The Monstrous Races*, 72.

53. Saint Augustine, *The City of God*, book 16, chapter 8, http://www.newadvent
.org/fathers/120116.htm. See Friedman's discussion of this passage in *The Monstrous
Races*, 90–91.

54. The project of Europeanization has its counterparts in Europe itself, most
obviously in fifteenth- and sixteenth-century Spain, where the *reconquista* involves
the resocialization and, of course, religious "reeducation" of Jewish and Muslim
populations.

55. For a history of one of the early explicit attempts at Europeanization and the
general sixteenth-century response, see Lewis Hanke's account of Las Casas's unsuc-
cessful efforts to establish utopian Indian communities in Hispaniola and Cuba (*First
Social Experiments in America*).

56. A parallel understanding obviously defines much of the trajectory of the
Europeanization project in Spain, as the contemporaneous development of the idea
of *limpieza de sangre* (literally, "purity of blood") shows. The descendants of converted Jews are excluded from public office and most universities in Spain at least
through the eighteenth century, merely on the grounds that they carry something "in
the blood" that cannot be altered even by centuries of "civilized" behavior.

57. Interestingly, in many parts of Latin America today someone who has lost their
temper will say, "Me salió el Indio"—"The Indian in me came out."

58. On the medieval and modern history of the idea of the inherited curse, see
Hannaford, *Race*, 91–92.

59. In the case of the Indians at least, the trope of skin color is sometimes employed
to mark this inward continuity in monstrousness. Though Indians are almost universally not seen as black by Europeans of the period under discussion, they are
nonetheless almost always marked as different in appearance from the Europeans
themselves, who in this period are paradigmatically seen as white, whether they be
English, Spanish, or Portuguese. Columbus and other early European explorers
often contrast the bronze or "red" color of American Indians (and Canary Islanders)
with the black color of Africans. Describing his first encounter with the Taino in
October of 1492, Columbus says, "they are of the color of the Canary Islanders, neither black nor white. . . . None of them are black." Regarding the Taino women of
Hispaniola, he remarks in a December 1492 entry that "as to beauty, [Columbus's]
men stated that they exceeded the [women of the other islands] beyond comparison,
both men and women being of a much lighter color, and that two young females
were seen as white as could be found in Spain" (Tyler, *Two Worlds*, 38–39, 73). In
contrast, at least since the late medieval era—and perhaps well before—those who
are seen as having black skin are often placed thereby beyond the pale of humanity.
The significance of black skin in the history of race is of course a complex matter,
deserving of its own study.

3. Beauty's Relational Labor

MONIQUE ROELOFS

"I adore Macabéa, my darling Maca. I adore her ugliness and her total anonymity for she belongs to no one. I adore her for her weak lungs and her under-nourished body," writes the Brazilian novelist Clarice Lispector (1925–77) in the voice of her fictional author, Rodrigo S.M.[1] The novella in question, *The Hour of the Star*, Lispector's last, is probably best known as an example of *écriture féminine* through the writings of the philosopher Hélène Cixous, or as the script of a successful movie by that name.[2]

In the novella, Lispector challenges beauty's operations in the service of economic disparity and social violence.[3] For Rodrigo, writing about Macabéa, his protagonist, amounts to writing about someone whose ugliness is part and parcel of her social expulsion. This endeavor is charged with the paradoxical task of making the insignificant matter, of having the existence of a disposable person count. How is this possible while retaining her insignificance? Rather than resolving this paradox, Lispector uses it to push the limits of the web of aesthetically mediated relationships surrounding Macabéa — relationships that are organized with the help of the concept of beauty. In challenging such aesthetic relationships, Lispector rewrites the connections of the beautiful and the ugly with the feminine, the body, the postcolonial, and race, and directs us toward an alternative economy of beauty. The force of Lispector's cultural critique stands out when considered in light of the relational frames in which philosophers historically have cast the beautiful.

Plato and Enlightenment philosophers have implicitly offered accounts of aesthetic relationality, a network of aesthetically mediated relationships that subjects entertain with one another and the material world.[4] Comprehended as a dimension of aesthetic relationships, beauty reveals conflicting moral and political commitments. It bears affiliations with the ethical as well as the unethical, with social justice as well as domination. This polyvalence appears to be a product, in part, of the relational workings and preconditions of the beautiful. Possibilities for altering the meanings of the beautiful and the ugly and for transforming the cultural labor of these concepts can then be expected to ensue from changes in the broader structures of relationality that harbor the aesthetic functioning of beauty and ugliness. Indeed, the menace and promise of the beautiful as a bearer of aesthetic value, a dimension of experience, and a category of cultural criticism turn on the ways in which we may dislocate its relational functioning. The project of reorienting beauty's relational workings necessitates a detailed engagement with the concept's historical difficulties. These difficulties continue to resound in its intricately racialized and gendered spell. They play a part in the entwinements of beauty with economic mobility and abandonment. They can also be recognized in the ties the beautiful sustains with constructions of cultural citizenship and liminality. *The Hour of the Star* explores these themes. I begin by indicating how Lispector responds to beauty's problems by indicting and unhinging modes of relationship it has served to orchestrate.

Beauty and Ugliness in *The Hour of the Star*

In the voice of its fictional author, Rodrigo S.M., *The Hour of the Star* tells the story of Macabéa, a young woman from the northeast of Brazil. Orphaned early in life and raised by her aunt, she moves to Rio de Janeiro, where she works as a typist with her boss and her co-worker, Glória. Rodrigo, whose narrative is said to create Macabéa, proclaims the masculinity of his authorship—a woman writer, he declares, would have cried "her heart out" chronicling this tale.[5] Lispector has Rodrigo profess his love for his character in the passage quoted above: "I adore Macabéa, my darling Maca. I adore her ugliness and her total anonymity for she belongs to no one. I adore her for her weak lungs and her under-nourished body."[6] This in-your-face aestheticization of poverty reverses the typical affective implications of ugliness. At the same time, Rodrigo's unqualified love of the victimized body stands out in its outrageousness, resisting assimilation in a sublimatory narrative that could confer moral legitimacy on his, Lispector's, and the reader's attitude toward the young female inhabitant of a third-world slum, a woman who appears indistinguishable from so many others. Abject poverty renders Macabéa's life superfluous. It is her lot to remain an insignificant residue, neglected by everyone but—as he imagines it—the author. This fate is in no small measure due to her sallow complexion, her drooping shoulders, her body odor, the grime underneath nails from which she has chewed away most of their bright scarlet lacquer. In short, it is a matter of her "ugliness." The only "really beautiful thing in Macabéa's life," we learn, is Donizetti's "Una furtiva lacrima," sung by the tenor Enrico Caruso, to which she listens on the radio.[7] She also finds pleasure in the crowing of a cockerel and the signals of cargo ships. Rodrigo tells us that Macabéa loves movie stars and wishes she were like Marilyn Monroe.

> Since nobody wanted to give her a treat, much less become engaged to her, she would give herself a treat. The treat would consist of buying a new lipstick she didn't really need: not pink like the one she was using, but this time bright red. In the washroom at the office she painted her lips lavishly beyond their natural outline, in the hope that she might achieve that stunning effect seen on the lips of Marilyn Monroe. When she had finished, she stood staring at herself in the mirror, at a face which stared back in astonishment. The thick lipstick looked like blood spurting from a nasty gash, as if someone had punched her on the mouth and broken her front teeth (small bang). When she went back to her desk Glória chuckled:
> —Have you taken leave of your senses, girl? What are you up to, wearing all that war-paint? You could be mistaken for a tart.
> —I'm a virgin! You won't find me going out with soldiers or sailors.
> —Excuse my asking: is it painful being ugly?
> —I've never really thought about it, I suppose it's a little painful. How do you feel about being ugly yourself?
> —I am not ugly!—Glória howled at her.
> Peace was soon restored between them, and Macabéa continued to be happy thinking about nothing.[8]

At one level, the text frames female poverty as ugly, putting bodily beauty, including its connotations of social desirability and potential for upward mobility, out of Macabéa's reach. Her efforts to partake of material tastefulness misfire, as in the lipstick scene, or when, having visited Glória's parents, she can barely refrain from throwing up the hot chocolate she has drunk, or when, at the sound of her own voice, her singing turns into weeping. Macabéa is granted no more than a grotesque or melancholic repetition of aesthetic achievements others pull off successfully, as a matter of course. The beautiful, the ugly, the malformed, and the grotesque are instrumental in construing her as extraneous to the sphere of ordinary subjectivity and sociality. These aesthetic markers seal her expendability, notwithstanding her love of Coca-Cola and Hollywood film stars such as Greta Garbo, which qualifies her as a competent reader of a transnational stream of cultural products, and constitutes a point of access to modernity.[9] When Macabéa asks her short-term boyfriend Olímpico, whose realist sensibilities unfailingly counter her disinterested, semiotic perceptions, "Did you know that Marilyn Monroe was the color of peaches?" he bluntly affirms the intersecting racial, medical, and economic registers of her aesthetic incorrigibility, replying that she, Macabéa, is the color of mud.[10] The signs and symbols she likes do not bring her the real things they refer to, their "designation," as Macabéa spells it. Indeed, the word "mimetism" (*sic*) worries her.[11] The unavailability of feminized and feminizing beautification represents an integral dimension of her disempowerment.

Via implicit and explicit notions of the beautiful, the ugly, the grotesque, and the malformed, *The Hour of the Star* attaches, then, a range of classical connotations to differentially positioned bodies. The experiences, evaluations, and desires captured by aesthetic categories help to weave a web of relationships between humans and among humans, objects, and places. Beauty and its antitheses are revealed to circumscribe operations of power and hierarchy, possibility and constraint, inclusion and exclusion.

Withholding the assurance of a corrective, Lispector suspends the applicability of the language of beauty and ugliness that helps to organize Macabéa's relationships with others and herself. In relation to the catastrophe exemplified by Macabéa, the grounds for a tenable ethical or political stance collapse. *The Hour of the Star* undercuts a normatively aestheticized vocabulary of poverty, wrenching from this lexicon a critical look at the terms and conditions of aestheticization. The reader is invited to reconsider beauty's role in the maintenance, discursive and otherwise, of poverty, global inequality, economic disparity, and social marginalization.

Grotesque, sad, or even horrific as they turn out, Macabéa's attempts at beautification and self-aestheticization cannot be read as mere failures. Provoking cruelty and indifference, they expose the violence of the regime of beauty and ugliness through which wealth and poverty are comprehended and inhabited by her companions and the author. Macabéa's grotesque performances exercise resistance, even if unemphatically and unconsciously, as evinced by Glória's and Olímpico's vehement censure. Defying normalized cultural meaning, her lipstick articulates an oppositional physicality. Her solitary urban, consumerist, and environmental perceptions fail to exhaust her aesthetic life, as can be witnessed in the "misspellings" she funnels into the documents she types, her voice that sings a love rhyme out of tune, her urge to expel from her body the hot chocolate she is offered—a substance that is comfortably internalized by the well-nourished, middle-class bodies of Glória and her parents. These acts and desires refract the city's and the cinema's construction of beauty. They instantiate a beauty of sorts in their own right, necessitating an alternative framing of the beautiful that exceeds the novel's normative alignments. Enveloping the reader in an aesthetic dynamic that the novel refuses to close, and drenching this dynamic in the urgency of disaster, Lispector articulates the need to subject structures of aesthetic relationality to transformation.[12]

Beauty and Moral Order: Plato, Shaftesbury, and Hutcheson

Beauty's philosophical history presents a dilemma. On the one hand, philosophers consider the beautiful of irrevocable significance to ethics, subjectivity, and the construction of culture. On the other hand, beauty's power to bring about what qualifies as freedom, goodness, truth, and the public sphere goes in tandem with its contributions to unjust constellations of difference. With the aid of analyses by Bernard Mandeville, Mary Wollstonecraft, and contemporary commentators, the following sections trace this dilemma to writings by Plato, Shaftesbury, Francis Hutcheson, David Hume, Adam Smith, and Edmund Burke, which locate the beautiful in a network of relationships beauty helps to orchestrate. Across these texts, beauty's organizational workings can be seen to give rise to constructions of hierarchically coded social difference.

The Scottish Enlightenment accords beauty great moral and political weight.[13] For Shaftesbury, Hutcheson, Hume, and Smith, among others, the beautiful stands in a direct relation to the morally good social order. Shaftesbury and Hutcheson comprehend this order as God's design. The human sense of beauty is able to register the presence of this design, recognizing in advance of personal benefit or utility and independently of rational comprehension—that is to say, in a disinterested fashion—those actions, traits of character, and forms that stand in a just proportion with the whole, and that, as such, qualify as good. In Shaftesbury's and Hutcheson's views, a person's sense of beauty intuitively perceives as beautiful those elements that are also moral and rational in the context of the larger whole.[14] This idea allows Shaftesbury (and, to a lesser extent, Hutcheson) to envision a process of aesthetic education that provides the individual a suitable place in the moral order and makes possible the collective attainment of that order at the level of the nation. Declaring the arts and virtues friends and recommending "morals on the same foot with . . . manners," Shaftesbury charges art with the task of rendering individuals morally praiseworthy.[15] He delineates the ethical and aesthetic trajectory that he envisions by way of comparisons with examples of inferior forms and tastes, which the virtuous and aesthetically apt agent is enjoined to avoid:

> Grotesque and monstrous figures often please. Cruel spectacles and barbarities are also found to please. . . . But is this pleasure right? And shall I follow it if it presents? not strive with it, or endeavour to prevent its growth or prevalency in my temper? . . . How stands the case in a more soft and flattering kind of pleasure? . . . Effeminacy pleases me. The Indian figures, the Japan work, the enamel strikes my eye. The luscious colours and glossy paint gain upon my fancy. A French or Flemish style is highly liked by me at first sight, and I pursue my liking. But what ensues? . . . Do I not for ever forfeit my good relish? How is it possible I should thus come to taste the beauties of an Italian master, or of a hand happily formed on nature and the ancients? 'Tis not by wantonness and humour that I shall attain my end and arrive at the enjoyment I propose. The art itself is severe, the rules rigid.[16]

Shaftesbury articulates the meanings of this severe art, these rigid rules,[17] and the enjoyment they provide in part by contrast with elements connoted pejoratively in terms of the grotesque, the monstrous, effeminacy, and barbarity. These denominations differentiate the ethical and aesthetic path that is to issue in beauty, goodness, and civilized status ("politeness") from models of subjectivity that are coded as feminine, vulgar, of suspect cultural origin, or formless. In Shaftesbury's fragmentary prose:

> Politeness in figures helped still to polish grace. . . . As beauteous forms polish (taking politeness with its consequences), so ugly barbarize. . . . But this assert: that neither Jew, Egyptian, nor Chinese polite.

This is a judgment of politeness. If polite; show me a picture, a statue, coin, proportion, nature. But arabesque! Japan! Indian! Savage. Monstrous. Even in their portraiture, pleasure-pieces, wanton pieces. Also gods monstrous, frightful according to Egyptian and Syrian models; or Turkish mosques, no architecture, or statuary, or figures: or as bad as none.

Frightful, horrid, cruel ideas entertained, advanced by such divine forms; soft gentle, humane ideas, by truly human forms, and divinity represented after the best, sweetest, and perfectest idea of humanity to the vulgar.

But without application to divinities, and simply viewed and contemplated in cities, groves, high-ways, places, gardens, forums, etc., *emollit mores.*

"Bad figures: bad minds." "Crooked designs: crooked fancies." "No designs: no thought." So Turks, etc.[18]

The above stipulations conjoin semantic emptiness with fullness, obscuring what precisely is being defined in terms of what, and why. The meanings of aesthetic and racial or ethnic concepts approximate one another closely. A clear example of this is the staccato sequence, "But arabesque! Japan! Indian! Savage. Monstrous." Shaftesbury's list of generic verdicts deploys notions of femininity, vulgarity, and formlessness, as well as multiple kinds of cultural difference, as stand-ins for morally and aesthetically objectionable meanings.[19] Minimally descriptive placeholders for understandings the reader is invited to supply, these concepts solicit the reader's collaboration in tracing the right path toward the beautiful and the good. Absent the reader's supplementary efforts, the language traces circuitous tautologies.

Shaftesbury's racial and ethnic preoccupations manifest themselves more concretely in his concern to keep citizens from dwelling on "prodigies of Moorish and Pagan countries," from hearing "monstrous accounts of monstrous men and manners," and from developing a love of "strange narrations." Part of this anxiety, which emerges in a reading of Othello, is that white, British women will fall for "a mysterious race of black enchanters, such as of old were said to creep into houses, and lead captive silly women." Shaftesbury worries that readers' curiosity about the messages they expect unusual objects of sight and hearing to convey will be transferred to the persons of the storytellers, rendering them "sacred and tremendous." He foresees the consequence that "[a] thousand Desdemonas are then ready to present themselves, and would frankly resign fathers, relations, countrymen, and country itself, to follow the fortunes of a hero of the black tribe."[20] Appropriate forms of art and artistic reception, accordingly, for Shaftesbury, outline itineraries of moral and aesthetic development that enable individuals to perform suitable roles in an adequately racialized and gendered national culture. Good art, accompanied by the right kind of interpretation, also helps to achieve an acceptable distribution of power and affect (feelings must be regulated so the right sentiments are felt for the right reasons, to the right degree, for the right persons). Furthermore, art's pedagogical function enables it to serve as a measure of civilization. For in the above passage on politeness, after identifying the civilizing effects of the beautiful and the barbarizing effects of the ugly, Shaftesbury proceeds to deploy judgments about the arts he attributes to a number of nations (including, implicitly, Britain) as comments on the moral stature of these nations, their level of civilization, and the quality of their imagination and thinking ("No designs: no thought."). Since art is expected to instigate a pedagogical track that issues in the realization of the beautiful and the good, it becomes indicative of a person's or nation's level of beauty and goodness. Accordingly, aesthetic designations ("beautiful," "luscious," "crooked") take on racial, gendered, and class-inflected meanings, as when Shaftesbury understands "polite figures" implicitly as figures created by, say, "the ancients" or the British, not the Turkish or the Chinese.

We encounter here an instance of the phenomenon I call "racialized (gendered, class-inflected) aestheticization."[21] This label describes the inflection of aesthetic concepts and elements by social categories, and designates the ways in which constellations of difference leave their marks upon aesthetic arrangements. This phenomenon is the correlative of the situation in which racial (gendered, class-inflected) forms of subjectivity and culture building are aestheticized, as when Shaftesbury employs art in the business of creating politeness, and witnesses the hand of "polite figures" and "beauteous forms" in the polishing of "grace" and the creation of "humane ideas," whereby what counts as politeness, grace, and humanity is comprehended in racial (gendered and economically hierarchical) terms. This latter condition I name "aesthetic racialization (gendering and class inflection)." This concept denotes the aestheticized nature of differential social constellations.[22] Both phenomena collaborate to establish what counts as a good moral order, for Shaftesbury. The closeness of their mutual cooperation can be witnessed, for example, in the idea that "polite figures" (forms generated by the British, among others, but not by the Japanese, and that, so conceived, bear the marks of racialized aestheticization) help to produce "grace" or "humane ideas," and other achievements exclusively available to a limited group of white Europeans (thereby operating as modes of aesthetic racialization).

Critics have observed that Shaftesbury's ethics legitimize problematic class and gender hierarchies. Bernard Mandeville contends that the realization of a virtuous society à la Shaftesbury, one that is also rich, flourishing, and civilized, ineluctably rests upon the imposition, by "law-givers and other wise men," of "violence" on others' desires.[23] Within this social scheme, Mandeville argues, politicians and rulers offer imaginary compensation for the violent self-denial demanded from subordinate subjects, in the form of flattering illusions about civilization and public-spiritedness. Assisted by these illusions, in conjunction with a hypocritical denial of their private interest in others' efforts to promote the public good, well-situated individuals, including leaders, are able to appropriate others' labor for their personal advancement.[24] *Contra* Shaftesbury, who considers virtue disinterested, such ambitious persons thereby satisfy their own, self-regarding concerns, such as a love of sensory gratification, desire for worldly possessions, and the pleasure of "the pomp and luxury [they are] served with."[25] At the same time, these comfortably positioned subjects exhibit a range of allegedly vicious qualities, such as selfishness, deception, ignorance, pride, vanity, envy, jealousy, lust, malice, and fraud.[26] Mandeville concludes that the field of disinterested, virtuous action is more limited than Shaftesbury would like to (have his readers) believe. He warns against Shaftesbury's "generous Notions concerning the natural Goodness of Man." These are "hurtful as they tend to mis-lead, and are meerly Chimerical."[27] Mandeville's argument breaks the connection Shaftesbury forges between an individual's tasteful, disinterested perceptions of beauty and his or her contributions to the achievement of the good moral order. His critique exposes the ways in which Shaftesbury's (and Hutcheson's) conceptions of disinterested moral and aesthetic perception rest upon a partial and reduced picture of the moral psychology and the division of labor underlying social arrangements. This challenge to disinterested beauty, already influential in the Scottish Enlightenment, stands today. Replies have not been provided in contemporary discussions of beauty, analogous and additional recent objections notwithstanding.[28]

Shaftesbury's and Hutcheson's idealized abstractions mask beauty's concrete symbolic functioning, which contradicts its allegedly univocal orientation toward a sensorily, rationally, and ethically commendable order of being. To the extent that the beautiful contributes to the good, as conceived by these thinkers, it also serves oppressive constructions of difference. This difficulty precedes eighteenth-century British and Scottish aesthetics. Broader conceptual grounds of this problem become visible if we approach the Enlightenment debate in light of the Platonic formations it replicates.

Shaftesbury's and Hutcheson's theories draw upon Plato's hierarchical theory of beauty. In Diotima's speech, which Socrates relays at the banquet in the *Symposium*, the virtuous soul progressively works its way through several stages of beauty.[29] Initially devoted to the beautiful bodies of young boys, the good soul moves on to a passion for beautiful minds. Via the love of beautiful activities and laws and states of affairs, and the beauty of knowledge generally, the soul arrives at a contemplative apprehension of the abstract idea of the beautiful, the form of Beauty itself. Only then is it possible for the soul to "give birth not to images of virtue (because he is in touch with no images), but to true virtue (because he is in touch with the true Beauty)."[30] In the *Phaedrus*, the soul's memory of eternal beauty, as this tends to be triggered in independent men by beautiful boys, initiates a process of moral, philosophical, and amorous development in relation to such beloved boys, empowering the rational part of these men's souls to supersede physical desire in favor of a more gratifying love for the world of eternally self-identical ideas, which is accessible through dialectical reasoning.[31] The result is a life of mutual philosophical edification, goodness, wisdom, and happiness.[32] Propelling an aesthetic, ethical, and philosophical process of soul building that is sustained by appropriately subjugated forms of bodily attraction and passion, as well as an appropriately dominant love of ideas, hierarchized instances of beauty, in this aesthetic scenario, enable the noble soul to renew its original, preembodied access to the idea of the Beautiful along with the other forms, including those of the True and the Good.[33]

The problematic hierarchies sustaining Plato's metaphysics and epistemology have received widespread attention.[34] Julia Kristeva and Luce Irigaray, among others, reject the gendered presuppositions of Plato's moral and aesthetic pedagogy. They argue that Plato valorizes a masculinist order of reason that sustains the appearance of being self-authenticating because it abjects, as its unthinkable other, its constitutive bonds with the feminized body, the passions, and the senses.[35] In their view, the Platonic scheme postulates significatory elisions that render the feminine and the body (which is connoted feminine) constitutively unrepresentable, and gives rise to a limited, exclusionary notion of (inter)subjective becoming. Indeed, making beauty's pedagogical ties to the true and the good contingent upon a dismissal of the body and the feminine,[36] Plato enlists the beautiful in the production and validation of diminished forms of subjectivity. Like Mandeville's objections to the notion of disinterested contemplation, this challenge has not been answered.

The failure of Plato's, Shaftesbury's, and Hutcheson's proposed aesthetic idealizations testifies to the impossibility of controlling beauty's moral orientation at high levels of abstraction. Beauty's ethical and epistemic capacities appear to reside not in its principled affiliations with the true and the good, but in operations that at the same time recruit the beautiful as a tool of exclusion, gearing it toward public and intimate forms of domination. This problem recurs in subsequent treatments of beauty.

Beauty and the Economy: Hume and Smith

Novel dimensions of beauty's relational functioning emerge in writings by David Hume and Adam Smith that explore beauty's effects within the market, the state, and other institutional forms. Hume updates the eighteenth-century Platonic heritage in aesthetics by modernizing beauty's relational operations. His secular analogue to Shaftesbury's and Hutcheson's divine order is the social, political, and economic structure of the state, which he considers dependent on beauty in the following ways. Hume's delicacy of taste—that is, the faculty that issues in correct experiences and judgments of beauty and ugliness and that is trained through the perception of "beauties" of various kinds—enables one to control one's passions, to assess one's companions' quality of character, and to find a virtuous kind of pleasure in one's consumptive behavior.[37] Incited by taste and refinement, middle-class men seek the civilizing influence of suitably positioned women and are able to deploy this to good effect. In these different capacities, taste lends a person's affective life an organization that fosters individual autonomy as well as a connectedness with desirable others.[38] It allows for the formation of deep bonds among white men as well as "easy and sociable" relations among the sexes that are conducive to further refinement.[39]

The cultivating bonds generated by taste are highly selective. Blacks are excluded from refined society, on account of their inability to acquire taste.[40] It is doubtful that peasants and Indians, whose tastes Hume deprecates, are able to acquire the requisite level of refinement to participate in civilized status.[41] Male and female contributions toward civilization are sharply differentiated, with white middle-class women softening white men while making experience available to them, and white men supplying white women with knowledge.[42]

Taste and refinement cast their social, political, and moral effects yet further, in Hume's view. They spur national productivity by allowing the manufacturing of commodities to take off, fostering reservoirs of labor that would otherwise go to waste.[43] Rewarding human activity with pleasure, taste motivates rather than disciplines the individual to work.[44] Accordingly, sloth and indolence, tendencies Hume considers natural, are kept within bounds; our pleasures are rendered virtuous.[45] As it fosters productivity and commerce, taste promotes the rise of a free middle class in the state. The result is a nation with a high level of knowledge, humanity, and civilization.[46] By way of his conception of taste, Hume renders beauty instrumental to the social, economic, and political well-being of the nation state.

Adam Smith tightens the connections between the beautiful and the economy in *The Theory of Moral Sentiments*. Like Hume, Smith gives beauty a place in an encompassing social, political, and economic order, for which it is also, in part, responsible:

> If we consider the real satisfaction which [wealth and greatness] are capable of affording, by itself and separated from the beauty of that arrangement which is fitted to promote it, it will always appear in the highest degree contemptible and trifling. But we rarely view it in this abstract and philosophical light. We naturally confound it in our imagination with the order, the regular and harmonious movement of the system, the machine or economy by means of which it is produced. The pleasures of wealth and greatness, when considered in this complex view, strike the imagination as something grand, and beautiful, and noble, of which the attainment is well worth all the toil and anxiety which we are so apt to bestow on it.
>
> And it is well that nature imposes upon us in this manner. It is this deception which rouses and keeps in continual motion the industry of mankind. It is this which first prompted them to cultivate the ground, to build houses, to found cities and commonwealths, and to invent and improve all the sciences and arts, which ennoble and embellish human life.[47]

According to this well-known passage, the appreciation of wealth and greatness is contingent on the imaginative experience we have of these conditions as we comprehend them as a result of the beautiful arrangement from which they stem. This regular and harmonious system, which is "fitted to promote" wealth and greatness, allows these states to appear beautiful, grand, and noble. This appearance, then, makes us willing to expend "the toil and anxiety" it takes to attain these states. Though somehow illusory, it is an aesthetic imaginary of wealth and greatness that, for Smith, motivates and, in our eyes, legitimates the cultivation of land and nation. More than that: Smith not merely claims that beauty drives the economy, leaving it open that the economy may be understood as an aesthetically neutral phenomenon, but propounds the far stronger thesis that this very economy substantially amounts to an *aesthetic* good: the arts and sciences "ennoble and embellish human life." Ennoblement and embellishment are ethically and aesthetically substantive goods: "It is *well* that nature imposes upon us in this manner." Significantly, Smith does not call these conjoined aesthetic and ethical achievements illusory, contrary to what the above quotation might lead us to expect. *The Theory of Moral Sentiments*, accordingly, sees beauty as serving the good, where this good is understood in terms of a combination of aesthetic, economic, moral, and political values.

Several points follow from this crucial passage. One, while a product of the imagination, the aesthetic dimension of the relevant goods is clearly *not* reducible to the other dimensions. Two, it represents a value that is non-derivative from the other values, one that emerges as a result of an imaginative surplus. Three, more than that, aesthetic value is a necessary ingredient of other values: economic goods matter to us, at least in part, on account of their aesthetic significance. For Smith, the aesthetic thus constitutes an indissociable dimension of the meanings and values we realize by way of labor and via the establishment of civic and (trans)national institutions, such as cities and commonwealths.

What follows is that the aesthetic and the economic are conceived as fundamentally complicit in one another. This understanding Smith shares with numerous other theorists, as cultural critics have argued.[48] In light of the widely documented, long-standing, and pervasive imbrications of aesthetics and political economy, the prospects of separating beauty's economic and political workings from its aesthetic functioning must be considered dim. Entwined aesthetic and economic values inform our imaginaries and desires, and constitute a structural dimension of social existence. They underlie the existential possibilities that are open to us and that we grant others. Beauty and its antitheses, such as the ugly, the formless, the grotesque, and the malformed, enter into a complex affective calculus. A politically neutral conception of beauty can only come at the price of ignoring an intricate system of aesthetically conditioned economic designs and economically embedded aesthetic plans. The complex operations by which beauty makes its polyvalent, often ambiguous effects should be a focus of our attempts to rethink the beautiful.

Beauty, Love, and the Body: Burke and Wollstonecraft

If Platonic concerns with love and the body to some extent retreat to the background in Hume's and Smith's theories of beauty, these dimensions return with full force in Edmund Burke's view. The latter offers a detailed picture of beauty's social functioning, particularly of its role in safeguarding "adequately" gendered, racialized, and eroticized social arrangements. For Burke, beauty is critical to love and sociality. The male passion of love, he argues, discriminates among the social qualities exhibited by females. While he defines love as a contemplative state that, in distinction to lust, does not involve a desire for possession, he also calls love a mixed passion.[49] As a mixed state, it combines the general passion of lust a man is said to direct toward all women with the specific (purely contemplative) passion of love he feels for the beauty of particular women. This type of beauty consists in the social qualities that distinguish women from one another. These qualities supply men with a basis for the discriminations that govern their social preferences and choices. They inspire men "with sentiments of tenderness and affection towards their persons; we like to have them near us, and we enter willingly into a kind of relation with them."[50] By attaching the mixed passion of male sexualized love via beauty to female social and bodily qualities, Burke genders and eroticizes society on aesthetic grounds.[51]

As with Hume's theory, the beautiful in Burke's account helps to organize relationships in conformity with norms of gender, race, and class.[52] Burke's gendering of the beautiful idealizes a decisively white and upper-middle-class form of femininity. Testimony to this is that the qualities he advances as beautiful, such as weakness, smoothness, softness, and so forth, readily signal bodily states connoting lives that are tended to, rather than the work of tending or other sorts of labor that are more typically associated with white and nonwhite working classes.

The racial specificity of Burke's gendering of the beautiful is emphasized further by his insistence on the "terrible" nature of the color black, an idea he applies to skin in his discussion of a formerly blind, presumably white boy who is "struck with great horror at the sight" of a black woman.[53] The boy had already seen a black object, which "gave him great uneasiness." Note the difference in intensity of experience in the shift from object to person. In accordance with Burke's definition of the sublime as a condition that is inspired by horror,[54] and *contra* the aestheticized norms of adequate gender performance, the woman would have to qualify as sublime. This is a possibility that commentators have indeed assumed to be true.[55] However, Burke does not say this explicitly, which is remarkable given his enthusiasm for reiterated articulations of sublime moments.[56] His silence has a number of effects. One, it suggests that a woman's body cannot be sublime. Read this way, Burke's silence preserves the masculine gendering of the sublime, and its stable contrast with the consistently feminized beautiful. Since the binary gendering of these qualities infuses their social functioning, the silence, in Burke's scheme, also supports the masculinizing workings of the sublime, and their distinction from the feminizing operations of the beautiful. Thus he safeguards the dual operations of gendered aestheticization and aesthetic gendering at the heart of his construction of the social order, phenomena we have also encountered in Shaftesbury.

Two, Burke's silence honors the animation of the sublime as a great and admirable aesthetic quality by construing it as racially white and masculine.

In tandem with this, Burke upholds beauty's social and aesthetic lovability by implicitly characterizing the beautiful as white, upon rendering the black woman horrific. Correlatively, the philosopher protects the social and aesthetic attractiveness of white femininity (and/or feminine whiteness) by allowing it a potential for beauty that he denies the black woman. Accordingly, the beautiful and the sublime are valorized as racialized concepts; it appears to be exclusively white femininity and masculinity (of a certain class and sexual preference) that are to be appreciated for their aesthetic qualities and social promise.

Three, construing black femininity (and/or feminine blackness) as an aesthetically irredeemable threat, he bans the woman *and* the color of her skin, *on account of* this color, to a realm beyond the gendered dichotomy of the beautiful and the sublime. The black woman is cast outside the boundaries of normatively aestheticized sociality. Burke understands her as an aesthetic nonbeing in the sense that he takes her to elude the aesthetic laws governing human affect and sensibility. Assuming that the perception of her as horrific implicitly constitutes an aesthetic judgment, one that deploys the horrific as an aesthetic concept, I would resist the conclusion that she is unqualifiedly expelled from the aesthetic realm. Nevertheless, in positioning the woman beyond the dichotomy between the beautiful and the sublime, he irrevocably characterizes her as a social nonentity, as someone who exceeds the norms of ordinarily aestheticized social subjectivity and intersubjectivity. In the case of the white boy and the black woman, Burke thus renders inapplicable the regularities he institutes by means of the binary of beauty and sublimity.[57] This exception exposes the racial constraints curtailing these alleged generalizations. Aesthetic principles function as racial disciplinaries, while racial regimes find support in an aesthetic system.

Four, Burke's racialization of the beautiful and the sublime carries over to that of the colors white and black. His *Enquiry* studies natural and universally valid principles that connect qualities of objects and states of affairs with human feelings. These principles he names aesthetic "laws," or "principles of Taste."[58] Whiteness and blackness, accordingly, function as sources of aesthetically produced emotion and are subsumed under aesthetic generalizations. Inscribing distinctions between beauty and sublimity into whiteness, and rendering blackness horrific, Burke then clearly racializes these colors' aesthetic qualities and functioning. The specific aesthetic nature and powers of whiteness and blackness depend on the racial coding they carry in Burke's system; at the same time, their racial meanings find elaboration in their aesthetic effects. The racialization of whiteness and blackness is thus to be understood, in part, as an aesthetic artifact, and the aestheticization of these concepts is to be seen partly as a racial construct. In other words, their racialization and aestheticization are entangled. We can recognize here structural elements of a frame of interpretation that understands whiteness and blackness as bodily signs of cultural identities. Burke's picture of normative sociality is informed by a conceptual apparatus that institutes complex collaborations between aesthetic and racial readings.

As the above consequences indicate, Burke's theory subscribes to the two interrelated phenomena of racialized aestheticization (aesthetic categories are racialized) and aesthetic racialization (racial categories are aestheticized) identified earlier in Shaftesbury. These forces intersect with the (aestheticized and aestheticizing) forms of gendering I have described.[59] The beautiful, as conceived in opposition to the sublime and the horrific, constitutes a vital ingredient of these processes. For Burke, it functions as a means of controlling the racial, class-inflected, and gendered ramifications of social life. In that capacity, it helps to put into place a constellation of sharply differential, hierarchical social relationships.

Mary Wollstonecraft prominently challenges Burke's notion of beauty. Considering the place of women's beauty in the context of the pleasures and temptations of property and the aestheticized economy pertaining to women's social roles, Wollstonecraft judges feminine beauty of the sort that is associated with weakness, passivity, and women's pleasing of men, or that "rests supinely dependent on man for reason," to be morally invidious.[60] Burke, as we have seen, valorizes the former kind of beauty; Hume comes close to endorsing the latter. Beauty of these kinds, Wollstonecraft argues, conflicts with women's virtue because it inhibits their ability to attain reason and understanding. It is incompatible with the development of strength of character and stands in the way of dignity.[61] In Wollstonecraft's view, the need to please by physical appearance causes women to surrender themselves to men's affections in order to attain what power is available to them, condemning them to a life of sensibility and immediate pleasure, that is to say, to an existence that is limited to the present moment.[62]

In Mary Poovey's reading of Wollstonecraft's critique of Burke, Wollstonecraft reveals the contradictions that a system which denies the mutual imbrication of aesthetics, politics, and the economy inscribes in "the figure of woman and the difference of sex," assigning women an impossible position.[63] Poovey indicates that this system ambivalently locates sex as a matter of providential proportion at the basis of social differentiation and judgment, and renders women objects of aesthetic appreciation in an eroticized market economy in which they function as commodities that are appreciated imaginatively and exchanged rather than as agents of aesthetic discrimination.[64] Regarding this dual positioning of women, she writes, "At the heart of this semiotic system of discriminations is the difference upon which Burke anchored aesthetics: women are 'the sex'; men discriminate among women and so found civilization."[65] It is this discriminatory authority that Burke brings to his reading of the white boy's fear of the black woman.[66] He constrains this power of judgment racially, rendering it a prerogative of white men. Furthermore, registering racial differentiations, this discriminating and culture-building propensity is revealed to constitute a capacity to identify racial differences that, filtered through the appropriate perceiver's observations, become formative of what counts as culture and cultural status. Burke's centering of beauty in a frame of white, upper-middle-class, heterosexual relationships manifests itself in the aesthetic figuration of subjectivities, forms, feelings, and bodies that elude these bonds, and are expelled from the social and natural order that is controlled by the opposition between the beautiful and the sublime.

Wollstonecraft's own conception of beauty lacks the resources to rectify these imbalances. She proposes an alternative form of beauty, "the beauty of moral loveliness," which is to replace aristocratic and upper-middle-class women's "false notions of beauty and delicacy," supplanting their false refinement and manners.[67] Such "true beauty" lays claim to virtue, as it arises from the mind and from dignified occupations, contrary to "mere beauty of features and complexion."[68] True beauty consists in the "harmonious propriety" exemplified by the "well-regulated" mind. As such, Wollstonecraft believes, it gives the subject access to the "privileges of humanity."[69]

A difficulty with this view is that it implicitly reinstates the ethical and aesthetic generalizations put forth by Plato, Shaftesbury, and Hutcheson.[70] Like Shaftesbury and Hutcheson, Wollstonecraft's proposal affirms the questionable coincidence of (true) beauty, interest, and pleasure with public and private virtue in the larger social whole and, more specifically, in the fabric of relationships binding white upper- and middle-class men and women.[71] The privilege Wollstonecraft accords beauty of mind over beauty of body replicates Plato's aesthetic subjugation of bodily desire, the passions, and the senses by reason. But the mind/body hierarchy, feminists have argued, functions as a marker of social position, translating the valorizations it sustains into normative distinctions of race, class, gender, and sexuality. Wollstonecraft's account is no exception to this.[72] Her alternative fails to free the theory of beauty from the problems identified earlier. More than that, it falls short of engaging the entangled economic, amorous, and social powers beauty carries as a cultural desideratum, demanding normative physiques, skin color, odors, dress codes, and facial expressions. Coming to terms with the force of these disciplinary effects requires a more complex strategy than she envisages.

Wollstonecraft's critique of Burke and company contests important aspects of gendered aestheticization and aestheticized gendering. Yet these phenomena cast a wider web of psychic, embodied, and social effects and admit of a broader span of oppositional possibilities than her duality between "mere" physical beauty and "beauty of moral loveliness" recognizes. Beauty's concrete functioning within strategies of oppression and resistance eludes Wollstonecraft's dichotomies of mind and body, and of reason and affect or sensibility, as evinced, for example, by Macabéa's oppositional materiality, such as her typos and lipstick.[73]

Reaestheticizing the Beautiful

Ostensibly lending beauty a one-directional orientation toward the good, Scottish Enlightenment thinkers and other Neo-Platonists in fact locate beauty at the heart of a detailed pattern of social differentiation that appears morally praiseworthy only within a radically idealizing vision. Plato, Shaftesbury, Hutcheson, Hume, Smith, Burke, and Wollstonecraft implicitly set the beautiful and its antitheses to work to orchestrate a system of relationships. For these philosophers, the beautiful functions as a regulative idea that installs acceptable trajectories of subjectivation and regiments the traffic of culture. Its tendencies to bring about goodness, truth, happiness, and freedom go hand in hand with its capacities to inspire unjust differentiation and hierarchy. Beauty's pleasures are of a piece with its participation in ethical and political devastation.

While the impulse to dredge beauty onto solid moral ground is comprehensible in light of the concept's momentous (inter)subjective powers, the relational history of the beautiful belies its abiding there. In lieu of what traditionally was conceived as an overarching moral order, the actual context for beauty's cultural operations consists in continually evolving relationships between humans, animals, objects, and environments. Such relationships are mediated by aesthetic elements, which they also help to shape. Unfolding within crisscrossing institutional dynamics, aesthetic relationships are formative of values, ends, and concepts that come to matter in concrete social conditions. This means that the moral and political project of the beautiful is to be a relational endeavor. Beauty's conceptual structures and its ethical valences cannot be insulated from its participation in formations of aesthetic relationality. Hence, a stable, morally secure notion of beauty that would be protected from the vicissitudes of aesthetic relationships is undesirable and untenable.

As Mandeville implies, the persuasive appeal of the ethical and aesthetic idealizations advanced by Plato, Shaftesbury, and Hutcheson rests upon forms of discipline and oppression, which they conceal. Like Shaftesbury's and Hutcheson's generalizations, the accounts proposed by Hume, Smith, Burke, and Wollstonecraft downplay the problematic valence of beauty's concrete social operations. To attribute an unequivocally good orientation to the beautiful is to write off its participation in conditions of economic disparity, poverty, and social disposability,[74] and to discount the hold beauty has on our imagination and desire. More than that, it is to obfuscate the endemic operations of racialized (class-inflected, gendered) aestheticization and aesthetic racialization (class-inflection, gendering), which are part of the cultural scaffolding against the backdrop of which we shape our identities and differences.

Beauty is not ready to be set aright; it never will be. The moral and political polyvalence of the beautiful is inseparably bound up with its relational operations, including its frictions and collusions with market rationality. Our multidirectional ties to beauty and its antitheses testify to the need to transform constellations of aesthetic relationality. A critical reaestheticization of the modes of relationality we inhabit is in order. This leaves us with a collective task of working through beauty's ambivalent history, a challenge that Lispector's novel takes up.[75]

Ensconced in the contours of normative sociality, beauty is differentially available to us to arrange our relationships for better and for worse. At the same time, the categories of the beautiful and the ugly exceed the realm of what standardized social existence valorizes or devalorizes under those rubrics. Unimagined aesthetic possibilities can be recuperated in the margins of normative culture. Expendable and superfluous, Macabéa is shown to find unscripted joy in the sounds of a cockerel, in hugging a tree, and in listening to the pings that make up her favorite radio program, *Radio Clock*.[76] Like many other artists, Lispector refracts relational forces that bind the beautiful to social and economic flourishing, and the ugly to subalternity. Abundant aesthetic resources envelop us that we can rally to redirect beauty's moral and political orientations, to tweak the meanings of the beautiful, and to dislodge the structures of relationality in which beauty exerts its effects.

Notes

I thank Elizabeth V. Spelman and Norman S. Holland for comments and discussion about this essay.

1. Clarice Lispector, *The Hour of the Star*, trans. Giovanni Pontiero (1977; Manchester: Carcanet, 1986), 68.

2. *A hora da astrela*, dir. Suzana Amaral (Raíz Produções Cinematográficas, 1986; released in the U.S. as *The Hour of the Star*, 1987).

3. As Jean Franco argues in "Going Public: Reinhabiting the Private," in *On Edge: The Crisis of Contemporary Latin American Culture*, ed. George Yúdice, Juan Flores, and Jean Franco (Minneapolis: University of Minnesota Press, 1992), 65–83, 75–76.

4. I develop this notion in "Racialization as an Aesthetic Production: What Does the Aesthetic Do for Whiteness and Blackness and Vice Versa?" in *White on White/Black on Black*, ed. George Yancy (Lanham, Md.: Rowman and Littlefield, 2005), 83–124.

5. Lispector, *The Hour of the Star*, 14.

6. Ibid., 68.

7. Ibid., 50.

8. Ibid., 61–62.

9. Ibid., 23.

10. Ibid., 53. The term "semiotic" refers here to Macabéa's enjoyment of the materiality of signs apart from their referential meanings (as when she delights in the smell of meat while lacking the means to buy meat itself [53]). See also Julia Kristeva, *Revolution in Poetic Language*, trans. Margaret Waller (New York: Columbia University Press, 1984), 21–89.

11. Lispector, *The Hour of the Star*, 15, 55.

12. I elaborate this reading of Lispector's novel in my book manuscript in progress, "The Cultural Promise of the Aesthetic."

13. I follow Alexander Broadie and others in seeing the Scottish Enlightenment as spanning roughly the eighteenth century. See his introduction to *The Cambridge Companion to the Scottish Enlightenment*, ed. Alexander Broadie (Cambridge: Cambridge University Press, 2003), 1, 6.

14. Anthony Ashley Cooper, Earl of Shaftesbury, *Characteristics of Men, Manners, Opinions, Times*, 2 vols., ed. John M. Robertson (New York: Bobbs-Merrill, 1964); and Francis Hutcheson, *An Inquiry into the Original of Our Ideas of Beauty and Virtue in Two Treatises*, ed. Wolfgang Leidhold (Indianapolis: Liberty Fund, 2004). According to Shaftesbury, the mind, which has "an idea or sense of order and proportion" (*Characteristics of Men, Manners, Opinions, Times*, 2:63), perceives and rationally enjoys beauty in itself, which coincides with goodness and truth (1:91, 1:94, 2:126–28, 2:144). Beauty depends on symmetry and order (1:92, 2:177, 2:267–69, 2:276), which we perceive without fully knowing this order (1:214, 2:65). The proportionality that makes for beauty is productive of utility, convenience, and advantage, but beauty does not depend on this. Rather, it depends on the "fountain of all beauty," which forms the minds that, in turn, form beautiful things (2:126, 2:131–33). Likewise, Shaftesbury argues that self-interest and virtue coincide (2:243–44,

2:274, 2:281–82), though virtue is not based on interest (1:66), but rather is disinterested (1:67, 1:69, 1:77–78).

Hutcheson echoes Shaftesbury's idea that the sense of beauty provides a disinterested pleasure in order and the just proportion of elements within the larger whole of which these elements are a part (*An Inquiry into the Original of Our Ideas of Beauty and Virtue*, 8–9, 45, 86, 112). This pleasure is immediate and prior to utility or rational comprehension (9, 25, 35, 100). At the same time, it is compatible with self-interest (186). More than that, self-interest is actually morally required (122).

15. Shaftesbury, *Characteristics of Men, Manners, Opinions, Times*, 1:217, 2:257, 1:214, 1:218, 1:228, 1:260–61, 1:279–82.

16. Ibid., 1:218–19.

17. John Barrell analyzes the gendered, sexual, artistic, and spectatorial requirements posed by art's moral and political task in Shaftesbury in "'The Dangerous Goddess': Masculinity, Prestige and the Aesthetic in Early Eighteenth-Century Britain," *Cultural Critique* 12 (1989): 101–32.

18. Anthony Ashley Cooper, Earl of Shaftesbury, *Second Characters; or, The Language of Forms*, ed. Benjamin Rand (London: Cambridge University Press, 1914), 103–105.

19. The designation *emollit mores*, denoting a softening of norms, points to the danger of feminization. See the link between softening and "effeminacy" in the previous set of quotations as well as in Shaftesbury's *Second Characters*, 104. Here the phrase occurs in connection with a concern about the weakening that may follow from polishing and refinement, and that Shaftesbury takes to result in effeminacy.

20. Shaftesbury, *Characteristics of Men, Manners, Opinions, Times*, 1:222, 1:224, 1:225.

21. These forms of differentiation intersect. See Elizabeth V. Spelman, *Inessential Woman: Problems of Exclusion in Feminist Thought* (Boston: Beacon, 1988).

22. For these two phenomena, see also my "Racialization as an Aesthetic Production."

23. Bernard Mandeville, *The Fable of the Bees; or, Private Vices, Publick Benefits*, vol. 1, ed. F. B. Kaye (Oxford: Clarendon, 1924), 42, 323–25, 331. Following Mandeville, Howard Caygill elaborates on the need for violence, forced labor, and political regulation in Shaftesbury and Hutcheson in his *Art of Judgement* (New York: Basil Blackwell, 1989), 43–45, 51–53, 57–62.

24. Mandeville, *The Fable of the Bees*, 48.

25. Ibid., 166, 149.

26. Ibid., 331, 68–69, 76–80, 124–65, 231–35.

27. Ibid., 343.

28. Besides broader critiques by, among others, Walter Benjamin, Cornel West, and Sylvia Wynter, see Caygill, *Art of Judgement*, 43–62; and Barrell, "'The Dangerous Goddess,'" 102–103.

29. Plato, *Symposium*, trans. Alexander Nehamas and Paul Woodruff (Indianapolis: Hackett, 1989), 210A–12C.

30. Ibid., 212A–B.

31. Plato, *Phaedrus*, in *The Collected Dialogues of Plato*, ed. Edith Hamilton and Huntington Cairns, trans. R. Hackforth (Princeton: Princeton University Press, 1961), 249e, 251a, 253c–54e.

32. Ibid., 256b, 156d–e.

33. Ibid., 247c–e, 248d–49b.

34. See, for example, Spelman, *Inessential Woman*, 9–13, 19–36, 126–28.

35. Julia Kristeva, "Manic Eros, Sublime Eros: On Male Sexuality," in *Tales of Love*, trans. Leon S. Roudiez (New York: Columbia University Press, 1987); Kristeva, *Revolution in Poetic Language*, 25–30, 45–51, 68–71; Luce Irigaray, *This Sex Which Is Not One*, trans. Catherine Porter (Ithaca: Cornell University Press, 1985), 86–118, 186–89; Luce Irigaray, *An Ethics of Sexual Difference*, trans. Carolyn Burke and Gillian C. Gill (Ithaca: Cornell University Press, 1993), 20–33; and Luce Irigaray, "The Female Gender," in *Sexes and Genealogies*, trans. Gillian C. Gill (New York: Columbia University Press, 1993), 109, 113–15.

36. Recall the violent subjugation in the *Phaedrus* of the bad horse, which stands for the soul's appetitive part, that is to say, its bodily desires, by the charioteer, who stands for the soul's rational part. For a discussion of somatophobia in Plato and the politicization of the distinctions between the rational and appetitive parts of the soul, see Spelman, *Inessential Woman*. On the gendered and racial connotations of figurations of the body and the links between Plato's views of embodiment and beauty, see especially 23–31 and 127.

37. David Hume, "Of the Standard of Taste," in *Selected Essays*, ed. Stephen Copley and Andrew Edgar, 141–44 (Oxford: Oxford University Press, 1998); David Hume, "Of the Delicacy of Taste and Passion," in *Selected Essays*, 10–13; and Hume, "Of Refinement in the Arts," in *Selected Essays*, 168–70.

38. Hume, "Of the Delicacy of Taste and Passion," 11–13.

39. Hume, "Of Refinement in the Arts," 169; Hume, "Of the Rise and Progress of the Arts and Sciences," in *Selected Essays*, 72–74; and Hume, "Of Essay Writing," in *Selected Essays*, 1–2, 4.

40. This follows from the role reason plays for Hume in taste (esp. in taste's dimension of "good sense" ["Of the Standard of Taste," 146–47; "Of the Delicacy of Taste and Passion," 11]) and from Hume's denial of reason to blacks (Hume, "Of National Characters," in *Selected Essays*, esp. 360 n. 120). For analysis, see my "Racialization as an Aesthetic Production."

41. Hume, "Of the Standard of Taste," 144.

42. Hume, "Of the Rise and Progress of the Arts and Sciences," 74; and Hume, "Of Essay Writing," 2.

43. Hume, "Of Refinement in the Arts," 168–69; and Hume, "Of Commerce," in *Selected Essays*, 160–63.

44. Hume thus avoids the violent self-denial that, Mandeville argues against Shaftesbury, is forced on working classes by politicians and thinkers who perpetuate hypocritical equations of public and private good, and of virtue and self-interest (Mandeville, *The Fable of the Bees*, 42, 323–24, 331). See also n. 23 above.

45. Hume, "Of Refinement in the Arts," 168–69.

46. Ibid., 174–75, 169–70. Thus, taste in Hume's philosophy exemplifies what John Guillory sees as its role in eighteenth-century moral philosophy generally,

namely that of regulating consumption without limiting "the commerce and industry upon which the nation depended" (John Guillory, *Cultural Capital: The Problem of Literary Canon Formation* [Chicago: University of Chicago Press, 1993], 307).

47. Adam Smith, *The Theory of Moral Sentiments* (Amherst, N.Y.: Prometheus, 2000), 263.

48. Regenia Gagnier, *The Insatiability of Human Wants: Economics and Aesthetics in Market Society* (Chicago: University of Chicago Press, 2000); and Mary Poovey, "Aesthetics and Political Economy in the Eighteenth Century: The Place of Gender in the Social Constitution of Knowledge," in *Aesthetics and Ideology*, ed. George Levine (New Brunswick: Rutgers University Press, 1994), 79–105.

49. Edmund Burke, *A Philosophical Enquiry into the Origin of our Ideas of the Sublime and the Beautiful*, ed. Adam Phillips (Oxford: Oxford University Press, 1990), 83, 39, 47.

50. Ibid., 39.

51. Burke, like Shaftesbury, keeps subjects in line via regulations without taking recourse to "totally banishing" or "prohibiting" (Shaftesbury, *Characteristics of Men, Manners, Opinions, Times*, 1:218–19; and Shaftesbury, *Second Characters*, 104).

52. On gender and race in Burke see, among others, Paul Mattick, "Beautiful and Sublime: 'Gender Totemism' in the Constitution of Art," in *Feminism and Tradition in Aesthetics*, ed. Peggy Zeglin Brand and Carolyn Korsmeyer (University Park: Pennsylvania State University Press, 1995), 28–29, 40–41; and Meg Armstrong, "'The Effects of Blackness': Gender, Race, and the Sublime in Aesthetic Theories of Burke and Kant," *Journal of Aesthetics and Art Criticism* 54, no. 3 (Summer 1996): 213–36.

53. Burke, *Philosophical Enquiry*, 131.

54. Ibid., 36, 47, 53–79.

55. See, for example, Armstrong, "'The Effects of Blackness.'" The assumption is reasonable, given that sublimity is the subject of Burke's discussion.

56. Moreover, the horrific or terrible is not necessarily sublime. This latter honorific state involves a measure of distance from danger and pain, which, "with certain modifications," allows for delight (Burke, *Philosophical Enquiry*, 36–37; see also 47). Possibly Burke takes the necessary distance and adjustments to be lacking in the case of the white boy's perception of the black woman. He associates a high degree of sublimity also with astonishment, and recognizes dimensions of admiration, reverence, and respect (53).

57. Armstrong argues that Burke casts the black female outside the boundaries he has established for the beautiful and the sublime and explores the racial and gender implications of the contradictions his theory incurs on these points ("'The Effects of Blackness,'" 215, 220–21).

58. Ibid., 12–17.

59. Such intersectionality is to be expected in view of the analytical interconnectedness of racial, gender, and class categories. See n. 21 above.

60. Mary Wollstonecraft, *A Vindication of the Rights of Woman: With Strictures on Moral and Political Subjects*, rev. ed., ed. Miriam Brody (London: Penguin, 1992), 144–47, 162. The argument may not apply to men's (or other non-female-identified individuals') aesthetic pleasing of men. For it is not clear that Wollstonecraft perceives

a problem with "equivocal beings" that offer men "something more soft than women" (254; see also 161).

61. Ibid., 156, 170, 150, 144. Wollstonecraft writes, "From the respect paid to property flow, as from a poisoned fountain, most of the evils and vices which render this world such a dreary scene to the contemplative mind," before insisting on the ways in which "the respect paid to wealth and mere personal charms" is destructive of women's virtue (257–58). Thus she explicitly discusses the question of women's beauty (the source of their personal charms) in the context of the market. See Poovey on connections with eighteenth-century debates on the relation between virtue and commerce ("Aesthetics and Political Economy," 91–98).

62. Wollstonecraft, A *Vindication of the Rights of Woman*, 152, 146, 163, 168.

63. Poovey, "Aesthetics and Political Economy," 98, 97.

64. Ibid., 92, 89–90.

65. Ibid., 96.

66. On this discriminatory authority, see also Armstrong, "'The Effects of Blackness,'" 217, 220.

67. Wollstonecraft, A *Vindication of the Rights of Woman*, 268, 225, 144, 153.

68. Ibid., 165, 227, 259–60.

69. Ibid., 268.

70. This is not to deny its distance from Shaftesbury's grounding of the artistic civilizing process in female beauty (see Barrell, "'The Dangerous Goddess'").

71. Wollstonecraft, A *Vindication of the Rights of Woman*, 259, 262. While Wollstonecraft presents upper- and middle-class women with the virtuous paradigm of working-class women who perform the labor it takes to discharge their responsibilities (174), she ultimately privileges the former. Lucinda Cole critiques Wollstonecraft's class hierarchy in "(Anti)Feminist Sympathies: The Politics of Relationship in Smith, Wollstonecraft, and More," *English Literary History* 58, no. 1 (Spring 1991): 107–40.

72. See Cole, "(Anti)Feminist Sympathies."

73. Lispector, *The Hour of the Star*, 26, 32.

74. This point applies also to beauty's associations with able-bodiedness and its conventionally assumed disconnection from aged and physically impaired bodies, and to its complicity in environmental destruction. See Anita Silvers, "From the Crooked Timber of Humanity, Beautiful Things Can Be Made," in *Beauty Matters*, ed. Peg Zeglin Brand (Bloomington: Indiana University Press, 2000), 197–221; and Yuriko Saito, "Ecological Design: Promises and Challenges," *Environmental Ethics* 24, no. 3 (Fall 2002): 243–61.

75. Irigaray, among others, alerts us to this task in the context of problematic gender constellations. For an illuminating approach to beauty's ambivalence, its entwinement with race, gender, and other dynamics of subjectivity, see Anne Anlin Cheng, "Wounded Beauty: An Exploratory Essay on Race, Feminism, and the Aesthetic Question," *Tulsa Studies in Women's Literature* 19, no. 2 (Autumn 2000): 191–217.

76. In my book manuscript, "The Cultural Promise of the Aesthetic," I discuss how pleasures of this kind critically implicate the reader in consequence of the novella's forms of address. In our joint book manuscript in progress, "Reclaiming the Aesthetic in Latin America," Norman S. Holland and I situate the novella's aesthetic modes in a broader cultural perspective.

4. Queer Beauty: Winckelmann and Kant on the Vicissitudes of the Ideal

WHITNEY DAVIS

Uranists often ornament their apartments with pictures and statues representing good-looking youths. It appears that they love the statue of Apollo Belvedere in a manner all their own.
—Albert Moll, *Perversions of the Sex Instinct*

The history of modern and contemporary art provides many examples of the "queering" of cultural and social norms. It has been tempting to consider this process of subversion and transgression, or "outlaw representation" (as Richard Meyer has called it), as well as related performances of "camp" or other gay inflections of the dominant forms of representation, to be the most creative mode of queer cultural production.[1] Whether or not this is true in the history of later nineteenth- and twentieth-century art, we can identify a historical process in modern culture that has worked in the opposite direction—namely, the constitution of aesthetic ideals, cultural norms that claim validity within an entire society, which have been based on manifestly homoerotic prototypes and significances. There has been little subversion or camp in these configurations. Indeed, perhaps there has been a surfeit of idealizing configuration and normalizing representation. But as Johann Joachim Winckelmann's art history and Immanuel Kant's aesthetics might suggest, such idealization can be no less queer than camp inflections or outlaw representations.

In this respect we might consider modern European replications of the Classical Greek pederastic imagery of ephebic male beauty. At Sanssouci at

Potsdam, his pleasure palace outside Berlin, Frederick II of Prussia erected the *Adorante* or Adoring Youth (fig. 4.1), acquired in 1747 and now understood to be an original bronze of the early Hellenistic period, at the end of a garden walkway that he could survey when seated in his private library. There Winckelmann saw it in 1752. The king was the only person who officially had access to this privileged view. But outside the building, visitors could readily see how the sculpture related to the king's quarters. Christoph Vogtherr has noted that observers could remark its association with the king's tomb, which stood nearby, readied for his eventual occupancy. Vogtherr has proposed that Frederick's art collections at Sanssouci tried "to make a synthesis between the norms of society and love," that is, Frederick's loves for men, especially Hans Hermann von Katte, special friend of the crown prince before his accession, executed for sodomy by Frederick's father (then the king) in 1730.[2] "Synthesis between the norms of society and love": Vogtherr uses this phrase to describe Frederick's gallery of paintings by Antoine Watteau and other contemporary artists. It could equally describe Frederick's collection of antiquities, specifically his installation of the *Adorante*.

But what exactly was this synthesis? Regardless of the personal connotations of the sculpture for Frederick, the *Adorante* (formerly owned by such collectors as King Charles I in London and the counts of Liechtenstein in Vienna) shows that pederastically determined imagery can achieve normative status—Vogtherr's synthesis of personal erotic love and social norms. Displayed by leaders of church and state in prominent public places, the imagery has signified and legitimated dynastic, national, and imperial aspirations. At Sanssouci, the *Adorante* certainly displayed the king's taste and learning. In figuring the eroticized (and infantilized) position of the worshipful young body politic in relation to the king's real person, it embodied Frederick's paternalistic (and incorporative) claims as king of Prussia— claims that had initially been threatened by the taint of homosexuality affixed to him in his youth.

We can pursue this particular image in later replications. In the 1880s, for example, the British sculptor Ronald Sutherland Leveson-Gower, a relative of Queen Victoria and an heir to the vast holdings of the dukes of Sutherland, recalled it in his figure of Prince Hal (later King Henry V) on the forward face of the Shakespeare Memorial at Stratford-upon-Avon, dedicated in 1888, one of England's few monuments to her greatest writer. On the Shakespeare Memorial, Hal served as the Allegory of History. Gower used the *Adorante*, which he had likely studied in a visit to Potsdam, to set the pose of his nude model, a young male studio hand. He went so far as to

Figure 4.1. *Adorante,* or Adoring Youth, installed in 1747 at Sanssouci, Potsdam, Prussia. Courtesy Stiftung Preussischer Kulturbesitz.

Figure 4.2. Ronald Gower's statue of Prince Hal as the Allegory of
History on the Shakespeare Memorial at Stratford-upon-Avon (unveiled
1888). PHOTOGRAPH BY CATHERINE WEED BEECHER, 1895. COURTESY OF
GEORGE EASTMAN HOUSE.

consider that he might show Prince Hal in the nude, although Shakespeare's
text gave no support for the idea. In *Henry the Fourth Part Two*, Prince Hal
takes the crown from his dying father's bedside in Westminster Abbey and
reveals himself to be "Harry of England," soon to be victor at Agincourt—the
very type, as the poet Algernon Charles Swinburne noted, of the "militant
Englishmen" who founded the British Empire in India, Africa, and elsewhere. Imperial and glamorous whether nude or not, Gower's Hal presents
a package with familiar pederastic and homoerotic associations (fig. 4.2).
In addition to dramatizing Hal's bulging crotch and clenched, muscular

buttocks, Gower paired the prince with Falstaff, the fat old knight who regarded the prince, the Achilles to his Centaur, as a fellow "minion of the moon" (that is, a follower of Diana and Bacchus) and Falstaff's "sweet wag," his "most comparative, rascalliest, sweet young prince."[3]

It is debatable whether these replications gained prestige and power *because of* their association with Greco-Roman and Elizabethan pederasty or *despite* it. But undeniably they were fully intelligible to many modern observers in pederastic terms. In 1808 Conrad von Levezow, a distinguished antiquarian, produced the first scholarly treatise on the ancient imagery of Antinous, the slave, lover, and companion of the Roman emperor Hadrian. In the same year, Levezow noted commonly accepted identifications of the *Adorante* as an Antinous or (even better) a Ganymede, cup-bearer to the gods and bedfellow of Zeus. (In fact, a special type of Antinous-Ganymede—a super-pederastic image, as it were—had been identified by another scholar in another sculpture that Levezow had not seen.) One or the other of these identifications had probably been accepted by Frederick, who also displayed an Antinous in the type of "benevolent Genius" in his garden.[4] On the basis of his comparative knowledge, Levezow felt that the facial features of the *Adorante* did not quite match those of an Antinous. The other features were a different matter. Levezow believed that ancient artists usually avoided the reputedly feminine aspect of Antinous's body, for these traits identified him as the emperor's catamite; they preferred to depict him to have an ideally male—an athletic or even Apollonian—character. In Frederick's statue, however, the ephebic grace of the figure was undeniable. In the end, Levezow left the iconography indefinite—it was a delicate topic—and chose to affiliate the statue with a rather obscure class of adoring figures, both male and female, which had a Classical Greek vintage. According to Levezow, the *Adorante* might be attributed to the sculptor Euphranor, who worked in the "beautiful style" of the fourth century BCE identified by Winckelmann. As such, it might be associated with the series of male statues of victorious athletes which had been arrayed at Olympia in Elis in the fifth and fourth centuries BCE and later—historical horizons to which I will return below.

Despite these broadly homoerotic and specifically pederastic connotations, the works in question could be admired as expressions of the highest ideals of truth, history, and beauty. If Gower literally dressed up his principal artistic source (as well as his real human model) for Prince Hal, Levezow's review of interpretations of the somewhat risqué iconography of the *Adorante* (he did not hesitate to mention the *Knabenliebe* attributed to Zeus and Hadrian and implicitly to Frederick) did not prevent its reproduction in plaster casts and other media throughout the nineteenth century.[5] As I have already suggested, such replications (whether Frederick's or Gower's or the cast industry's) proffered what might be called queer beauty. I use the term "beauty" in its specifically Kantian sense to denote a normative communal-ization of judgments of taste which claims deep aesthetic agreement, gains wide social assent, and relays an entire community's ideals *of* itself *for* itself. The *Adorante* at Sanssouci is the Prussian people — Frederick's lover.

It would seem that there should not be any queer beauty in this Kantian sense. That is, there should not be any *queer* beauty or queer *beauty*. But clearly there was. In the late 1750s at his villa in Rome, Cardinal Alessandro Albani installed a striking relief of Antinous, found at Hadrian's villa at Tivoli in 1737, in a public salon. According to Winckelmann, Albani's art advisor at the time, the relief from Tivoli did not quite reproduce the "high style" of beauty in Classical Greek sculpture of the fifth century BCE, identified above all with the sculptor Phidias. The voluptuousness of Antinous in Hadrian's relief departed from (or, alternatively, had yet to be fully idealized in) the tranquility of the most elevated works of Greek style. Needless to say, the relief had not been made by Classical Greek artists in the first place: though perhaps made by an ethnic Greek sculptor, obviously it had a specifically Hadrianic vintage and meaning.

Following in the footsteps of the Roman emperor, Winckelmann prob-ably appreciated the relief of Antinous from Tivoli in the same way that he fetishized the pseudo-Polykleitan head of a faun which he installed in his apartment in the Villa Albani, his "Ganymede," as he called it, "whom I would kiss before the eyes of all the saints."[6] As in the case of Frederick's *Adorante*, however, and given Albani's highly visible ecclesiastical position, the cardinal's installation of the relief from Tivoli did not have to imply that *he* adored it pederastically. Perhaps he did; historians have amassed circum-stantial evidence for a homoerotic social network headquartered at the Villa Albani. But if this social network was a distinctive subculture, as some his-torians have concluded, it was equally *Kultur*. The Tivoli relief belonged to a complex sediment of many kinds of ancient and modern beauties dis-played at the Villa Albani, beauties that could be the objects of antiquar-ian devotion or aesthetic *Kult*. Regardless, Albani's installation of the relief certainly showed that he judged it to be beautiful. And so did many other viewers, whether homoerotically interested or not. Edward Gibbon, who condemned sodomy, found it "admirably soft, well turned and full of flesh."[7] In Pompeo Batoni's portrait of an unknown patron, perhaps one of the wealthy British, German, or Scandinavian gentlemen who were guided around Rome by Winckelmann, the young Grand Tourist (painted circa 1760) was not simply affiliating himself with Greco-Roman pederasty when he displayed—and gestured at—the relief of Antinous from Tivoli placed on the table beside him.[8] He did not have to position himself as a Hadrian to this Antinous. Rather, he positioned himself as a Winckelmann or an Albani to this Antinous: he displayed his correct contemporary taste for Classical beauty, originally homoerotic in its sexual aesthetics, as a newly canonical cultural norm. This norm had emerged in a historical process, the synthesis identified by Vogtherr at Sanssouci, that had moved in the duration of one generation or less from Winckelmann's eroticized and even "homosexual" enthusiasm to Albani's catholic, cultivated approbation and finally to Batoni's recognition of a virtually universal standard, a cultural beacon, which had recently been established among a pan-European class of elite young men. To explore this process, we must start with Winckelmann's eroticized enthusiasm for ancient art.

Despite his veneration of Socrates, Winckelmann (as Bernard Bosanquet and Benedetto Croce realized) was an anti-Platonic Platonist. Like Socrates and Plato, Winckelmann believed that erotic desire promotes human knowledge of—and participation in—the ideal; *eros* is the ladder of the ideal. But unlike the mature Plato, and perhaps more like Socrates in Xenophon's sympathetic and worldly portrayal of him, Winckelmann did not really believe that the artistic realization of an ideal involves transcendence of erotic desire, its wholesale conversion into a love of the good, the just, and the beautiful, as the strict-constructionist Platonist tended to suppose.[9] (This Platonist was a figure as much imagined by Winckelmann and his generation as actually to be found in the ancient Academy or the modern schools. But this problem need not detain us here; each generation has produced the Plato and the Platonism that it thinks it needs.) Instead, *eros* is always required, even in the ideal or as the ideal. Indeed, Winckelmann could not take the ideal to be the end point of human knowing, that is, the end point of erotic desire. As his art-historical writings implied, Winckelmann imagined—and here is the distinctively anti-Platonic note— that there is something to be sensed beyond the ideal and, as it were, by way of the ideal, even if it is difficult to realize and represent this condition or horizon in the ideal: namely, the continuous movements of desire toward ideality, in ideality, and around ideality. It is these movements, rather than their supposed aim or putative issue in ideal forms, which constitute the primal conditions of knowing in human being.

To be specific, Winckelmann's history of the process of aesthetic idealization offered a reconstruction of the creation and display of sculptures in the ancient *palaestra,* or wrestling grounds, especially at the pan-Hellenic gaming grounds at Olympia. (In his meditations on Greek civilization in the *Phenomenology of Spirit* and the *Lectures on Aesthetics,* G. W. F. Hegel relocated the history in question at these sites to the Greek temple, which was surrounded by sculptural dedications, and the Greek theater, in which human actors performed as if in the form of sculptures; Winckelmann's history of art and the politics and erotics that it marked never fully recovered from these tendentious deflections.) Of course, in the absence of scientific excavation of these sites (which would later discover, for example, the situation of statue bases), Winckelmann's reconstruction was largely speculative; it was based primarily on Pausanias's description of Greece and other texts. Indeed, in the *History of the Art of Antiquity,* Winckelmann's description of the display of sculpture at Olympia took the form of a report of a "dream," an imaginative or hallucinatory visualization of its original aspect.

According to Winckelmann, the sculptural displays of victorious athletes erected in the *palaestra* inspired young men to physical and moral achievement. In turn, the beautiful bodies of athletes who had cultivated these artistic ideals were used as material prototypes for the sculptor's representations of them, images that eventually returned to the *palaestra* and other contexts of display in which they could be admired and imitated in due course by the next generation (and all later generations) of young male athletes admired by *their* lovers, philosophers and artists included. Winckelmann imagined this continuous historical cycle of idealization in sculpture (and the human bodies correlated with it) in terms of the ancient Greek practice, embodied in Pindar's odes, of singing the praise of the successive generations of Olympian victors, the framework that Pliny had adopted in his *Natural History* to narrate the history of ancient art. (Along with Pausanias, in the eighteenth century Pliny was the principal ancient authority on the chronology of Greek art; before Winckelmann worked out his stylistic chronology, the dating of Classical sculpture depended on Pliny's enumeration of the works of sculptors arranged in terms of their place, as makers of sculptural commemorations of victors, in the continuous sequence of Olympiads.) At the heart of the cycle, its motivation or engine, was the institution of pederasty.[10] Winckelmann's account of pederastic *Nachahmung* in ancient Greek art and culture—the construction of artistic ideals as literal relays of and templates for homoerotic ideals—was based in large measure on certain ancient sources and modern commentaries that were not well known to Winckelmann's contemporaries. Chief among these were Gottlob Zeibich's *Athleta paradoxos* of 1748, which dealt with the role of ancient statues (especially of naked or near-naked young men) in producing models or paradigms for real-life emulation, and Johann Gesner's *Socrates sanctus paederasta* of 1752, which dealt (albeit in a sardonic mode) with Socrates' aesthetic and ethical valorizations of temperate, modest pederasty, which was literally incarnated in Socrates' practice of holding philosophical conversations (many of them about the self-management of homoerotic love) at the perimeter of the *palaestra* where the young athletes trained for games and for war and where (as Winckelmann had it) the sculptors came to study their ideally beautiful naked bodies. These sources were not explicitly cited by Winckelmann (although both works were available to him in the library of Count Bünau) and so far as I can tell they were overlooked by Justi and other scholars of Winckelmann's career; they do not appear in the bibliography to the recent Getty translation of Winckelmann's *History of the Art of Antiquity*. But as we will see below, they were soon to be codified in a somewhat shadowy strand of post-Winckelmannian materialism in Enlightenment aesthetics and by nineteenth-century sexologists. In books such as Richard Payne Knight's *Discourse on the Worship of Priapus*, published in 1786, and Friedrich Karl Forberg's commentaries on the erotic epigrams of Antonio Beccadelli (a Renaissance imitator of Martial and Petronius), published in 1824, ideality—art as the morally elevated perfection of beauty—was more or less rudely recalled to its origins in erotic fantasy and sexual attraction, including homosexual lust. Although Winckelmann himself did not write in public with such frankness, he would not have been surprised by Knight's or Forberg's researches; both scholars depended on him.

Setting aside his history of the homoerotic dimension of Greek art, Winckelmann's social and political history of Greece and its art was widely acceptable and relatively familiar to readers at the time. To some extent it had already been stated by the Baron de Montesquieu and other historians. In particular, the putative interdependence of the high style associated with supreme beauty (on the aesthetic side) and Periklean politics associated with maximum freedom (on the political side)—that is, the supposed affiliation of the ideals of Phidian art and the ideals of Athenian democracy— appealed to the political sentiments of many eighteenth-century readers. Insofar as eighteenth-century liberalism could not imagine any society more free than democracy, more ideally expressive of the interests of its individual citizens synthesized in the harmoniousness of collective self-government, it was impossible to conceive of an art (putatively it represents such citizens in such a state of political self-organization) possessing any greater ideality. To be sure, one had to idealize Periklean democracy in order to admire it, overlooking its imperial adventurism and restricted franchise; and it was understood that the democracy instituted in Athens in the fifth century BCE manifested an ideal liberal democracy in the modern sense only *in nuce.* Oddly enough, however, one could admire Phidian art without qualification: supposedly it represented the zenith rather than the origin of all possible ideality in art. Regardless, the overtly political correlation of ideal art in Greece was widely recognized and widely applauded by scholars and political activists who echoed Winckelmann. Moreover, in some respects Winckelmann's model of *Nachahmung* in ancient culture—of the cycles of imitation and emulation instituted in pederasty—would have been familiar, or not unexpected, to readers who had been educated in such texts as Pomponius Gauricus's *De sculptura et pictura antiquorum,* published in 1504, and the Baron de Longepierre's *Discours sur les anciens,* published in 1687. Based in large measure on literary evidence, these treatises noted the replicatory and imitative cycles that had constituted ancient art. (As we have already seen, Winckelmann liked to cover his tracks in presenting some of his most fundamental proposals: much as he remained silent about Zeibich and Gesner, he cited neither of these writers of previous centuries, though probably both were well known to him because the relevant works were available to him in the library of Count Bünau.)

But Winckelmann's refinement of his predecessors was more important than his repetition. In keeping with his Lucretian perspective, Winckelmann understood that the historicity of *Nachahmung,* of art "coming after" an ideal of the past, need not always be imagined (indeed, it cannot coherently be imagined, and it cannot be reconstructed historically) as a progressive, univocal, and unilinear improvement of formality inclined toward a single supreme ideality. *Nachahmung* devolves historically as a cycle rather than unfolding teleologically as a sequence. And as a cycle rather than a sequence, it displays a complex rhythmic movement toward and away from aesthetic formalizations that temporarily stabilize a community's sense of the ideal. In its hundreds of pages, Winckelmann's *History of the Art of Antiquity* made it clear that history of art in culture recognized many deviations of the artistic *clinamen,* that is, many revolutions and devolutions of Classical style. The art historian can find, for example, an original or primitive protoclassicism in the panegyric modes of early Greek poetry and monuments; as noted, Pindar's odes (contemporary with the earlier horizons of Greek sculpture known to Winckelmann) served Winckelmann as a model of ancient

Nachahmung, and he knew that classicism in Greek sculpture had been preceded by an epoch of crafting figures in "rough stones." Further, we can find a disjunctive or bifurcated classicism in the fifth and fourth centuries BCE; as noted, Winckelmann identified two major styles of Classical Greek art, the "high" and the "beautiful" styles of the Phidian and Praxitelean schools, respectively. Again, we can find an innovative if imitative classicism—both regressive and progressive—in the second century CE: Winckelmann admired certain inventions of Hadrianic or neo-Attic Hellenism despite its association with Roman despotism and imperialism. Finally, we can find a decadent classicism in the fourth and fifth centuries CE. Winckelmann ended his *History* with a striking description of the decline and disappearance of Greek art in the age of Justinian, its supposed disappearance and loss in the art of the Byzantine manuscript painters. But he also admitted the melancholy beauty of the crepuscular images in question.[11]

By the same token, there might be similar oscillatory movements—disjunctions, deflections, declines, returns, and revisions—in all the new classicisms of modernity. Abetted in due course by Kant's choice of ancient examples of the perfected ideal of beauty in fine art, the modern academies of art took Winckelmann to recommend that the modern artist should imitate the grandeur of Classical Greek art in the Phidian age or the "high" style associated with the constitution of supreme ideal beauty. (As I will show below, Kant explicitly correlated the perfected ideal of beauty in ancient fine art with the Polykleitan *Kanon*, a crucial technical buttress of the high style in the late fifth century BCE.) But Winckelmann's complete portrayal of ancient *Nachahmung* in his full narrative of Greco-Roman art history did not entirely encourage this restriction of the Classical prototypes to be admitted for *Nachahmung* in modern times. A Praxitelean or a Hadrianic, even an Alexandrian or a Justinianic, moment might be possible in modern art. Such temporary stabilizations in the movements of formality could relay certain erotic, ethical, and political horizons of the ideal; they might be valid movements of the ideal in the cycle of its ethical realization, in the parabolas of its formal development, and in the routes of its social communication.

Sophisticated antiquarian artists in the modern tradition understood this lesson: modern neoclassicism from the 1770s through the 1930s has never simply been an imitation of the Phidian high style. Anne-Louis Girodet's *Sleep of Endymion*, painted in Rome in 1791 and exhibited in Paris in 1793, might be taken as one influential example. Contesting Jacques-Louis David's preference for Phidian ideality (and the Platonic transcendence associated with Phidian ideality), Girodet's painted figure of Endymion overtly imitated

Praxitelean prototypes that were known by eighteenth-century viewers to be affiliated with the idealized ephebic masculinity—somewhat androgynous, perhaps even feminized—which tended to be bound to pederastic aesthetics in ancient and modern culture. Indeed, Girodet's painting resisted a comprehensive contemporary sublation of the eroticized ideality of such youths: it explicitly recalled paradoxes in the Platonic theory of the reincarnation of the soul (the supreme moment of an absolute transcendence of human life) figured by Socrates in his citation of the myth of sleeping Endymion in the *Phaedo*, which had been David's text for the *mise-en-scène* of his 1787 painting of the death of Socrates. (It is possible that Girodet, one of David's assistants in the mid-1780s, had worked on a preparatory version of this picture; certainly he knew it well.) Even if the body of Socrates as painted by David could not help but figure the erotic as well as the "elenchic" or self-transcending philosophic body of the philosopher, and even if the painting referred unmistakably to the pederastic context of Socrates' dialogues with friends, Girodet's figure of sleeping Endymion was a manifest refutation of David's image: Endymion is not—precisely not—divided between his sensual or erotic and his intellectual or philosophic selves, standing pictorially for the endless if unconscious sensual-sexual responsiveness of the desirable male body.[12]

Most important, and in general, a modern "Greek" should not imitate, or he should not merely imitate, ancient Greek forms of art and culture. He should imitate the ancient Greek mode of cultural becoming, the entire cultural cycle rather than the select formal precipitates of *Nachahmung*. This point was grasped in the most famous contemporary statement of Winckelmann's project by readers in the generation which followed him: according to Goethe, one "learns nothing" from Winckelmann, but nonetheless he "becomes" something.[13] Goethe meant that one becomes someone who comes-to-himself in the same way as the Greeks became themselves in coming-after themselves in the history of their self-culture in art. A similar point was made in elaborate detail in Hegel's *Phenomenology of Spirit*, published in 1805, in a dialectical or "logical" restatement of Winckelmann's history of ancient culture as *Nachahmung*, even if Hegel's push to describe the *Aufhebung* of the self-conscious Greek self (and Greek works of art as an image of that self) reintroduced an essentially Platonic element—a dynamic of sublation or negation-transcendence and supersession-absorption—in Winckelmann's rather more Lucretian or stochastic portrayal of the surprising (the dialectically unpredictable) swerves of Greek art. A dialectical analysis of the history of ideality as *Aufhebungen* in the realization of an immanent Absolute evidently cannot suffice to represent these bifur-cations and recursions; at any rate, Hegel's description of Greek culture (despite its recognition of the "new organ" of historical observation intro-duced by Winckelmann) did not fully recognize and pursue the differentia-tions Winckelmann had identified.

In the never-completed ethical project of the *Nachahmung* of *Nachahmung*, of the coming-to-be of oneself in coming-after another who admires and imitates his image modeled in turn on someone coming-after-his-image . . . surely the ideal will be attenuated and transformed. Probably, in fact, it will mutate beyond what would have been admired by its previ-ous adherents, even if its immediately contemporary exponents—its adher-ents at a particular moment in its inclination—accept it as the most valid manifestation of ideality. The ideal will be continually detached from itself and it will be continually returned to itself. As I will show below, this (re)cycling need not always amount to—it need not always issue in—the decay, decomposition, or destruction of the ideal, though "deconstruction" is continually required as a normal process in idealization, de-idealization, and re-idealization, serving as the anabolic agent in its catabolism. As Kant recognized, the cycles of *Nachahmung* can sometimes advance the univer-salization of the ideal. But these nuances were lost on academic idealists. In relation to Winckelmann's model of the aesthetic swerves of ancient art, cul-ture, and personality, the epigones of Kant and Hegel stressed that the tele-ology of aesthetic judgment in Classical society was progressively idealizing, the invincible rise of a supreme world-historical constant of ideal formality—countered by no inclinations or swerves in any countervailing, idiosyncratic, or unpredictable directions—that should be repeated in all subsequent arts, typically in the form of the "grand style" recommended by such art theorists in the late eighteenth-century academies of art as Sir Joshua Reynolds. It remained for Schopenhauer, as a philosopher, and especially for Friedrich Nietzsche, as a philologist and historian, to emphasize the counterthrust-ing movements of *Trieb* in ancient culture toward ecstatic or unconscious disintegration, decadence, and destruction. Indeed, a "Darwinian" history, the modern representation of a Lucretian natural history, is more suitable to Winckelmann's model than a Hegelian history.

It has often escaped notice that the "perfected ideal of beauty in fine art" described by Kant in section 17 of *The Critique of the Power of Judgment*, pub-lished in 1790, could have been read at the time virtually as a blow-by-blow account of the vicissitudes of the contemporary Winckelmannian taste I have already described. Whether or not Kant had read Winckelmann in close detail, like other educated readers in the 1780s and 1790s, he had grasped Winckelmann's perspective on ideality in art. It was well known to readers, and not only from Winckelmann's scholarly writings on the history of ancient art. In Kant's day, one could also acquire a clear sense of it from Winckelmann's painfully romantic letters to his young friend Friedrich von Berg, published in 1784 and widely read. Winckelmann had addressed an important meditation, "On the Ability to Perceive the Beautiful in Art," to von Berg; it had already been published in 1763 as a complement to his original essay on *Nachahmung* in 1754.[14] (Probably we see an aristocratic gentleman like von Berg in the youthful Grand Tourist in the portrait by Pompeo Batoni mentioned above.) After 1784, most educated readers probably had to agree with Goethe's assessment of Winckelmann's aesthetics: attending to the evidence of Winckelmann's letters as well as his essays and treatises, in *Winckelmann und sein Jahrhundert*, published in 1805, Goethe did not shy away from acknowledging its homoerotic affective and social contexts. As we have seen, however, these contexts were transmuted when Winckelmannian taste became a cultural norm: if Winckelmann allowed himself an eroticized description of the relief of Antinous installed at the Villa Albani, Cardinal Albani (let alone the visitors and tourists who viewed it) simply expressed good taste in admiring it. In Kant's terms, an *interested* judgment of taste had been succeeded by a *canonical* judgment.

According to section 17 of Kant's Third Critique, the judgment of ideal beauty (*le beau idéal*) cleaves individual expressions of interested pleasure, such as a pederastic appreciation of the youthful male body, from the increasingly "disinterested" accumulation of multiple judgments rendered on the same or similar objects by the same person or by other people. These judgments emerge, then, in the community. And they are increasingly unconcerned, Kant supposed, with the empirical existence (including the sexual availability) of the worldly object of judgment for the human subject of judgment, especially for the first subject in the chain or palimpsest of judgments. This process of accumulation and modification in aesthetic judgment, constituted and communicated socially, is neither mysterious nor sinister. It need not have the oppressive character that present-day (and supposedly post-Kantian) accounts of aesthetic transgression and cultural subversion seem to assume in putative opposition to normative (or Kantian) aesthetic judgment in culture. In fact, Kant supposed that the perfected ideal of beauty constitutes a desirable horizon of human freedom: the perfected ideal might unbind us from the empirical conditions of judgment, that is, from both its object and its subjectivity, whether or not this freedom, this liberation from the cares of the self, can be attained in every case by all parties who have been socially involved in constituting the ideal. In turn, Schopenhauer returned Kant's abstract notion to the concrete affective life of the bodily ego, to appropriate a term devised by Richard Wollheim. Like Socrates before him, Schopenhauer understood the value of aesthetic idealization, of ideality in art, to consist in the relief of human suffering. This condition surely included the pangs of unrequited homoerotic love and romantic hypostasis which had plagued Winckelmann and which readers like Goethe had detected in his letters and essays.

In the ordinary course, many interested judgments of taste, maybe even all interested judgments of taste, should turn out to be incompatible with communalized judgment—that is, with so-called subjective universality. On the one hand, the psychic and social history of subjective universality implies that the interested judgments of individual subjects have been "queered" in the direction of supposedly disinterested normative judgments. But on the other hand, it equally implies that disinterested judgments of ideal beauty effect a queering of personal interested judgments of taste. The psychic and social process in question must be a transitive one, whether or not Kant drew attention to the fact. Each order of judgment in the subjective consolidation and social transmission of an ideal, then, harbors possibilities not only of fulfilling but also of transmuting, even transgressing, the other order of judgment. In Winckelmann's dynamic historical terms, each collation of judgment encourages, even demands, the transformation of other judgments. And the continuing cultural cycle of *Nachahmung* sustains the replication of aesthetic judgments of both types (that is, personal and relatively interested on the one hand, and communal and relatively disinterested on the other) as new members of the community, new objects of judgment, and new judgments of taste enter the mix. We make a logical and psychological mistake only when we describe this cycle as a unidirectional, univocal teleology, a one-way development from personal feelings to communal norms—a development that can be described all too easily, of course, as the suppression of personal feelings by communal norms. Winckelmann did not make this mistake, and neither did Kant despite his psychological explication (respecting the ideal of beauty in fine art) of the collation and transformation of aesthetic judgment in communal life. It was a sub-Kantian idealist abstraction. Academic Kantians were so impressed by the cognitive power of subjective universality—the collation, amalgamation, and consolidation of diverse sensations, impressions, and images in the constitution of the perfected ideal of beauty in art—that they forgot about its origins and echoes, its detours and declines, and its reversions and reversals. To be sure, Kant himself did not emphasize these recursions and oscillations; in the model presented in section 17 of the Third Critique, he ordered them in such a way as to issue in the perfected ideal of beauty in art as a symbol of the morally desirable, the worthy or the good. But they had been placed, as I have already argued, at the heart of Winckelmann's history of the vicissitudes, the various formal inclinations and different historical declensions, of ideal beauty in the traditions of Classical art.

In section 17 of the Third Critique, Kant cited the example of the perfected ideal of beauty realized in the *Kanon* of Polykleitos of Argos. Around 440 BCE, this Greek sculptor supposedly wrote a treatise and cast a bronze figure of a spear-bearer, the *Doryphoros*, in order to expound his theories about the correct proportions of the male body when represented in a statue. In explaining how the *Doryphoros* might have been produced, and given the lack of hard evidence for Polykleitos's theoretical propositions, Kant proposed to imagine one's judgments of taste regarding a "thousand full-grown men," that is, men such as the youthful athletes who might have served as the prototypes for Polykleitos's famous sculpture, copies of which were not discovered until several years after the publication of Kant's treatise. As Kant wrote somewhat cryptically, he invoked an "analogy to optical presentation": "in the space where the greatest number of [these judgments] coincide and within the outline of the place that is illuminated by the most concentrated colors, there the average size becomes recognizable, which is in both height and breadth equidistant from the most extreme boundaries of the largest and smallest statures; and this is the stature for a beautiful man."[15] In the *Doryphoros*, Polykleitos supposedly discovered and replicated this configuration as what he called *Kanon*, Rule or Norm.

Kant's quasi-technical description of "canonical" idealization in art as analogous to a concentration of superimposed images (each image relays the aesthetic approbation of an observer regarding the object and the canonical concentration "averages" them) probably responded to Winckelmann's emphasis on the outline-contour of freestanding or fully three-dimensional Classical Greek sculpture. As I have already noted, traditional accounts of the technique of idealization in art repeated the simplistic notion, derived from Greco-Roman legends of artistic practice, that idealizing artists such as the ancient Greek painter Zeuxis must have combined the discrete parts of different bodies that he and his peers had found to be beautiful in those parts (and maybe *only* in those parts). At times Winckelmann invoked this implausible scenario, notably in his presentation of his formal doctrine of supreme beauty. But mere combination of this kind is not the same thing as the "concentration" cited by Kant. The traditional stories referred to a material procedure used to piece together a depiction, perhaps echoing ancient sources that mentioned the piecework production of certain ancient statues. Winckelmann and Kant, however, referred to a psychological process, an operation in consciousness. (As Kant took care to say, the explication in terms of "optical presentation" is simply an analogy.) And whereas the traditional legends of the practice of Zeuxis and similar artists seemed to imply that one artist had collated his impressions of many different bodies and parts of bodies, Kant's model acknowledged that different judgments of the same body—rendered by the same person or by different people and somehow collected, collated, consolidated, and concentrated by the artist—might constitute the relevant images which eventually constitute the ideal. In this respect Kant's account of the technique of Polykleitos was closer to Winckelmann's cyclical (and to an extent stochastic) model of *Nachahmung* than to the simplistic stories of artistic idealization as a piecing together of the discrete beauties to be found in objects and bodies or in their separate parts.

Winckelmann thought that Greek sculptors had imitated the handsome bodies and noble characters of young men regarded in the *polis* as beautiful and honorable. Specifically, as already noted, he imagined that artists such as Polykleitos and Phidias had observed the human prototypes for their sculptures at the gymnasia and *palaestra* where the youngest generation of athletes, candidates for beauty and honor, trained for games and for war. Indeed, according to Winckelmann the ancient sculptors imitated the imprints left by the wrestlers in the sand, images reproduced in the contour of the sculpted figure as it constituted a visual image for observers (including athletes in later generations who would attempt to incorporate the ideal it relayed to them). Needless to say, Greek sculptors could not actually have worked in this way. Winckelmann's highly eroticized scenario found no support in the evidence compiled by his principal scholarly source for the replicatory structure of *Nachahmung*, namely, Gottlob Zeibich's 1748 treatise on Greek athletes and athlete-statues as paradigms, as models or templates for one another.[16] I suspect that Winckelmann intended his readers to recall the only Classical Greek text which refers to judgments of taste specifically rendered by observers on imprints of the bodies of athletes: in *The Clouds*, Aristophanes joked that old men in Athens rushed to examine the impressions of genitals and buttocks left behind by good-looking boys sitting in the sand at the gymnasium.[17] Winckelmann probably meant his readers to get the joke: in his model of *Nachahmung*, Phidias and Polykleitos (and at another level Socrates and Plato) acted like the pederastic lechers, for despite the placid ideality of the sculpted figures they eventually produced the sculptors carried the fascinated enthusiasm of pederastic fetishism into art.

In certain respects, then, it is Kant's model of idealization that helps explain why the lechers must be seen as ridiculous, as Aristophanes made clear, while the sculptors, if Winckelmann is right, must be applauded. Kant's narrative of the crucial outline of the perfected ideal of beauty in section 17 of the Third Critique echoed Winckelmann's allusion. But Kant did not reproduce its comic erotic ground—the original sexual joke—or the historical gloss that Winckelmann had given to it in his portrayals of Socrates and Phidias in his *Reflections on the Imitation of Greek Works in Painting and Sculpture*. In fact, Kant entirely skipped over the logically primitive stage (or stages) of the erotically fascinating images of an ideal, such as those pursued by Aristophanes' lechers or admitted in Winckelmann's letters. In Kant's model of Classical Greek imaging of the ideal, we jump immediately to our "dynamic" imaginative (literally imagistic) experience of a male beautifulness derived from discrete images and energized by them, but not identical with any of our impressions and thus with our real interest in the actual objects in question (namely, this, that, or the other boy who might be judged by us to be beautiful in this, that, or the other respect).[18] In turn or in the next stage of its projection and recursion, Kant's emergent norm (if it is to be the subjective universality of a community such as the African, Chinese, and European groups mentioned in section 17) would have to move from the imaginative palimpsest constituted in a single person's dynamic judgment of a thousand men: it would have to be transported into the more extensive palimpsest constituted dynamically—in a kind of social interaction, conversation, or intercourse—in a thousand different people's dynamic judgments of the beautifulness of a single man, or, indeed, a thousand different people's thousands of dynamic judgments of a thousand different men. As this dynamic image of beauty emerges communally, it must be increasingly less vested in one person's image of one man's beauty. Correlatively, it must be increasingly relayed in a thousand times a thousand, a million, judgments. In the psychological terms of Kant's narrative, this "universalization" can be analyzed as the mnemic millionization of our fleeting single impression of one beautiful man in the immediate activity of our erotically interested personal taste. This millionization, the "normal idea," produces a necessary condition for beauty which Kant called "correct[ness]." According to Kant's model as we might reconstruct it, then, Polykleitos's *Kanon* was not just his collation of his judgments of taste, his judgment about the beauty of boys in the gymnasium. The sculptural image relayed in the *Doryphoros* collated an entire community's history of judgments achieved in the historical cycle of *Nachahmung*.[19]

As Winckelmann had stressed, the judgments of taste collated by the sculptor in his canonical representation of a beautiful man had been incorporated by the sculptor's living models. The young man judged by the sculptor to be more or less beautiful to him had already been motivated by aesthetic considerations. After all, he was an athlete who had attracted attention, whether pederastic or not, in light of model athletes praised by previous generations of lovers, poets, and sculptors. And as an athlete, he labored to present a more or less canonical beauty for a contemporary social admiration not limited to the sculptor's personal judgment of taste: the community of judgment toward which the athlete oriented himself included such personages as the old lechers parodied by Aristophanes and the courtly adult admirers who attended their young friends at the gymnasium. If a contemporary sculptor found this young man to be beautiful, then, he could not help but partly ratify a norm which had already partly emerged long before the artistic encounter itself. According to Kant, this canon achieved its final "perfected idealization" when its corrected beauty, as we might call it, expressed virtues—strength, moderation, courage, modesty, benevolence, and the like—that did not require the "sensuous charm" of the original objects (wherever and whenever we might locate them in the historical cycle of canon-formation) to inflect the delight which we might properly take in such worthiness. In brief, Kant's doctrine of the idealization of beauty requires that the sensuous erotic pleasure we take in certain impressions be converted into a non-sensuous moral admiration of correctly consolidated images of them. As I have urged throughout this essay, this is a rereading—a specifically Kantian reading—of Winckelmann's established understanding of the canons of Greek culture based on the concrete corporeal cycles of *Nachahmung*.

In Greco-Roman and early modern European societies, as Kant's example of the *Kanon* of Polykleitos might suggest, pederastically determined judgments were not always incompatible with an emergent ideal, because sometimes they were already universalized or universalizable. (Of course, certain pederastic tastes or homosexual practices were condemned in ancient sexual aesthetics and ethics, especially those in which an older man occupied a passive sexual role or a younger man submitted to anal penetration—an important feature of the topography of ancient pederasty to which Michel Foucault frequently adverted. But obviously the condemnation required homoerotic ideals against which it could be judged.) The institutions and mores of pederasty relayed an approved notion, although not the only approved notion, of masculine moral identity. For this reason a judgment of pederastic beauty could be made not only in a sensuously invested and sexually interested context, for example, in the infatuations of Socrates' friends and in the loves of Socrates himself, such as the affairs narrated by Xenophon and parodied by Aristophanes. In principle a pederastic judgment could also be made disinterestedly. In a sufficiently concentrated aesthetic of pederasty—a culture, strictly speaking—one could see what another man found to be beautiful in a youth without taking an erotic interest in it himself. In turn, such judgments did not have to be sloughed off as unwanted parochialisms in the palimpsest which constituted the ideal. They could smooth the way for its conversion into a general morality in a norm that remained valid and could be properly applied beyond the specific historical context and the particular social community of male lovers and their male objects of desire. In some cases (such as Lord Gower's representation of Hal's self-transformation) they might figure that conversion, imaging the erotic passage of the ideal (and to that extent preserving the visibility of its sexual basis) as well as its final moral perfection. Whatever Winckelmann's erotic self-interest might have been, he insisted that Classical Greek images of admirable young men served to steer individual interests in sensuous pleasure toward the erotic temperance preached (if not always practiced) by Socrates. Winckelmann's Platonizing tendency, as it has sometimes been called, was not—it was quite specifically not—the suppression of pederastic love. It was the normativization of pederastic love.

In a brilliant essay, "Parergon," Jacques Derrida has offered a deconstruction of Kant's doctrine. Despite idealist abstraction of the canonical form, aesthetic disinterestedness cannot be fully detached from its origins in sensuously appealing images; in life or in art, a "pure cut," as Derrida calls it, cannot be made between erotic charm and ideal beauty.[20] According to Derrida, then, Kant's moral paragon of perfected correct beauty in art cannot be disembedded from the mosaic of sexual identifications within which the ideal supposedly emerged, even though Derrida did not explicitly identify the Winckelmannian context of Kant's remarks in section 17—that is, Winckelmann's identification of the pederastic parergonality of Greek ideality.

Derrida's perspective has been widely adopted in cultural studies; his deconstruction of idealist aesthetics would seem to be logically and

psychologically irrefutable within its purview. Today cultural criticism therefore insists that where Kant saw aesthetic transcendence attained in ideal art,
we must notice the erotic entanglements of art in its social milieu. In turn
this has suggested that aesthetics must retrieve—because it cannot avoid—
its art-historical moment. In historical and social terms, then, queer beauty
can be explicated simply by calling it "Kantian beauty—queered": queer
beauty is reified or perfected canonical beauty relocated in its corporeal and
communal contexts of affective, cognitive, and social significance. These
contexts include the possibility that some proportion of a thousand people's
dynamic judgments on the beauty of a thousand men will be homoerotically
determined, a relation that must inhere in the emergent norm because it was
dynamically integrated in its canonical form all along.

Derrida's counter-Platonizing approach was anticipated to some extent
within a philosophical anthropology that had responded specifically to Kant.
In 1792, shortly after the Third Critique appeared, one of Kant's students,
Friedrich Karl Forberg, published a laudatory exposition of transcendental
aesthetics. In 1798, accused of atheism, Forberg left his teaching post. In
1824, working as an obscure librarian, he surfaced with a remarkable commentary on the notorious *Hermaphroditus* of Antonio Beccadelli, printed in
1460, a Latin compilation of erotic epigrams and quotations from ancient
sources—Martial, Petronius, and other authors—about all kinds of sex acts
not bound to procreative heterosexual relations. (In fact, Forberg's text was
organized in terms of the categories of *fellatio, irrumatio, pedicatio,* and
the like, whether homosexual or heterosexual.) The text of Beccadelli had
been rigidly suppressed in the Renaissance, but Forberg edited a surviving
manuscript printed in Paris in 1791, the year before his Kantian disserta-
tion had been published.[21] Forberg's commentary emphasized the homosexual relations that occurred in Greco-Roman society—relations sometimes
approved and sometimes condemned. His book, like Beccadelli's, was con-
fiscated by many national and municipal police forces, and indeed soon
became one of the rarest books of sexual arcana in clandestine circulation
among collectors of erotica. Nevertheless, for nineteenth-century readers it
served as the single most detailed source for the history and terminology
of unorthodox sexual practices. Between 1824 and the early twentieth century, the results (and sometimes even the literal text) of Forberg's *Manual
of Classical Erotology,* as it was called when translated into English in the
1880s, were much repeated and replicated:[22] first by Julius Rosenbaum in his
1839 treatise on sexually transmitted diseases in antiquity, *Die Lustseuche im
Alterthum;* then by Heinrich Kaan in 1844 in the first *Psychopathia sexualis,*

which rewrote Forberg's *Apophoreta* as a compendium of vice in modern cities, a *Satyricon* for Paris, London, and Berlin; after 1848 by several influential European scholars of sexual hygiene and psychosexual disorder, notably Ambrose Tardieu in France and Johann Ludwig Casper in Germany; by the Viennese psychiatrist Richard von Krafft-Ebing in his version of a *Psychopathia sexualis*, first published in 1886; and finally by Sigmund Freud in his psychoanalytic revision of the nosology of sexual medicine and of Krafft-Ebing's psychopathology. In his book of 1824, Forberg stated that he had taken up the history of sexuality because he had become disillusioned by what he called the "solipsism of modern philosophy," that is, by Kant's system. He meant *inter alia* that the doctrine of the *beau idéal* as a morally elevated norm had wrongly abstracted the cultural form, the work of art, from the real social relations of admiration, love, contest, status, and sexual desire which had organized it in such institutions as pederasty and prostitution in the ancient and modern worlds. To drive home his point, the 1824 edition of his book was illustrated with ancient gemstones and modern replications, rendered in the impeccable Winckelmannian "high style" of Phidian and Polykleitan age, depicting homosexual sexual practices. These images reminded his readers (if they needed it) that the canonical ideals of beauty explicated by Kant inhered in pederastic and homoerotic sociability, just as the Winckelmannian account transmitted to Kant had intimated.

Derrida's critique of Kant's theory of the perfected ideal of beauty makes a powerful general case. But it has a defect in the special case of the homoerotic contexts of queer beauty in the sense explored in this essay. If the concentration of judgments of taste produces a norm in the mental region in which "the greatest number of them coincide," then some judgments—namely, those that are not replicated by other judgments in any respect—cannot be registered in the ideal, the admirable canonical configuration, even though they belong to its dynamic conditions of possibility. Indeed, certain judgments can be kept out of the overlay, perhaps even forced out of it. In other words, many normative aesthetic teleologies work by excluding homoerotic and other unorthodox affections. In turn, these norms can only be queered by forcibly (re)introducing into the overlay what has been eliminated or excluded—beauty queered. This is not what we find, however, in the peculiar but prevalent case of queer beauty in my sense. In queer beauty, specifically as opposed to beauty queered, homoerotic significance has not been excluded. It has not even been substantially occluded. In queer beauty, homoerotic significance flows smoothly into and provides a manifest dynamization of the norm (as Kant's model presumed) even if it no longer constitutes its sole imagistic content, insofar as many other layers of significance have also been integrated into the perfected ideal. This is not quite the possibility that Derrida tells us Kant had overlooked. It was a seeming *impossibility* that Kant had accepted. He accepted it, as we have seen, because it was manifest in public culture.

Derrida did not notice that in its own terms Kant's account can explain why Frederick's *Adorante*, Albani's Antinous, or Gower's Prince Hal became ideals of beauty in the fine arts. Indeed, in view of the Winckelmannian background of Kant's remarks in section 17 it would appear that his "psychological" model of aesthetic idealization (based on the "analogy of optical presentation") was included in the overall system of the Third Critique partly in order to handle Winckelmannian cultural materials even if, perhaps especially when, they constituted possible counterexamples to the general architecture of Kant's argument.[23] To be sure, Derrida's strictures on Kant's exclusions do not apply only to the artifacts adumbrated by Kant in section 17. To that extent Derrida's most general claim (namely, that Kant overlooked the *parerga* of pure aesthetic judgment) escapes the consideration raised here. In section 17, the "pure cut" to which Derrida objected does not occur between sensuous charm on the one hand and ideal beauty on the other hand. It occurs within the construction of ideal beauty between a correct or canonical image on the one hand and its significance as a moral symbol in a perfected work of fine art on the other hand. For this reason, it is entirely possible to imagine an immoral but correct, canonical image as a deconstructive counterexample to the artifacts cited in section 17. These would not be the kinds of images, of course, displayed in public by Frederick of Prussia, Cardinal Albani, and Lord Gower and accepted within their communities; strictly speaking, formally correct or canonical but immoral artworks cannot be included in the purview of Kantian subjective universality in fine art. But the pornographic illustrators of Forberg's *Manual of Classical Erotology* produced striking visualizations in which canonical formal devices were used to depict immoral acts.[24] Their intent was to transgress public culture and to subvert its ideals—beauty queered rather than queer beauty— and perhaps to begin to constitute the possibility of an alternate culture. These ambitions had artistic and political value. But they did not create queer beauty, which proffers a repetition of an ideal of beauty rather than its deconstruction. (Needless to say, in repetition there may be deconstruction in the end.) If queer beauty is an ideal of beauty in the full Kantian sense, by definition it cannot subsist as a clandestine art.

In the Castro in San Francisco, in Chelsea in New York, or in Soho in London, to dress queer today is not to dress queerly. It is to subscribe to correct canons of aesthetic presentation and implied sociability. Of course, queer beauty in the Castro in San Francisco, Chelsea in New York, or Soho in London cannot be exactly the same as the beauty approved and appreciated by the men, youths, and *hetairai* (female prostitutes) who primped for a pederastic symposium in fifth-century Athens. These beautiful people, as they called themselves, did not really have queer beauty, despite occasional citation of their art by makers of queer beauty in modern times. There is an obvious catch—a deconstructive and perhaps disabling twist—in the constitution of queer beauty in modern art and culture. Classically ideal beauty can be replicated in modern society. But pederastically disinterested judgments in the sense required by Kant's model could be made only in the ancient Greco-Roman world and possibly in certain milieux in late medieval and early modern Europe. In the modern world, a manifestly homosexual judgment can only be idiosyncratic. Because it is socially proscribed, it must be defined as asocial, possibly even sociopathic. Because it has no conceivable warrant or fulfillment in modern morality, it can only subsist as a sensuous fixation and erotic enthusiasm emanating from a sodomite, a libertine, a criminal, or a madman. It issues from him, but it achieves no social agreement and no communal generalization. In the end, then, it can only be seen as utterly self-interested: it manifests the "narcissistic" character that Freud thought he could identify in an anonymous Classical archaeologist who conjoined his homosexual pursuit of young actors and waiters with a supposed Winckelmannian "infatuation with statues."[25]

In modern queer beauty, a diffused acceptance of homoerotically determined judgments of taste despite moral proscription of their sexual imagism, we can find a moment of what might be called self-sanctioning. I intend the double meaning of this term: self-sanctioning is both the restriction and the release of erotic interest. Kant's theory of judgments of taste made as others would make them implies that modern queer beauty typically presents homoerotic love and beauty inflected by the kinds of love and beauty preached by church and state. As Winckelmann and Levezow recognized, Antinous with his crown of lotuses from the Nile and his reins of apotheosis (both motifs indicated that he drowned himself to save his emperor) was the deified Antinous of Hadrian's cult, not the Bithynian slave of his bedroom. Antinous stood for ultimate sacrifice and self-denial—a pagan Jesus. (It was partly for this reason that Antinous and similar figures became beloved avatars of later nineteenth-century Decadence.) By the same token,

Gower's Prince Hal was not merely the wild prince of Falstaffian revelry. As
Gower took care to say when he provided an inscription for the statue, quoting the Archbishop of Canterbury in *Henry the Fifth*, "consideration like an
angel came, and whipp'd th'offending Adam out of him." The "offending
Adam," the "old Adam," is human wickedness in sexual temptation. And as
we are meant to recall from Shakespeare's Henriad, in the end Hal denied
Falstaff ("I know thee not, old man") to assert himself as rightful holder of
the crown, beloved by all the people of his island: "we few, we happy few,
we band of brothers." Observers can see these self-sanctioning features of
the images quite as well as, though not at the expense of, the pouty lips of
Antinous, Hadrian's sexual favorite, or the bulging crotch of Hal, Falstaff's
"sweet wag." Hal's tumescent phallus does not compromise his accession to
kingship. Indeed, in reaching for the crown of his father he displays a phallic power in which all his people (so Shakespeare and Gower imagined)
can properly take interest and delight. But nor does Hal's worthy destiny
occlude his special friendship with Falstaff. His homoerotic initiation provides the very source and dynamic of his masculine and English and royal
self-becoming. Needless to say, however, if queer beauty normativizes judgments of taste, it leaves itself open to queering in its own turn. Just as Gower
condemned the cold, correct beauty of the neoclassical sculpture praised in
his day, heating it up notably in his statue of Prince Hal, Oscar Wilde radicalized Gower's aesthetic point of view in the amoral homosexual character
of Lord Henry Wotton, the aristocrat (modeled in part on Gower) responsible for the corruption of young Dorian's taste and morals in *The Picture of
Dorian Gray*.

Whether Gower queered neoclassical conventions or Wilde queered
Gower, queering a norm cannot bring a culture back to non-normativ-
ized or prenormativized conditions. It can only recalibrate it in queering it
toward a newly emergent norm. In this regard the makers of queer beauty
in my sense hoped their art could survive the Kantian teleology of aesthetic
judgment, rather than subvert it. Whether queer beauty has done valuable
cultural and political work, or conversely whether it has inhibited a more
radical modern queer ethics and aesthetics, is an open question. The question remained fully open for Foucault, the most radical queer ethicist of the
twentieth century; Foucault conceived a post-gay homoerotic friendship as
a complex declension of Greek pederastic homoeroticism. Many testimonies suggest that queer beauty enabled homoerotically inclined viewers in
the past two hundred or more years to reconstruct themselves: in engaging
the images projected in certain works of art, they could retrace the teleology

of queer beauty, presented as an aesthetic and social norm, back to its echo and origins or its content and conditions in homosexual judgments of taste. In it they could find interests as yet unknown to them — as yet inaccessible to them *as* their deepest interests, as what Richard Wollheim has called the "depths" of their minds — until queer beauty had collated it in culture. Modern homosexual cultures probably could not have come into being without this Kantian bridge, whatever their subversive, transgressive, or outlaw claims today.

NOTES

The epigraph is from Albert Moll, *Perversions of the Sex Instinct: A Study of Sexual Inversion*, trans. Maurice Popkin (1891; Newark, N.J.: Julian, 1931), 71.

1. For representative applications of the terminology in art history and cognate fields of visual and cultural studies, see Richard Meyer, *Outlaw Representation: Censorship and Homosexuality in Twentieth-Century American Art* (New York: Oxford University Press, 2002); Jonathan Goldberg, ed., *Queering the Renaissance* (Durham, N.C.: Duke University Press, 1994); Moe Meyer, ed., *The Politics and Poetics of Camp* (London: Routledge, 1994); Gordon Brent Ingram, Anne-Marie Bouthillette, and Yoland Retter, eds., *Queers in Space: Communities, Public Places, Sites of Resistance* (Seattle: Bay Press, 1997); and Sophie Fuller and Lloyd Whitesell, eds., *Queer Episodes in Music and Modern Identity* (Urbana: University of Illinois Press, 2002). This essay is a version of chapter 1 in my *Queer Beauty: Sexuality and Aesthetics from Winckelmann to Freud and Beyond* (New York: Columbia University Press, 2010).

2. Christoph Vogtherr, "Absent Love in Pleasure Houses: Frederick II of Prussia as Art Collector and Patron," *Art History* 24, no. 2 (2001): 239. The situation of the statue was described for contemporary readers in M. Oesterreich, *Description et explication des groupes, statues, . . . formant la collection de S. M. le Roi de Prusse* (Berlin: Decker, 1774), 110, no. 113. For the sculpture itself, see Gerhard Zimmer and Nele Hackländer, eds., *Der Betende Knabe: Original und Experiment* (Frankfurt am Main: Peter Lang, 1997); and Stephanie Gerlach, *Der Betende Knabe* (Berlin: Gebr. Mann, 2002).

3. For a full examination of the figure of Prince Hal in the context of Gower's career (it was marked by homosexual scandals that eventually ruined him), see Whitney Davis, "Lord Ronald Gower and 'The Offending Adam,'" in *Sculpture and the Pursuit of a Modern Ideal in Britain, c. 1880–1930*, ed. David John Getsy (Aldershot: Ashgate, 2004), 63–104. Sculptural prototypes for *Prince Hal* included Benvenuto Cellini's *Perseus*, but it clearly replicates the distinctive pose of the *Adorante*.

4. For the *Adorante*, see Conrad von Levezow, *De iuvenis adorantis signo ex aera antiquo* (Berolino: Kuhn, 1808). For Frederick's Antinous-Genius, restored by the sculptor Bartolomeo Cavaceppi, see Conrad von Levezow, *Ueber den Antinous dargestellt in der Kunstdenkmaelern des Alterthums* (Berlin: J. F. Weiss, 1808), pl. 6.

5. For these replications, see Jörg Kuhn, "Der 'Betende Knabe' von Sanssouci: Die Rezeptionsgeschichte des Knaben vom 18. Jahrhundert bis heute," in Zimmer and Hackländer, *Der Betende Knabe*, 35–50. Oddly, however, Kuhn does not discuss Levezow.

6. For the faun, see J. J. Winckelmann, *Monumenti antichi inediti* (Rome: A spese dell'autore, 1767), vol. 1, 73, and vol. 2, plate 59; and Hans Diepolder and Walther Rehm, eds., *Briefe* (Berlin: Walter de Gruyter, 1952–55), 2:309, 2:316. The sculpture was probably a Roman copy of a Hellenistic original. And it was not wholly Phidian or Polykleitan ("high style") in stylistic vintage. A hint of voluptuousness in the faun's smile, although not as lascivious as one can find in Hellenistic satyrs and similar sculptures known to Winckelmann, inflects its bland high-classicistic beauty. Moreover, the youth's head (probably intended to represent an ephebic athlete) bore faun's horns. Apparently it had been reworked to add these details, although I have not been able to ascertain whether the reworking dates to the eighteenth century. Possibly it should be attributed to the circle of Winckelmann's colleagues and friends, which included sculptors and sculpture-restorers such as Cavaceppi. One might even imagine (though there is no forensic evidence for this speculation) that Winckelmann himself had commissioned the elaboration.

7. For the relief of Antinous from Tivoli and its reception in the eighteenth century, see Francis Haskell and Nicholas Penny, *Taste and the Antique: The Lure of Classical Sculpture, 1500–1900* (New Haven: Yale University Press, 1981), 144–46, from which I draw my quotations. For the display of the collections at the Villa Albani, see Herbert Beck and Peter C. Bol, eds., *Forschungen zur Villa Albani: Antike Kunst und die Epoche der Aufklärung* (Berlin: Mann, 1982).

8. For the painting, see Anthony M. Clark, *Pompeo Batoni: A Complete Catalogue of His Works with an Introductory Text*, ed. Edgar Peters Bowron (Oxford: Phaidon, 1985), no. 230; a life study also survives (ibid., no. 229). Batoni's sitter was incorrectly said at one time to be Emperor Joseph II of Austria (painted by F. H. Drouais); he is not definitively identified. It is reasonable to speculate, however, that he was someone known to Winckelmann.

9. Winckelmann admired Xenophon's portrayal of Socrates; his studies of Xenophon's *Memorabilia* and *Symposium* began when he was a schoolteacher in the mid-1740s (Winckelmann MSS., Bibliothèque Nationale, Paris, vol. 63, fols. 27, 66–115; cf. vol. 71, fols. 75–78, which might be a later text).

10. I have explored these relations in more detail in Whitney Davis, "Winckelmann's 'Homosexual' Teleologies," in *Sexuality in Ancient Art*, ed. Natalie Boymel Kampen (New York: Cambridge University Press, 1996), 262–76; in the interest of economy I will not repeat the account here. As it is crucial to the perspective pursued in this essay, however, the reader might wish to consult it.

11. For the Justiniac decline of Greek art (the moment of its final morbid efflorescence was the very affirmation of the value and beauty of the entire Classical tradition in ancient art), see Whitney Davis, "Winckelmann Divided," in *Replications: Archaeology, Art History, Psychoanalysis* (University Park: Pennsylvania State University Press, 1996), 232–43. I consider natural and cultural decadence in relation to the possibility of historical continuity and artistic development in more detail in chapter 4 of my *Queer Beauty*.

12. For this argument, see Whitney Davis, "The Renunciation of Reaction in Girodet's *Sleep of Endymion*," in *Visual Culture: Images and Interpretations*, ed. Norman Bryson, Michael Ann Holly, and Keith Moxey (Hanover, N.H.: University Press of New England, 1994), 168–201; Abigail Solomon-Godeau, "Ist Endymion schwul?" in *Männlichkeit im Blick: Visuelle Inszenierungen in der Kunst seit der Frühen Neuzeit*, ed. Mechthild Fend and Marianne Koos (Cologne: Böhlau, 2004), 15–34; and Satish Padiyar, "Who is Socrates? Desire and Subversion in David's 'Death of Socrates' (1787)," *Representations* 108, no. 1 (2008): 27–52.

13. J. W. von Goethe, *Conversations with Eckermann*, introd. Wallace Wood (New York: M. W. Dunne, 1901), 188.

14. J. J. Winckelmann, *Abhandlung von der Fähigkeit der Empfindung des Schönen in der Kunst, und dem Unterrichte in Derselben* (Dresden: Walther, 1763). For von Berg, see Carl Justi, *Winckelmann und seine Zeitgenossen*, 5th ed., ed. Walter Rehm (Cologne: Phaidon, 1956), 3:74–78; for the letters to von Berg that could have been read by Kant, Goethe, and others, see J. J. Winckelmann, *Lettres familières de M. Winckelmann*, 3 vols. (Yverdon: n.p., 1784). Surveys of Winckelmann's reception in the two generations after his death can be found in Henry C. Hatfield, *Winckelmann and His German Critics, 1755–1781: A Prelude to the Classical Age* (New York: King's Crown Press, 1943); and Henry C. Hatfield, *Aesthetic Paganism in German Literature from Winckelmann to the Death of Goethe* (Cambridge, Mass.: Harvard University Press, 1964).

15. Immanuel Kant, *Critique of the Power of Judgment*, trans. Paul Guyer and Eric Matthews, ed. Paul Guyer (Cambridge: Cambridge University Press, 2000), 118.

16. Gottlob Erdmann Zeibich, *Athleta paradoxos e monimentis Graeciae veteris conspectui expositus* (Vitemberg: Ahlfeld, 1748).

17. Aristophanes, *The Clouds*, ll. 973–76.

18. As Kant noted in pursuing the "analogy of optical presentation," these images could be compiled and averaged in a mechanical fashion, perhaps in a literal overlay. But our imagination collates the ideal "in the repeated apprehension of such figures on the organ of inner sense," building it up over time and adjusting it, or averaging it, as we go along (Kant, *Critique of the Power of Judgment*, 119). This process of assimilation can properly be characterized as dynamic in contrast to the mechanical procedure of overlaying an array of images in a discrete, final operation of superimposition.

19. In this regard neither Winckelmann nor Kant proposed that the perfected ideal of beauty in fine art constitutes a pan-human universal, as some critics of the idealist tradition have claimed. (For a culturalist and historicist critique of Kant's art theory as supposedly "essentialist" or "universalist," see Keith Moxey, "Politicizing the Canon in Art History," *The Encyclopedia of Aesthetics*, ed. Michael Kelly [Oxford: Oxford University Press, 1999], 1:338–41.) Kant's theory implied only that the norm must be relative to the history of a particular community; likely enough, as Kant specified, it will vary between historically disjunct societies. (In the psychological terms adumbrated in section 17, it will be exceedingly difficult to extract a single canonical image from the process of "concentration" if the starting points of individual judgments to be registered in the matrix are extremely diverse; the cultural diversity of ideals follows from the fact that the ideal must be based on the empirical comparisons

and amalgamations making up the *Normalidee,* the "normal idea" or correctness.) In fact, if Winckelmann or Kant must be charged with an error, it must be the error not of universalism but of culturalism, with its tendency to reify racial or ethnic characters: subjective universality might be taken to denote a shared habit of mind, literally a sharing of mind, that is characteristic of particular social groups defined in terms of their racial, ethnic, religious, or national identity. In Hegel's aesthetics, this essentialist culturology tended to take over the dialectical history: according to the *Phenomenology of Spirit* and the *Lectures on Aesthetics,* the imagistic consciousness of the ancient Egyptians was disjunct from the consciousness of the Classical Greeks. In turn, sub-Hegelian historians correlated these dialectical phases of human consciousness with the essential cognitive characters of well-defined ethnic and racial groups or *Volken.* But Winckelmann and Kant had only gone so far as to remark the plain empirical fact of cultural variation in the historical constitution of perfected ideals. Their approach might be taken to have laid some of the groundwork for the very emergence of the anthropological concept of culture later in the nineteenth century.

20. Jacques Derrida, "Parergon," esp. pt. 3, "The *Sans* of the Pure Cut," in *The Truth in Painting,* trans. Geoff Bennington and Ian McLeod (1978; Chicago: University of Chicago Press, 1987), 15–148. In French, Derrida wrote *sans pur*—the "without of the pure cut"—to describe Kant's "framing" of the ideal artwork. As the translators note (ibid., 83), the term is homophonic with *sens pur* (pure sense) and *sang pur* (pure blood).

21. Friedrich Karl Forberg, "Dissertatio philosophica de aesthetica transcendentali" (diss., University of Jena, 1792); Friedrich Karl Forberg, *Apologie seines angeblichen Atheismus* (Gotha: J. Perthes, 1799); and Friedrich Karl Forberg, *Antonii Panormitae Hermaphroditus: Apophoreta* (Coburg: Meusel, 1824). For the Latin text of Beccadelli corrected by Forberg, see Barthélemy Mercier de Saint-Léger, *Quinque illustrium poetarum: Ant. Panormitae . . . lusus in Venerem* (Paris: prostat ad pistrinum in vico suavi ["Chez Molini, rue Mignon"], 1791).

22. [Friedrich Karl Forberg,] *The Manual of Classical Erotology (De figuris Veneris)* ("Manchester" [i.e., Brussels]: "privately printed for Viscount Julian Smithson and friends," "1884" [prob. circa 1895–1900]). Forberg's *Manual* (i.e., the text of Beccadelli and Forberg's commentary or *Apophoreta*) was later edited by Friedrich Wolff-Untereichen and Alfred Kind and published as *Antonii Panormitae Hermaphroditus . . . mit einem sexualwissenschaftliche Kommentar* (Leipzig: Adolf Weigel, 1908). This edition reflected the researches conducted by sexologists following in Forberg's footsteps (and often simply repeating his philological and archaeological labors).

23. As Paul Crowther pointed out to me in a discussion of an earlier version of this essay, section 17 of the Third Critique has often been seen as the "ugly duckling" of the text, difficult to integrate analytically with the conceptual architecture of the whole treatise and often ignored by commentators despite its immense influence in providing a theoretical rationale for—in modernizing the conventional idealisms of—the practices and prescriptions of the European academies of art. (This might be contrasted with the sensitive commentary that has been devoted to section 16 and its exposition of Kant's doctrine of "adherent beauty.") In Paul Guyer's brief remarks on

section 17 in his introduction to the new translation of the Third Critique, it is not fully clear that in section 17 Kant referred not simply to an "object" of beauty—a natural object or a human being—but specifically to the represented human figure in fine art (*Critique of the Power of Judgment*, 273). (Admittedly Kant made the odd but prescient suggestion that Nature herself uses the normal or correct ideas of objects, the *Normalideen*, as "the archetype[s] underlying her productions in the same species [of animal]," and it is no surprise that in addition to Polykleitos's *Doryphoros* Kant cites Myron's *Cow*.) From the point of view of the present essay, a brief observation by Christian Helmut Wenzel is the most germane: "Winckelmann wrote about Greek Art and singled out the human body as an object of ideal beauty, [and] so did Kant; but Kant was less interested in the human body and the Greek spirit of physical education in the *gymnasium* than he was in morality, and so he took over Winckelmann's praise for the human body by modifying it, establishing its ground not in beauty as such but in morality instead" (Christian Helmut Wenzel, *An Introduction to Kant's Aesthetics: Core Concepts and Problems* [Oxford: Oxford University Press, 2005], 75). Most commentaries on section 17 of the Third Critique, or on the Third Critique as a whole, do not mention Winckelmann at all.

24. The illustrations to Forberg's publication in 1824 were reproduced wholesale from a pornographic publication by P. F. Hugues d'Hancarville, a colleague and collaborator of Winckelmann (*Monumens de la vie privée des douze Césars* ["Capri," i.e., Nancy: "Chez Sabullus," 1780]). Hancarville's pornography, like Forberg's *Apophoreta*, partly functioned as a pungent satire of earnest antiquarian Winckelmannianism. (For the complex bibliography and reception of these works, see Whitney Davis, "Homoerotic Art Collection from 1750 to 1920," *Art History* 24, no. 1 [2001]: 247–77.) Similar points could be made about the pornographic illustrations produced for various editions of various works of the Marquis de Sade.

25. See Whitney Davis, "Narzissmus in der homoeroticischen Kultur und in der Theorie Freuds," in Fend and Koos, *Männlichkeit im Blick*, 213–32, and Whitney Davis, "Love All The Same," in *Queer Beauty*, 233–48.

5. Worldwide Women

ELEANOR HEARTNEY

In a season rife with related events [i.e., 2007], the Brooklyn Museum's "Global Feminisms: New Directions in Contemporary Art" is an eagerly anticipated component of a nationwide reevaluation of feminist art. It takes its place alongside the presentation of "WACK! Art and the Feminist Revolution" at the Museum of Contemporary Art in Los Angeles, and the installation of Judy Chicago's *The Dinner Party* (1974–79) and opening of the Elizabeth A. Sackler Center for Feminist Art at the Brooklyn Museum, for which "Global Feminisms" acted as the opening salvo; there are also numerous panels, lectures, and other activities around the country. While "WACK!" reviews the contributions of feminist artists in the late 1960s and '70s, "Global Feminisms" is meant to bring the story up to date with work by a generation of women artists born after 1960, and to represent the global sweep and diversification of the feminist art movement. As such, it was designed to appeal to a younger generation that has been resistant to the feminist label.

In the process, it promised a timely assessment of advances made and obstacles remaining, reflecting a climate in which it is no longer startling for a woman to curate a major international exhibition or appear as the subject of a solo show at a major museum. On the other hand, as the curators note in the hefty catalogue, women still lag far behind men in terms of representation in galleries, museums, and international exhibitions, as well as price tags and sales at auctions.

The curatorial team for this project was intriguing—its senior member was Linda Nochlin, whose 1971 essay "Why Have There Been No Great

Women Artists?" sounded a clarion call for a reconsideration of the institutional obstacles historically placed before women artists. Her landmark exhibition "Women Artists, 1550–1950," co-curated with Ann Sutherland Harris, was the first comprehensive survey of the work of women artists from the Renaissance to the modern era; it opened at the Los Angeles County Museum of Art in 1976 and had its final stop at the Brooklyn Museum the following year. For the current Brooklyn show, which marks the earlier exhibition's thirtieth anniversary, Nochlin was paired with the younger scholar Maura Reilly, who taught art history and women's studies at Tufts University before becoming the Sackler Center's first curator. Together they promised to combine historical perspective and contemporary observation, connecting the work on view with earlier currents in feminism while suggesting how feminist art had evolved to address present situations.

However, "Global Feminisms" is not likely to be the watershed event its organizers and supporters had envisioned, for a variety of reasons. First, of course, is the fact that no exhibition could fulfill all the varied expectations this show generated. But beyond that there were problems with the organization of the material on view and with the strangely shaped and rather cramped space in which it was placed, and unresolved contradictions in the underlying concept. The plus side includes the introduction of a number of noteworthy artists from diverse locales who are little known to American audiences. These are intermingled with better-known artists, though to the organizers' credit this is by and large not a parade of already sanctioned art stars. Altogether there are almost ninety artists in the show, hailing from fifty countries and working in mediums that range from painting, sculpture, and installation to photography, video, and performance.

Problems begin with the title and with the way its promise is realized. "Global Feminisms," as Reilly notes in her extensive catalogue essay, points to two important aspects of the show. One is that it represents the first effort to examine feminist art's global impact, in full recognition of the very different obstacles and circumstances women face in different cultures. Second, it was designed to refute the notion of feminism as a monolithic entity, with the use of the plural *feminisms* suggesting the possibility of myriad definitions of the term. The catalogue is organized in a manner that admirably furthers these ideas, with a pair of introductory essays by the curators followed by seven essays by non-American critics dealing with the situation of feminism and women's art in Africa, India, Japan, Asia, Central America, Western Europe, and Central and Eastern Europe. These essays indicate the different ways that feminism has evolved across the globe, ranging from

Africa and Central America—where political struggle and even survival frequently trump feminism, which tends to be viewed as a foreign imposition—to Japan, where feminism is a homegrown phenomenon developing out of women's discontent with rigid and restrictive roles at a time of rapid modernization and economic expansion. In Eastern and Central Europe, feminism still carries a taint from Soviet days, when nominal equality forced women into the workplace while failing to relieve them of their domestic responsibilities.

These accounts offer a fascinating glimpse of the unequal march of feminism internationally. However, the exhibition itself places contributors within four categories that have nothing to do with distinct global conditions. Artists from different countries were scattered throughout each section, making it difficult to discern some of the rather interesting observations made by the essay writers on specific geographical manifestations of feminism. This arrangement reflects the curators' reluctance to use globalism as an organizing principle for fear of simplifying nationality and reinforcing the binaries of mainstream and periphery. But by abandoning a geographical organization, they were left with an arbitrary set of categories that lacked conceptual clarity.

The show is introduced by "Life Cycles," which is shoehorned into an awkward space on the edges of the shrinelike environment devoted to the permanent display of Judy Chicago's epic *The Dinner Party.* "Life Cycles" includes works that deal with the stages of life from birth to death. Despite Reilly's catalogue demurrals, recurring images of motherhood and the victimization of women hark back to discredited essentialist notions of the commonality of female experience. Meditations on birth and maternity include various riffs on the traditional Madonna and Child, ranging from Catherine Opie's photograph of herself—heavy-set, naked, scarred, and heavily tattooed, tenderly nursing her child—to Australian artist Patricia Piccinini's startling, realistic fiberglass sculpture of a mutant orangutan/human hybrid similarly engaged, to Dutch artist Margi Geerlinks's photographs of nursing women of a grandmotherly age. In a more humorous mode, Japanese artist Hiroko Okada contributed a video of a purported "Delivery by Male Project" and a doctored photo of a couple of hugely pregnant Japanese men smiling broadly in a hospital setting. At the other end of the spectrum are a variety of images of death. Several are horrific and graphic, notably German artist Claudia Reinhardt's photographic re-creation of the death of Sylvia Plath, depicting the poet sprawled on her kitchen floor with her head in the oven, and Swedish artist Annika von Hausswolff's similarly staged images of apparent rape/murder victims lying half hidden on country roads or fields. More subtle is Mexican artist Teresa Margolles's hollow plaster impression of the head and torso of a corpse whose chest is marked with a stitched-up autopsy scar.

In between are other stages of life. The confusions of childhood are acknowledged in Anna Gaskell's *Untitled #35 (hide)*, 1998, in which an adolescent girl in a loose nightie stares down at her legs, covered in white pantyhose that extend beyond her toes, the ends tied together to create a kind of prison. The sacredness of marriage comes in for a cynical drubbing in Serbian artist Tanja Ostojic's *Looking for a Husband with an E.U. Passport* (2000–2005), which documents the artist's ultimately successful search for the desired object. Along with her initial advertisement and various responses, Ostojic includes the nude photograph of herself that served as a come-on and her wedding portrait with the successful suitor (whom she divorced once she obtained her passport). Old age was given a positive spin by Japanese artist Miwa Yanagi, who contributed a photo from a series titled "My Grandmothers," in which young women were asked to imagine their old age. In the image on view, the participant, made up to look like a hot granny with a lined face and bright red hair, screams exultantly from the sidecar of a motorcycle driven by her young lover.

The other sections of the show appear in a string of galleries leading off those containing *The Dinner Party* and "Life Cycles." The next, "Identity," is the most coherent segment and seems most in keeping with the emphasis in Reilly's essay on the contemporary bid for a more fluid and hybridizing definition of female (and male) identity. This section is full of works that blur distinctions between races, genders, and ethnicities. Cross-dressing is a common theme. Israeli artist Oreet Ashery offers *Self-Portrait as Marcus Fisher I* (2000), a photograph of herself decked out in the black hat, beard, and payos of an Orthodox Jewish man as she pops a swollen breast out of her shirt and examines it with bemusement. Moroccan artist Latifa Echakhch morphs into a young Muslim boy in a skullcap sitting on a prayer rug with a slightly come-hither look in *Pin-Up (Self Portrait)*, 1999–2002. Trolling similar territory, Cass Bird offers *I Look Just Like My Daddy* (2004), in which an androgynous young girl wears a baseball cap emblazoned with the titular text. Indian artist Tejal Shah presents a two-channel video in which a young Indian man and woman transform themselves into fairly credible replicas of each other.

What seem to be more painful gender transformations appear in *Binding Ritual, Daily Routine* (2004), the video contribution of Mary

Coble, a butch-looking woman who tightly binds and unbinds her breasts with silver duct tape, which leaves an angry red mark. A more entertaining take on cross-dressing appears in Polish artist Katarzyna Kozyra's *Il castrato* (2007). This is a video of a performance at an annual Gender Bender festival in which a group of men in eighteenth-century female drag coalesce around a woman (the artist herself) in similar garb. She is undressed to reveal a fake male chest and genitals, which are cut off to turn her into a castrato. The performance ends with a stirring rendition of "Ave Maria." This becomes a video within a video, watched from a bathhouse by the same group of men who acted in it, now swathed in towels and sans drag costumes. Related to if not exactly about cross-dressing, German artist Julika Rudelius's *Tagged* (2003) is a three-channel video installation in which young Muslim men in Germany display a surprising obsession with designer fashion.

Other works move into the more startling territory of transgender. Jenny Saville contributes a big gestural painting of a nude figure with female breasts and face and male genitals. More intriguing is Indian artist Dayanita Singh's photo essay on the life of a self-castrated eunuch. In a series of candid and often painfully revealing black-and-white photographs, Singh captures stages in this figure's life, from early residence in a community with other eunuchs and the adoption of a young girl to isolation and despair after the child is taken from him.

The racial construction of identity serves as subtext for South African artist Tracey Rose's *Venus Baartman* (2001), a photograph that pays homage to the so-called Hottentot Venus, a native Khoisan who captivated British audiences in the nineteenth century with her exaggerated sexual and racial characteristics. Here the artist crouches naked in the African bush in a pose that draws attention to her presumably digitally enhanced buttocks and breasts. In a similar allusion to the mythical power and seductiveness of African women, Kenyan-born, New York-based artist Wangechi Mutu assembles a collage of a primitive goddess figure from fragmentary print-media images of body parts.

Finally, a number of works in this section deal in a humorous way with the multiplication of identity, which might be read as a commentary on the kind of narcissism that makes all other humans an extension of oneself. This monstrous sense of self appears in a photo from Japanese artist Tomoko Sawada's "School Days" series (2004), in which the artist has imposed her own youthful face on those of all the identically dressed Japanese schoolgirls posing for a class picture. Amy Cutler similarly riffs on uniformity and narcissism in *Army of Me* (2003), a precisely drawn gouache in which a large representation of the artist faces down a crowd of miniaturized versions of herself. British artist Tracey Emin clones herself for a different purpose in *The Interview* (1999). For this video, Emin assumes the roles of both a slightly haggard, aging party girl (a character close to her own public persona in Britain) and a hectoring, straitlaced interviewer who takes her alter ego to task for her hedonistic lifestyle. The interview ends in a stalemate, with the interviewer stalking off and the interviewee giving a nonchalant shrug as she puffs on a cigarette.

The "Identity" section also contains one of the most disturbing works in the show, a 1998–99 video by Serbian artist Milica Tomic, who stands calmly in front of us in a white shift, introducing herself by name in various languages and then claiming the appropriate nationality ("I am English," "I am German," etc.). With each statement, a new wound or bloody welt appears on her exposed flesh, until she stands placidly before us, lacerated and bleeding. Tomic makes a connection between nationalism and political violence, and it is not clear why her work appears in "Identity" and not in the next section, "Politics."

The selection of works in "Politics" begs the question of how the show defines feminism, as it contains a number of pieces that, though created by women, have no discernible connection to feminist theory, gender issues, or female identity. For instance, Australian artist Fiona Foley's *HHH #4* (2004) is a photographic portrait of a member of an obscure political group the artist claims was founded in 1965 to counter the Ku Klux Klan. The Hedonistic Honky Haters (HHH) wear subverted Klan outfits, including a black pointed hood emblazoned with their acronym and colorful flowing gowns printed with patterns of stylized African masks. Since we can't tell if the eyes behind the hoods are male or female, it's hard to see how this admittedly comic send-up of a notorious hate group is particularly feminist. Similarly, Emily Jacir's video *Crossing Surda (A Record of Going to and from Work)*, 2002, is a surreptitiously filmed documentation of the obstacles faced by ordinary Palestinians who must cross daily through Israeli checkpoints in the West Bank. The video dramatizes, as does most of Jacir's work, the difficulties confronting Palestinians in the occupied territories, without making a distinction between men and women. A counterpart to Jacir's piece, Israeli artist Sigalit Landau's *Barbed Hula* (2000), deals with the same situation from the other side, and is marginally more feminist; it presents the bloody marks a barbed-wire hula hoop leaves on the torso of a naked woman, whose actions are explained in the catalogue as references to the geographic barrier between Palestine and Israel.

Other works here deal with oppression directed more specifically at women. Iranian artist Parastou Forouhar has covered one wall of the gallery with wallpaper featuring tiny stylized images of women being flogged, hanged, stoned, beaten, and otherwise tortured, one assumes in the name of sharia. Canadian artist Rebecca Belmore's *The Named and the Unnamed* (2002) is an installation documenting a performance memorializing fifty women, many of them sex workers, who disappeared and remain missing in Vancouver. Projected on a wall studded with small light bulbs that seem to function like votive candles is a video of the artist performing various ritualistic actions on urban streets, under the gaze of curious onlookers. In a related homage to the often invisible victims of AIDS and sex trafficking in Thailand, Skowmon Hastanan has covered a wall with a lightbox collage in which images of alluring hostesses in traditional Thai dress are set within bubbles referring to the blood corpuscles and pharmaceutical capsules that are central to AIDS infection and treatment.

Several artists also incorporate the female body into works dealing with nationalism. Congolese artist Michèle Magema presents a two-channel video, one channel of which is documentary black-and-white footage of young girls marching in parades under the eye of dictator Mobutu Sese Seko, who ruled the country from 1965 to 1997; the other channel is a video of the artist in a blue shift with white stripe, marching in place to military music. In Russian artist Zoulikha Bouabdellah's video *Let's Dance (Dansons)*, 2003, by contrast, the female body subverts nationalistic cant, rather than serving as an instrument of propaganda. Here, the camera pulls in close as a woman winds a spangled belly-dancing outfit in the colors of the French flag around her waist and proceeds to shake seductively to the strains of "La Marseillaise." Bouabdellah, who was raised in Algeria before moving to France, refers in this video to the problematics of ethnic and political identity in her adopted country.

The last section, "Emotions," seems almost an afterthought—a catchall for works that didn't fit elsewhere. The rationale given is that the material here was chosen to demonstrate how women artists self-consciously parody conventional ideas about female emotionalism. The piece that most closely fills this bill is Australian artist Tracey Moffatt's hilarious video *Love* (2003), a compilation of quick cuts from Hollywood movies in which both men and women behave emotionally, and badly, succumbing to sexual passion, arguing, pulling weapons, and finally killing each other. By contrast, real-life emotions are the subject of an hour-long video by Julia Loktev that analyzes and acts out the complexities of her relationship with her partner,

Vito Acconci. More of a stretch are works like Shahzia Sikander's delicate updated Persian miniatures, Ghada Amer's sex-themed embroidery, and Costa Rican artist Priscilla Monge's *Room for Isolation and Restraint* (2000), a small room padded with sanitary napkins.

The critical reception of "Global Feminisms" has been bumpy. Roberta Smith (in the *New York Times*) questioned the validity of the term "feminist art," while Peter Schjeldahl (in the *New Yorker*) found the work too didactic, too heavy on video and new media, and insufficiently focused on aesthetic pleasure. The latter critique seems somewhat beside the point for work that deliberately flouts conventional standards of beauty and eschews traditional mediums. More distressing was the curious erasure of the 1980s, a decade referred to, in the catalogue, simply as a time of gathering interest in postcolonial issues. Reilly notes, "The year 1990, then, was chosen as the starting point of the exhibition to designate the approximate historical moment when this mandate began; which is to say, when the linked issues of race, class, and gender were placed at the forefront of feminist theory and practice."[1] This perspective slights the lively feminist debates that took place in the '80s over issues like difference, gender construction, and the ideology of representation, and which formed a bridge between the feminism of *The Dinner Party* and the feminisms of today. Perhaps because this backdrop was dispensed with, the show offered little or no insight into the continuing debate over the use of sexually explicit and racist imagery in art by women, and particularly over whether such practices reinforce or undermine the power of this imagery in the larger world. The debate is often styled as a standoff between "bad girls" like Lisa Yuskavage, Cecily Brown, Renee Cox, and Kara Walker (who is represented in this show, but not by the sexually explicit and racially provocative imagery for which she is best known) and older feminists for whom such work is unambiguously a mark of complicity with patriarchal culture.

Similarly absent is a sense of the infiltration of feminist ideas into mainstream Western art. Arguably the greatest triumph of feminist art is the way it pried art open to hitherto verboten themes, materials, and approaches — among them narrative, autobiography, low art, craft, and unconventional materials — and inserted these into the center of art production. Feminist art's impact on art today is visible everywhere in developments as diverse as the interest in abjection and the grotesque, the continuing debates over the politics of identity, and the focus among younger artists on fantasy and narrative. Indeed, the work of celebrated male artists like Matthew Barney, Robert Gober, and Mike Kelley is unimaginable without feminism.

"Global Feminisms" skirts these issues while failing to fully round out its global vision. The unconvincing thematic arrangement hinders its potential to capitalize on the intriguing connection between *The Dinner Party*, which can be viewed in this context as perhaps the first effort to embrace a transnational feminist vision, and the worldwide spread of feminist art today. But even with these shortcomings, "Global Feminisms" succeeds in bringing forward an intriguing array of geographically diverse female artists. As such, it serves notice that women have entered the art world on a massive scale internationally, and that their contributions are no longer being ignored.

Notes

This essay was originally published in *Art in America* 95, no. 6 (June–July 2007): 154–65. "Global Feminisms" was exhibited at the Brooklyn Museum from March 23 to July 1, 2007. The Brooklyn Museum offers an array of images, the Feminist Art Base, associated with the exhibit plus Judy Chicago's *The Dinner Party* at the Elizabeth A. Sackler Center for Feminist Art: http://www.brooklynmuseum.org/eascfa/feminist_art_base/index.php.

1. Maura Reilly, "Introduction: Toward Transnational Feminisms," in *Global Feminisms: New Directions in Contemporary Art*, ed. Maura Reilly and Linda Nochlin (London: Merrell; New York: Brooklyn Museum, 2007), 32.

PART 2.

STANDARDS OF BEAUTY

6. Jenny Saville Remakes the Female Nude: Feminist Reflections on the State of the Art

DIANA TIETJENS MEYERS

After school I walked home across the football field. . . . I carried my big black leather binder full of notes in front of me, hugging it to my chest with both arms, my textbooks piled on top of it. All the girls did this. It prevented anyone from staring at our breasts, which were either too small and contemptuous, or else too big and hilarious, or else just the right size—but what size was right? Breasts of any kind were shameful and could attract catcalls. . . . But not to have any at all would have been worse.

—Margaret Atwood, "My Last Duchess"

When I was young, my mother read me a story about a wicked little girl. She read it to me and my two sisters. We sat curled against her on the couch and she read from the book on her lap. . . . The girl in the story was beautiful and cruel. . . . Because I sat against my mother when she told this story, I did not hear it in words only. I felt it in her body. I felt a girl who wanted to be too beautiful. I felt a mother who wanted to love her. I felt a demon who wanted to torture her. I felt them mixed together so you couldn't tell them apart. The story scared me and I cried. My mother put her arms around me. "Wait," she said. "It's not over yet. She's going to be saved by the tears of an innocent girl. Like you." My mother kissed the top of my head and finished the story and I forgot about it for a long time.

—Mary Gaitskill, Veronica

Margaret Atwood's vignette tells a familiar tale of endemic female body shame. The schoolgirls are already locked in the double bind of feminine narcissism—at once needing attention and being humiliated by it. Unsure of what constitutes bodily perfection, they are tormented by uncertainty about how to be physically okay, let alone lovable. Mary Gaitskill traces this syndrome back into childhood. Her parable of the wicked beauty's fall from grace and her redemption warns of the perils of investment in physical beauty. Because Alison, the listening child, is in fact beautiful and prizes her beauty, the fairytale treats her to a premonition of her own damnation. As Gaitskill writes this scene, Alison not only hears the lesson that her self-love is a curse, the lesson resonates through her mother's body, and her own tiny body absorbs it.

What makes these passages an apt introduction to a discussion of the aesthetics of the female nude is that they narrate how gendered beliefs, norms, and values become somatic. Atwood and Gaitskill, more than most writers, are attuned to what I call the psychocorporeal dimension of women's experience, and they are exceptionally adept at depicting it. In my view, contemporary British artist Jenny Saville paints visual analogues of these literary scenarios. She reconfigures the female nude, I argue, by endowing her figures with psychocorporeal attributes.

Shaun Gallagher's distinction between the body image and the body schema provides a framework for my argument. Because the body image and the body schema are corporeal phenomena that are also meaningful dimensions of subjectivity, I use the term "psychocorporeal" to designate the crosscutting category in which they belong. They are psychological because the agentic capabilities of the body schema and the grasp of one's physical body that is captured in the body image are comparable to but not equivalent to mental capabilities.[1] Although they are not merely physiological processes, the body image and the body schema are embodied; hence they are corporeal.[2] By attending to psychocorporeal capacities, we can better understand the phenomenology of gendered bodies as well as the liabilities and potentialities of the female nude.

After reviewing feminist critiques of the female nude in Western art, I take up a selection of Saville's paintings. A self-proclaimed feminist whose work feminist critics often praise, Saville is concerned with body image issues, and I discuss how she reconfigures representational practices with respect to feminine body images. However, the most exciting potential for feminist analysis of the state of the female nude derives from the concept of the body schema, for it recognizes the agency of the human body. My key question, then, is by what pictorial means and to what extent Saville succeeds in representing feminine body schemas. Although Saville has not fully explored psychocorporeal interpersonal agency in her nudes, I argue that she radically remakes the female nude by painting psychocorporeal agentic capabilities into her images. Moreover, I suggest that the success of her transfiguration of the female nude—her success in representing gendered psychocorporeity—owes much to her reflexive art practice.

Current Theory of the Body

Recent philosophical work on the body lays to rest the dualist, misogynist dogma that the body is the tool of the mind. The enculturation of the body is necessary to the formation of a self.[3] Corporeal disciplines reproduce gender, class, race, and other hierarchy-enforcing components of identity.[4] Abstract knowledge and thought depends on physical "scaffolding" that incorporates the organic body and extends beyond it to supplementary equipment.[5] The animate body is the locus of practical knowledge of objects in space.[6] Dispensing with rational deliberation, the skilled body generates behavior that is appropriately coordinated with situations.[7] Mind is in the body, these theorists maintain; it is not merely contingent on brain functioning.[8] Or, as I prefer to put it, the human body has psychocorporeal as well as biological properties.

In this section I consider one strand of work on psychocorporeity—Shaun Gallagher's neuroscientifically informed, phenomenologically motivated distinction between the body image and the body schema. Gallagher contends—rightly, in my view—that a great deal of philosophical mischief stems from conflating these two systems. I present his distinction between the body image and the body schema in preparation for using it, first, to sharpen Lynda Nead's critical analysis of the female nude in Western art and, second, to analyze the advances that the nudes of Jenny Saville signal.

According to Gallagher, the body image is a "system of perceptions, attitudes, and beliefs pertaining to one's own body." It includes your visual picture of your appearance, your conception of the workings and state of your body, and your feelings about your looks, your health, and other aspects of your physical condition. You have short-term body images—your self-image in this situation right now—and a long-term body image—your cumulative and projected self-image. Although you are not constantly aware of your body image, you can bring it to consciousness at will.[9] The body image is what social psychologists and clinical psychologists are talking about when they speak of body image distortions as contributing to self-esteem deficits and eating disorders. The self-assessment component of the body image is the source of the anxiety of Atwood's young protagonist, and it is the subject of Gaitskill's fairytale.

The body schema is a "system of sensory-motor capacities that function without awareness or the necessity of perceptual monitoring." According to Gallagher, conscious control over your actions takes place at the level of intentions and objectives—for example, intending to go home from school via the football field—not at the level of orchestrating the neuron firings, muscle contractions, and so forth that must happen to carry out intentions, nor at the level of the body schema. By organizing perception according to your purposes and by pragmatically controlling and adjusting posture and movement, the body schema's "preconscious, subpersonal processes" mediate between your goals and physiological processes.[10] The body schema reduces the need for conscious planning and eliminates the need for supervising the minutiae of movement. Comprised of countless skills and competencies, your body schema ensures that you hold yourself erect while showering, stand at a socially acceptable distance from conversation partners, flirt in a manner that communicates your attraction, drive your car without crashing, and much more besides. The unnamed girl in Atwood's story who clutches her books to conceal her bosom has acquired a self-protective bodily routine that is part of her body schema and that is constitutive of her gendered identity.

Whereas the body image is primarily an imagined self-portrait that secondarily affects choice and action, the body schema is primarily an agentic apparatus that may be partially represented in the body image. The body schema can never be fully accessible to consciousness, and, to the extent that it can be brought to consciousness, it becomes part of the body image.[11] At the time Atwood's self-conscious schoolgirl was hiding behind stacks of books, she acted automatically. Her body schema maintained her self-protective practice, and she thought nothing of it. Writing about her adolescent experience later, she notices that she could have carried her books differently, and she realizes that she had an ulterior motive for carrying her books in that particular way. Now she is recording her behavior and its significance in her long-range body image. The body schema and the body image reciprocally influence one another. Your body image rules out the development of some body schema capabilities and encourages the development of others, and your body schema's capabilities frame how you see yourself.

I find it helpful to isolate four dimensions of the body schema: cognition, virtue, versatility, and memory. Psychocorporeal cognition is the sensitivity of the body schema to the use-value of affordances as well as its sensitivity to the meanings of ambient affect, attitudes, and the like. Thanks to her body schema's sensitivity to affordances, Atwood's schoolgirl makes use of her books to manage her anxiety. Thanks to her body schema's kinesthetic apprehension of meaning, the perils of beauty are viscerally implanted in Alison's impressionable body. By psychocorporeal virtue I mean corporeally encoded values that install a basic motivational structure in the body schema that facilitates and enhances agency. Courage, curiosity, prudence, patience, communicativeness, modesty, dignity, respect, friendliness, empathy, compassion, kindness, and generosity are among the values that might be integrated into your body schema. What we see in the Atwood and Gaitskill stories is the perversion of corporeal virtue. Modesty and kindness are twisted into distrust and secretiveness that permeate the characters' body schemas. Psychocorporeal versatility has several forms. It includes your physical vigor—energy, stamina, strength, agility, suppleness, and so forth—as well as the extent of your accumulated know-how. It also includes somatic mood—that is, your sense of bodily competence. Psychocorporeal mood depends on at least two factors: 1) the safety spectrum, which ranges from trust to fear, and 2) the comfort spectrum, which ranges from being at ease and relaxed to being stressed and taut. The fictional passages I have quoted say little about vigor, but both depict a wary and tense psychocorporeal mood.

Alison's body is the body of the traditional female nude—a body that is beautiful on the surface and yet at war with itself. Psychocorporeally, Alison never for a moment forgot the story of the cruel, beautiful girl, although she didn't consciously recall it until much later. The reading infuses her body schema with conflict-laden corporeal knowledge of the meaning of feminine beauty. As an embodied memory, this knowledge inflames her body image. Throughout her life, Alison is either disproportionately enamored of her beauty or disproportionately derisive of it. Embedded in her body schema, the memory of the story skews Alison's perception of circumstances as well as her comportment when interacting with others. In the first pages of *Veronica*, then, we witness a dysphoric, dysfunctional body image and a dysphoric, dysfunctional body schema in the making—the genesis of one kind of feminized person. None of this psychocorporeity finds its way into the canonical female nudes of Western art history.

The Problem of the Female Nude

Jenny Saville expresses ambivalence about the female nude:

Could I make a painting of a nude in my own voice? It's such a male-laden art, so historically weighted. The way women were depicted didn't feel like mine, too cute. I wasn't interested in admired or idealised beauty.[12]

And for good reason. Lynda Nead's study of the nude in Western art history accounts for Saville's chariness.

According to Nead, the prefeminist female nude "is meant to transcend the marks of individualized corporeality by means of a unified formal language." Manhandled in this way—that is, contained by patriarchal artistic conventions—the naked female body is converted into a beautiful object of (presumptively male) contemplation and connoisseurship.[13] In other words, archetypal paintings of nude women are the antithesis of the living and lived body, for the artist strips individualized psychocorporeity from the image. In many instances, no sign of reflexive awareness subjectivizes the figure as she gazes at nothing and no one in particular. Other works impose an alien subjectivity on the figure. Anticipating Alison's patriarchally poisoned narcissism, they lock the figure's eyes on a mirror image that casts doubt on her beauty.[14] Because they lack evolving body images as well as working body schemas, no hint of bodily vitality or motility spoils the static splendor of these female forms. Because depriving a human figure of an authentic body image deprives it of any simulacrum of self-ownership, this pictorial maneuver grants viewers permission to stare and to scrutinize. Because depriving the figure of any semblance of the power of self-movement relieves beholders of the need to read cues of incipient action, they are freed to enter the elevated zone of aesthetic appreciation. Exemplary nudes of the Renaissance and Baroque suspend interpersonal demands while spotlighting a bare female body.

In the Western painting tradition, Manet's much discussed *Olympia*[15] is a liminal work in which the conceit of peeking in on an unclothed woman in a private moment is jettisoned and in which some practices of objectification, though not idealization, are revised. Manet gives Olympia eyes with a strange bidirectional gaze that forthrightly addresses viewers while also appearing distracted from the scene before her.[16] Starkly delineated, her tensile, pale body lacks the yielding softness of earlier works in this genre. As a result, Olympia's body hints vaguely at resistance to the viewer's desire. Yet this figure is unmistakably on display as to-be-consumed.

Manet paints as idealized a body as any premodern nude.[17] Olympia's— or rather, the model and artist Victorine Meurent's—own body image does not enter into this tableau. An ideal image of female corporeal perfection replaces it.[18] Olympia's body schema, as expressed by her pose and Manet's facture, reinforces the message of feminine availability. Awaiting inspection, Olympia complies with the proprieties of feminine modesty and conceals her pubis with one hand. No proclamation of female sexuality or demand for sexual reciprocity spoils the viewer's pleasurable dalliance. Moreover, Olympia's smooth, unmarked body betrays no memory of her previous encounters with clients in this boudoir. Devoid of desire and experience, the figure of Olympia reduces psychocorporeally animate flesh to an idealized cipher. At most, her complex glance and her porcelain body suggest dissociation from her demeaning profession—the defensive agency of the powerless in the presence of the powerful. To discern a form of agency unencumbered by Olympia's subordinate social position, you must look elsewhere in the painting. If you construe the black cat with its sharp glare and its angry arched back as Olympia's familiar, it is arguable that Manet exports her active psychocorporeal agency to this feline attendant.

Nead picks up the story of the female nude in her discussions of several second-wave feminist strategies for contesting the idealizing, as well as the objectifying, heritage of this pictorial theme.[19] Some feminist artists challenged the denial of female sexuality in traditional nudes by foregrounding an iconography of female genitalia. Taking aim at the ubiquity of youthful, white, heterosexual female bodies in Western female nudes, others attacked the racist, ageist, heterosexist attitudes presupposed by these works and trumpeted the diversity of female bodies. Performance artists used their own nude bodies to insist on corporeal interiority, to reject the value of feminine purity, and to stage transgressive agency.[20] Photography, sculpture, textile and needlework, collage, installation art, and performance art were the principal media in which feminist artists lodged their protest and proffered alternative visions.

Still, some feminist artists favored paint on canvas and wrung feminist statements from this medium.[21] Joan Semmel painted a nude that shows (surprise!) how her body looks from her own point of view—*Me without Mirrors* (1974). Alice Neel painted all-but-unprecedented nude portraits of women—seven of pregnant women and one of herself as an octogenarian artist.[22] Semmel and Neel seized the prerogative of self-definition. Other painters opted for indirect tactics. Engaging in a bit of table-turning, Sylvia Sleigh parodied Ingre's seraglio pictures by painting a roomful of lounging, full frontal male nudes (*The Turkish Bath*, 1973).[23] Late in the 1980s, Sue Williams appropriated the pictorial and narrative conventions of comic strips to represent decidedly imperfect bodies in lewd states of undress, scabrous poses, and abusive scenarios.[24]

With the exception of Semmel's painting, this work digresses from the issue of the female nude. Neel is a portraitist; Sleigh takes on the male nude to comment implicitly on the female nude; Williams inveighs against violence in heterosexual relations. I do not gainsay the originality of these approaches or the trenchancy of these images. However, none of these artists is chiefly concerned with bending the topos of the female nude to feminist purposes.

It was not until well into the 1990s that the project of recuperating the female nude in painting really took off. That is when Jenny Saville (along with other young women artists, notably Lisa Yuskavage and Cecily Brown) made their presence felt in the artworld. Critics have dubbed Saville's images cruel. I prefer to say that she is a painter of the not-demure. Her images are confrontational. They exult in the "too-muchness" that, according to Susan Bordo, drives women into obsessive dieting and exercising, even life-threatening eating disorders.[25]

Banishing orthodox, aesthetically validated conceptions of feminine allure from her pictures, Saville paints fantastic female bodies. Of course, the titans of the Western female nude—Titian, Velázquez, Rubens, Manet, Degas, Renoir, Bonnard, Modigliani, Matisse, Picasso, to name but a few— depict fantastic female bodies too. Like Saville, they enlist fanciful hues to represent skin tones, and they elongate and truncate the anatomical form of their models. But the great male artists depict eerie states of bodily vacuity and confine inwardness to facial expressions (if the figure is accorded any trace of subjectivity at all). In contrast, Saville psychocorporealizes female flesh and makes female nudes that are imbued with credible body images as well as potent body schemas.

Prop, Hem, and Fulcrum

There is a litany of points that virtually every commentator makes about Jenny Saville's work, and they are worth reiterating here. She paints "gargantuan," "gigantic," "mountainous" figures that are blemished, pocked, bruised, scabbed, venous, bulging, obese, wounded, riven, and occasionally sutured. A stylistic descendant of Francis Bacon and Lucian Freud, her painterly technique is superb. Her "ugly," "monstrous," "grotesque" subjects clash with the manifest beauty of her painting. She doesn't paint from live models. She works from photographs of her own body, sometimes photographs of friends or models, and from images found in medical texts and news sources. She is well versed in feminist theory and acknowledges this influence.

In interviews Saville is highly articulate about her feminist, aesthetic, and art-historical concerns. Her theoretical and pictorial sophistication with respect to feminine body image issues is beyond doubt. Although she has relatively little to say in interviews about the body schema per se, I argue that her paintings speak volumes on the subject. All of her full-length nudes represent subjectivized bodies—that is, psychocorporealized figures. Some of her images replay normalized feminine body images and body schemas as painfully awkward enactments of culturally prescribed gestures or inscriptions. Of greater interest is her painterly treatment of flesh itself. I discuss one painting, *Hem*, in which her pictorial description of the organic density of flesh adumbrates the human body's potential for intelligent, innovative agency and a second, *Fulcrum*, in which her representation of flesh discloses the emotional strains and bonds that undergird a trio of body images and correlated body schemas.

Saville's Account of a Negative Feminine Body Image

Saville's 1992 suite—*Propped, Prop*, and *Untitled* (each is oil on canvas, 84 × 72 in.)—is a sustained and probing meditation on the woes of feminine body images. Unprepossessing nude giantesses are stationed on little stools. Thick legs pretzel around slender stanchions into positions that supposedly keep them from falling off. Ponderous hip flab droops over the edges of the stool seats. Pendulous breasts, elephantine thighs and calves, mounded stomachs, and bloated buttocks occupy most of the picture plane. Small heads recede above these avalanches of flesh. The *Propped* figure (plate 5) gazes down from high above, daring you to look at her and revile her body, yet she squishes her breasts between her arms and digs her fingertips into her thighs, clumping the flesh. The *Prop* figure (fig. 6.1) gazes into the distance above viewers' heads, her lips set in a grim pout, while her arms and hands conspire to conceal her breasts. In *Untitled* (fig. 6.2), the figure's eyes are closed tight, her forehead is gnarled, and one arm is flung around her chin to hide her mouth—hers is an expression of unbearable anguish and shame. Not one of these figures caresses herself. Not one takes any delight in her body.

It is no accident that I have described the torsos and legs of these figures before describing their heads. The former are huge and protrude aggressively toward the viewer. They fill the lower three quarters of these works. The heads are small and pushed to the top margin of the canvases. These placements and proportions suggest two interrelated ways of reading these images.

There is reason to regard these images as projections of the contours of a common type of negative feminine body image, as opposed to images of bodies that actually look this way from a certain angle. Only virtuoso yogis of this girth could assume these positions. As a viewer, you sense the artifice of these poses because you kinesthetically register the tug of gravity, the

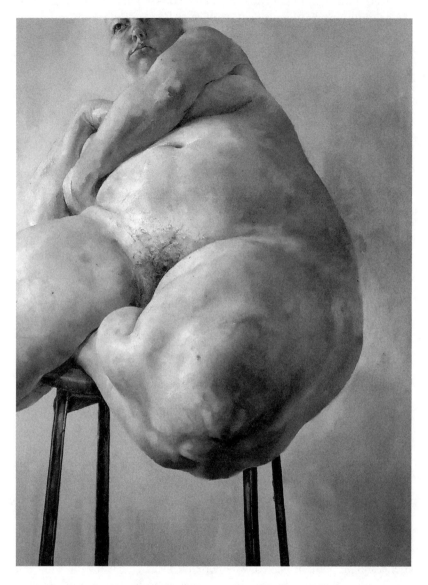

Figure 6.1. Jenny Saville, *Prop*, 1992. Oil on canvas, 84 × 72 in.
© JENNY SAVILLE. COURTESY OF THE GAGOSIAN GALLERY, NEW YORK.

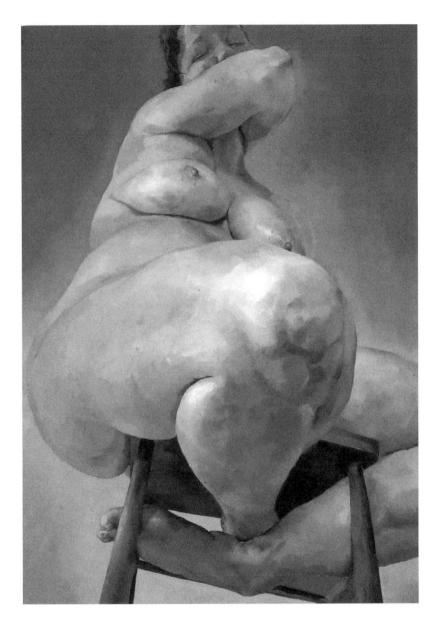

Figure 6.2. Jenny Saville, *Untitled*, 1992. Oil on canvas,
84 × 72 in. (pictured 84 × 60 in.). © JENNY SAVILLE.
COURTESY OF THE GAGOSIAN GALLERY, NEW YORK.

strain on joints, and the crush of avoirdupois. At the same time, Saville invokes the feminist trope of the pedestal. Symbolizing the disempowering, heterosexist adoration that is conferred on "proper" women and that is underwritten by beauty ideals that inflict a malign narcissistic syndrome on women, the pedestal all but impales the figure in *Propped*.[26] Coupled with the unstable disposition of the pictorial volumes, this metaphor transports viewers into the psychic world in which emotional investments and disinvestments determine what things look like—the world of the gendered body image. For the women whose body images Saville portrays, body dysphoria wildly exaggerates the dimensions of their hips and thighs.[27] So vast are these fantasized bodies that self-concealing gestures leave almost everything exposed. Their mottled, bruised coloration exudes consternation—they are deemed insufferable, and they are suffering.

It is also possible to interpret these images in light of Saville's use of perspectival devices. If you focus on her foreshortening of the figures in these paintings, they read as representations of large women seen from the standpoint of a Lilliputian. This interpretative slant not only extends what I have said about negative feminine body images, it also discloses a challenge these images level at the art-historical tradition. Assuming that each of these paintings depicts a woman's body image and that she is the implicit minuscule viewer, the pictures convey the power of feminine body images to overshadow actual women and distort their self-understandings.

With respect to art history, underscoring Saville's foreshortening of her figures clarifies how her paintings challenge the typical male artist's objectification of women's bodies. The placid faces and lounging bodies of the most revered nudes of the Renaissance and Baroque periods invite the spectator's stare, no questions asked. Although Manet's *Olympia* ushers in a more ambiguous transaction between the viewer and the female nude, its deindividualized, idealized treatment of the nude figure still allows the viewer to visually ravish the figure without feeling gauche or, worse, prurient. Saville's *Prop* suite nullifies this scopophilic entitlement. Her foreshortened, foregrounded bodies command your attention and then embarrass you in the act of staring.[28] In Holmes's words, "For the viewer who has already gawked at the body, it's decidedly uncomfortable to arrive at the face and confront the psychological presence of this thinking and feeling human being."[29] You are staring, but you have no right to stare.

Yet Saville is not content to regale us with intimidating images of massive female bodies or poignant images of feminine body dysphoria. She wants viewers to find beauty in these works:

There is a thing about beauty. Beauty is always associated with the male fantasy of what the female body is. I don't think there is anything wrong with beauty. It's just that what women think is beautiful can be different. And there can be a beauty in individualism. If there is a wart or a scar, this can be beautiful, in a sense, when you paint it. It's part of your identity. Individual things are seeping out, leaking out.[30]

Saville resists aesthetic orthodoxy. The *Prop* suite critiques the norms that contribute to rampant body dysphoria among women and also undertakes to redeem overlooked beauty in the figures she portrays. Saville discovers beauty in individual persons whose bodies are marked by life, as opposed to the formulaic beauty of idealized nudes. Importantly, she does not accomplish her goals of resistance and redemption by air-brushing and prettifying those of her subjects' attributes that are widely considered ugly. Such cosmetic manipulation would falsify her images and reproduce the very ideals that damage women's body images in the first place. Instead she expresses the beauty she perceives in her subjects through the quality of her painting—exquisite brushstrokes tenderly daub the figure, and unstinting swaths of oil salve it. By deploying her painterly technique to represent her figures with care and respect for their distinctiveness, she articulates her repudiation of customary beauty norms without erasing or camouflaging the ostensible flaws of her figures. "I made a body that was too big for the frame, literally too big for the frame of art history," Saville remarks.[31] I would add that her beauteous application of pigment on canvas bursts the constraints of the aesthetic regime of the female nude and proffers an alternative understanding of beauty along with a vehicle for aesthetic appreciation of it.

Saville's Organicism and a Feminine Body Schema

Before I consider what I take to be Saville's major achievement with respect to portraying female body schemas, I briefly review the more pedestrian, though not ineffective, strategy that she employs in the *Prop* suite. Saville defines her project as follows: "I'm interested in the physical power a large female body has—a body that occupies a lot of physical space, but also someone who's acutely aware that our contemporary culture encourages her to disguise her bulk and look as small as possible."[32] The subjects of *Propped*, *Prop*, and *Untitled* are women who are disconsolate because they are overweight. They fold their calves under their thighs, and they flatten their breasts or squeeze their thighs together. The reddened, jutting knee and elbow joints in *Prop* attest to the strain of deflecting social scorn. The figures' efforts to compress and conceal their bodies betoken stunted body schemas—innumerable skills foregone, energy diverted from productive exertion, chronic stress and insecurity. These bodies have internalized the cultural ideology that equates slenderness with desirability—indeed, with bare acceptability. To their lasting, possibly irreparable detriment, this censorious message permeates and impairs their body schemas.

In contrast, the figure in *Hem*[33] is unbowed by beauty norms despite her naked hugeness (fig. 6.3). Staged from a puny mortal's point of view, the painting shows a warrior goddess who towers over viewers.[34] Her bearing is operatic. No waif weakling, she stands erect, her shoulders thrown back, her breasts high, her eyes intent on the distance. A descendant of ancient statues of Nike and Athena (e.g., the *Agora Nike*, Stoa of Zeus, late fifth century BCE; *Nike* by Paionios, 420–410 BCE; the *Pergamene Athena*, second century BCE), her thighs are massive, and her torso is propelled forward. But unlike the female inhabitants of Olympus, Saville's figure is multidimensional—she is a mother as well as a warrior, and her sexuality is intact.

The hem that gives the painting its name is the figure's cesarean scar.[35] Yet the rust-tinged red streak separating her pubis from an abdominal roll of fat initially appears to be nothing more than a crease in her ample flesh. Availing herself of this ambiguity, Saville discloses the figure's maternity without so accentuating it that her womanhood becomes equated with her motherhood. Below the scar, strands of wiry pubic hair squiggle every which way. Here Saville acknowledges the figure's sexuality without courting the male gaze. By layering semitransparent paint over the figure's mons veneris, Saville blurs the hairs and deflects pornographic voyeurism. Fertile, but not reducible to her fertility; sexual, but not reducible to her allure for men; powerful, but not reducible to the misogynist fantasy of the engulfing mother—this figure is styled after a lioness whose cubs are playing nearby. She is a vigilant, militant, fierce defender of the innocent and helpless.

What I have just described is a representation of feminine psychocorporeity that is consummately agentic. The key to this achievement is what I call Saville's "organicism." Reflecting on her artistic development, Saville notes, "Paint mixed a flesh color suddenly became a kind of human paste."[36] In Saville's practice, oil paint stands in for living tissue, and one function of painterly technique is to convey corporeal density, temperature, and exertion—that is, flourishing or thwarted psychocorporeal agentic capabilities. Her art is a sustained inquiry into the chromatics and textures of embodiment and embodied agency. I make my case for this claim through a close reading of *Hem*'s facture.

Figure 6.3. Jenny Saville, *Hem*, 1999. Oil on canvas, 120 × 84 in.
© JENNY SAVILLE. COURTESY OF THE GAGOSIAN GALLERY, NEW YORK.

The *Hem* figure is partitioned into two sections defined by distinct palettes and painterly qualities. The figure's right side, from her shoulder down through her torso and into the rear of her thigh, is composed of chilly whites, putties, khakis, and Persian blues.[37] Big multidirectional brushstrokes—including zigzags and crisscrossing shafts punctuated by little blobs—join with thick impasto to endow the surface of the cool section with tingling energy.[38] The figure's left side is composed of warm yellows, beiges, pinks, and pale turquoise blues. A central set of unidirectional, diagonal brushstrokes reinforced by fine ridges of paint define the contours of her right thigh. Concave, horizontal sweeps of paint undergird the figure's belly, while a line-up of rounded brushstrokes arcs down from her waistline to give volume to the roll of flesh above her pubis. Dabs of orange are scattered on her upper torso, which, like her bosom, is modeled in smaller, more blended, less salient brushstrokes. All together, the calmer colors, moderated paint handling, and firm volumes of the warm section produce an effect of solidity, strength, and competency. The orange dappling that seems to emanate from deep in the figure's flesh hints at bodily potentials that are held in reserve.

Two small patches of solvent-induced, tendrilous paint stand out from the rest of *Hem*'s facture because there are only two of them in the painting. Because of their distinctiveness, they function visually as the painterly equivalent of exclamation points. Moreover, they call attention to additional dimensions of the figure's agency.

One of these patches is in the middle of the warm side of the figure's upper torso—right where you'll find your solar plexus. If someone socks you in the solar plexus, your diaphragm is likely to go into painful, disabling spasms, and you'll probably report that you've had the wind knocked out of you.[39] In this atypical little passage, Saville marks a vulnerable spot that must be protected to preserve agentic control. Magnificent though she is, this figure is not armored against violence and injury.

The second of these patches of curdling paint is located at the intersection between a prominent band of pure white that runs along the figure's waist in the cool section and a pinkish line in the warm section that continues along her waist. This passage highlights a site of exchange between the energy of the cool section and the powers of the warm section. Feelings of coldness can be invigorating, as when one steps into a cold shower after a session in the sauna. They can also destabilize a warm-blooded creature's equilibrium and prompt it to seek heat. In both ways, chilliness animates the body. But unless this energy is harnessed to well-honed agentic capabilities, it cannot give rise to anything but chaotic, counterproductive behavior.

The discipline and practical intelligence of the body schema are necessary to agency. To depict an agentic woman, Saville inserts a striking transitional, transactional passage where energized, unruly impetus converges with an individual's repertoire of psychocorporeal capabilities to give rise to action. At this juncture, motivation combines with the body schema to support agency.

Two features of Saville's drawing augment and refine her treatment of the body schema in *Hem*. At the outer edge of the cool section, Saville uses a soft dark line to outline the shape of the figure's body. This line subtly but definitely distinguishes the figure's back from the background. Whatever is behind her is past and is not subject to her will. In contrast, Saville fudges the boundary of the warm side. On this side, the painting of the figure and the background frequently interpenetrate. Whatever might lie ahead for her is still amorphous. The contrast between the two sides gives the impression that this undeniably stationary figure is nevertheless projecting forward, heading into the future in a spirit of openness to change.

To bring my interpretation into focus, I return to the four aspects of the body schema that I identified earlier—psychocorporeal memory, cognition, virtue, and versatility. The *Hem* figure's cesarean scar indexes her psychocorporeal memory of giving birth. This is an experienced body that remembers the pain of labor and the preciousness and fragility of life. With respect to psychocorporeal cognition, Saville presents a kinesthetically alert and attuned figure who, despite being still, is manifestly ready to go into action. The figure's unflinching, proud demeanor betokens the psychocorporeal virtues of courage, resoluteness, and self-assurance. This is not a submissive or easily intimidated woman. Saville conveys psychocorporeal versatility through the painting's facture as well as through the form of the figure. The scintillant energy of the cool side and the concentrated power of the warm side imbue the figure with its dynamism—that is, the synergy between her vigor and know-how. Although Saville does not show the slightest trace of the figure's musculature, her flesh does not appear to be blubbery, nor does it appear to be weighed down. You picture this woman striding, not waddling or shuffling. The figure's posture suggests a psychocorporeal mood that is best characterized negatively—she is not in repose, but neither is she tense or alarmed.

On the whole, the figure comes across as prepared to encounter new situations resourcefully, and as capable of formidable endurance if need be. Her bearing connotes uncompromising determination backed up by colossal might. Hers is a body that refuses to be contained, suppressed, manipulated, or controlled by anyone else. In no uncertain terms, *Hem's* figure defies the beauty ideals that Gaitskill's Alison fulfills so perfectly but that beleaguer her agency. Whereas *Hem's* figure is a paragon of psychocorporeal agency, Alison is a victim of psychocorporeal asphyxiation.

Saville's Organicism and Relational Psychocorporeity

I conclude this section with a word about a possibility that Saville has not yet pursued as far as she might—the body schema's relational capabilities. *Fulcrum* (plate 6) is typical of Saville's multifigure works to date.[40] Three nude female bodies lying in alternating directions are piled on a gurney, forming a pyramid. Thirty-year-old Fiona lies on her back at the bottom; Saville's twenty-nine-year-old body curls into a semifetal position facing viewers on top; Sadie, the titular fulcrum, who is Fiona's sixty-year-old mother, lies on her back between them, twisting her upper body toward viewers. At the feet of the middle figure and just below the shoulders of the upper and lower figures, a cord ties this "body pile" together and secures it to the gurney. According to Saville, "It's different generations of flesh touching one another."[41]

The key term here is "touching": "It's not about the primacy of vision, it's about using paint, its materiality, in a way that can evoke tactility."[42] In an infantile, somnolent gesture, the top figure's left arm circles the middle figure's ankles, her pudgy hand shoved between the middle figure's left leg and the bottom figure's belly. Less than a hug, more than a dangling limb, this arm is in contact with all three figures. Elsewhere, Saville elaborates on the theme of touching in painterly terms. At several places along the line between Fiona's right thigh and Sadie's left thigh, and along the line between Sadie's and Jenny's right thighs, patches of paint disobey the law of the sovereignty and separateness of bodies. In these passages, Saville uses one and the same mark to simultaneously construct two ostensibly distinct forms. To touch is to blur boundaries and blend into another. In other words, to be a person committed to interpersonal relationships is to have a body image that is not altogether separable from those whom you touch and who touch you.

That these figures haven't met up freely introduces a motif that is at odds with the concept of the unitary self. Bound together, the figures are compelled to touch. Indeed, the lashing is pulled so tight that it pinches their ample flesh and forces it to bulge. It hurts them to touch. Thin, rigid, vertical strips of paint traverse the three bodies. A blood-red strip runs from above Jenny's eye to Fiona's shoulder. A shower of gray-blue strips thread their way in and out of Sadie's head and chest and Fiona's lower legs. Saville strings these women together like popcorn garlands. Touching penetrates deep into their flesh, and touching is inextricable from their selfhood and subjectivity.

Yet each of the bodies has its own painterly and agentic personality, its own body schema. Serrated, diagonal palette strokes accented by linear ridges of paint model Fiona's torso and define the directionality of her muscular exertion. Her body strains against the others' weight and struggles against being squashed. Horizontal lines predominate in Sadie's thighs and make them into a platform. Yet swirls of thickened paint in her abdomen suggest the torsion she musters to turn her upper body toward the viewer and resist being sandwiched between the younger women. Jenny's body has the smoothest texture and most delicately modulated coloring. It is the most relaxed of the three. Yet her face and the arm she wraps around Sadie's ankles bespeak neediness. Although Saville individualizes the three *Fulcrum* figures and assigns them different positions in their relationship, it is clear that their relationship conditions their agentic possibilities.

Fulcrum is a portrait of a triadic relationship, as opposed to a depiction of three women interacting. Sensory tactility, emotional intimacy, and agentic interdependency are privileged over active exchange. The configuration and qualities of the volumes symbolize mother/daughter bonds and tensions more than they depict lively interaction among individuals at different stages of life. I do not mean to deny the power of this image, nor do I mean to belittle the urgency of its subject matter. This painting accomplishes what it sets out to accomplish, and the three figures are far from psychocorporeally vacant. However, I wish to point out that there is a key dimension of female body schemas that Saville has yet to broach—namely, the capacity to engage collaboratively or conflictually with another person apart from a close relationship. As yet, her multifigure works disregard the possibility of representing this aspect of feminine psychocorporeal interpersonal agency.

Reviving the Female Nude—Saville's Reflexive Practice

Saville has said that the subject of her work is "extreme humanness"— a conceptualization that goes a long way toward explaining the pictorial foment of her work.[43] Extreme humanness is a paradoxical expression. It suggests both the utterly and typically human and the marginally and atypically human.[44] Saville's work neglects no permutation of humanity. Her oeuvre portrays gendered, sexed bodies that are extremely human, that push humanity to extremes, and that in some instances are *in extremis*.

In the cultural imaginary that underwrites traditional female nudes, the female body is a neatly bounded entity that is covered in smoothly curved, alabaster or golden skin. Her pose is redolent of come-hither languor or narcissistic indulgence. Her body is on display for the visual delectation of men, albeit disguised as aesthetic contemplation.

What is a woman artist at the end of the twentieth century to do? Saville's de-idealizations and de-normalizations of the female body, however alienating they may be at first blush, are crucial to her struggle with the Western art-historical tradition. As well, they are indispensable to her recuperation of the female nude as a subject for women artists and as an object of aesthetic interest for women.

In three respects, Saville creates female nudes that repudiate patriarchal domination and comport with feminist values. In Saville's hands, the female nude becomes a vehicle for representing existential states that are depressingly familiar to many Western women. In her *Prop* series, the eruption of psychocorporeal insecurity and anxiety about one's bodily defects comes as a disconcerting burst of realism and pathos to anyone accustomed to female nudes that erase or displace feminine subjectivity. In a related gambit, Saville appropriates the female nude to challenge feminine stereotypes and norms. The figure in *Hem* is an unapologetically big woman, who takes her space and stands her ground. Neither pretty nor acquiescent, this figure is stunning—a redoubtable, raw, nonidealized vision of feminine beauty as grandeur. Most importantly, Saville's nudes are vibrantly psychocorporeal. Her figures have individualized body images and body schemas—interiority and agency. Saville constructs unconventional, yet legible, poses for her nude figures, and her gestural, expressive handling of pigment enlivens the bodies she depicts. Her nude bodies are stamped with memories, sensitized to social norms, and imbued with cognition, virtue, and versatility. Whether hobbled by social norms (the *Prop* suite) or thriving despite them (*Hem*), Saville's nudes are equipped with psychocorporeal agentic intelligence.[45]

I suspect that one reason that Saville plumbs the human body as deeply as she does is that she frequently bases her paintings on her own body.[46] Her artistic process precludes treating human bodies as inert matter. "I use my body as a prop," she says. "It's like loaning my body to myself. So the flesh becomes like a material."[47] To transform her own flesh into *nature morte* would be to repress and betray her own experience of the subjectivity of personhood—her psychocorporeal being. Particularly for an artist whose huge canvases entail highly skilled, whole-body activity.[48]

Eschewing the detached, spectatorial perspective of the painter contemplating "his" model, Saville's self-sourcing personalizes her working methods. As she puts it,

> I don't like the idea of just being the person looking. I want to be the person. Because women have been so involved in being the subject-object, it's quite important to take on board and not be just the person looking and examining. You're the artist but you're also the model. I want it to be a constant exchange all the time.[49]

The evidence of the paintings suggests that this role reversal has been remarkably productive. Fully identified with the image of flesh she confides to canvas, Saville strives to overcome the inner and outer, mental and physical polarities:

> It's because the nervousness of revealing is inherent that I'm interested in it. . . . It is about being brave enough with myself to offer up that anxiety.[50]

Bodying forth different dimensions of her self-understanding in different works, Saville makes psychocorporeal nudes that rescue the hoary female nude from somatic vacuity.

NOTES

The first epigraph is from Margaret Atwood, "My Last Duchess," in *"Moral Disorder" and Other Stories* (New York: Doubleday, 2006), 59–60. The second epigraph is from Mary Gaitskill, *Veronica* (New York: Pantheon, 2005), 3–4.

I am grateful to the University of Connecticut for a sabbatical leave that gave me time to work on this essay and for a University of Connecticut Provost's Research Excellence Award that gave me funding to revisit two of the paintings I discuss. I am also indebted to the editor of this collection for her valuable comments on an earlier draft and to Kristina Grob for her indispensable assistance in preparing this manuscript for publication.

1. Because you can retrospectively articulate what goes on psychocorporeally in the form of a planning narrative, intelligent corporeity is analogizable to the mental. But because you don't actually "talk to yourself," silently or out loud, when your body schema is organizing your conduct, and because making decisions psychocorporeally isn't equivalent to a verbalized decision-making process, intelligent corporeity is not assimilable to the mental.

2. Shaun Gallagher stresses the peculiar neither-fish-nor-fowl status of the body image and the body schema in *How the Body Shapes the Mind* (New York: Oxford University Press, 1995), 235–37.

3. Elizabeth Grosz, *Volatile Bodies: Towards a Corporeal Feminism* (Blooming-ton: Indiana University Press, 1994).

4. See Judith Butler, *Gender Trouble* (New York: Routledge, 1990); Judith Butler, *Bodies That Matter* (New York: Routledge, 1993); and Shannon Sullivan, "Reconfiguring Gender with John Dewey: Habit, Bodies and Cultural Change," *Hypatia* 15, no. 1 (Winter 2000): 23–42.

5. Andy Clark, *Being There: Putting Brain, Body and World Together Again* (Cambridge, Mass.: MIT Press, 1999).

6. See Maxine Sheets-Johnstone, *The Primacy of Movement* (Amsterdam: John Benjamins, 1999); and Sean Dorrance Kelly, "Merleau-Ponty on the Body," *Ratio*, n.s., 15 (December 2002): 376–91.

7. Hubert L. Dreyfus, "Intelligence without Representation," Cognitive Sciences Initiative at the University of Houston, http://www.hfac.uh.edu/cogsci/dreyfus.html (1998).

8. Recent work in neuroscience reinforces this philosophical trend. For example, Antonio Damasio, in *The Feeling of What Happens: Body and Emotion in the Making of Consciousness* (New York: Harcourt Brace, 1999), maintains that experiencing emotion depends on your sensory-motor and hormonal systems.

9. Gallagher, *How the Body Shapes the Mind*, 24, 25, 35, 38.

10. Ibid., 24, 26; see also 33, 38, 139, 142–45, 239–41.

11. Ibid., 35, 38.

12. Suzie Mackenzie, "Under the Skin," *Guardian*, October 22, 2005, http://www.guardian.co.uk/artanddesign/2005/oct/22/art.friezeartfair2005.

13. Lynda Nead, *The Female Nude: Art, Obscenity and Sexuality* (New York: Routledge, 1992), 22, 24, 55. There are fascinating parallels between Nead's account of the female nude and Susan Bordo's account of the slender female body in *Unbearable Weight: Feminism, Western Culture, and the Body* (Berkeley: University of California Press, 1993), 195–212; however, I do not have space to explore them here.

14. Diana Tietjens Meyers, *Gender in the Mirror: Cultural Imagery and Women's Agency* (New York: Oxford University Press, 2002), 106–15.

15. Édouard Manet, *Olympia*, 1863, oil on canvas, 130.5 x 190 cm, Musée d'Orsay, Paris.

16. For helpful discussion of the complexity of Olympia's gaze, see Alexander Nehamas, *Only a Promise of Happiness: The Place of Beauty in a World of Art* (Princeton: Princeton University Press, 2007), 111–12, 116–20; and Charles Harrison, *Painting the Difference: Sex and Spectator in Modern Art* (Chicago: University of Chicago Press, 2005), 49–51, 56–58. What concerns me about their accounts of Olympia's subjectivity, however, is that they treat subjectivity as if it were all in the head and revealed by the face. They overlook proprioception as a form of bodily self-awareness, and this faculty of the body schema is not well represented in *Olympia*.

17. For an alternative view of idealization in this work, see Nehamas, *Only a Promise of Happiness*, 107–108.

18. Arguably Manet is less guilty of objectifying and idealizing his nude models into abject anonymity than his predecessors. Still, it is worth comparing his individualized portrait of Victorine Meurent (1862, oil on canvas, 42.9 x 43.8 cm, Museum

of Fine Arts, Boston) with the idealized face in his depiction of Victorine Meurent as Olympia.

19. Also see Rosemary Betterton, *Intimate Distance: Women, Artists and the Body* (New York: Routledge, 1996), especially chapters 4 and 6; and Jo Anna Isaak, *Feminism and Contemporary Art* (New York: Routledge, 1996), especially chapter 6.

20. Nead, *Female Nude*, 65, 72–81, 67–69.

21. For documentation and discussion of this work, see Norma Broude and Mary D. Garrard, *The Power of Feminist Art* (New York: Harry N. Abrams, 1994); and Helena Reckitt and Peggy Phelan, *Art and Feminism* (New York: Phaidon, 2001).

22. For discussion of Neel's images of pregnant nudes, see Pamela Allara, "'Mater' of Fact: Alice Neel's Pregnant Nudes," *American Art* 8, no. 2 (Spring 1994): 6–31; and for a discussion of her self-portrait as an aged painter, see Meyers, *Gender in the Mirror*, 153–54.

23. Arguably, Semmel's *Intimacy/Autonomy* (1974) also partakes of this turn-about strategy. This painting is a double nude of a woman and a man who are lying slightly apart on a bed, presumably after sexual intercourse. The table-turning feature of this image is that his detumescent penis, not her breasts or pubis, is the most conspicuous pictorial element.

24. More recently, Williams slyly inserts miniature orifice motifs into paintings that appear to be lyrical abstracts until you get up close. In these works, Williams comments on the inescapability of the erotic in painting and perhaps on the fantasies undergirding pretentious claims about the sublime that some members of the Abstract Expressionist movement put forth. In any case, she no longer seems to be interested in reclaiming the female nude for any feminist purpose.

25. Susan Bordo, *Twilight Zones: The Hidden Life of Cultural Images from Plato to O.J.* (Berkeley: University of California Press, 1997), 127–38.

26. For discussion of the cultural underpinnings of feminine narcissism and feminist artists' resistance to this malady, see Meyers, *Gender in the Mirror*, chapter 5.

27. For related discussion, see Alison Rowley, "On Viewing Three Paintings by Jenny Saville: Rethinking a Feminist Practice of Painting," in *Generations and Geographies in the Visual Arts: Feminist Readings*, ed. Griselda Pollock (New York: Routledge, 1996), 95; Michelle Meagher, "Jenny Saville and a Feminist Politics of Disgust," *Hypatia* 18, no. 4 (Autumn 2003): 34; and Mackenzie, "Under the Skin."

28. Lynda Nead, "Caught in the Act of Staring," *Women's Art Magazine*, no. 58 (May–June 1994): 18; Pernilla Holmes, "The Body Unbeautiful," *Art News* 102, no. 10 (November 2003): 145; Meagher, "Jenny Saville," 38–39.

29. Holmes, "The Body Unbeautiful," 145.

30. David Sylvester, "Areas of Flesh," in *Jenny Saville*, by Jenny Saville (New York: Rizzoli, 2005), 15.

31. Simon Schama, "Interview with Jenny Saville," in Saville, *Jenny Saville*, 127.

32. Martin Gayford, "A Conversation with Jenny Saville," in *Jenny Saville: Territories*, ed. Mollie Dent-Brocklehurst (New York: Gagosian Gallery, 1999), n.p.

33. Jenny Saville, *Hem*, 1999, oil on canvas, 120 × 84 in., Vicki and Kent Logan Collection.

34. Linda Nochlin describes the figure as a fertility goddess—a giant *Venus of Willendorf* "seen in an ant's eye perspective" in "Floating in Gender Nirvana," *Art in*

America 88, no. 3 (March 2000): 96. But the posture and the body of this statuette and the figure in *Hem* differ markedly. The fertility goddess hunches slightly forward, her breasts heavy with milk. Although there is a certain resemblance between the two treatments of the rolling abdomen and pubic area, the resemblance goes no further.

35. Although she has occasionally depicted moments in stories, e.g., *Plan* (1993), Saville is not for the most part a narrative painter. Nevertheless, there is a narrative dimension to her art. Reflecting on her conception of the body and her artistic practice, Saville comments, "Most of the marks are like inscriptions on the flesh. As we go through life traces or memories both physical and psychological are left on the body; they almost help to 'produce' your body" (Gayford, "A Conversation with Jenny Saville"; also see Holmes, "The Body Unbeautiful," 144). By portraying scars, wounds, and other vestiges of the body's susceptibility to experience, Saville evokes the events that produced them. Moreover, she endows her figures with a kind of embodied memory and knowledge that is necessary for psychocorporeal practical intelligence and hence for agency.

36. Schama, "Interview with Jenny Saville," 124. Saville often returns to this theme in interviews, e.g., "I mean, people who are seen as fat or overweight . . . usually have circulation problems, so there's a coldness of flesh. I think a lot of people don't think about how the body is made up" (Sylvester, "Areas of Flesh," 15); "I wanted the paint itself to be kind of obese" (Schama, "Interview with Jenny Saville," 127); "For me it's about the flesh and trying to make paint behave the way flesh behaves," and "Close up I want you to feel the heat of the bodies" (Gayford, "A Conversation with Jenny Saville").

37. Because this cool section resembles modeled plaster, it calls to mind plaster casts of Greek and Roman sculpture and provides support for connecting *Hem* to ancient goddess statuary.

38. Saville's ambivalence about large women comes out in her explanation of her use of white in *Hem* to try to "thin out this big body—paint the background into the body or the body into the background" (Schama, "Interview with Jenny Saville," 127). Ironically, though, the vigor of Saville's painting on this side of the figure counteracts her attempt to render this part of the body recessive.

39. Anatomists will point out that the celiac plexus is located within the body at the same spot. The celiac plexus is the motherboard of the part of the sympathetic nervous system that controls the operation of abdominal organs, and its functioning is indispensable to life without mechanical assistance.

40. Jenny Saville, *Fulcrum*, 1999, oil on canvas, 9.5 × 16 ft., Gagosian Gallery.

41. Gayford, "A Conversation with Jenny Saville."

42. Ibid.

43. Holmes, "The Body Unbeautiful," 145.

44. For lack of space, I have not discussed two strands of Saville's work—her paintings of transsexual bodies and her paintings of battered bodies. However, it is important to consider these works to grasp Saville's conception of extreme humanity.

45. Perhaps this is what Linda Nochlin has in mind when she comments ("Migrants," in *Jenny Saville* [New York: Rizzoli, 2005], 11) that Saville's work presents a "painterliness pushed so far that it signifies a kind of disease of the pictorial, a symptom of deeper disturbances lurking beneath the visible relation of paint to

canvas." The disease of the pictorial, I suggest, is the purging of psychocorporeity from traditional female nudes.

46. In *Propped* (1992), Saville inscribes a reminder of the need for reflexivity in reverse writing on the surface of the painting. For this purpose, she chooses a text from Luce Irigaray's essay "This Sex Which Is Not One": "If we continue to speak in this sameness, speak as men have spoken for centuries, we will fail each other again" (Holmes, "The Body Unbeautiful," 146). The text, says Saville, is supposed to act as a mirror, in which "I could see my own position" (Gayford, "A Conversation with Jenny Saville").

47. Elton John, "Elton Talks to Jenny Saville," *Interview*, October 2003, http://www.eltonjohnworld.com/protected/webspecials/BACKSTAGEPaintItRed.html.

48. Alison Rowley makes a similar point in asserting that Saville's *Plan* produces "a rearticulation of Western modernism's discourse of the 'body of the painter.' The represented body is no longer 'the supine female object body' but the active *female* creative body examined in the practice of the 'woman's body'" (Rowley, "Three Paintings by Jenny Saville," 94).

49. Sylvester, "Areas of Flesh," 14. Elsewhere she reiterates this point: "I don't like to be the one just looking or just looked at. I want both roles" (Mackenzie, "Under the Skin").

50. Mackenzie, "Under the Skin."

7. Indigenous Beauty

PHOEBE M. FARRIS

When I was asked to write an essay about beauty from a gendered or ethnic perspective, two Native American expressions came to my mind and served as inspiration: "Beauty surrounds us" and "Walk in beauty." "Walk in beauty" is a well-known Navajo saying and philosophical outlook. It encompasses both inner beauty and carrying oneself in a dignified manner that brings harmony to one's environment. The phrase is applicable to both women and men.

The phrase "Beauty surrounds us" is also well known, although I do not know if it has a specific tribal origin. However, "Beauty Surrounds Us" was also the title of a 2006 exhibit at the New York branch of the National Museum of the American Indian (NMAI). The exhibit celebrated the grace, elegance, and aesthetics present in various everyday Native American tools, games, clothing, etc., from a variety of cultures in the Western hemisphere. For me personally, it was a wonderful reaffirmation that Native Americans in the past and present have always surrounded ourselves with objects of beauty, including those that adorn our bodies.

So, too, the beauty of the indigenous human form can be celebrated as it appears in everyday life as well as on special occasions when we wear our regalia. For the purposes of this feminist anthology, I will mainly focus on the beauty inherent in the female form, but I have to include some male examples as well to achieve the male/female balance that is so essential to native life.

At the "Beauty Surrounds Us" exhibit, certain phrases and subtitles on the exhibit walls and display cases also resonated with me, such as "Nurturing

Identity," "Elegance of Presentation," "Containing Culture," "Expressions of Movement," and "Design as Identity." From an indigenous woman's perspective, adorning ourselves can be an expression of who we are, of where we originate in this hemisphere now called the Americas, and of our tribal identity when we are traveling outside of our home environments. When we are elaborately dressed for a powwow, our movements can be enhanced by the sound of jingle cones or bells, the gentle blowing of feathers, or the swaying of leather fringes. As we have adapted material objects from Europe, Asia, and Africa into our art and clothing, we have transformed our indigenous aesthetics and created new ways of visually expressing our beauty.

For me, one of the most effective ways to document indigenous beauty is visually; therefore, this is a photo essay highlighting the beauty of Native American women (and a few men). These photographs, shot at various pow-wows and cultural events on the East Coast as well as in the private domestic sphere, reflect the tribal diversity and dynamic, electrically charged beauty and vitality of contemporary Native Americans. Because all of the people photographed have their tribal roots in one or more of the tribes or nations on the eastern coast of the United States, their physical appearance may differ from what the dominant culture identifies as looking American Indian.

The dominant images of Native Americans, past and present, tend to focus on two geographical and cultural areas, the Plains and the Southwest. These images became fixed in the American media as "typical." Physical and cultural characteristics of Native Americans east of the Mississippi River are often ignored. These concerns have led me to use photography as a means of documenting various aspects of Native American cultures in the eastern United States and in the Caribbean. I am especially interested in those nations on the Atlantic coast who had early contact with Europeans, Africans, and "free people of color" (a broad category encompassing racially mixed nonwhites) and absorbed aspects of those cultures while still maintaining a firm Native American identity.

My photos are from my travels and interactions with family, friends, and the public at various cultural events and institutions, such as the Powhatan-Renape Rankokus reservation in New Jersey, the Pamunkey and Mattaponi reservations in Virginia, the Haliwa-Saponi Cultural Center in North Carolina, the Shinnecock reservation in New York, the Narragansett reservation in Rhode Island, the Mashantucket Pequot reservation in Connecticut, the American Indian Community House Gallery in New York City, and the National Museum of the American Indian in Washington, D.C., and New York City. The people profiled in this photo essay, dressed in both regalia and everyday attire, reveal the diversity prevalent among eastern tribes. They represent a broad, encompassing view of "indigenous beauty": a beauty that surrounds us in all aspects of our lives, at all phases in our lives from infancy to elderhood, and in health as well as infirmity.

Figure 7.1 is of Ms. Foggo, who was born in Bermuda but whose ancestry is Mashantucket Pequot. Ms. Foggo and families like hers from St. David's Island in Bermuda participate in the annual Pequot Powwow in Connecticut. The group shot (fig. 7.2) includes members of her family at the 2007 Schemitzun Feast of Green Corn and Dance. Her shining white hair, which so many American women dye as they age, is perhaps one of her most distinguishing beauty characteristics.

Figure 7.1. Ms. Foggo (Bermudan Pequot), Pequot Powwow in Connecticut, 2007. PHOTOGRAPH BY PHOEBE M. FARRIS.

Figure 7.2. *Ms. Foggo and Family Members, 2007.*
PHOTOGRAPH BY PHOEBE M. FARRIS.

Another elder with an ageless beauty is Lorraine Nunn Briscoe (fig. 7.3), shown visiting the Powhatan-Renape Rankokus reservation in New Jersey during one of their spring festivals. Her tan skin, with the fine lines often associated with aging, reveals a seriousness of expression and wisdom. The blue-and-white blouse and turquoise necklace contrast beautifully with her pink lips and rosy cheeks.

The copper-brown skin of the young mother and her toddler-aged daughter (fig. 7.4) is offset by their dazzling white regalia. The male dancers, in contemporary Day-Glo-colored regalia, exemplify male standards of beauty. This group of dancers was also photographed at the 2007 Pequot Powwow in Connecticut.

The next set of images is from the 2007 Mills-Boston family reunion at Algonquin Park in Northern Virginia. The families share a Powhatan heritage and have intermarried since the 1800s. The woman in the tiger-print blouse wearing a turquoise necklace is Keziah Boston, who is in her eighties (fig. 7.5). She is hugging her cousin, Susie Boston Miles, who is in her nineties, another white-haired beauty.

Another image of Keziah Boston (fig. 7.6) shows her at home, engaged in the simple task of spreading butter on bread. Wearing turquoise jewelry

Figure 7.3. *Lorraine Nunn Briscoe, Powhatan-Renape Rankokus Reservation, New Jersey, 2006.* PHOTOGRAPH BY PHOEBE M. FARRIS.

Figure 7.4. *Young Mother and Daughter, Pequot Powwow in Connecticut, 2007.* PHOTOGRAPH BY PHOEBE M. FARRIS.

Figure 7.5. *Keziah Boston and Susie Boston Miles, Family Reunion, Virginia, 2007.* Photograph by Phoebe M. Farris.

Figure 7.6. *Keziah Boston at Home, Virginia, 2005.* Photograph by Phoebe M. Farris.

and a "Still Here" native-designed sweatshirt, she appears in deep thought. This photo was shot in Keziah's Virginia log cabin home during a meeting and pot-luck gathering of the Confederated Powhatans of Washington, D.C., Virginia, and Maryland. Figure 7.7 shows Thelma Boston, in a wheelchair and also in her eighties but still active, with me, her younger cousin, leaning next to her. The Indian elder in figure 7.8 wearing a brown blouse, turquoise necklace, and dangling earrings is artist Georgia Mills Boston Jessup with her nephew-in-law, Carl Briscoe, Jr., who is wearing an NMAI tee shirt. All four of these female elders have faces that express character, deep thought, and vitality.

Another artist in this photo essay is Nadema Agard (Lakota, Cherokee, Powhatan), who is shown standing in front of her mixed media installation at a New York gallery (fig. 7.9). The rich reds in her artwork are also reflected in her clothes and makeup.

The dancing woman draped in a red blanket (fig. 7.10) exemplifies beauty in motion. Her profile, caught in mid-movement, emphasizes a stoicism that is often associated with the male Indian image. Her dance performance took place at the Schemitzun Feast, as part of an exhibit of a traditional woodland village outside the dance competition area.

Figure 7.7. *Phoebe Mills Farris and Thelma Boston, Family Reunion, Virginia, 2007.* PHOTOGRAPH BY PHOEBE M. FARRIS.

Figure 7.8. *Carl Briscoe, Jr. and Georgia Mills Boston Jessup Family Reunion, Virginia, 2007.* PHOTOGRAPH BY PHOEBE M. FARRIS.

Figure 7.9. *Nadema Agard (Lakota, Powhatan, Cherokee), New York Solo Exhibit, 2006.* PHOTOGRAPH BY PHOEBE M. FARRIS.

Figure 7.10. *Woman in Red Blanket, Pequot Powwow in Connecticut,* 2007. PHOTOGRAPH BY PHOEBE M. FARRIS.

Also in bright red is a dancer repairing the beadwork on her regalia (plate 7). A fellow dancer wearing bright blue, with lime-green hair accessories, has a smile that lights up her entire face (fig. 7.11). The pair of dancers sitting down (fig. 7.12), especially the young woman facing the viewer with the wide smile and glittering gold sleeves, are wearing clothing that incorporates new materials, reflecting the new realities of indigenous clothing aesthetics. All of these young dancers (in their teens and early twenties) have an "elegance of presentation."

The sleeping baby (fig. 7.13) captures that beauty of innocence, that quiet time that mothers embrace when a child's activity has ceased for the day. The baby is Sienna Captola Farris, photographed in 1974 or 1975. The exuberantly smiling infant and mother in figure 7.14 were photographed at the groundbreaking 2002 NMAI Powwow in Washington, D.C. Also in attendance at the event was my now deceased mother, Phoebe Mills Lyles (fig. 7.15), shown sitting on a bench wearing a blouse made in Uganda by descendants of immigrants from India, the people Columbus thought he encountered in 1492. She was seventy-five when the image was shot, and I see beauty in her generous smile, her prominent forehead veins, and the laugh lines around her eyes . . . beauty at any age.

Figure 7.11. *Dancer in Blue and Green Regalia, Pequot Powwow in Connecticut, 2007.* PHOTOGRAPH BY PHOEBE M. FARRIS.

Figure 7.12. *Two Dancers, Pequot Powwow in Connecticut*, 2007. PHOTOGRAPH BY PHOEBE M. FARRIS.

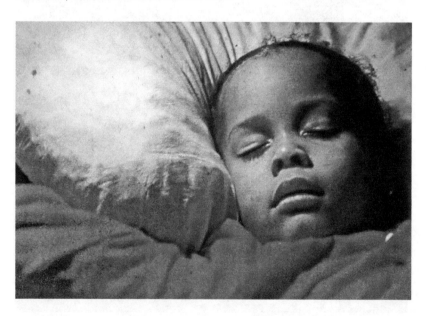

Figure 7.13. *Sienna Captola Farris*, 1970s.
PHOTOGRAPH BY PHOEBE M. FARRIS.

Figure 7.14. *Smiling Mother and Child, NMAI Powwow, Washington, D.C.*, 2002. PHOTOGRAPH BY PHOEBE M. FARRIS.

Figure 7.15. *Phoebe Mills Lyles, NMAI Powwow, Washington, DC,* 2002. PHOTOGRAPH BY PHOEBE M. FARRIS.

As this essay visually demonstrates, beauty is multigenerational and age-less, and occupies both private moments and public events; it can be seen in a smile or a more serious countenance. Although the photo essay highlights Native Americans, particularly women, the same essence can be found around the globe if we embrace a broader concept of beauty, if we listen to the Navajo and other indigenous peoples and "walk in beauty."

Plate 1. Soody Sharifi, *Mariam*, 2008.
Fine art inkjet print, 29 × 36 in.
COURTESY OF SOODY SHARIFI AND THE
ANYA TISH GALLERY.

Plate 2. Photograph by Michael Kamber,
New York Times, July 12, 2008.
COURTESY OF THE *NEW YORK TIMES.*

Plate 3. Lida Abdul, still from *White House* (one of six),
2005–2006. Cibachrome print, 29 ⅝ × 40 ¼ in.
Single-channel video, color, sound, 5 min.
By permission of Lida Abdul.

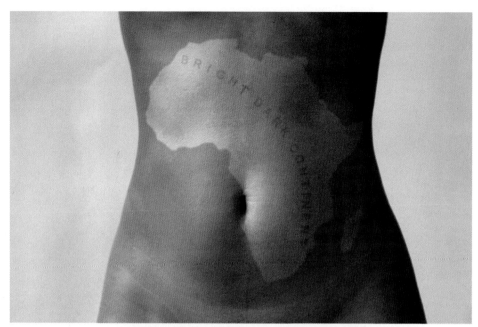

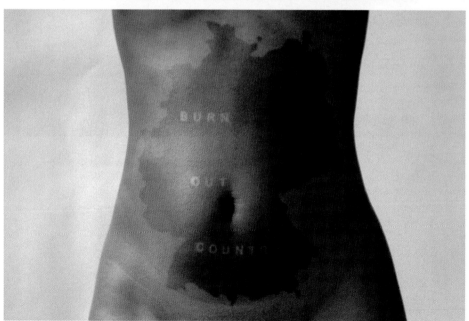

Plate 4a and b. IngridMwangiRobertHutter, *Static Drift*, 2001.
Two chromogenic prints mounted on aluminum (edition of five), each 29 ½ × 40 ¼ in.
Collection of Heather and Tony Podesta, Falls Church, Va.

Plate 5. Jenny Saville, *Propped*, 1992. Oil on canvas, 84 × 72 in. © JENNY SAVILLE. COURTESY OF THE GAGOSIAN GALLERY, NEW YORK.

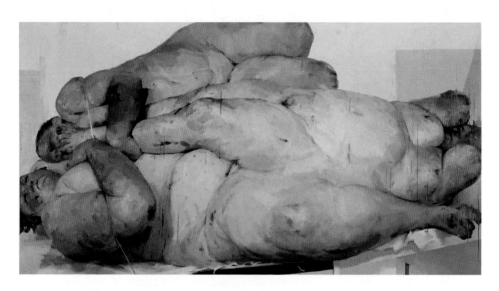

Plate 6. Jenny Saville, *Fulcrum*, 1999. Oil
on canvas, 103 × 192 in. © JENNY SAVILLE.
COURTESY OF THE GAGOSIAN GALLERY, NEW YORK.

Plate 7. Woman repairing beadwork, Pequot powwow in Connecticut, 2007. PHOTOGRAPH BY PHOEBE M. FARRIS.

Plate 8. Cok Ratih dances *legong jobog.*

Plate 9. Breda Beban, still from *The Most Beautiful Woman in Gucha*, 2006. Two-screen video for gallery projection. Courtesy of Breda Beban. Reprinted by permission of the *Louisville Eccentric Observer*.

Plate 10a and b. Keith Lehrer, *Horizon*, 2005. Acrylic on
canvas board, 16 × 20 in. Plate 10b is inverted.
COURTESY OF THE ARTIST.

Plate 11. George Catlin, *White Cloud: Head Chief of the Iowas*, 1844–45. Oil on canvas.

Plate 12. ORLAN, *Painting Portrait of Wash-Ka-Mon-Ya, Fast Dancer, a Warrior, with ORLAN's Photographic Portrait, Refiguration, American-Indian Self-Hybridization, no. 3*, 2005.
Digital photograph, 124.4 × 152.4 cm.
© ORLAN.

Plate 13. Soody Sharifi, *Honeymooners*, 2005.
Fine art inkjet print, 29 × 36 in.
BY PERMISSION OF SOODY SHARIFI AND THE
ANYA TISH GALLERY.

Plate 14. Soody Sharifi, *Frolicking Women in the Pool (detail)*, 2007. Fine art inkjet print, 34 × 40 in. By permission of Soody Sharifi and the Anya Tish Gallery.

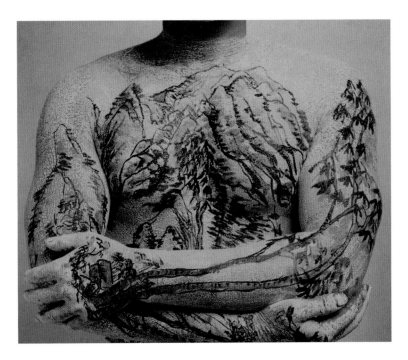

Plate 15. Huang Yan, *Chinese Landscape: Tattoo*,
1999. Chromogenic print, 31½ × 39 ⅜ in.
Collection of Arthur Walter.

Plate 16. Cui Xiuwen, *Sanjie*, 2003. Digitally
manipulated chromogenic print mounted on
plexi, 18 ⁷⁄₁₆ × 118 ¹⁄₁₆ in. (mounted size:
20 ³⁄₈ × 120 ¹⁄₁₆ in.). A. J. Japour Gallery.
Courtesy of Cui Xiuwen.

8. Is Medical Aesthetics Really Medical?

MARY DEVEREAUX

Medicine is the art of healing, aesthetics the study of our response to art and beauty. What happens when the two come together in the practice of cosmetic surgery? This is my question, a foray into what I will call "medical aesthetics." In what follows, I examine how practitioners of cosmetic surgery and related specialties have appropriated the language of medicine and healthcare to reframe and legitimize various nonmedical elective procedures designed to modify appearance.

I begin with a short discussion of the history and terminology of cosmetic surgery. Against this background, I critically assess the claim that cosmetic surgery qualifies as a form of healthcare, and hence a legitimate branch of medicine.[1] The argument for this claim takes a variety of forms, the main variants of which I consider in turn. Of particular relevance is the relation of the norms of beauty and health. It is the human attraction to attractiveness—to beauty, good looks, and social acceptance—that impels popular demands for cosmetic interventions of seemingly endless variety. That it is to medicine that we turn to meet this need is, as we will see, not surprising. But the effort to wed health and beauty creates challenges both for the medical aesthetician, or "beauty doctor," and for medicine. In pressuring medical professionals to place beauty above health, cosmetic surgery and related specialties such as cosmetic dentistry unavoidably raise questions about the definition of medicine itself. In particular, patient demand for what I am labeling "medical aesthetics" may collide with the Hippocratic requirement that physicians "do no harm." It is to those harms and related concerns that I turn in the final section.

History and Terminology

The field of cosmetic surgery has its roots in medical techniques developed to treat noses ravaged by syphilis, a disease epidemic by the end of the sixteenth century, and the facial wounds incurred by soldiers in the trenches of World War I. As Sander L. Gilman and other medical historians have noted, surgical skills first honed in the repair of disease and war-related injuries eventually found employment in altering ethnic noses and eradicating signs of aging.[2] Cosmetic surgery, its chroniclers point out, evidences a pattern typical of medical technology: techniques invented with strictly medical ends in mind soon became adapted to broader goals. Rhinoplasty, for example, a surgery designed to treat the ravages of war or disease, soon finds a new task: "making the body beautiful," more socially acceptable, or otherwise more in line with individual preference.

In part this shift arose with the aesthetics of the Renaissance. The emerging emphasis on the beauty of the human form only heightened the stigma of syphilitic disfiguration and other "unaesthetic" deformities, defects that helped fuel the rise of aesthetic surgery.[3] From early on, charges of quackery and debates about the legitimacy of their field spurred practitioners of "aesthetic" surgery to create medical terminology and a serious rationale for work that replaced health with other priorities: the creation of a "beautiful" face, the correction of ugliness, the erasure of signs of disease, and the creation of a façade of health.[4]

In contemporary medicine, "cosmetic surgery" or "plastic surgery" serves as a generic or umbrella term, covering both reconstructive procedures aimed at restoring basic function, e.g., repairing a hand maimed in an industrial accident, and elective procedures such as Botox injections, meant simply to better appearance. To avoid ambiguity, in what follows I reserve the term "cosmetic surgery" solely for procedures that are both elective and aimed primarily at non-health-related goals, such as a younger appearance.[5] I adopt the standard use of "reconstructive surgery" for interventions undertaken to reconstruct the body's normal appearance or repair functional deficits.[6] In some cases it may be difficult to draw a clear distinction between cosmetic and reconstructive surgery because the line between health-related and non-health-related goals is not sharp.[7] But for now, a rough distinction will suffice.

The proposed distinction between cosmetic and reconstructive surgery aligns with the oft-made distinction between therapy and enhancement. Here too the effort is to differentiate between health-related and non-health-related uses of medical tools and procedures. In some cases, we can easily tell the two apart. So, for example, administering human growth hormone to a child with growth hormone deficiency is health-related or therapeutic. Using the same hormonal therapy to make normal, healthy children taller classifies as enhancement. Other cases may fall less neatly on one or other side of the enhancement/therapy divide. Therapies used to restore an ill person to health may also result in a more radiant complexion or a brighter eye, hence improving appearance. But in this case, this outcome is a secondary effect, not the goal of the medical intervention.

Medicine as a profession is meant to operate under professional norms that rank health and bodily function over beauty. Patients know that, of necessity, health-restorative interventions may at times alter or even impair appearance. Surgery may scar, and drugs may damage hair, skin, or muscle tone. In some cases, the ravaging effects of medicine may diminish or disappear with a return to health. But in others, a missing limb or disfiguring marks continue to indicate the price paid for curing or managing disease.

The notable exception to ranking health over beauty is cosmetic surgery and its cousins, cosmetic dermatology and dentistry. Here aesthetic ends have more status. Medical risk is balanced not by medical benefit, but by the hoped-for improvement in appearance. The cosmetic surgeon employs the scalpel to reshape the human face and body, making of skin, muscle, and bone a "clay" to create human beauty. Indeed, in many cases there is no disease or defect to "fix." As Kathy Davis discovered in her study of cosmetic surgery patients, rarely do those seeking such procedures have features warranting drastic corrective measures.[8] The surgeon is presented not with obvious departures from standard appearance or objective reasons for surgery, but with subjective desire. This desire is complex. The urge to alter the body—to achieve a smaller nose, a flatter abdomen, or larger breasts—may reflect a drive to make the normal "better," to alter identity or "pass," to find happiness, or simply to look more youthful.

This is not to say that such desires are unnatural or necessarily misguided. Nor are the cosmetic surgeons who aim to satisfy such wants unconcerned with health or a safe outcome. Far from it. No cosmetic surgeon who wishes to remain in practice would or could ignore the physiological well-being of her patients. Still, the use of invasive, often risky, procedures such as liposuction and repeated injections of toxins such as Botox for non-health-related ends raises a number of issues that receive comparatively little attention despite their importance to the topic of women's health—and to the professional norms of medicine.

Legitimacy

The very nature of cosmetic surgery gives rise to questions about its legitimacy as medicine. What justifies the use of painful, potentially dangerous medical procedures in the absence of disease or impairment? What explains the allotment of scarce medical expertise and resources to aims that have little or nothing to do with healthcare? Unlike biopsies, heart surgery, and appendectomies, beauty surgery lacks an obvious medical rationale. The "patient" is not sick. The aim is not to treat or prevent disease or disability. The improvement of appearance falls outside the parameters of medicine as defined by the Hippocratic tradition. Indeed, cosmetic surgery is rarely covered by health insurance on the grounds that it fails to meet the standard of medical necessity.

While now professionalized and a recognized specialty,[9] cosmetic surgery still raises questions of legitimacy. Nor, in the face of a flood of advertising for a growing menu of options, some of questionable merit, are such questions likely to disappear.[10] Consider four attempts to provide a medical rationale for cosmetic surgery.

"It's Just Medicine"

The first argument is that cosmetic surgery is just ordinary medicine. In operating on the body, e.g., tightening facial muscles, cosmetic surgeons perform surgery. The surgery they perform differs in no important respect from cardiac surgery or the removal of gallstones. Both kinds of operation require the acquisition and exercise of skills specific to medicine, e.g., knowledge of physiology, surgical technique, and the ability to control infection. Insofar as cosmetic surgery is just another branch of medicine, it needs no special justification.

This line of argument doesn't stand up under scrutiny. Unlike procedures aimed at correcting functional impairment, e.g., a hip replacement, or reconstruction of bodies shattered by war, cosmetic interventions expose patients to the medical risks of anesthesia, blood loss, and infection without obvious therapeutic benefit. Even successful cosmetic surgery does not improve the health of the patient, except incidentally. Surgery aimed at aesthetic improvement or socially more acceptable features is thus different from medicine.

This is not to deny that cosmetic procedures can have therapeutic side effects. The American Headache Society reports that several clinical trials substantiate anecdotal reports that patients receiving Botox injections experience fewer headaches.[11] While Botox was not originally marketed for this purpose, the FDA recently approved a form of the toxin for use with adults with chronic migraine. Thus, while some cosmetic procedures may be said to belong within "the core of medical practice" because they confer health benefits, this fact, as Miller, Brody, and Chung convincingly argue, "has no bearing . . . on the vast majority of purely cosmetic surgery procedures performed on normal bodies."[12]

Proponents of the "it's just medicine" argument point out that all surgical procedures, including those clearly aimed at treating illness and disease, carry risks. So, they maintain, an element of risk cannot itself make cosmetic surgery problematic. The difference is that in the former case health risks are undergone for the sake of health *benefits*. Subjecting healthy people to medical risks is a morally different proposition from subjecting people who are ill or disabled to the same risks. A medical practice that exposes sound bodies to unnecessary hazard stands in considerable tension with the physician's promise to "do no harm." What then justifies cosmetic surgery that does not produce incidental therapeutic benefits?

"It Answers Consumer Demand"

A second line of argument is that cosmetic surgery satisfies consumer needs. Like cell phones and the latest iPod app, face-lifts and breast implants are consumer goods. They mark status, improve social position, and reflect personal taste. From this perspective, cosmetic surgery is justified because cosmetic surgeons provide a service people want.[13] Cosmetic surgery remains a part of medicine because the techniques it uses, such as suturing and wound management, are taught in medical schools.[14]

One may of course wonder whether physicians should be in the beauty business. Defenders of commercial medicine will answer that the business of physicians is business. If physicians can meet consumer demand for beautification, why shouldn't they? Like other businesses, medicine follows the market.[15] So long as doctors employ safe and effective procedures, and patients consent to the risks, cosmetic surgery is justified.

The problem with this line of justification is that it abandons the traditional idea of medicine as a profession. What makes a profession a profession is that, in contrast to business (a purely commercial enterprise), it has an internal end, or telos. An internal end is not only the goal one wants to achieve, but also what defines the enterprise itself. In the case of medicine, that telos is health. The goal of furthering health is distinct from meeting consumer demand. Medicine also has internal, health-related norms that include standards of expertise (exemplified in board certification) and standards of care. These technical and ethical standards are part of what makes medicine a profession and part of what makes it the specific profession it is. The normative force of these standards is not contingent upon market forces or consumer demand. Were there a market niche for medical services made cheaper by the elimination of routine hand washing, a doctor would still have an obligation to wash her hands.

This is not to say that physicians are required to forego profit. Medicine is a profession, not a charity. But there's more to being a doctor than having a set of marketable skills. That this is so is witnessed by the fact that the use of medical skills in execution by lethal injection conflicts with the requirements of being a doctor.[16] If medicine were just a business, there would be nothing wrong with using physicians to execute prisoners on death row. The same is true of the deployment of medical knowledge to facilitate the torture of "enemy combatants." The point is that the conception of medicine as a profession precludes the idea that medicine is just business, or simply a set of skills.

The proper aim of medicine is to meet the medical needs of one's patients. The sphere of medical needs is much smaller than the sphere of human wants. Even if medicine satisfies legitimate human desires, the satisfaction of desire, as such, isn't medicine. So, while my middle-aged patients may beseech me to inject "more and more" Botox or to siphon off yet another quart of accumulated fat, it doesn't follow that I should comply with their requests, any more than I ought to provide growth hormones to my short, but healthy, children simply to improve their chances of a basketball scholarship. Recommendations for medical treatment ought to be based on medical judgment about medical need. One cannot simply replace professional medical judgment with the desires expressed by clients. This remains so despite arguments by Kathy Davis and other "agent-centered" feminists that women use cosmetic surgery to meet their own needs: that in exercising choice over her body, a woman may achieve a more authentic embodiment, become more "herself."[17] Such arguments, however compelling, don't—indeed mustn't—trump medical judgment. A patient may have a long-standing desire to have Mona Lisa's smile or horns on her head, but it doesn't follow that such desires, however authentic, should overcome sound medical judgment. Hence questions about the medical ethics of the French physicians who agreed to perform multiple cosmetic surgeries in the service of ORLAN's performance art.[18]

None of this is meant to deny that medicine in the United States operates within a market economy and that doctors make their living by responding to economic pressures.[19] But it is possible to acknowledge these realities without abandoning the idea of medicine as a profession, as an enterprise constrained by professional and ethical norms.

The next two conceptions of cosmetic surgery can be thought of as responses to the failure of the two previous approaches. They recognize the ways in which cosmetic surgery differs from much of traditional medicine while nonetheless attempting to find ways of understanding its practices as consistent with established conceptions of medicine.

"Using the Blade to Cure the Soul"

This third conception represents cosmetic surgery as a form of psychological healing. Elective procedures, such as rhinoplasty and face-lifts, serve psychological ends, e.g., the relief of emotional distress caused by unlucky genes, undesired features, or signs of aging. On this view, cosmetic surgery is warranted because it "heals" self-consciousness or low self-esteem. The claim is that "using the knife" results in "measurable and meaningful improvement in psychosocial functioning and psychological well being in the long term."[20] Cosmetic surgery, understood in these terms, is in effect a form of psychotherapy. The beauty doctor, in Sander Gilman's classic formulation, "creates beauty to cure the soul."[21]

This historically prominent line of argument reframes cosmetic surgery as a natural extension of the medical arts. After all, modern medicine takes care not only of the body, but also of the mind, treating disorders such as agoraphobia, depression, and bipolar disorder. In addressing these conditions, psychopharmacological drugs provide patients with goods that balance possible side effects. Similarly, the argument goes, in removing or refashioning features that distress their owners, the cosmetic surgeon provides a psychological benefit that justifies the risks of surgery.

Two problems arise with this rationale. The first is that not everything that makes people happy or augments their subjective well-being qualifies as a health benefit. Cigarette smoking may improve adolescent self-esteem by making smokers feel cool. It may help control weight. Money, too, works wonders in increasing confidence and bolstering self-regard. But a physician who handed his patients fistfuls of money or packs of cigarettes wouldn't be practicing medicine. The point is not that doctors are or should be indifferent to the happiness of their patients, but that subjective well-being is distinct from healthcare. In short, the proper goal of medicine is health, not happiness. The claim that cosmetic surgery makes people happy, even if true, hence fails as medical justification.

A second concern is that problems of self-esteem or depression born of social or work-related rejection may be better met by therapies that directly address the problems that caused them. A desire for breast implants or genital reshaping may reflect less an authentic sense of self than the internalization of rigid, often demeaning, standards for what the female body in particular is meant to look like—and be. In "treating" departures from these standards, cosmetic surgery may help to foster the very conditions it pretends to alleviate. Moreover, if, as a variety of feminist and cultural critics charge, prevailing beauty norms often rest upon insidious gender, racial, and ethnic representations, with such consequences as a "need" to Westernize Asian eyes, then the price of the psychological well-being cosmetic surgery provides may be the cultivation of a false sense of self.

Advocates insist that, for many patients, cosmetic surgery offers a release from years of suffering caused by unwanted or inadequate aspects of the bodily self. Shyness, lack of confidence, and social anxiety may create real distress, leading to isolation, depression, or even self-harm. Surgical modification presumably alleviates this suffering, creating greater assurance and feelings of self-worth by altering the body.

Important, then, is the question whether cosmetic surgery delivers what it promises. Do elective procedures such as breast implants, altered noses, and body contouring result in demonstrable long-term psychological benefits? A 2004 review of the literature measuring psychosocial outcomes found generally good results, but noted several methodological limitations in this research. Of most significance, researchers stress the distinction between patient satisfaction with their change in appearance following surgery (being happier about their looks) and "measurable and meaningful improvement in psychosocial functioning and psychological well-being in the long term" (being happier). As they report, studies attempting to measure long-term outcomes reach conflicting conclusions, with some interview-based studies reporting positive outcomes, while others note no change or negative consequences.[22]

A related issue is the potential psychological complications arising from the surgery itself. A 2009 national survey of 312 board-certified plastic surgical nurses found that patients perceived higher rates of psychological complications, including anxiety and mild depression, than of physical complications such as surgical site pain. Patients with preexisting psychological conditions were at higher risk, thus indicating the need for better screening, support, and psychological treatment for plastic surgery patients.[23] The absence of randomized clinical trials comparing surgical intervention with no treatment or with alternatives such as psychotherapy, exercise, or expanded social interaction present another limitation. Such a study would of course be difficult to enroll and to carry out. But even researchers who conclude that cosmetic surgery is psychologically effective acknowledge that without such comparisons it is difficult to know whether the reported improvements resulted from the surgery, other aspects of the intervention, or unrelated changes in circumstance. Nor can the possibility of a placebo effect be ruled out.[24]

In short, existing outcome measures fall short of establishing reliability or causality. With the popularity of "makeover" television shows downplaying the risks of body-altering cosmetic procedures and claiming that such procedures can have life-altering effects, increasingly unrealistic expectations may lead to decreased patient satisfaction.

"It's a Kind of Optimization"

The last line of justification strives to validate cosmetic surgery by going back to the body. Its claim is that cosmetic surgery is a form of optimization, of qualitative improvement. The unattractive face can be made ordinary or average, the average made beautiful. This conception of cosmetic surgery depends upon an expanded notion of health—one that goes far beyond the idea of health as the attaining or maintaining some average or agreed-upon capacities, e.g., a specified resting heart rate, hemoglobin level, or blood pressure. It may define health as the attainment of maximal "species-typical functioning" or as the transcendence of species-typical limitations altogether.[25] One goal of optimization is to give all of us the capability to run at Olympic speeds and enjoy the skills now possessed by only the very gifted. Another is to transcend even the far range of normal function, allowing human beings to regrow severed body parts, stay awake for seven days, and enjoy an unwavering feeling of contentment.[26] If this seems over the top, it is. Yet these are claims that advocates of optimization actually make.

In this context, providing individuals with the necessary surgical and pharmaceutical means to make the average body beautiful seems small potatoes by comparison. To the objection that optimizing human function or appearance lies beyond the original brief of medicine, its defenders reply, so what? Why must we restrict ourselves to a traditional conception of medicine? The same benevolent regard that motivates restoration of function also motivates its optimization. Prior to the twentieth century, medicine did not include prevention, research into the causes of disease, public health campaigns, or education to eradicate the chronic conditions that plagued modern societies.²⁷ Much of what belongs quite comfortably to contemporary medicine—vaccination programs, epidemiology, psychotherapy, anesthesiology, even regular hand washing—required an expansion of medicine's reach. Why not go further? Why stop at restoring health and normal function when the technical know-how exists to do more? Why not use biological manipulations, where available, to extend memory, raise average life span, and, while we're at it, remove unsightly bumps and bulges? This is certainly a tempting vision. It promises to make us all faster, smarter, and, yes, more fetching.

Philosopher Julian Savulescu goes so far as to contend that enhancing biological and psychological characteristics may be ethically required.²⁸ Particularly with respect to children, he argues, choosing not to alter ears that stick out or features that others find "funny" may cause avoidable harm. Just as it would be medically wrong to withhold a good diet or vaccinations for early childhood diseases, so too, defenders of enhancement like Savulescu maintain, physicians ought not to forestall the benefits of cosmetic interventions so long as these are reasonably safe and plausibly in the child's interest.²⁹

This reasoning may convince some that it is justifiable to make broader use of ear tucks, eyelid surgery (to make eyes look more "Western"), and surgery aimed at normalizing the appearance of children with Down syndrome. Others will balk not only at the risk of side effects, but also at subjecting the young to procedures intended to "optimize" or normalize appearance, which is often defined as erasing ethnicity, race, or other forms of "difference." Children with crossed eyes may need surgery in order to learn to read. They can study perfectly well, however, without a nice nose or surgically pinned ears.

One can easily predict the response to this last objection. Although protruding ears may not directly interfere with education or professional success, such features can negatively impact self-confidence and social interaction. In so doing, they "disable" individuals in ways that diminish quality of life and that surgery can fix. So characterized, the smaller (or less ethnic) nose, tucked ears, and other proposed enhancements offered by the cosmetic surgeon are motivated by the impulse to do good. The idea is that a change in features will increase self-assurance and the likelihood of success.³⁰

Despite its appeal, the optimization rationale faces a number of philosophical and ethical hurdles. First, while some efforts to better human appearance may strike us as morally unproblematic (e.g., the possibility of reversing the effects of sun damage), others, such as the possibility of elective face transplants, may give at least some of us pause. What the enhancement controversy reveals is the need for a principled means of establishing the boundaries of professional obligation, the limits of private and public health insurance, and the proper sphere of biomedical research.[31] Traditional medicine has tended to fix these boundaries by appealing to notions of health and disease, or notions such as "species-typical function." While problematic, such notions assume that at some level the limits of the human (and hence of medicine) are biologically fixed. New biotechnologies have opened up the possibility that we may soon be in a position to change many of the biological limits assumed by traditional medicine. But this possibility raises a host of questions about the permissibility and desirability of making such changes. The friends of optimization push hard for these developments. They assume answers to questions they don't pause long enough to ask.

Even if some forms of optimization, including new beauty treatments, are an acceptable goal for medicine, the employment of scarce medical resources for this purpose raises moral and political questions that a commitment to the principle of individual choice obscures. The financial and human resources available for healthcare are limited. The use of these resources to meet the demand for cosmetic procedures means that fewer resources are available for basic healthcare. With the American population increasing, and the number of physicians remaining largely constant since 1980 (an artifact of limiting medical school enrollment), the diversion of large numbers of MDs into cosmetic surgery and boutique specialties has obvious costs.[32] Does this distribution of resources reflect good medical judgment? Does it reflect medical judgment at all? Is it just?

The optimization argument is subject to a further—foundational—difficulty: that it trades on a basic error. That error consists in maintaining the idea that cosmetic surgery and other appearance-based modifications actually expand human functionality. This is rarely the case. Breast implants don't increase cancer resistance or boost lactation. Smaller noses don't improve breathing. Whitening does not strengthen the teeth. What cosmetic surgery—and medical aesthetics in general—deliver is something other than functional improvement. Nor is functional improvement the aim. The goal, as both patients and doctors know, is aesthetic (and social) enhancement. The effect of the procedures responsible for these enhancements is often reduced functionality, e.g., decreased breast sensation, paralyzed and expressionless facial muscles, bright but also painfully sensitive teeth. In many standard cosmetic procedures, health is compromised or put at risk in exchange for non-health-related ends.

Concerns

We have been focusing on the kind of cosmetic or aesthetic surgery that qualifies as medical enhancement. The term "medical enhancement" suggests a practice that adds something to health and healthcare. But this assumption merits scrutiny. Presenting cosmetic surgery as something extra, a supplement to basic healthcare, provides a misleading and misguided picture. It leads us to make two seriously erroneous assumptions: the first concerning the concept of enhancement, the second concerning its costs.

First, much of the debate over the benefits and risks of medical enhancement centers on the question "How far beyond good health should we go?" Casting the question this way assumes that good health and good healthcare remain fixed while we pursue the dream of enhancement, defined as improving "human form or functioning beyond what is necessary to sustain or restore good health."[33] What we have seen, however, is that the growth of the practice of medical aesthetics may actually lead to a worsening of health. Patients undergo the injury of surgery itself and its short- and long-term risks. Some forms of cosmetic surgery, e.g., liposuction, raise especially serious questions about whether the benefits are worth the risk. Survey results obtained from board-certified plastic surgeons indicate a 1 in 5000 mortality rate from liposuction, often from pulmonary thromboembolism.[34] Other forms of cosmetic surgery, while unlikely to cause death, can result in long-term crippling effects. One such surgery is toe shortening—cutting the foot to fit the shoe rather than the reverse—a procedure that cannot but strike an impartial observer as perverse. Talk of medical enhancement thus obscures the fact that the dimension along which things are enhanced is not medical. As these and other cases illustrate, much of what gets called enhancement "enhances" neither health nor function.

One therefore has to ask to what extent medical enhancement can properly be classified as healthcare. The tendency to redefine each new cosmetic procedure as a cure for some freshly minted disease or disorder, e.g., cellulite, dermatochalasis (the presence of excess upper or lower eyelid skin), asymmetrical breasts, or gynecomastia (enlargement of the male breast), is evidence of the profession's awareness of the need to provide a medical warrant for the imposition of health risks in the service of refashioning "unfashionable" and "unaesthetic" bodies. That increasing numbers of cosmetic procedures take place outside hospitals, in offices, spas, and shopping malls—with little or no regulation—exacerbates the problem.[35]

The second error in characterizing cosmetic surgery as "enhancement" lies in the assumption that its effects on the healthcare system are minimal. Putting medical energy and resources into making people pretty and keeping them "young" when a significant percentage of the national population lacks even basic healthcare has real implications for patients, their caregivers, and society at large. Patient demand for Botox injections and a host of new cosmetic procedures has, as report after report indicates, risen exponentially in the United States, the United Kingdom, and other developed countries. The call for drugs such as Rogaine and Viagra is also mushrooming. If leading scientists are correct that ever more powerful biotechnology, including brain/machine interfaces and cosmetic neurology, will be widely available within ten to fifteen years,[36] competitive demand for such services will only increase, putting growing pressure on medical resources already stretched thin.

Changes in patient demands aren't the only explanation for shifts in the allocation of medical resources. Physicians too find these new and lucrative specialties attractive. Surgeons trained on the battlefield find themselves moving into cosmetic surgery. Those specializing in hand reconstruction find themselves pressured to provide "hand-lifts" to erase signs of aging skin. Medical students and residents increasingly hear of the headaches inherent in the managed care system and are warned of comparatively low salaries in primary care fields such as family and internal medicine. Diminished control and lowered income not surprisingly lead more and more physicians to elect service specialties such as cosmetic dermatology, areas of medicine that offer regular hours, a better-educated clientele, and more remuneration. One result is the increasing competition for residencies in cosmetic specialties. The shift in medical personnel from basic healthcare to "medical aesthetics" may come to be a public health problem.

Conclusion

The human desire to be beautiful, to refashion ourselves according to some inner vision, has ancient roots. In the United States, we wish to be our own Pygmalion, to craft the selves we want to be. But the tools we need for this project lie in the hands of others; they rest in the hands of medical experts. It is to surgeons and other "medical aestheticians" that we turn in pursuing our vision of physical beauty, in trying to become the person we hope others will desire. That physicians agree to assist in the physical remaking of the self is not by itself unethical. But when patient demand for improved appearance defeats or compromises medical judgment about physical health and safety, the inclusion of beauty among the professional ideals of medicine does raise ethical concerns.

That physicians stand to profit from providing procedures that are not medically necessary, but not from advising against them, only adds to the ethical and professional tensions inherent in cosmetic medicine.[37] Whether the human desire for beauty and self-transformation can be better met by nonmedical means is a question for another time.

NOTES

1. The argument presented here draws substantially on my earlier work on cosmetic surgery, material that originally appeared as "Cosmetic Surgery," in *Medical Enhancement and Posthumanity*, ed. Bert Gordijn and Ruth Chadwick (Heidelberg: Springer, 2008), 159–74.

2. Sander L. Gilman, *Making the Body Beautiful: A Cultural History of Aesthetic Surgery* (Princeton: Princeton University Press, 1999), 8–10, 169–72.

3. The beauty of the human form was appreciated long before the Renaissance. However, as sociologist Kathy Davis points out, until the availability of anesthesia and sterile technique, cosmetic surgery would have been an excruciating, dangerous, and sometimes deadly endeavor. For more on the complex interplay of cultural and medical issues leading to the establishment of cosmetic surgery as a profession, see both Gilman, *Making the Body Beautiful*, and Kathy Davis, *Reshaping the Female Body: The Dilemma of Cosmetic Surgery* (New York: Routledge, 1995), 14–18.

4. Gilman, *Making the Body Beautiful*, 15–16.

5. Note that not all of what falls within the common understanding of cosmetic surgery is surgical. Botox injections involve no cutting. A number of newer techniques for face-lifts avoid the knife by using lasers or radio waves. While my discussion centers primarily on surgical forms of bodily modification, many of these less invasive procedures carry their own medical risks and raise many of the same ethical and social issues.

6. As Sander Gilman argues, the distinction between reconstructive and "plastic" or cosmetic surgery is as old as the profession itself. See his *Creating Beauty to Cure the Soul: Race and Psychology in the Shaping of Aesthetic Surgery* (Durham, N.C.: Duke University Press, 1998), 3.

7. As a number of medical historians and others have noted, our notion of what constitutes good health (or basic healthcare) alters as biological science and biotechnology advance. A healthy pregnancy now includes prenatal care; measles and chicken pox are no longer an expected part of childhood. Nor are the toothless grins of the aged any longer regarded as normal parts of aging, at least not in developed nations. These are complicated issues, about which I will have more to say later.

8. Davis, *Reshaping the Female Body*, 68–70.

9. On the organization of plastic surgery as a profession, see Elizabeth Haiken, *Venus Envy: A History of Cosmetic Surgery* (Baltimore: Johns Hopkins University Press, 1997), 44–90; and Gilman, *Making the Body Beautiful*, 5–8.

10. While widely popular, hair transplants, buttock implants, and face-lifts for younger and younger women, and the advertisements for such procedures in popular magazines, taint cosmetic surgery with the air of quackery. Many reputable cosmetic surgeons naturally wish to distance themselves from such practices.

11. Sheena K. Aurora, "Implications of Current Clinical Trials Focused on Medication Overuse and Therapeutic Prophylaxis," *Headache* 51, suppl. 2 (July–August 2011): 93–100, doi:10.1111/j.1526-4610.2011.01956.x.

12. Franklin G. Miller, Howard Brody, and Kevin C. Chung, "Cosmetic Surgery and the Internal Morality of Medicine," *Cambridge Quarterly of Healthcare Ethics* 9, no. 3 (July 2000): 358.

13. Surgical procedures have come into favor as gifts. So husbands purchase gift certificates for their wives to have breast implants, daughters arrange face-lifts for their mothers, parents provide rhinoplasty for their children. Extreme instances of patient-driven medicine include the procedures carried out by the highly controversial Scottish doctor Robert Smith, who agreed to amputate healthy limbs in response to patient demands. These patients were not physically sick, nor were they incompetent, according to psychiatrists. Recent work on the brain, however, suggests that they may suffer a neurological problem in the right parietal lobe, the part of the brain responsible for body integrity and identity, that causes them to fervently wish to have a limb removed. For a fascinating discussion of the reasoning behind Smith's actions, see Carl Elliott, "A New Way to Be Mad," *Atlantic Monthly* 286, no. 6 (December 2000): 72–84.

14. Cosmetology, massage, and mortuary professionals also require training in areas such as dermatology, physiology, and the use of certain medical tools, devices, or products. Medical training and equipment do not by themselves make a doctor.

15. Deborah A. Sullivan, *Cosmetic Surgery: The Cutting Edge of Commercial Medicine in America* (New Brunswick: Rutgers University Press, 2001), 79–80.

16. American Medical Association, "Policy E-2, 06 Capital Punishment," http://www.ama-assn.org/ama1/pub/upload/mm/369/e206capitalpunish.pdf.

17. Davis, *Reshaping the Female Body*, 112–14.

18. Andy Beckett, "Suffering for Her Art," *Independent*, April 14, 1996, http://www.independent.co.uk/arts-entertainment/suffering-for-her-art-1304810.html.

19. Many of those who opt out of the managed care system, often by engaging in fee-for-service specialties such as cosmetic surgery, see themselves as experts, trained at great personal expense, and expecting a return on investment. On the importance of the shift from "social trustee professionalism" to "expert professionalism," see Dennis F. Thompson, *Restoring Responsibility: Ethics in Government, Business, and Healthcare* (Cambridge: Cambridge University Press, 2005), 267–70.

20. Roberta J. Honigman, Katherine A. Phillips, and David J. Castle, "A Review of Psychosocial Outcomes for Patients Seeking Cosmetic Surgery," *Plastic and Reconstructive Surgery* 113, no. 4 (April 1, 2004): 1229.

21. Gilman, *Creating Beauty to Cure the Soul*.

22. Honigman, Phillips, and Castle, "A Review of Psychosocial Outcomes," 1229–37.

23. Marlene Rankin and Gregory Borah, "Psychological Complications: National Plastic Surgical Nursing Survey," *Plastic Surgical Nursing* 29, no. 1 (January–March 2009): 25–30.

24. Marlene Rankin, Gregory L. Borah, Arthur W. Perry, and Philip D. Wey, "Quality-of-Life Outcomes after Cosmetic Surgery," *Plastic and Reconstructive Surgery* 102, no. 6 (November 1998): 2139–45.

25. For the notion of "species-typical function," see Norman Daniels, *Just Health Care* (New York: Cambridge University Press, 1986), 33. For a critique of the use of "typicality" as a medical standard, see Anita Silvers, "A Fatal Attraction to Normalizing: Treating Disabilities as Deviations from 'Species-Typical' Functioning," in *Enhancing Human Traits: Ethical and Social Implications*, ed. Erik Parens (Washington, D.C.: Georgetown University Press, 1998), 93–123.

26. Joel Garreau, *Radical Evolution: The Promise and Peril of Enhancing Our Minds, Our Bodies and What It Means to Be Human* (New York: Doubleday, 2005). Garreau maintains that the acceleration of advances in computing and biology will bring dramatic changes in our lifetimes and almost certainly in the lifetimes of our children. Garreau and others describe the emergence of creatures "no longer like us," creatures he calls Transhumans or Posthumans. See, for example, 21–22.

27. Roy Porter, *Blood and Guts: A Short History of Medicine* (New York: W. W. Norton, 2002), 157–59.

28. Julian Savulescu and Guy Kahane, "The Moral Obligation to Create Children with the Best Chance of the Best Life," *Bioethics* 23, no. 5 (June 2009): 274–90, doi:10.1111/j.1467-8519.2008.00687.x.

29. Savulescu also outlines a number of other conditions that must be met for enhancement to be ethical in children. In particular, where possible, the intervention should be delayed until the child is of an age to make his or her own decisions. The problem here is that, if the harm of not enhancing is as great as Savulescu maintains, then rarely will the importance of the child's autonomy overrule the presumed mandate to intervene in childhood, making decisions that the child might or might not have made when grown.

30. At this point, the optimization defense comes very close to the idea that cosmetic surgery is justified because it provides the means to make us subjectively happy. On the psychological model, a finer appearance makes us feel better about ourselves. The optimization model introduces an intermediary step. Improved appearance leads to personal or professional success, which in turn is presumed to enhance personal satisfaction or "happiness." While this point cannot be pursued here, the biomedical discussion of enhancement would profit from a more philosophical reflection on what constitutes human flourishing and some attention to the history of this discussion.

31. Eric T. Juengst, "What Does 'Enhancement' Mean?" in Parens, *Enhancing Human Traits*, 29.

32. Norman M. Wall, "Stealing from the Poor to Care for the Rich," editorial, *New York Times*, December 14, 2005, http://www.nytimes.com/2005/12/14/opinion/14walln.html.

33. Juengst, "What Does 'Enhancement' Mean," 29.

34. Frederick M. Grazer and Rudolph H. de Jong, "Fatal Outcomes from Liposuction: Census Survey of Cosmetic Surgeons," *Plastic and Reconstructive Surgery* 105, no. 1 (January 2000): 436–46.

35. Fred Schulte and Jenni Bergal, "Lack of Regulations Heightens Surgical Risks—Cosmetic Office Procedures Largely Go Unregulated Because the State Has No Way to Track Them," *Fort Lauderdale Sun Sentinel,* November 30, 1998, http://articles.sun-sentinel.com/1998-11-30/news/9811250800_1_tummy-tucks-surgeons-plastic.

36. Garreau, *Radical Evolution*, 35–38.

37. For recommendations on addressing these concerns, see my "Cosmetic Surgery," 170–72.

9. The Bronze Age Revisited: The Aesthetics of Sun Tanning

JO ELLEN JACOBS

In an episode of *The Twilight Zone* entitled "The Eye of the Beholder," a woman has plastic surgery to become "beautiful."[1] Yet, when she is unwrapped, her classically symmetrical face appalls the other characters. This society believes that asymmetrical faces are beautiful. When asked which kind of face they prefer, the characters always select the lopsided; they even undergo surgery to achieve unevenness. The television audience finds this evaluation odd, at best. We want to know if there was some utilitarian, religious, or other nonaesthetic basis for these judgments, since the aesthetic preference for symmetry is universal, and is *not* in the eye of the beholder.[2]

The preference for women with pale skin is also universal. Anthropologist Peter Frost surveyed over seventy cultures in his book *Fair Women, Dark Men: The Forgotten Roots of Color Prejudice*, and discovered that in every culture, in every era, in every ethnic group, women's beauty is linked with the lightest complexion found within the group.[3] This is true except for one bizarre culture: European and American Caucasian culture of the past one hundred years, in which there has been a strong preference for women with tanned skin. This is just as unexpected a preference as one for crookedness, so why do these particular people prefer women with browner skin rather than coloring that occurs without sun exposure?

Other than symmetry and paleness of women, there are few other judgments of bodily beauty that are universal.[4] Most beauty practices, e.g., tattooing, makeup, hair ornamentation, and clothing fashion, are notoriously variable, differing from one culture to another and sometimes changing quickly within a given culture. A preference for bellbottoms gives way to one for skinny jeans, heavily made-up eyes yield to a natural look, pierced ears give way to pierced noses, perms lose ground to straightened hair—all such styles can change in a few years or even a few weeks in a commercially driven culture such as the United States. People may either resist or follow a fad for both political and aesthetic reasons; reasons for disparaging universal marks of beauty in favor of the opposite must be even more compelling than those for complying with fashion. In this essay I hope to answer several questions: Other things being equal, why are the lightest women considered the most beautiful? Why have Caucasian women preferred dark skin during the past century?[5] What does tanning mean in the context of current beauty norms? I argue that sun tanning is deeply tied to questions of race, class, and gender in ways that make this behavior a reflection of women's struggle to define themselves in twentieth-century Euro-American culture.

The Universal Desire for Light

Marc Lappe is correct when he points out that "the adornment and beautification of the skin is a fundamental cultural need."[6] Changing our skin color may be one of the earliest human decorative acts. Recently, scientists discovered that South African women altered their body color with makeup made from "reddish or pinkish-brown" crushed rock as early as 164,000 years ago.[7] Whether through tattooing, piercing, dying, or applying makeup, humans have sought to beautify themselves by altering their skin, usually in ways that heighten their sexual attractiveness.[8]

Furthermore, nearly all animals sunbathe. Although scientists are not sure why, William Hamilton notes, "one is tempted to conclude that the advantage [sunbathing] provides, whatever it may be, is available to all animal life."[9] Scientists know that some humans desire to lie in the sun or in a tanning booth because they are getting high on the experience. In fact, researchers at Wake Forest University have shown that one can be addicted to the endorphin production that is triggered by exposure to UV light, explaining why tanners sometimes report, "It makes me feel alive," "It makes me feel like there's nothing that can go wrong," and "I always felt better about myself."[10] Exposure to UV light, either from the sun or in a booth, also makes us feel sexier.[11] These biochemical changes may also explain why humans in all cultures have consistently worshipped the sun.

However, despite these physical reasons for being attracted to being in the sun and a deeply ingrained desire to change skin color, humans have universally rejected the aesthetic of tanned women—in every ethnic group, whether subjected to colonization or not. Ten thousand years ago, all humans were brown;[12] then two separate mutations led to the development of lighter-colored peoples in Europe and Asia.[13] Yet all ethnic groups around the globe prefer the palest females in the group, with the notable exception of Euro-Americans in the last century.

In addition to producing different skin tones among groups of people, evolution has resulted in fairer-skinned women than men in every ethnic group.[14] This difference may be due to women's greater need for previtamin D3, which is required to support pregnancy and which is produced through exposure to sunlight. Furthermore, men's sexual arousal is, well, pretty obvious to anyone around, but women's is more subtle. Women demonstrate their sexual readiness through blushing and flushing—features that are more readily apparent in lighter women. One example is Karen Connelly, a Caucasian Canadian who, in a journal of her year in Thailand, writes about her crush on a Thai teacher: "because I'm so white, my blushing is even worse than a Thai girl's."[15] In another example, various cultures, including Victorian England, have denigrated makeup for women because it hides this sexual signal—or proof of innocence, as they perceived it.

In addition, babies are the most fair skinned within each ethnic group. The instinct to protect the young is hard-wired in adults, so, by choosing to remain as pale as possible, women may be trying to signal the same need for protection (particularly in monogamous societies). And women's skin darkens during pregnancy and remains marginally darker after pregnancy, so the palest skin advertises nulligravidity.[16] Finally, women are palest during the most fecund part of their cycle, signaling their sexual availability.[17] For whatever evolutionary reason, sexual dimorphism of skin color is a fact. It appears with puberty and is heightened during ovulation. Biology in this case gives rise to or supports an aesthetic, since there is a universal preference for lighter-skinned women.[18] (This sexual dimorphism has been recognized by every painting tradition in the history of the art.)

Just as the biological fact that men are hairier than women may be culturally enhanced by shaving, plucking, or waxing, so the biological differences in skin tone have been enhanced by makeup, sun avoidance, and other means of heightening the paleness of women's skin throughout human history. From ancient history until today, from Africa to Asia to Oceania, the vast majority of women in the world try to acquire as light a skin as they can, by avoiding sun exposure, by using parasols, long sleeves, gloves, and hats, or by using billions of dollars' worth of skin bleaching or lightening creams. There are even lotions to make nipples pinker, and underarm deodorants with skin whiteners! (Ironically, some of these are as harmful as sun tanning.)[19]

Although there may be biological foundations for a preference for paleness, there are cultural reasons for it as well. The preference for lighter skin is discussed and decried by African American and Asian American authors as well as by African, Latina, and Asian women. For example, in *Is Lighter Better? Skin-Tone Discrimination among Asian Americans*, Joanne Rondilla and Paul Spickard write, "The worship of tanned bodies is a Euro-American fetish, not one honored by Asian American families and communities," in part because of the colorism in Asian and Asian American groups.[20] Marita Golden, throughout her memoir *Don't Play in the Sun*, chronicles her resistance to the preference for light skin within her African American community.[21] And Margaret L. Hunter analyzes colorism among African Americans and Mexican Americans in *Race, Gender, and the Politics of Skin Tone*.[22] Light skin is seen as more beautiful and results in better pay and better marriage opportunities, among other social and economic consequences. Lawrence Otis Graham describes the ways that African American associate light skin with higher class status in *Our Kind of People*.[23] Others have argued that the association of pale skin with the need for protection has racial overtones in a multiracial society in which a white aesthetic "implicitly supported the defamation and sexual abuse of black women by white men."[24] Finally, Cedric Herring, Verna Keith, and Hayward Derrick Horton have put together an anthology to discuss the economic, social, and political elements of skin tone in *Skin Deep: How Race and Complexion Matter in the "Color-Blind" Era*.[25]

An ethnic group's preference for pale skin among its members has complex roots, including colonialism and favoritism shown to the lighter-skinned children of darker slaves and their lighter owners. It is a painful reminder of the racism that simmers in American culture and of the remnants of colonialism around the world. However, the desire for lighter-skinned women appears even in cultures that have never experienced either of these sad practices. The aesthetic preference that women's skin be as light as possible is not politically neutral, but it is (nearly) universal. Most Caucasian women in Europe, the United States, and Australia shared this aesthetic taste for paleness until the turn of the twentieth century. In all these cases, the desire for light skin is produced by a combination of evolutionary predispositions and cultural pressures.

I must leave a more complete discussion of the aesthetics of skin lightening to more capable hands, and turn to the other two questions of this paper:

what happened to change the desire for lightness in one group of people during one historical period, and what does this change mean?[26]

Social Class and Sun Tanning

The development of a cultural preference for tanned Caucasian women begins in the early twentieth century. The history of tanning reveals that this practice has several sources: medical prescriptions to tan as a means to cure tuberculosis, the invention of the vacation and the development of travel technology that allowed the middle classes to spend time on beaches, advertising that sold middle-class women a look that had originally been adopted by the upper class, and the industrial revolution that changed class perceptions, plus the added effects of youth culture, sports and beach culture, and consumer culture. As in a game of pick-up sticks, we need to carefully distinguish each part of this story—a story in which class plays an omnipresent role.

Fair skin had always been associated with the upper class, since peasants are the ones relegated to working in the sun, and this association continues to be the reason most cultures cite as a reason to prefer lighter skin. However, the industrial revolution meant the working classes began working in factories during daylight hours and hence were pallid, while the upper classes were free to enjoy leisure by playing tennis, riding horses, and yachting in the sun. The changed settings of work and play meant that the upper classes could redefine beauty as something other than fair skin.

In this same period there were advances in transportation, in particular the railroad, and increases in disposable income for the middle classes that allowed changes in their leisure activity as well, including more people flocking to warmer, sunnier climates, such as the south of France, for vacations. Even the concept of a "vacation" itself, for working people, was developed at this time.

The shift in aesthetic for the upper class is recorded in the bronzed skin of the characters in F. Scott Fitzgerald's *Tender Is the Night*, which is set on the Riviera. The novel begins with a description of a hotel near Cannes in June 1925. This hotel had generally catered to northern Europeans during the winter, but had begun opening in the summer two years before. Rosemary, a teenage American film star, arrives at the hotel with "her pink palms and her cheeks lit to a lovely flame, like the thrilling flush of children after their cold baths in the evening. . . . the color of her cheeks was real," but she immediately heads for the beach, where "a tanned woman with very white teeth looked down at her" making her "suddenly conscious of the raw whiteness of her own body." Rosemary wastes no time "broiling" her skin to the "ruddy, orange brown" color of Mrs. Diver's, despite being warned by "the untanned people . . . about getting burned the first day, . . . because *your* skin is important."[27] When we compare these passages to Elizabeth Barrett Browning's *Aurora Leigh*, written in 1857, the difference is astounding. Browning writes that "he, in his developed manhood, stood / A little sunburnt by the glare of life; / While I . . . it seemed no sun had shone on me."[28] Browning's association of suntan with activity contrasts with Fitzgerald's record of the birth of a new aesthetic among the upper classes in the 1920s.

As the century progresses, the look, like most fashion trends, gets sold to the middle and lower classes. Since tanning could be done on weekends in the backyard or up on the roof, it was equivalent to a free makeover. As the middle classes earned more money after World War II, they could even take up beach culture. The bourgeois girls beat a path to the beach along with the boys.

Countless sources credit the legendary French fashion designer Coco Chanel with originating the fashion for deliberate "sun tanning." According to various versions of the story, in the 1920s Chanel was sailing with the Duke of Westminster and (supposedly accidentally) exposed her face to the sun. Making lemonade out of lemons, she reportedly cultivated the fashion of the suntan, by using "bronzed models" as mannequins for her clothing designs.[29] In his study of sun tanning, Kerry Segrave debunks this myth, since he can find no facts to support the claim, and credits the myth to an article in *Mademoiselle* magazine.[30] But Chanel clearly exhibited a feeling of freedom and advocated an abandonment of fashion rules that had corseted women's lives and kept them shrouded in cloth while in the sun. Chanel was a fashion icon, which meant she both reflected upper-middle-class cultural values and helped solidify them.

The other fashion guru of 1920s Paris was singer Josephine Baker, whose golden body suggests the possibility of a fashion preference for hybridity and the exotic, an issue that is discussed below.

Gender and Sun Tanning

Among several factors leading to the practice of intentionally exposing one's self to the sun for the purpose of changing the color of one's skin, otherwise known as "sun tanning," is a medical prescription. For centuries the sun has been worshipped for power but, as Segrave argues in *Suntanning in 20th-Century America*, "the single most important reason for the change (in attitude towards sun tanning) started around 1890 with the first medical reports that promoted the scientific view that the sun is a healer, with respect to tuberculosis, initially, and later rickets and various other ailments."[31] The 1903 Nobel Prize in Physiology or Medicine was given for the invention of the sun lamp.[32] Tuberculosis and syphilis both involve skin eruptions, and so the earliest dermatologists were also syphilologists. Tanning, prescribed for these and other skin diseases, came to be recommended more widely to help with the ultimate horror for women: zits.

In a book called *The Body Project*, Joan Jacobs Brumberg discusses the history of acne. Her thesis is that the Victorians stressed the "beauty" of good works over physical beauty for young girls, but that this began to change with the 1920s and Coco Chanel's emphasis on makeup, eyelash curlers, etc., including the compact mirror, "which allowed women to scrutinize and 'reconstruct' the face almost anywhere at a moment's notice."[33] In an era that introduced beauty pageants, women started becoming obsessed with pimples. Acne became medicalized and more or less cured by the beginning of the twenty-first century. Brumberg points out that "skin care was the first of many different body investments made by middle-class parents. Orthodontia, weight-loss camps, contact lenses, and plastic surgery all followed, revealing how parental resources have been harnessed in the twentieth century to a new ideal of physical perfection."[34]

Scientists now know that it is a very specific two-color combination of light waves that kills bacteria and helps heal acne. The full spectrum that would give you a tan is not required, although tanning involves exposure to these two helpful kinds of rays.[35] Tanning serves as both a kind of makeup to hide zits and a cure for the disease that might make you ugly. So an obsession with acne intertwines with an obsession with tanning.

The concern with acne combined with changes that took place in white, middle-class women's lives, as they were no longer secluded and protected but became part of the outside (and inside) work world and needed clothing that allowed such activity, and that therefore showed more skin. In addition, a new interest in sports, including swimming by both men and women, meant that uniforms and "costumes" were required that exposed more of the body. Every woman alive knows the agony of trying on a bathing suit. As we show more skin, the need for more self-discipline is required. As Brumberg notes,

This new freedom to display the body was accompanied, however, by demanding beauty and dietary regimens that involved money as well as self-discipline. Beginning in the 1920s, women's legs and underarms had to be smooth and free of body hair; the torso had to be svelte; and the breasts were supposed to be small and firm. What American women did not realize at the time was that their stunning new freedom actually implied the need for greater internal control of the body, an imperative that would intensify and become even more powerful by the end of the twentieth century.

The seeds of this cultural and psychological change from external to internal control of the body lie in vast societal transformations that characterized the move from agrarian to industrial society, and from a religious to a secular world.[36]

Fashion, including the fashion for sun tanning, reflected both the desire to be active and to be free of Victorian constraints, and the need for a new body discipline.

The Meaning of Tanning

What do tanned women mean? What political signal is being sent by their tan? Why would anyone choose to practice tanning, especially since it opposes the universal aesthetic preference? To answer these questions, I begin with the more fundamental question: What is it like to be a creature with skin?

A phenomenology of living with/in a skin is complex. The French performance artist ORLAN and transsexuals have taught us that the connection between our skin's shape and our identity is fluid.[37] Those at the edges—women and ethnic and sexual minorities—are often uncomfortable in their skin, the organ that both conceals and reveals us, that both holds us up for visual scrutiny and offers us a means of contact with others. Skin records time's passage yet sometimes allows time to reverse itself; we marvel as our wounds heal, sometimes without a trace. Skin allows us to receive and explore others. It protects and imprisons us.[38]

Our skin is more than a wrapper containing our innards; it is the biggest organ we have and the one that we spend the most time considering. Entire days go by without my thinking about my heart or liver, but most people, especially most women, think about their skin several times a day. And we pay for our skin with our money as well as our time. In fact, "depending on our age and social class, Americans spend 6–10 percent of their expendable income on cosmetic products."[39]

The hide that we hide in is also our vehicle of touch. We reach out to the world with our skin, and touch conveys a sense of reality unparalleled by our other senses. Pygmalion's Galatea gains her senses one by one, but it is only when she gains touch that she becomes real.[40] More than "life's traveling bag,"[41] skin allows us to fold in the world and unfold toward it—it is our "worldliness of being," according to Sara Ahmed and Jackie Stacey.[42]

Morris Berman points to the creation of the "I" when a child shifts from a kinesthetic to a visual way of being in the world. In our culture, fetuses move from the symbiotic "cosmic anonymity" to a childhood in which they are not in constant skin-to-skin contact with parents.[43] We expect babies to sleep separately and to eat on a schedule that is convenient for others, and so we nurture a self/other divide that gives rise to a recognition that I am here and that is there.

According to Berman, this shift to a visual sense of self results in what John Fowles calls a "nemo," an emptiness at the core, a void that demands to be filled.[44] Because no one wants to be a nobody, we fretfully avoid being silent or alone, for fear that we might have to confront our emptiness. So we experiment with religion, ambition, or consumerism, or we fill our days with television, text messaging, or telephoning. We no longer trust our "lower" senses, the senses of touch, smell, and taste, but see ourselves through mirrors, literal and metaphorical, as others see us, not as we live in our bodies. For example, we determine that we are overweight not from feelings of sluggishness, but by the mirror of mannequins at the mall. We have become schizoid, according to Rollo May, anesthetized, incapable of feeling from the inside.[45] I am simultaneously alienated from and reduced to the visual body.[46] As long as a judgment of beauty is merely a visual judgment of a body, we will continue to feel alienated from our bodies. Instead of feeling the joy of melding with another, I am an other for other others, and I know my body will never measure up as a visual object.

Visual Meaning

Let's explore the visual self. I look at my face in a mirror and see acne or wrinkles, and I make a judgment that the self is stressed or over the hill. Peiss joins Berman in claiming that the visual body has become a central paradigm for the self in the twentieth century. Beauty questionnaires ask women to rate "the real you—not as you think you are—but as others see you."[47] These questionnaires simply reflect the cultural emphasis on the visual as opposed to the kinesthetic. If we are visual selves, we can turn that vision into power. Leon Wurmser coins the term "delophilia" for "the desire to express oneself and to fascinate others by one's self-exposure, to show and to impress."[48] The phenomena of beauty pageants, strip clubs, the red-light district of Amsterdam, and porn booths that display women behind glass (as in the film *Paris, Texas*) are part of a culture that demands to see women without touching them, and in which women can gain some amount of power through visual display. By putting on an itsy-bitsy, teeny-weenie yellow polka-dot bikini and getting a great tan, a woman can create a visual surface that may yield power.[49]

That is, as long as the woman is young. The problem is that the visual surface starts to fall apart and reveal the real when she ages. Time materializes on the body.[50] The body is an archive.[51] It records a person's experiences of the world both permanently, through plastic surgery, tooth straightening, scars, piercings, tattoos, wrinkles, and sags, and temporarily through our decisions to dye our hair, wear contact lenses, bleach our teeth, apply makeup, or tan our skin. People offer their bodies to the world as a souvenir of their journey through life and the decisions they have made about what to do, what they care about, and how they see themselves. No desperate applications of Botox will prevent the accumulation of marks on the visual archive known as skin. Although skin has a remarkable ability to reverse time by darkening and then fading, or being scratched and then healing, ultimately time is unidirectional. The sags, wrinkles, and lines will become visible. Delophilia is a young person's game.

The Visual Goal Is Glow

Women who tan report that they desire to be a very specific color: not orange, nor brown per se, but golden, bronze, always glowing. The desire for radiance and luminescence reflects (pun intended) a spiritual connection that is worth exploring. Both Umberto Eco and Richard Dyer have recently highlighted the connection between beauty and light. Eco notes, "In the late Middle Ages Thomas Aquinas said . . . that beauty requires three things: proportion, integrity, and *claritas*—in other words clarity and luminosity." At this period of European history, light was associated with God, so beauty shared this characteristic of God. Light was also associated with the rich, whose jewels and clothes shimmered among the drab poor. According to Isidore of Seville's *Etymologies*, the word for physical beauty, *formosus*, is related to the word *formus*, denoting the heat that moves the blood and results in a beautiful complexion that is "not pale, but healthily pink."

Here we get an explicit statement of and justification for the beauty of pink skin and perhaps the beginning of the association of light with what would later be called "white" identity. Light is an aspect of the soul—a colorless, luminous being—whereas color is merely light reflected by the opaque body. Sweat shines and light is reflected off a body, whereas glow is part of the inner radiance that signifies the soul. Today's Caucasians' dread of shine and their hunger for glow mirrors this medieval aesthetic.[52]

Richard Dyer suggests that at the end of the nineteenth and the beginning of the twentieth century, with the development of artificial light and photography, Anglo-European culture had begun to equate knowledge and power with seeing.[53] In this century, light is not God's knowledge but human's. This technological development has not been blind to skin color. According to Dyer, "the photographic media and, *a fortiori*, movie lighting assume privilege and construct whiteness."[54] Film stock has and continues to be chosen specifically according to how well it records beige skin. From Hollywood to school pictures, to see is to see images of lighter people in a good light (literally) and darker people in a bad light. Photography and film also use light itself. In a slide show or movie theater we are seeing colored light on a white screen. In this medium, white subjects appear "illuminated and enlightened" and "without substance."[55]

In particular, "white" women were expected to glow, not shine. Dyer argues convincingly that "idealised white women are bathed in and permeated by light. It streams through them and falls on to them from above. In short, they glow."[56] Cosmetics aim to avoid shine while increasing radiance and luminescence. Glow is enhanced by blond hair and white clothing, as is especially seen in wedding attire—weddings are the ultimate photo op, in which the already discussed technical bias toward pale skin is enhanced with backlighting, soft focus, and gauzes to flatter the shimmering bride. Dyer offers examples of film stars, ballerinas (and their light-diffusing tutus), even photos of Diana, Princess of Wales, as examples of this ongoing desire to infuse white women with light.[57] I might add that the current obsession with sparkling white teeth is another way of accentuating "glow." All this adds up to the claim that women's desire to be radiant is concocted by a culture that has constructed whiteness as a dematerialized, virginal light that is best exemplified as a glowing woman. So, oddly, women might tan—if the result is that their blond hair, the whites of their eyes, their white teeth, and their white clothing increase their inner glimmer. They don't want to be brown; rather, they want to be luminescent, thus accentuating their visual whiteness.

The Visual Goal Is Hybridity

Or is tanning the opposite? Is tanning about women's rejection of the pale angel in the house? In short, is tanning about hybridity, about what Nalini Bhushan called "shrugging off race?"[58] Is there a conscious or unconscious urge to attain a universally recognized skin color, like the one depicted on a 1993 *Time* cover as "the new face of America"—a computer-generated combination of racial characteristics?[59] Dyer argues that hybridity is not a likely goal, since "the point about tanning is that the white person never becomes black. A tanned white person is just that—a white person who has acquired a darker skin. There is no loss of prestige in this . . . it also displays white people's right to be various."[60] Or, as Marita Golden writes in *Don't Play in the Sun,*

> I had seen the famous Coppertone ads for suntan lotion. I knew that White people worshipped the same sun that my mother warned me against. But I also knew that Whites' desire to possess a glaze of color in the summer did not mean they wanted to be Black. I knew that Whites could despise blackness and yearn for some measure of it at the same time.[61]

Compare the eagerness to darken pink skin to the ridicule heaped on darker-skinned people who lighten theirs—think of Michael Jackson, for example. Whites assume skin lightening is for the purpose of "passing," but tanning is not thought of as an attempt to pass for black. Tanned Caucasian women never dye their hair black, perm it into an "afro" hairstyle, and wear dark brown contact lenses in order to adopt a "black" aesthetic (although many blacks and whites mock those whites who wear dreadlocks or who aspire to become rappers).

Yet tanning allows white women to flirt with hybridity. After Coco Chanel, the second most influential woman of the 1920s in France was Josephine Baker, the African American jazz singer whose lightly bronzed skin was admired for its beauty. Just as many Caucasian women today cite Halle Berry as possessing the ideal skin color, so Baker became the hallmark of beautiful skin. The taste for the exoticism of tanned skin might be traced back to Flaubert's and Hugo's fascination with *les orientales* in the first half of the nineteenth century, accompanied by the golden figures in Delacroix's painting "Women of Algiers (in Their Apartment)" and other coffee-colored visions that contrasted sharply with the pale women of more conventional paintings from the period.[62] Here the aesthetic taste in literature and painting may have filtered into the real-world preferences for Josephine Baker and Coco Chanel fashion half a century later. Then Baker and Chanel spark the aesthetic choice of Caucasian women for nearly the next hundred years. The yearning for the exotic either in literature, painting, or the real-life choices of fashion are not merely to be scorned. Brown women had something more than a look to offer pale women.

White women might use tanning to paint on some substance, to go beyond the emptiness of their lives. Toni Morrison writes, "Whiteness alone, is mute, meaningless, unfathomable, pointless, frozen . . . senseless, implacable." Dyer comments, "Through the figure of the non-white person, whites can feel what being, physicality, presence, might be like, while also dissociating themselves from the non-whiteness of such things." Tanned women often highlight or bleach their hair, and the most beautiful also have blue eyes. They may be searching for just enough symbolic skin color to feel "alive," as the angels in the house are not, while never giving up the privileges of being labeled as white. If "the purity of whiteness may simply be the absence of being," then tanning may be an attempt to add some substance to this lack, to add some kinesthetic being by darkening their visual surface.[63]

The Visual Goal Is Resisting Patriarchy

Rose Weitz discusses how visual choices like hairstyles might be a way that women "seek power through resistance and accommodation," to paraphrase the subtitle of her essay. Weitz defines resistance as "actions that not only reject subordination but do so by challenging the ideologies that support that subordination." Makeup styles, tattooing, piercing, and other visual signals protest the system that imposes disciplinary practices, according to Weitz. "Like slaves' rebellious songs, women's rebellious hairstyles can allow them to distance themselves from the system that would subordinate them, to express their dissatisfaction, to identify like-minded others, and to challenge others to think about their own actions and beliefs."[64] Recall the earlier discussion of Rosemary's rejection of "the untanned people" at Cannes in 1925 in favor of the more risqué copper-colored crowd in Tender Is the Night.

The early-twentieth-century women's movement that gained American women the right to vote resulted in rebellion in the fashion world as well as the political arena. Porcelain beauties were read as vulnerable, weak, and refusing to be exposed, while tanned women were and are seen as physically fit, sexually powerful, and strong—in fact, these women have chosen to become closer in color to the average man, as I discussed earlier. As one ad claims (fig. 9.1), tanning is a way of literally getting even. Physiologically, that is correct.

Figure 9.1. Advertisement for a spray-on tanning product. By permission of Rimmel.

A tanned body is a kind of costume that a woman can temporarily adopt that says, "I don't need protection." A tan is a superwoman suit. A bronzed woman is powerful. As a fair woman, I can't help but exhibit my sexual feelings, thus giving up my power to the observer, while a bronzed woman is more in control of her sexual display. The woman decides when to have sex. Naomi Wolf goes so far as to characterize the contemporary warnings against skin cancer as a kind of fear-mongering intended to drive women back inside.[65] Women who tan seem to be making a conscious choice about their identity, choosing to control their image in a kind of living self-portrait.

The Visual Goal Is Accommodating Patriarchy

On the other hand, playing along with the visual game will also yield power through accommodation. Blondes do get the guy, pretty girls do get the job, skinny women do get promoted, and tanned females are seen as more alluring. This kind of accommodation is nevertheless "circumscribed, fragile, bittersweet, and limiting,"[66] and this becomes clear as we think further about tanning.

The late-nineteenth-century death of God leads to materialism and obsession with the body as opposed to the soul. Beauty is found only in the body. Forget "inner beauty." Women exchanged the outward control of their bodies by men — first father, then husband — for the inner self-control necessary to sculpt the body that they display to gain men's approval. Instead of an arranged marriage, the culture has created a meat market of women searing, steaming, sweating, suctioning, injecting, starving, and otherwise mutilating their bodies to attract men and keep them. Foucault's disciplinary practices, a hardship many women see as inevitable, lead to self-surveillance and self-conscious performances; they believe that control comes from changing their bodies for men's pleasure.[67] Tanning is simply one of the ways that this narcissism displays itself, and it happens in conjunction with a whole host of other disciplines of the body: makeup, revealing clothing, skin care, shaving, hair care, high-heeled shoes, stockings, contact lenses, plastic surgery, orthodontia, etc.

Margaret Hunter, in *Race, Gender, and the Politics of Skin Tone*, notes, "Beauty as an ideology also serves the interests of men because it maintains patriarchy as it divides women through competition and reduces their power."[68] Women who tan are always holding their arms next to each other to compare their tans or judging the progression of their tan by checking their tan lines, which serve as a meat thermometer for the skin. There is clearly a competition to achieve the perfect tan. A young male student of mine noted that when his peers hang out together they make comments like "She's a 6 [out of 10], but she'd be an 8 if she had a tan." Clearly men are aware that women compete for their attention, and women are aware of this competition as well—and skin color is an important determinant of desirability.

The visual meaning of tanning is confusing. A tan may suggest both a glow that highlights the special qualities of a white woman and, on the other hand, the desire for hybridity. Tanning both accommodates and resists patriarchal desire for women to look a particular way. When we turn to the kinesthetic meaning of tanning, is the message clearer?

Kinesthetic Meaning

The split between the visual self and the kinesthetic is one that begins in childhood and, according to Berman, results in everything from religious fundamentalism to a makeup industry whose profits could feed the world. The hunger for something more than the visual might paradoxically be the desire to tan the visual. But the kinesthetic can be cultivated. We can learn to live through our skin even as we tan.

Our body surface is what allows us to feel the other, whether it is sand, wind, sun, lotion, or the touch of another. We yearn to be marked by the environment. Lady Chatterley's lover isn't the only admirer of the smell of grass or the feel of rain or the hug of a friend. We want to have our borders crossed, to be touched, to be marked invisibly on the memory skin.[69] Those beauty practices designed only to prepare a visual surface are often painful, e.g., eyebrow plucking, bikini waxing, sleeping in hair rollers (am I dating myself?), eyelash curling, orthodontia. But there are beauty practices that feel good, e.g., having massages, applying moisturizers, and tanning while sitting at the edge of an ocean.

When people live in their skin and through their skin, they are deeply embodied, not existing merely as a thin surface. Beauty arises as an epiphenomenon of wholeness. And a person overcomes many paradoxes. She is deeply animalistic and spiritual simultaneously. When people do tai chi or yoga, they are a breathing body living that body fully, and yet they find spiritual understanding and peace. Meditation and sensuality, mind and body, are commingled. At the moment that people are most in their bodies, they are closest to sleeping, dreaming, and imagining.

This meditative sensuality can occur while tanning. The historical connection to sun worship is not to be overlooked. Lying in the sun on the grass in a park, or on a beach with the breeze on one's skin, feels good. Wiping on a tan would be like drinking nonalcoholic beer—what's the point? (And yet we do it.) Both tanning and drinking are supposed to be slightly intoxicating.

One other element of the erotic quality of tans is that whether in or out of the sun, becoming tanned almost inevitably involves touching others or ourselves. We massage oil, potions, lotions, sprays, and ointments into our own and each other's skin in order to tan and to maintain the color afterward. Seeing a tanned body—and of course smelling suntan lotion—brings to mind the sensuality of that contact just as Proust's madeleine does. Mattel sells a Cali Barbie that smells like the suntan lotion which she holds in her hand, but sun worshippers know that just a whiff of their favorite suntan oil suggests memories as pleasant and vivid as Proust's. In a visual age such as ours, any connection to human touch and smell is a welcome relief from the sterility of sight. The visual tan may be seen as beautiful merely because it offers a means of recalling the sensuality of attaining the tan—the kinesthetic beauty of tanning as a verb. We might not see our own tan or others' as beautiful if tans no longer pointed to the experience of tanning—if, for instance, we could take a pill to attain an instant tan, thus erasing the connection between tan and touch.[70]

Humans often are just "here and now" when they lie or sit in the sun. They stop fussing about their ambitions, worrying about their finances, or even considering how good their hair looks. Everyone feels beautiful as they are massaged or lie in the sun or practice tai chi. These practices are about not creating a vision for others, but realizing the body/mind connection, i.e., making it real. People feel wholly present. They stop resisting and judging others. They are open to the world as they care for—even mother—themselves. In a recent survey of American women carried out by Dove as part of the company's Campaign for Real Beauty, those who responded claimed that helping others made them feel beautiful.[71] They understood beauty not merely as a judgment of an object, but as a way of being in the world. Beauty stopped being an adjective describing a noun—whether face, body, or hair—and became an adverb modifying a verb—a way of living, moving, being. Seeing one's skin as an organ of sense rather than only a visible surface has moral implications. People who understand skin this way must touch others and ask to be touched, sensitively and respectfully. Beauty is a judgment of a life, not a visual surface.

The Contradictory Meaning of Tanning

Lying on the beach slathered in SPF 50 suntan lotion to prevent tanning will offer only sensual joys, while a trip to a salon for a spray-on tan will result only in visual accommodation. Usually those in Euro-American culture are caught between these symbolic acts. Women taking off most of their clothes in public and jogging down the beach might be protesting the patriarchal preference for the Victorian pale flower in the house, yet they might also be competing with other women for men's attention. Tanners thumb a bronzed nose at capitalism's pursuit of the almighty dollar by celebrating a free beauty enhancement and cure for acne, but feed capitalism by buying billions dollars' worth of lotions, tanning beds, and bikinis. A tanned woman denies men the ability to read her sexual excitement and demands the right to display her body and to play with sexuality, even touch herself erotically in public, yet must discipline her body into anorexia to look acceptable in a swimming suit as she plays the pinup. Tan skin says "I'm not a child" and reflects the play of time (forward and backward) on our skin, allowing a woman to recall the endorphin rush that attaining this color involved, while it also indicates a willingness to risk skin cancer.

In *Accommodating Protest*, Arlene Macleod relies on Foucault's analysis to understand why the contradictory emerges in the struggle to confront modern power. She asks the question that all women today face: "How can we deal with the somewhat disturbing realization that women are active, yet ambivalent, actors who wish to accommodate as well as resist?"[72]

This ambivalence is particularly apparent in beauty practices: we function between the "poles of victimization and self-invention, prison of beauty and play of makeup," as Peiss puts it in *Hope in a Jar*.[73] Thus, many women would agree with Susan Douglas, who says in *Where the Girls Are*, "I want to look beautiful" while simultaneously noting, "I think wanting to look beautiful is about the most dumb-ass goal you could have." Douglas argues that this ambiguity is the result of a generation's growing up in the age of mass media.

> American women today are a bundle of contradictions because much of the media imagery we grew up with was itself filled with mixed messages about what women should and should not do, what women could and could not be. . . . The media, of course, urged us to be pliant, cute, sexually available, thin, blond, poreless, wrinkle-free, and deferential to men. But it is easy to forget that the media also suggested we could be rebellious, tough, enterprising, and shrewd. And much of what we watched was porous, allowing us to accept *and* rebel against what we saw and how it was presented.

This double message was particularly true in the commercial response to the women's movement after the 1960s.

> The appropriation of feminist desires and feminist rhetoric by Revlon, Lancôme, and other major corporations was nothing short of spectacular. Women's liberation metamorphosed into female narcissism unchained as political concepts and goals like liberation and equality were collapsed into distinctly personal, private desires. . . . Get *truly* liberated: put yourself first.[74]

This narcissism leads to working on your tan rather than finishing your philosophy paper or volunteering for a domestic violence shelter.

Commercialization also plays a role in whether a practice is resistant or accommodative. "One of capitalism's great strengths—perhaps its greatest—is its ability to co-opt and domesticate opposition, to transubstantiate criticism into a host of new, marketable products."[75] It did this with fitness as well as tanning. Even if a fashion was initially intended to challenge, the more widely it is adopted, the more it loses power as a protest. Spiked green hair, pierced lips, and masculine clothing (like Annie Hall's) cease to indicate a refusal to play the standard visual game and become just another fashion sold to the masses and diluted in the process.

When Euro-American women first tanned in the 1920s, the fashion was part of women's choosing to bare their legs, cut their hair, wear makeup, and vote. It was a declaration of independence, of the right of every woman to be mobile and public. But by the time tan lines became a feature of Playboy centerfolds in the 1960s, a tan was just another beauty discipline of the ideal body: anorexic, smooth-skinned, blonde, with long straight hair and tan skin. Caucasian women had to "work" on our tans just as we had to worry about our zits and wash out the orange juice cans with which to roll our hair—and just as African, African American, Asian, and Asian American women had to work to stay out of the sun. "Turning on its head the feminist argument that the emphasis on beauty undermines women's ability to be taken seriously and to gain control over their lives, advertisers now assured women that control *comes* from cosmetics"[76]—including tanning beds, bronzers, self-tanners, spray-on tans, and tanning pills.

So why have Caucasian women preferred to have tanned skin during the past century? Originally these women were loudly and visibly protesting an identity foisted on them—an identity that is still urged on women around the globe where the biology of sexual dimorphism is insisted upon in an aesthetic prescription for paleness. Those who tanned were defining a new woman who was visually different and who reflected the unity of mind and body, of kinesthetic sensuality and meditative quality. They discovered a competing biology to which to attach this new aesthetic, the endorphin surge provided by UV light. Yet this original impulse to resist the Victorian patriarchal aesthetic was diluted as tanning became absorbed in the commercial world, and women ended up accommodating a visual game not of their own making.

What does tanning symbolize? What it symbolizes depends on the era and the woman. It usually points toward resistance to as well as accommodation of patriarchal values. It signifies Caucasian women's insecurity as well as their desire to be autonomous; they hide behind a coat of copper so that they have some ability to paint their own self-portrait. It may signal a desire for hybridity or an assertion of their white luminescence. The aesthetics of tanning is as complex as women themselves.

The Future of Tanning

What is the future of tanning? In United States publications, particularly at the high end of the product and brand spectrum, extremely white ("glowingly white") models have recently begun appearing (fig. 9.2). Does this signal a change in the standards and ideology of beauty? Is it a backlash of "whiteness," with class and racial significance? Recent advertisements for Evian water ("Return to Purity") featuring a very white woman lying in snow, Burberry advertisements with collections of very pale men and women, and shots from the latest *Vogue* may indicate that tanning is only a hundred-year blip in Euro-American aesthetics.[77] Perhaps, if Susan Faludi is correct, the aftermath of 9/11 involves a return to Victorian values, including—although Faludi does not mention this—pale women.[78] Perhaps the vicissitudes of the global economy may be driving advertisers to embrace the more widely accepted aesthetic of light skin for women. With these images surrounding them, will Europeans and Americans abandon the bronze age? Or will Asians join the fad for tanning? Both Chinese and Japanese women have recently shown interest in tanning. Or maybe the giant Revlon makeup corporation's choice of Halle Berry and Julianne Moore as representatives points toward more tolerance of differences.

But the future isn't just in the hands of the advertisers; it is in women's hands as well. Macleod asks, "How can alternatives not only emerge, but gain the power to engage belief and encourage action?" Her answer: in order to change the world, people need alternative views of how humans

Figure 9.2. Advertisement for Evian spring water.

exist in the world and social structures to support those views.[79] I am suggesting that one alternative view is a view of ourselves as whole, embodied humans. Embodied means not a fixed identity or impermeability but an ongoing penetration of outer and inner, and a recognition of the fluidity of identities. People change who they are by changing how they look, and they reflect who they are in how they look to others. The fact that people reflect and change their identities through their appearances is not to be regretted. Humans are visual beings in the world and they see themselves as well as seeing others see them. This is part of their identity. But the kinesthetic experience of the world needs nourishing. The media focus on the visual can be overwhelming. The danger is that humans will accommodate patriarchy without any protest.

Kinesthetic beauty is a kind of *wabi* aesthetic. It acknowledges the passage of time and the ongoing changes that result from the materialization of time in objects and in people. Visual perfection is not the goal. In fact, perfection is boring, even ugly. The tan lines that allow a person to remember activity in the sunlight and allow others to imagine that past activity are visual reminders of an endorphin rush. These visual imperfections will fade and be replaced by other marks, scars, lines, and creases, each of which enhance the patina of my life in skin—no matter what color my skin is "naturally."

NOTES

1. This example and many of the ideas in this paper were suggested by Constance Kirker. We collaborated on a presentation on this topic for the International Aesthetics Conference in Turkey, July 2007. Although the writing in this paper is mine, a great deal of fruitful discussion preceded it. This paper would not exist without Constance's input.

2. Preference for symmetry is not merely cultural; it can be found, for example, among the hunter-gatherer Hadza people as well as those from the United Kingdom (Anthony C. Little, Coren L. Apicella, and Frank W. Marlowe, "Preferences for Symmetry in Human Faces in Two Cultures: Data from the UK and the Hadza, an Isolated Group of Hunter-Gatherers," *Proceedings of the Royal Society B* 274, no. 1629 [December 22, 2007]: 3113–17).

3. Peter Frost, *Fair Women, Dark Men: The Forgotten Roots of Color Prejudice* (Christchurch, New Zealand: Cybereditions, 2005), vii. Frost notes only three exceptions: preference for dark women because they are seen as harder workers, bias against albinos, and the sun tanning cultures I discuss.

4. Other universally approved features might include smoothness of skin, skin luminosity, and ratio of distance between the eyes to distance from eyes to mouth.

5. I will focus in this section only on those who wish to darken their skin through tanning. Usually these are European or Euro-American Caucasians—but not exclusively, since Jennifer Lopez, Selma Hayek, and Halle Berry, for example, all tan.

6. Marc Lappe, *Body's Edge: Our Cultural Obsession with Skin* (New York: Henry Holt, 1996), 169.

7. Curtis W. Marean et al., "Early Human Use of Marine Resources and Pigment in South Africa during the Middle Pleistocene," *Nature* 449 (October 18, 2007): 905–908.

8. Lappe, *Body's Edge*, 170–71.

9. William J. Hamilton, *Life's Color Code* (New York: McGraw Hill, 1973), 75.

10. Mandeep Kaur, Anthony Liguori, Wei Lang, Stephen R. Rapp, Alan B. Fleischer, and Steven R. Feldman, "Induction of Withdrawal-Like Symptoms in a

Small, Randomized, Controlled Trial of Opioid Blockade in Frequent Tanners," *Journal of the American Academy of Dermatology* 54, no. 4 (April 2006): 709–11.

11. "Animal studies suggest that increased exposure to sunlight is a stimulant to sexual drive. . . . In humans, exposure to sunlight over the body often results in a sense of well-being and improved self-esteem which, in turn, may affect sexual self-esteem" (Loren R. Pickart, "Compositions and Methods for Skin Tanning and Protection," U.S. Patent 5,698,184, filed August 23, 1996, and issued December 16, 1997, http://www.patentstorm.us/patents/5698184-description.html).

12. Nancy Etcoff, *Survival of the Prettiest: The Science of Beauty* (New York: Anchor, 1999), 115.

13. Rick Weiss, "Scientists Find a DNA Change That Accounts for White Skin," *Washington Post*, December 16, 2005; and Nicholas Wade, "Gene That Determines Skin Color Is Discovered, Scientists Report," *New York Times*, December 16, 2005.

14. Frost, *Fair Women, Dark Men*, 54–60.

15. Karen Connelly, *Touch the Dragon* (Winnipeg: Turnstone, 1992), 150.

16. Claudia Benthien, *Skin: On the Cultural Border between Self and the World* (New York: Columbia University Press, 2002), 177.

17. Nancy Etcoff, *Survival of the Prettiest* (New York: Anchor Books, 1999), 105.

18. In *Primates and Philosophers* (Princeton: Princeton University Press, 2006), Frans de Waal argues for recognition that morality evolved from some basic emotions already seen in some apes and chimps. The universal aesthetic preference for luminescent women is perhaps also based in biology.

19. Thomas Fuller, "A Vision of Pale Beauty Carries Risks for Asia's Women," *New York Times International*, May 14, 2006. The 1887 *White House Cook Book*, by F. L. Gillette and Hugo Ziemann (Chicago: Werner, 1887), includes a concoction of horseradish and sour milk that promises to "[bleach] the complexion . . . and [take] off tan" (531).

20. Joanne L. Rondilla and Paul Spickard, *Is Lighter Better? Skin-Tone Discrimination among Asian Americans* (New York: Rowman & Littlefield, 2007), 2. "Colorism" is a prejudice for lighter skin within an ethnic or "racial" group.

21. Marita Golden, *Don't Play in the Sun: One Woman's Journey through the Color Complex* (New York: Doubleday, 2004).

22. Margaret L. Hunter, *Race, Gender, and the Politics of Skin Tone* (New York: Routledge, 2005).

23. Lawrence Otis Graham, *Our Kind of People: Inside America's Black Upper Class* (New York: HarperPerennial, 2000).

24. Kathy Peiss, *Hope in a Jar: The Making of America's Beauty Culture* (New York: Henry Holt, 1998), 208.

25. Cedric Herring, Verna Keith, and Hayward Derrick Horton, *Skin Deep: How Race and Complexion Matter in the "Color-Blind" Era* (Urbana: University of Illinois Press, 2004).

26. Much more needs to be done on the aesthetics of skin lightening, but the main focus of this paper is on skin darkening.

27. F. Scott Fitzgerald, *Tender Is the Night* (New York: Charles Scribner's Sons, 1933), 3–7.

28. Elizabeth Barrett Browning, *Aurora Leigh* (London: J. Miller, 1864), book 4, ll. 1139–41.

29. The claim about Coco and the beginning of sun tanning is nearly ubiquitous on internet sites on the history of sun tanning, always without citing any source. It appears in books as well, again without a source citation. For example, in *Art Deco of the Palm Beaches* (Charleston, S.C.: Arcadia, 2007), Sharon Koskoff claims, "In 1920s France . . . Coco Chanel was 'bronzed' on a yacht" (2).

30. Kerry Segrave, *Suntanning in 20th-Century America* (Jefferson, N.C.: McFarland, 2005), 4. The title of the chapter is "Coco Chanel Had Nothing to Do With It."

31. Ibid., 180.

32. Lappe, *Body's Edge*, 191.

33. Joan Jacobs Brumberg, *The Body Project: An Intimate History of American Girls* (New York: Random House, 1997), 70.

34. Ibid., 94.

35. Does the fact that the use of drugs and phototherapy has made acne far less prevalent mean that we can now stop tanning?

36. Brumberg, *The Body Project*, 98.

37. Sara Ahmed and Jackie Stacy, *Thinking through the Skin* (New York: Routledge, 2001), 8–9. ORLAN's work can be seen at http://www.orlan.net.

38. Benthien, *Skin*, 236.

39. Lappe, *Body's Edge*, 172.

40. Benthien, *Skin*, 197.

41. Ibid., 241.

42. Ahmed and Stacey, *Thinking through the Skin*, 3.

43. Morris Berman, *Coming to Our Senses* (New York: Bantam, 1990), 19–62.

44. Ibid., 20.

45. Rollo May, *Love and Will* (New York: W. W. Norton, 1969), 13–33.

46. Benthien, *Skin*, 31.

47. Peiss, *Hope in a Jar*, 144.

48. Ibid., 100.

49. There is a debate about the visual role of tan lines. Those who like tan lines insist that they involve erotic play. Tan lines reveal which parts have been exposed, and which hidden. They play with the observer's imagination — which is at the heart of any sense of beauty. A "farmer's tan," with white legs and torso but darkened hands, face, and neck (a literal "redneck"), signals our work, not our play — thus these tan lines are seen as a curse. Tan lines from a bathing suit reveal just how much of your body you were willing to display to get the tan and thus hint at your willingness to offer yourself up, luxuriating in the sun and seducing others with the result.

50. Ahmed and Stacey, *Thinking through the Skin*, 2.

51. Paul Solomon, "The Body as Archive," display of photographs at the Allens Lane Art Center, Philadelphia, 2001. Two of these photographs are available at http://www.cfa.wmich.edu/dearts/solomon/bodyas/index.html.

52. Umberto Eco, *History of Beauty* (New York: Rizzoli, 2005), 100, 102–104, 105–10, 113, 129.

53. Richard Dyer, *White* (New York: Routledge, 1997), 103–104.

54. Ibid., 89.

55. Ibid., 110. Crime videos literally show police (typically white) "in a better light" than any (darker-skinned) criminal. Compare this with the ways that Chilean-born Alfredo Jaar displays his photos, using backlighting, mirrors, and reflections from water as a way of showing the beauty of the dark skin of Rwandan Africans and South American gold miners (http://www.alfredojaar.net/).

56. Ibid., 122.

57. Ibid., 125–42.

58. Nalini Bhushan, "An Indian in Paris: Toward the Development of a Cosmopolitan Aesthetic in Colonial India," paper presented at the annual conference of the American Society for Aesthetics, November 2007, and published as "Toward a Development of a Cosmopolitan Aesthetic," in "Aesthetics and Race: New Philosophical Perspectives," ed. Monique Roelofs, special volume 2, *Contemporary Aesthetics* (2009), http://www.contempaesthetics.org/newvolume/pages/article.php?articleID=557.

59. *Time*, November 18, 1993, cover available at http://www.time.com/time/covers/0,16641,19931118,00.html.

60. Dyer, *White*, 49.

61. Golden, *Don't Play in the Sun*, 10.

62. Alain de Botton, *The Art of Travel* (New York: Pantheon, 2002), 69–91, discusses exoticism in nineteenth-century France, but doesn't connect it to tanning.

63. Dyer, *White*, 80.

64. Rose Weitz, "Women and Their Hair: Seeking Power through Resistance and Accommodation," in *The Politics of Women's Bodies: Sexuality, Appearance, and Behavior*, ed. Rose Weitz (Oxford: Oxford University Press, 2003), 137.

65. Naomi Wolf, *The Beauty Myth: How Images of Beauty Are Used Against Women* (New York: Doubleday, 1991), 105–106.

66. Weitz, "Women and Their Hair," 141.

67. Sandra Lee Bartky, "Foucault, Femininity, and the Modernization of Patriarchal Power," in Weitz, *The Politics of Women's Bodies*, 37.

68. Hunter, *Race, Gender, and the Politics of Skin Tone*, 5.

69. Benthien, *Skin*, 220; and Ahmed and Stacey, *Thinking through the Skin*, 42.

70. Scientists at the University of Arizona created a pill to increase the production of melatonin—that is, to actually make people tanner, not just paint on a dye, which is what "sunless tanning" products do. The goal was to enable light-skinned people in areas where they are particularly susceptible to sunburn, such as Australia (because of ozone depletion), to take the pill to become tan and hence avoid the sun damage that leads to skin cancer. Little did they know that the "side effects" would be to make one thinner, reduce pain, and heighten the libido! If the point of tanning is the aesthetic look of tanned bodies, this pill will be the answer—a true tan without the sun's damage (Wil McCarthy, "Thin! Tan! Hotter Than Hell!" *Wired* 10, no 6 (June 2002), http://www.wired.com/wired/archive/10.06/melanotan.html; for a scientific analysis, see the article on Melanotan-II on WebMD.com).

71. Dove is a maker of makeup products; its Campaign for Real Beauty includes an advertising campaign to promote healthy conceptions of beauty as well as research

into perceptions of beauty around the world. The survey was discussed in Nancy Etcoff, Susie Orbach, Jennifer Scott, and Heidi D'Agostino, "The Real Truth about Beauty: A Global Report," white paper commissioned by Dove, September 2004, 30–42.

72. Arlene Elowe Macleod, *Accommodating Protest: Working Women, the New Veiling, and Change in Cairo* (New York: Columbia University Press, 1991), 142, 162.

73. Peiss, *Hope in a Jar*, 268.

74. Susan J. Douglas, *Where the Girls Are: Growing Up Female with the Mass Media* (New York: Three Rivers, 1994), 9, 246.

75. Ibid., 260.

76. Ibid., 254.

77. The change from tanned to pale models occurred in 2007. Sampling the Louis Vuitton advertisements in *Vogue*'s May issues from 2003 to 2007, for example, we find that the models are all tanned until 2007 (*Vogue*, May 2003, p. 79; May 2004, pp. 6–7; May 2005, pp. 2–3; May 2006, pp. 6–7; and May 2007, pp. 6–7). One Burberry advertisement appears in *Vogue*, August 2007, pp. 54–55. Evian's "Return to Purity" ad can be found in many magazines, including *Allure*, September 2006, p. 120.

78. Susan Faludi, *The Terror Dream* (New York: Metropolitan, 2007).

79. Macleod, *Accommodating Protest*, 162.

10. ¿Tienes Culo? How to Look at Vida Guerra

KARINA L. CÉSPEDES-CORTES AND PAUL C. TAYLOR

> I am a marked woman but not everybody knows my name. "Peaches" and "Brown Sugar," "Sapphire" and "Earth Mother," "Aunty," "Granny," God's "Holy Fool," a "Miss Ebony First," or "Black Woman at the Podium": I describe a locus of confounded identities, a meeting ground of investments and privations in the national treasury of rhetorical wealth. My country needs me, and if I were not here, I would have to be invented.
> —Hortense J. Spillers, "Mama's Baby, Papa's Maybe" (1987)

Vida Guerra (fig. 10.1) is a Cuban model from northern New Jersey. She made her name in hiphop videos and in "gentlemen's magazines" but quickly became an intermedial supermodel, with her own calendars, making-of-the-calendar DVDs, official website, fan websites, television show, and controversy over a "leaked" nude photo.[1] Unlike most of the other women who appear in these settings, she has managed to gather admirers from multiple sites for the consumption of heteromasculine erotica despite the underappreciated racial divides between them. She has moved from white-owned "laddie" magazines like *FHM* and *Maxim* to the analogous black and Latino publications, like *King* and *Open Your Eyes* (*OYE*); she has appeared in black hiphop videos, in a Comedy Central parody of a black hiphop video (on "The Chappelle Show"), and on Spanish television's top celebrity show, *El gordo y la flaca*; and she has starred in a straight-to-video sex farce from National Lampoon—a fact that earned a film largely by and for young white men a cover feature in *Black Men* magazine.[2]

Figure 10.1. Vida Guerra, *FHM* 8, no. 1
(January–February 2007), 109.

The editors of *OYE* explain the key to Guerra's popularity by reminding their readers that

> when Sir Mix-A-lot introduced the phrase "I like big butts and I cannot lie"
> into the psyche of the horny American male, [the] idea of classic, stick-fig-
> ured beauty was shucked aside for rumps with bumps. . . . Jennifer Lopez,
> whose ass carries more earthquake insurance than all of Southern California,

has carried the burden of our desire for butts everywhere. You may now move over J-Lo, and make way for Vida.[3]

Vida, in short, *tiene culo*, to borrow the Spanish slang that adorns one of her virally distributed Internet images.[4]

Of course, this information about Guerra's body explains her popularity by raising additional questions. If the shape of her body makes her popular, what makes that shape popular? Specifically, what accounts for the shift in body fashions that raises the stock of female *culos*—"rumps with bumps"—at the expense of "stick figures"? And what further shift requires J-Lo to "make way for Vida"?

These are questions specifically about the conditions that make Vida Guerra a public figure and that constitute her body as beautiful. There are many such conditions, from the hard facts of human political arrangements to the more elusive facts of ideology and psychocultural fixation. These conditions converge to produce a distinctive set of rules for using norms like beauty and ugliness to evaluate and shape human bodies—call this a regime of "somatic aesthetics." The somatic aesthetic that concerns us here focuses on the female *culo*, or posterior, and constitutes it as a cultural object that warrants specific forms of evaluation and display. We will refer to the aesthetic privileging of the *culo* as "culocentrism," in the spirit that moves some theorists to refer to the metaphysical privileging of sight as "oculocentrism."[5] Culocentrism can have various normative valences, so we will also have occasion to use terms like "culophilia" and "culophobia."

Culocentrism is, among other things, a way of looking at and valuing women's bodies. It is, more precisely, a collection of ways of looking, a collection that has taken shape over time, on an evolving "meeting ground of investments." These investments concern such things as the utility and politics of female beauty, feminine virtue, and social identity, and they frame the ways we look at, think about, and use racialized female bodies in social life, public policy, and visual culture. We will explore some different ways of looking at Vida Guerra, on the theory that understanding her will help us understand the burdens of looking, the promise of beauty, and the prospects of ethical subjectivity for people who *quieren culo*.

Before we move on, a word about terminology is in order. We will consistently use expressions like "U.S." and *estadounidense* (literally "United-Stater") where terms like "America" and "American" might seem adequate. We do this because we draw on traditions that question and resist the tendency to conflate the geographic areas known as "the Americas," and the symbol of freedom and newness known as "America," with the political and administrative fact of the United States. In a way, this essay chronicles the convergence of several different Americas on the meeting ground of one woman's body. We mean for our language to reflect this aspect of the work.[6]

First Look: Titillating, but Not Beautiful

One way of looking at Vida Guerra searches in vain for any sign of beauty. The point is not simply that she can be found unattractive. The spectator we have in mind can grant Guerra's attractiveness, perhaps feel personally drawn in by it, and still deny that it has anything to do with beauty. This is the approach of the aesthetic purist—someone for whom aesthetic theory must be disinterested and cleansed of any attachment to animal inclinations like desire. For someone like this, "bodily beauty" is a misnomer. Real beauty, on this view, requires the free play of our cognitive faculties (with that hoary Kantian formula suitably updated by contemporary cognitive psychology).[7]

For proponents of this cognitive approach to beauty, Ms. Guerra might seem to offer a kind of counterfeit beauty. She simply titillates, they might say, by presenting observers with stimuli that provoke judgments of physical and sexual attractiveness. If recent biological studies of physical attractiveness are correct, this sort of provocation will have less to do with the free play of cognition than with being, as a *Newsweek* review of these studies puts it, "viscerally attuned to small variations in the size and symmetry of facial bones and the placement of weight on the body."[8]

Looking at Vida Guerra in this way obscures more than it illuminates. For one thing, distinguishing beauty from attractiveness in this way overlooks the strong and vital links between purified aesthetics and somatic aesthetics (links suggested, if nothing more, by the way we speak of "beauty" in both contexts). For example, it is impossible to understand how judgments of bodily beauty function without subjecting cultural representations of the body to some of the techniques of traditional—purified—aesthetic criticism. And it is difficult to understand the history of Western figurative art without understanding the broader histories of the practices by which we assign meanings to human physiognomy. In these and other ways, the study of art-beauty and the study of bodily beauty in certain ways require each other.

In addition, aesthetic purism sometimes reflects and obscures deeper forms of uneasiness about the body. A complex, ambivalent relationship to corporeality runs through much of Western cultural history. This is a twice-told tale, one version of which begins with Plato and complains through the ages that the body's untidy functions and rebellious impulses weigh down the higher, rational functions. One extension of the story links the problem of the body to certain problem people, thereby populating our films, literature, and visual art with femmes fatales, passive white female nudes, and hot-blooded native "girls," among other characters. These characters then escape from our artworlds and insinuate themselves into our social interactions and public policy. These considerations provide all the more reason to analyze body-beauty and art-beauty in light of each other.

We can start toward a more adequate way of looking at Ms. Guerra by taking a cue from Alexander Nehamas. He says that "beauty" is "the name we give to attractiveness when what we already know about an individual . . . seems too complex for us to be able to describe . . . and valuable enough to promise that what we haven't yet learned is worth even more."[9] To say this is to begin rather than to end an argument. But it also shows how to register the enormous public fascination with Vida Guerra's *culo* while using the vocabulary of beauty.

Second Look: An "Ornament That Signals [Genetic] Quality"?

It may be that the beauty of Ms. Guerra's body seems to hold some promise for us only against the backdrop of evolutionary imperatives. If we were among the new biological scientists of beauty, we would say things like this: Humans, like other animals, use their bodies to attract mates. The bodies of human females tend to store fat in the breasts and buttocks more assiduously than the bodies of human males. So for reasons related, in the mists of prehistory, to the way these fat stores signal the genetic quality of potential mates, these areas of the female body became crucial to male judgments of female attractiveness. Ms. Guerra fascinates because her body sounds the ancient alarms and activates preconscious, animal instincts that have been engineered, so to speak, to respond to signs of "honest male value."[10]

Looking at Ms. Guerra through the lens of evolutionary theory also obscures at least as much as it reveals. For one thing, it evades the question of just who is doing the looking. Ms. Guerra's principal admirers may be heterosexual men, engineered to do the bidding of their selfish genes. But what about her queer female fans?

While the question of sexuality will recur somewhat later, it is an instance of a broader shortcoming of the "evolutionary signal" perspective.

Proponents of this perspective tend to elide the social, cultural, and histori-cal circumstances under which the criteria of female attractiveness get their content.[11] Human communities have *invented* breasts and buttocks as "sec-ondary sexual characteristics" when we have bothered with these attributes at all. And we have done this over time, with different visions of attractiveness in different places. For example, Western cultures have eroticized the breast only since the early modern period, and most vigorously since 1940. The Japanese have by and large come even more recently to the idea of eroticiz-ing the female breast, thanks in large part to U.S. postwar influences. (Until then, images of women in Japanese erotica tended to bypass the breasts and buttocks altogether, and focused instead on the nape of the neck or directly on the genitalia.)[12]

It is not unforgivably misleading to say, with some aesthetic surgeons, that "the gluteal region has . . . its place in the concept of beauty in all com-munities."[13] But the nature of the place varies considerably across space and time—as do the normative shapes of the bodies that play the role well. Even if we are as a species drawn to such basic things as facial symmetry, a great deal of local variation remains to be explained.

One local variation is particularly important for looking at Ms. Guerra. Hegemonic "Western" ideas about the shape and relative importance of the female buttocks diverge rather clearly from continental and diasporic African norms. The aesthetic surgeons tell us, "Well-rounded buttocks are highly prized . . . in South America and Africa," while dominant Western norms have preferred "a flat buttock."[14] This hegemonic Western preference grows out of the modern uptake of classical sculptures like the Callipygian Venus (fig. 10.2) as "the model for the normal."[15] And this preference dove-tails with the same somatic aesthetic that subordinates the buttocks to the breasts in places like the U.S. and UK. Call this "the *Playboy* aesthetic," after the U.S.-based men's magazine, and think of Venus Callipygos as modeling the portion of this aesthetic that contemplates the *culo*. This aesthetic fails to account for the popularity of Vida Guerra, which means that we need to look at the cultural history of "secondary sexual characteristics" more closely than does the evolutionary picture.

Third Look: Hottentot Vida

If Vida Guerra's emergence is a cultural and historical phenomenon, and if the Callipygian Venus points us to the wrong parts of the culture, then perhaps we should compare her to another Venus figure. Western

Figure 10.2. Aphrodite (Venus) Callipygos, first century CE.
Museo Archeologico Nazionale, Naples, Italy. PHOTOGRAPH
BY LUCIANO PEDICINI. PHOTO CREDIT: ALINARI / ART RESOURCE,
N.Y. IMAGE REFERENCE: ART102070.

Figure 10.3. Aaron Martinet (1762–1841) and Louis Francois Charon (1783–1831), satire of the Hottentot Venus (Sara Baartman), exhibited in Paris naked except for a loincloth, with two Scottish soldiers, a young Parisienne, and a well-dressed gentleman admiring her, September 1815. Hand-colored etching. British Museum, London. © THE TRUSTEES OF THE BRITISH MUSEUM / ART RESOURCE, N.Y. IMAGE REFERENCE: ART389770.

culocentrism began in the early nineteenth century with the drama of the so-called Hottentot Venus. With its uptake and denigration of an alternate, "steatopygian" bodily aesthetic, this tragic episode of psychocultural fetishization made clear what was at stake for Western standards of *culo*-normativity (fig. 10.3).[16]

The Hottentot Venus Episode

Sara Baartman, a Khoisan woman from South Africa, like many Khoisan women, had what European viewers would consider to be large buttocks and extended labia. These traits are common in southern Africa, the way blue eyes are ordinary in Scandinavia. And a Khoisan practice of bodily modification led to labial hypertrophy. But for nineteenth-century Europeans, determined to conflate body, race, and destiny, this "excess" flesh proved puzzling. Accordingly, entrepreneurially minded white men brought

Baartman to London in 1810, convinced that they could profit from scientific and popular curiosity about the shape of her body. After years of popular and degrading appearances as "the Venus of the Hottentots"—typically in what we now call "freak shows"—Baartman died penniless and depressed in France in 1815.

Baartman's death simply opened the next act of the drama. Other African women assumed her stage name and her place in various popular artworks and bizarre public exhibitions. Meanwhile, Baartman received even greater scrutiny from the burgeoning "sciences" of human difference. Eminent naturalists dissected her body, publicly presented their results, and left her disembodied genitals in the care of the Musée de l'Homme, where they remained on display for more than a century. (In the third act to this drama, the postapartheid leaders of South Africa demanded the repatriation of their countrywoman's remains.)

The Hottentot Venus story puts culocentrism into a broad social context, only some elements of which we can discuss here. There were oppressive institutions like imperialism and slave trading, male supremacy, white supremacy, and (what we can retrospectively call) heterocentrism. There was a widespread epistemological commitment to studying society by studying the body, a commitment embodied in anthropometry, comparative anatomy, and medical studies of pathology. And the broad phenomena we know as capitalism, liberalism, and Victorian culture were emerging or changing in ways that would have profound consequences for ideas about human freedom, identity, and sexuality.

All of these forces, and many more, collided in the Hottentot Venus drama, making a certain kind of human body into a spectacularly effective metonym for a distinctive phase of European modernity. When Baartman arrived in Europe, the dominant Western societies were fascinated by the idea of freedom, but also by the realities of empire, the natural hierarchies of class, race, and gender, and the various benefits of the trade in enslaved Africans. The sciences of the body promised to help reconcile these tensions, by finding in the contours of the human form the natural mechanisms of social and ontological stratification. Old myths about inferior peoples provided the intuition that drove these "sciences" in their readings of the body: that a deficit of rationality and excess of lasciviousness was what distinguished the savage types from the civilized. In this context, when Baartman arrived in Europe—a black, female, colonial subject and worker whose protruding buttocks marked her as irredeemably and paradigmatically inferior—it took little work to turn her into a commodity and an ethnographic artifact. More than this, through her central role in popular entertainments that were both consumer spectacles and imperialist exhibitions, she became a cultural icon, transcending any of the individual women who represented her.[17]

The Hottentot Venus was such an effective emblem for certain modern conditions that we might speak of her as a kind of fetish object. Modern Europe inscribed important social meanings onto her, it pretended that she was the source of the meanings, and it used this pretense to resolve certain psychosocial contradictions. The pretense then proved so useful that the icon at its center was invested with intense emotion and began to reappear in an almost ritualistic fashion.[18]

Specifically, the Hottentot Venus episode was fetishistic insofar as it helped Europeans reconcile their insistence on liberty and virtue with their determination to exploit, oppress, and abuse others. The key mechanism was the transposition of the relevant rationalizations into the viscerally affecting domains of the aesthetic and the erotic. The Hottentot's ugliness—an objective, natural fact, Europeans thought, not a projection or cultural artifact—made the inferiority of abject peoples a matter of immediate perception. And her lasciviousness—as objectively evident to her European contemporaries as her ugliness—provided an excusable and public outlet for the sexual fascinations of otherwise "temperate" men. The relevant precincts of European culture became so passionately invested in the Hottentot's buttocks that she began to show up everywhere—perhaps in the emergence of the bustle in women's fashion, but certainly in popular art and state-of-the-art science. This ritualistic recurrence went so far that prostitutes in Europe and Cuba became the subject of scientific studies reading their bodies and morals in light of the Hottentot template.[19]

The Hottentot Analogy

Seeing Ms. Guerra as a modern-day "Hottentot" does explain some aspects of her rise to prominence. The appeal to history fills in the gap between general accounts of "secondary sexual characteristics" and the specificity of culocentrism. It explains the peculiar tinge of exoticism that attends Guerra's displays, and it explains why Guerra goes places—*Maxim*, *FHM*—that darker women with similar builds do not. Guerra has, as one writer says of Jennifer Lopez, a "black butt," which, as an emblem of difference and otherness, freighted with historic ideas about African hypersexuality, remains puzzling and exciting all at once. But she also has light skin, which keeps her "black butt" from being *too* different and becoming grotesque.

But there are limits to the Hottentot analogy. Sara Baartman's tragic fate was to become a fetish object for a certain phase of European modernity. Quite specific cultural forces were in play, and without appeal to these her experience becomes inexplicable. A very different society, with very different material conditions and somewhat different psychocultural needs, has fetishized Ms. Guerra. Twenty-first-century culocentrism, although not fully disconnected from its nineteenth-century origins, does powerfully gesture toward a need to theorize the complexities of the material conditions and psychocultural needs that have fetishized Ms. Guerra. We can begin to identify the dimensions of this task with two remarks. First, Guerra is Cuban, and within the U.S. she is racialized as "Latina," not Khoisan. So the specific myths that informed the European uses of Baartman's body—myths, for example, about "Hottentots" as the "missing link"—are unlikely to figure as directly in the uses of Guerra's body in the U.S. Some more specific cultural narrative is likely to be in play now—although this cultural narrative is not disconnected from marking her body as occupying a racially luminal space that is suggestive of a "missing link." Second, where Baartman was isolated from the cultures that found her straightforwardly beautiful, Guerra remains rooted in multiple aesthetic communities. She has many black and brown fans, whose admiration remains uncomplicated by cover stories about grotesqueness and otherness, but who are still expressing their desire in the form of a confession that signals a transgression: in the words of the OYE editorial (and Sir Mix-A-Lot) quoted above, they "cannot lie" about J-Lo, and now Guerra, having "carried the burden of [their] desire."

Fourth Look: J-Lo 2.0

The limits of the Hottentot analogy suggest another way of looking at Vida Guerra. Perhaps she has simply benefited from the decade-long revival of culocentrism in mainstream U.S. culture that we associate with that famous *Puertorriqueña* Jennifer Lopez. A revival was made necessary as a response to hegemonic standards of female beauty. But in recent years the *culo* has become a vital part of the hegemonic conception of feminine beauty in the U.S. Women's fitness and beauty magazines now offer advice on how to improve the "glutes"—where "improvement" no longer means "buns of steel" but "round and shapely."[20] And aesthetic surgeons report "a distinct return to the more rounded female shape . . . particularly in the buttocks"—and a corresponding uptick in "butt lift" surgeries.[21]

As with any broad cultural shift, there are many forces at work in the rejection, or complication, of the Callipygian aesthetic.[22] But one indisputable element was the emergence of Jennifer Lopez as an A-list star and beauty icon. As one women's fitness authority puts it, while lumping Lopez with another star who emerged in her wake, "The butt is back. (Thanks, Beyoncé and J.Lo!)"[23] Because Lopez is a public figure, her image becomes publicly intelligible against the backdrop of the postcolonial social conditions that led to and emerged from the mainstreaming of hidden cultural transcripts for somatic aesthetics. (It would of course take detailed empirical work to demonstrate that these factors are in play. In advance of that work, we aim simply to refine the intuitions that call for empirical study, and perhaps to formulate a guiding hypothesis.)

Rewriting the Public Transcript

A hidden transcript emerges when, as historian Robin Kelley puts it, "oppressed groups challenge those in power by constructing . . . a dissident political culture . . . [in] the submerged social and cultural worlds of oppressed people."[24] It is the alternative to a public transcript, or the body of social norms that govern "the open interaction between subordinates and those who dominate.[25] By establishing the ugliness and lasciviousness of women with protruding buttocks, and enjoining that women with this trait be treated and treat themselves accordingly, Westerners were articulating a public transcript for white supremacist and colonialist modes of feminine objectification. But here as elsewhere, the public transcript "is unlikely to tell the whole story about power relations."[26]

There are several reasons to think that hidden culocentric transcripts, both on the African continent and in the diaspora, have long contested the official Western message of black ugliness. First, bodies like Baartman's were prized in southern Africa, and, as K. A. Appiah points out, colonial regimes tended to leave wide swaths of the colonized life-world untouched (while making it perennially vulnerable to violation).[27] Second, the "submerged cultural worlds" of African vernacular dance in the "New World" have long featured culophilic practices like the eighteenth-century "shaker" or "toe" dances, where "toe" seems to be a creolization of West African words for hips or buttocks. And third, general assertions of black and brown beauty have long been central to antiracist and anticolonial activists and artists.

Whatever the fate of hidden aesthetic transcripts in the immediate aftermath of the Hottentot Venus episode, they were clearly in evidence in the twentieth century. They appear in the descendants of the shaker dances, where "the dual celebration and objectification of the black female behind" links calypso, hiphop, dancehall and other music-related movement practices.[28] And they come into view in the archives of subaltern visual culture (in, for example, *Jet* magazine's "beauty of the week" feature) and with Puerto Rican performer Iris Chacon, who danced, sang, and shook her *culo* for the camera on her own Spanish-language television show, which aired in Puerto Rico and the continental U.S.

With these counterhegemonic norms already in place, the sociocultural transformations of the postcolonial and post–Civil Rights eras helped insert culocentrism into the U.S. public transcript. As "Anglo conquest . . . boomeranged back to U.S. shores" after 1940, overlapping groups of Latin American migrants came to the United States, or were transplanted from the "colony" to the mainland, as was the case for Puerto Ricans.[29] And the social and economic transformations in black life during and after the end of the Jim Crow era brought African Americans more squarely into mainstream public consciousness. Thanks to these and other developments, a couple of generations of *estadounidenses* have grown up, to paraphrase Trey Ellis, not only accustomed to black and brown bodies, but also hungry for them.[30]

The mainstreaming of the hidden transcript does not signify a seamlessly victorious struggle by the subaltern. It also involves the reconstitution of certain forms of hegemony. Black and brown bodies not only became more visible, they also become commodified and consumerized, facilitating the crossover of formerly suppressed aesthetic practices. In *Black Skin, White Masks*, Fanon points out that one's very "soul" can become the constructed "artifact" of social forces and desires.[31] The commodification of "black souls" encourages these subjugated peoples to accept, mirror back, and buy back the artifactual versions and visions of themselves. This creates the cultural and market conditions for the hidden and public transcripts to publicly converge.[32] Accordingly, the *culo* has in many settings become a public artifact, shaped by the hegemony of heteronormativity, colorism, capitalism, and more, and packaged for sale with hypersexual visions of *Latinidad*, or with the strip-club aesthetic of Two Live Crew.

In these ways, hidden culocentric transcripts represent what Gloria Anzaldúa called a "counterstance": they accept the terms of engagement and the stakes set by the stance they oppose, thereby merely escalating the "duel of oppressor and oppressed."[33] In this case, both "oppressor" and "oppressed" have agreed to manipulate women's bodies in the service of heteronormative masculinity and, in the process, to sidestep questions about how many live beauty and experience the erotic.

Borderlands and Bridges

The emergence of hidden culocentric transcripts, along with the convergence of these transcripts with fetishistic public transcripts, is among the conditions of possibility for people like Jennifer Lopez and Vida Guerra. But the public lives of these women also have a great deal to do with different strategies for negotiating the tension between stance and counterstance. Considering these strategies will help clarify the nature of Lopez's achievement, and its distance from what Guerra has accomplished.

Anzaldúa explains the best strategy. To offer a counterstance, she says, is "to stand on the opposite river bank, shouting questions." To move beyond this antagonism, one must "leave the opposite bank, [with] the split between the two mortal combatants somehow healed so that we are on both shores at once." In this way, "divergent cultures, paradigms, and worlds meet not to become combatants . . . but to become something more."[34] All this happens, she says, on "the borderland." This third space becomes part of what Anzaldúa theorized to be a marker of *la conciencia de la mestiza,* or mestiza consciousness. The "something more" can be articulated as a form of disidentification, or as a third space, that is not conciliatory, not simply "put on" or "performed, " but is instead transgressive. Because of this, to occupy the borderlands is to hold multiple identifications in their entirety and to make space for fusing them, in a way that exposes limitations while also, in this case, revealing the full meaning of beauty to an abject population.

One moment in Lopez's career embodies this idea of borderlands and demonstrates the transformative potential of the *culo.* When she won the lead in the 1997 film *Selena,* her "big rear end [became] . . . an identification site for Latinas to reclaim their beauty."[35] Women from many different Latin American backgrounds and communities reveled in seeing on the big screen a woman who, like them, was more curvaceous than Hollywood's usual suspects. Their fascination grew to the point that Lopez discovered an odd question recurring during the film's publicity tour of Spanish media: was her *culo* real? (She settled the matter on one show by standing up, turning her back to the audience, patting her behind and saying, "Todo es mio," it's all mine.[36])

In contrast with Lopez's transformative claim *que todo esto es mio,* she unfortunately models a different form of rapprochement between stance and counterstance, one that is more like a bridge than like Anzaldúa's borderland. Since mulattas and mestizas are able to pass both into whiteness and into blackness, they can pass out of the black/white binary of the U.S. and enter an alternate category that does not challenge white supremacy and may instead actively distance its gestures and postures from blackness. Such enactments of *mulataje* are not without their own particular types of transcendence, or even moments of "liberation," but they fall short of Anzaldúa's third space. They might reach a kind of interstitial or transitional space, but this space can also be a haven for opportunistic shape-shifting, for strategically variable identifications rather than dis-identification.

Lopez is more bridge than borderland when it comes to the darker precincts of the U.S. racial landscape because she has passed into whiteness and out of blackness, even as she has solidified the pan-Latin credentials she began to earn in *Selena*. She has, in a sense, had three different public careers. Her early, "black" career unfolded in close proximity to black media spaces, like BET, and black media figures, like the Wayans brothers and P. Diddy. She effectively concluded this phase and started another by "whitening" herself, with roles in cinematic assimilation fantasies like *Maid in Manhattan* (2002) and ties to Anglo leading men like George Clooney and Ben Affleck. And she has all along cultivated a third public life as a Latina, beginning in earnest with *Selena* and culminating in her professional work and romantic relationship with singer Mark Anthony. By effectively becoming a "white Hispanic" on film, she has not only forsaken the borderland, with its promise of transcendence, for the bridge, but she has also made the bridge between white and black a one-way passage.

Here Lopez and Guerra start to diverge. Where Lopez passes out of blackness and limits herself to bridging whiteness and *Latinidad*, Guerra continues to pass between white, black, and Latino communities. More specifically: Lopez's intertextual public identity, forged on film and in tabloid journalism, connects her to white men in romances of bourgeois assimilation, thereby creating a bridge out of abjection; and her "ideal 'Latin' beauty," with skin "neither too dark nor too light" and a prominent *culo*, creates a site for pan-Latin identification.[37] Guerra, by contrast, connects subaltern masculinities to each other and to the "mainstream" masculinity affirmed by *Maxim* and *Playboy*. (There are, to be sure, other differences between these women, in class, migration experiences, and skill set, and perhaps in preparation, social capital, and so on. But we are concerned here with public figures, with the cultural processes that embody themselves in these women and that go by their names. The rest is the subject matter of a different kind of study.)

Fifth Look: Guerra, *Sandunguera*

Vida Guerra may be less like Jennifer Lopez than like the Cuban dancer and actress Tongolele. Tongolele was a contemporary of Josephine Baker who modeled, acted, and danced in Cuban and Mexican cinema, and whose claim to fame was that she, as contemporary performance artist Alina Troyano (a.k.a. Carmelita Tropicana) put it, could put a tray of daiquiris on her behind and walk across a room without spilling a drop.[38] During the 1930s and 1940s Tongolele assumed postures similar to the ones that Guerra assumes now, and that both share with the rest of Cuba's *sandungueras* and *rumberas* (magazine pinup girls and club performers known for their witching charm and allure). Where Lopez aspires to the glamour of an old Hollywood star (on the cover of *Vogue*) or of Latina royalty (in her work and relationship with singer Mark Anthony), Guerra carries forward the tradition of the *sandunguera*, which inherits the templates of both Hottentot "lasciviousness" and mestiza shape-shifting. And both women signal their cultural locations and, so to speak, their vocations with the positions of their bodies, and with the role of the *culo* in the composition of their images.

Filming the Low Life

It is obvious that the images of Lopez and Guerra differ in print and on screen. Lopez's early assimilation fantasies, for example, demonstrate the kind of fetishistic ambivalence one expects in the wake of the Hottentot episode. Films like *Out of Sight* (1998) and *Enough* (2002) make sure to remind the viewer why this woman is the female lead, with gratuitous shots of her posterior. But these shots are isolated, relegated to diegetically inert scenes that could vanish from the film without any consequence for the embodied life of the character. Her *culo* becomes a device that adds a little extra *frisson* to roles that any white Hollywood actress could play.

Compare this ambivalence to the tone of Guerra's SPEED-TV reality show, *Livin' the Low Life*. As host, she visits and interviews black, Latino (Caribbean, Chicano, and Mexicano), and some working-class white men, all involved in the competitive art of automobile modification and display known as "low-riding."[39] Guerra is the live-action version of the models that adorn the covers of magazines for automobile enthusiasts, and, as the visual style of the show makes clear, a stand-in for the cheesecake silhouettes and painted images that constitute so much of this world's iconography of automobile adornment. She is the visual "hook" for the show, and her *culo* is the always-visible marker of the ethnoracial identity that fits her for this role.

She interacts with the mostly black and brown men, in their garages and elsewhere, using forms of speech, gestures, postures, and clothes that would utterly defeat any attempt at whitening herself. But these ethnic markers disqualify her from doing more—the voice-overs that explain and connect the show's segments fall to another, more "polished" female voice, one with no accent to tie it to New Jersey's working-class Latino neighborhoods.

Guerra's *culo* may be as central to the existence of her show as it is to her role on it. The men in these garages dramatize the kind of homosocial bonding that the show promotes, by gathering around Guerra to show her their cars. It is hard to imagine the white NASCAR fans that sustain the SPEED channel joining in, supporting a show about working-class black and brown lowriders, without some demonstration of common ground. Enter Guerra, whose career has been made possible by the simultaneous emergence of music videos, "laddie" magazines, Internet marketing and storefronts, "pornified" pop culture, "hiphop porn,"[40] and post-Lopez mainstream culophilia. Whether through BET, *Maxim*, *OYE*, or her own website, she has found her way into the semisegregated communities that these men inhabit. And now she facilitates the homoerotic encounter between and across these heteromasculinities.

Interestingly, Guerra guides the cable viewer through a version of the low-rider phenomenon that is, like her, thoroughly commodified. The show visits garages that customize cars for enthusiasts who seem willing to pay well for their passion. What is in some ways most interesting about the low-riding phenomenon emerges from its "post-work" forms, in which clubs of car owners organize mutual help activities—exchanging parts and services—as well as social activities and leisure get-togethers. In these cases, an object of private consumption which should, by its nature, isolate consumers becomes the centerpiece for a form of sociality and an occasion for proximity that is, in a sense, "incomprehensible," based on "non-wage labor, intensity, and solidarity."[41] We take this as support for the suspicion that Guerra, despite her own commodification, might also occasion a complex form of solidarity.

Poses, Postures, Gestures

The distance from Lopez to Guerra registers also in the ways they pose, or are posed, for magazine images. As Janell Hobson notes, back when Lopez still did cheesecake and provocative glamour photos, her images referenced the Callipygian aesthetic, explicitly citing classical sculpture in her poses.[42] Guerra, meanwhile, often references excavated hidden transcripts, using these to inflect the conventional near-porn suggestions of sexual availability, enthusiasm, and expertise.

The Callipygian aesthetic recommends a representational code that we might call "presenting," after the name, in the biological sciences, for the way female animals in some species display their hindquarters when they are ready to mate. This code governs the famous wartime pinup of Betty Grable and communicates feminine availability by depicting the subject with her back completely turned to the spectator. The "steatopygian" aesthetic, by contrast, sometimes recommends what we can call "profiling." This code requires that the subject appear in profile, or in other poses that make the fact—the "aimless fact," de Beauvoir would have us say[43]—of the naked posterior less important than its size; it often governs the "backshot" feature that (as of this writing) closes every issue of *King* magazine. An image from *Show* magazine (fig. 10.4) reveals the steatopygian code at work, as one Temeca Freeman evokes and transforms Grable's evocation of the Callipygian Venus. In heteromasculine contexts, both poses communicate sexual availability. (They may present a sexual challenge or critical intervention in certain feminist or womanist contexts.)[44] But while presenting is about general attractiveness as reflected in the buttocks, profiling is about the *culo*, first and foremost.

Guerra's culocentric poses not only mark her distance from Lopez, but also reflect the historical and cultural location of the social forces unfolding under her name. Both women strike their poses in the wake of the Hottentot episode, for example. But while Lopez's poses explicitly reject that inheritance, Guerra's recall it. The episode created a sign in Western culture that conflated protruding buttocks, sexual deviance, racial difference, and sexual availability. The theoretical underpinnings for this conflation have fallen away, but the sign lives on in the postures and gestures that have become associated with it. In this way, it invites us to imagine what lies behind the image, the unseen more at which it only gestures.

In fact, we read these gestures and postures as an insistence, by both the viewer and the viewed, on remembering and recounting unequal power relations. As such, these hieroglyphics of the mulatta or mestiza body are signs that point beyond the sign system itself to that which cannot be figured, captured, or resolved by it. These postures and gestures hail other meanings, something *más allá* than what the image/object, the artifact/art(y)fact, seems to be. It is here that the Cubana, Latina, or mulatta resides, at the crossroads between existing purely as a commodity and insisting that the image and its postures recount a history of unequal power relations, of bodies under dissection, commodification, and exploitation.

We find here, at this crossroads, a renewed possibility of Anzaldúa's dialectical transcendence. Guerra recalls a tradition of Cuban women

Figure 10.4. Temeca Freeman, in *SHOW
Black Lingerie* 1 (August 2007).

performing hyper-heterosexual *Latinidad* in order to make a living, and like
them she is tragically obligated to take on and take in the artifacts of blackness, of *Latinidad,* of whoredom, and perform them to the specifications of
the visual market's demands. But it is also true that this performance and its
consumption reveal what both the spectator and the performer have in common, and why both have come to the same geographical and ideological
space, at the same exact time, to reenact the problematics of an unresolved
legacy of colonialism and white supremacy.

Conclusion: From Looking to Bearing Witness

Latinas, mestizas, and mulattas (being both imaginary and "real" subjects)
are doubled sociocultural icons that in effect transport us to the sociopolitical
ordering that is the West. This sociopolitical order or historical ground represented for African and indigenous peoples (as well as their "Latina" descendants) a scene of actual mutilation, dismemberment, and exile. The postures
taken on by women like Vida Guerra serve as markers of a "New World"

diasporic plight and mark a theft of the body—a willful and violent severing from its will and desires. These mark the simultaneous absence and presence of just those bodies and make visible what is systematically declared invisible, thereby permitting an archive, of sorts, and a process of historical reconstruction via highly alternative, trivialized, and typically dismissed means.

Ultimately the representations of women like Vida Guerra can be read as attempts to "evoke [a] person/persona in the place of a 'shady' ideal."[45] Evoking a person in this case means recognizing and historicizing the burdens that women of African descent face as they resist the states and markets that seek to make their bodies nothing short of an attraction. In this way, we begin to see the lives of women of African descent in the Americas beyond the shady ideals of service and hypersexuality.

Having pointed beyond the shady ideal of Guerra's beautiful body, and having invoked the *más allá* that we see there, we should say more. We should, specifically, extend the task of disentangling complex persons from shadowy abstractions by distinguishing the spectators we have been theorizing from the viewers we have been. We have, in a way, been exploring resistant spectatorship in U.S. markets for heteromasculine erotica. We have described a multiply hegemonic gaze, a way of looking at *culos negros* that positions spectators as white, masculine, heterosexual, and in the position of colonial mastery. We have pointed to the social locations from which other spectators might emerge, spectators conversant with hidden transcripts that find protruding buttocks beautiful *simpliciter*, not grotesque-yet-exotic, or fascinating-yet-disturbing, or any other compound of colonial ambivalence. And we have suggested that these once-hidden transcripts have converged with the mainstream—that they have crossed over and now inspire another generation of white-Anglo *and* subaltern voyeurs, eager to "eat the other."[46]

With all of that said, though, the spectator is "a textual point of address," while the viewer is "an empirical unit," a flesh-and-blood person.[47] The semiotic machinery of a visual text does not so much position viewers as invite us, as viewers, to position ourselves, to identify with currents of meaning that run along familiar and well-charted paths. If we are unwary, if the machinery has effectively hidden itself and mythologized its subject matter, then the invitation will not register as such, and will seem obligatory. But even for viewers who are inured to the text's mythological spin, resistant spectatorship is hard work. It is, in particular, the kind of hard work that defines an ethic of self-care, or of self-excavation. And it is the ethical imperative—an ethic, we'll say, of witness—that lies at the heart of critical engagements with the experience of beauty.

The ethic of witness that we have in mind involves, as Kelly Oliver puts it, "an ongoing process of critical analysis," a process "that contextualizes and recontextualizes what and how we see." It is what we do when we pair an eye-witness report of an event with an attempt to bear witness to what we cannot see—to the context that framed the action, motivated the participants, and gave meaning to the entire transaction. Broadcast journalism routinely fails to bear witness in this sense, by refusing to "challenge [the] stereotypes, pre-conceptions, or expectations" that shape our familiar narratives about issues like war, crime, and poverty. To bear witness is to "move beyond what we recognize in visual images to [examine] . . . the subjectivity and agency, along with the social and political context . . . of the 'objects' of our gaze, *and* our own desires and fears." This process never ends; it is "an opening rather than a closure," a "perpetual questioning" that remains open to "alternative interpretations" and aware of "the impossibility of ever completely . . . understanding ourselves."[48]

Kobena Mercer shows the aesthetic function of the ethic of witness in his reading and rereading of Mapplethorpe's black male nudes. After criticizing the photographer for using his black male subjects to play out the same colonial ambivalence that we found in the Hottentot Venus episode, Mercer makes an about-face. The ambivalence was not in the photographic texts, he says, but in the "complex structure of feeling" uniting authors, texts, and readers in a web of dynamic relations. Mapplethorpe's work, Mercer now thinks, highlights and insists on the *cultural* ambivalence that frames our dealings with race, gender, and sexuality. More than this, the work makes spectators consider their own orientation to that culture. Having failed to do this himself—having failed to consider the role his own investments and resentments played in his earlier reading—he succumbed to moralism where he aspired to criticism. Moralism fails, he now thinks, because Mapplethorpe's aesthetic strategy makes it impossible to answer the moralistic question, "Is he reinforcing stereotypes or undermining them?" The viewer is instead forced to confront his or her own responses and social identities.[49]

Like Mercer with Mapplethorpe, we have had to reconsider our initial responses to Vida Guerra to undertake this project. The seductions of theory led us to suppress our own investments, which in turn struggled to express themselves moralistically. We wrestle with pride at Guerra's vindication of Afro-Cubano aesthetic transcripts, or at her ability to complicate familiar narratives about Latina and Cuban identity; with alarm at the centrality of feminine objectification in these advances, if they are that, and at the residues of nationalism in our reactions; with distress at the desires she provokes in us; and more. Following a suggestion from Eve Oishi, the next step in this inquiry would involve "outing" ourselves.[50] We should step back from theory and revisit our experiences of Vida Guerra, in order to insist on the experiential and ethical importance of the middle ground between viewer and spectator, the space that criticism must open, where the work of witnessing must unfold. We will have to leave that work for another time.

NOTES

The epigraph is from Hortense J. Spillers, "Mama's Baby, Papa's Maybe: An American Grammar Book," *Diacritics* 17, no. 2 (Summer 1987): 64.

1. Intermedial images or symbols have their meanings constituted across the boundaries between traditional media formats. See Kaarina Nikunen and Susanna Paasonen, "Porn Star as Brand: Pornification and the Intermedia Career of Rakel Liekki," *Velvet Light Trap*, no. 59 (Spring 2007): 31.

2. "Meet the Girls of Dorm Daze 2," *Black Men* (August–September 2006), 34–44.

3. "Mi Vida Guerra," *Open Your Eyes*, http://www.oyemag.com/vida.html, par. 1. The print version of the story is "The Story of the Derriere That Shook the World," *Open Your Eyes*, no. 31 (June–July 2004).

4. "Tienes culo?" photo uploaded by user CUBAN0L0C0, December 12, 2006, http://flickr.com/photos/53564922@N00/321023043/. References to the *culo* carry different meanings in different versions of Spanish slang. In some places, talk about the *culo* is a particularly raunchy way of discussing female sexual organs. That is of course not our meaning here. We are grateful to Mariana Ortega for encouraging us to make this clear.

5. Martin Jay, "Scopic Regimes of Modernity," in *Vision and Visuality*, ed. Hal Foster (Seattle: Bay Press, 1988), 3–28; David Michael Levin, *The Opening of Vision* (London: Routledge, 1988); Philippa Berry, "The Burning Glass," in *Engaging with Irigaray*, ed. Carolyn Burke, Naomi Schor, and Margaret Whitford (New York: Columbia University Press, 1994), 244 n. 6; and Victoria Best, "Mastering the Image: Photography and the Elusive Gaze," *French Cultural Studies* 8, no. 23 (June 1997): 173–81.

6. The conflation of America and the United States of America has been a matter of considerable critique within Latina(o) studies for at least the last two decades. This critique can be traced back to the writings of the nineteenth-century Cuban independence leader and poet José Martí, who proposed the concept of "Nuestra America" (Our America) as part of his critique of colonization and imperialism. *See* José Martí, *Our America: Writings on Latin America and the Struggle for Cuban Independence*, ed. Philip Foner, trans. Elinor Randall, Juan De Onís, and Roslyn Held Foner (New York: Monthly Review, 1977); and Jeffrey Belnap and Raúl Fernández, ed., *José Martí's "Our America": From National to Hemispheric Cultural Studies* (Durham, N.C.: Duke University Press, 1998).

7. See Jennifer McMahon, "Perceptual Principles as the Basis for Genuine Judgments of Beauty," *Journal of Consciousness Studies* 7, nos. 8–9 (August–September 2000): 29–35.

8. Geoffrey Cowley and Karen Springen, "The Biology of Beauty," *Newsweek* 127, no. 23 (June 3, 1996): 60.

9. Alexander Nehamas, *Only a Promise of Happiness: The Place of Beauty in a World of Art* (Princeton: Princeton University Press 2007), 70.

10. Randy Thornhill and Karl Grammer, "The Body and Face of Woman: One Ornament That Signals Quality?" *Evolution and Human Behavior* 20, no. 2 (March 1999): 105.

11. This culture-blindness is merely a tendency, though an overwhelmingly dominant one, because some studies do better. One that does is Martin J. Tovée, Viren Swami, Adrian Furnham, and Roshila Mangalparsad, "Changing Perceptions of Attractiveness as Observers Are Exposed to a Different Culture," *Evolution and Human Behavior* 27, no. 6 (November 2006): 443–56.

12. Laura Miller, "Mammary Mania in Japan," *positions* 11, no. 22 (Fall 2003): 272–79.

13. Douglas Harrison and Gennaro Selvaggi, "Gluteal Augmentation Surgery: Indications and Surgical Management," *Journal of Plastic, Reconstructive and Aesthetic Surgery* 60, no. 8 (August 2007): 922.

14. Ibid., 927.

15. Sander Gilman, *Making the Body Beautiful: A Cultural History of Aesthetic Surgery* (Princeton: Princeton University Press, 1999), 211.

16. Marisa Meltzer, "Venus Abused," *Salon*, January 9, 2007, http://www.salon.com/books/review/2007/01/09/holmes/singleton. The account developed here owes a great deal to Janell Hobson, "The 'Batty' Politic: Toward an Aesthetic of the Black Female Body," *Hypatia* 18, no. 4 (Fall 2003): 87–105; Harriet Washington, *Medical Apartheid: The Dark History of Medical Experimentation on Black Americans from Colonial Times to the Present* (New York: Doubleday, 2006), 82–86; Sander Gilman, "Black Bodies, White Bodies: Toward an Iconography of Female Sexuality in Late Nineteenth-Century Art, Medicine, and Literature," in "'Race,' Writing, and Difference," ed. Henry Louis Gates, Jr., *Critical Inquiry* 12, no. 1 (Autumn 1985): 204–42; and Janell Hobson, "Hottentot Venus," *Encyclopedia of Race and Racism*, ed. John Hartwell Moore (Detroit: Macmillan Reference USA, 2008), 2:112–14.

17. James Smalls, "'Race' as Spectacle in Late-Nineteenth-Century French Art and Popular Culture," *French Historical Studies* 26, no. 2 (Spring 2003): 351–82.

18. Laura Mulvey, "The Carapace That Failed," in *Reading the Contemporary: African Art from Theory to Marketplace*, ed. Okwui Enwezor and Olu Oguibe (Cambridge, Mass.: MIT Press, 1999), 400–20; and Anne McClintock, *Imperial Leather* (New York: Routledge, 1995).

19. Gilman, "Black Bodies, White Bodies"; and Amalia Lucia Cabezas, "Discourses of Prostitution: The Case of Cuba," in *Global Sex Workers: Rights, Resistance, and Redefinition*, ed. Kamala Kempadoo and Jo Doezema (New York: Rutgers University Press, 1998), 80.

20. Denise Austin, "Redo Your Rear View," *Prevention* 58, no. 2 (February 2006): 115–16. See the cover of a special issue of *Oxygen* entitled "Oxygen Glutes Special" (Spring 2008), http://www.shopmusclemag.com/product.asp?productid=1954.

21. Harrison and Selvaggi, "Gluteal Augmentation Surgery," 927.

22. Some of these will have to do with the consolidation of the female fitness

aesthetic; some will have to do with the sexualization of popular culture, in the wake of the technological revolution in the porn industry; and some may be credited to the impact of the women's movement of the 1960s and what can be described as a complicated result of a feminist aesthetic that rejected or complicated the Callipygian aesthetic.

23. Austin, "Redo Your Rear View," 115.

24. Robin D. G. Kelley, "'We Are Not What We Seem': Rethinking Black Working-Class Opposition in the Jim Crow South," *Journal of American History* 80, no. 1 (June 1993): 77.

25. James Scott, *Domination and the Arts of Resistance* (New Haven: Yale University Press, 1990), 2.

26. Ibid.

27. "The experience of the vast majority of . . . citizens of Europe's African colonies was one of an essentially shallow penetration by the colonizer" (Kwame Anthony Appiah, *In My Father's House* [New York: Oxford University Press, 1992], 7).

28. Chadwick Hansen, "Jenny's Toe Revisited: White Responses to Afro-American Shaking Dances," *American Music* 5, no. 1 (Spring 1987): 1–19; and Jennifer Thorington Springer, "'Roll It Gal': Alison Hinds, Female Empowerment, and Calypso," *Meridians: Feminism, Race, Transnationalism* 8, no. 1 (2008): 111.

29. Juan Gonzalez, *Harvest of Empire: A History of Latinos in America* (New York: Viking, 2000), 78.

30. Trey Ellis, "The New Black Aesthetic," *Callaloo*, no. 38 (Winter 1989): 237.

31. Frantz Fanon, *Black Skin, White Masks* (New York: Grove, 1952), 108–10.

32. Chela Sandoval, *Methodology of the Oppressed* (Minneapolis: University of Minnesota Press, 2000), 85, 97.

33. Gloria Anzaldúa, *Borderlands/La Frontera: The New Mestiza* (San Francisco: Aunt Lute, 1987), 148–49.

34. Ibid, 78–79.

35. Frances Negrón-Muntaner, "Jennifer's Butt," *Aztlán: A Journal of Chicano Studies* 22, no. 2 (Fall 1997): 192.

36. Ibid., 186.

37. Ibid., 183.

38. Alina Troyano, "Milk of Amnesia/Leche de Amnesia," in *I, Carmelita Tropicana*, ed. Alina Troyano, Uzi Parnes, and Chon A. Noriega (New York: Beacon, 2000), 55. A video and image of Tongolele are available at http://unvlog.com/ignominia/2010/1/1/yolanda-montes-tongolele, posted by user ignominia on January 1, 2010.

39. *Livin' the Low Life* ran for two seasons in 2008–2009. Low-riding is an elaborate art and an act of reinvention that emerges from communities that have been labeled *rasquache, chusma,* or ghetto. Communities of color within the U.S. have turned discarded and unattractive cars into coveted pieces of art that are then displayed, raced, and shown in community-based car shows and competitions. The art form is based on the premise that one may not have the economic resources to purchase a brand-new and expensive car, but may have the collective and community resources to transform an unwanted and discarded vehicle into a show-stopping piece of art; moreover, into a representation of the aesthetic that moves a

community. The art form has been associated with "low-lifes," working-class men of color assumed to be somehow connected to gangs, hence the title of Guerra's show.

40. Mireille Miller-Young, "Hip-Hop Honeys and Da Hustlaz: Black Sexualities in the New Hip-Hop Pornography," *Meridians: Feminism, Race, Transnationalism* 8, no. 1 (2008): 261–92.

41. María Milagros López, "Post-work Selves and Entitlement 'Attitudes' in Peripheral Postindustrial Puerto Rico," *Social Text*, no. 38 (Spring 1994): 130, 125.

42. Hobson, "The 'Batty' Politic," 97.

43. Simone de Beauvoir, *The Second Sex* (New York: Vintage, 1989), 158, quoted in Negrón-Muntaner, "Jennifer's Butt," 189.

44. Springer, "'Roll It Gal,'" 102–15; and Hobson, "The 'Batty' Politic," 98–103.

45. Hortense J. Spillers, "Changing the Letter: The Yokes, the Jokes of Discourse, or, Mrs. Stowe, Mr. Reed," in *Slavery and the Literary Imagination*, ed. Deborah McDowell and Arnold Rampersad (Baltimore: Johns Hopkins University Press, 1989), 29.

46. In her classic piece "Eating the Other," bell hooks makes a case for the ways in which the desire for the racialized Other can be exploited in a manner that reinscribes power relations. In exploring how desire for the Other is expressed, manipulated, and transformed by encounters with difference and the different, hooks reveals a critical terrain that can be used to indicate whether these potentially revolutionary longings are ever able to be fulfilled. We are extending her theorization to also include subaltern masculinities (bell hooks, "Eating the Other: Desire and Resistance," *Black Looks: Race and Representation* [Boston: South End Press, 1992], 21–39).

47. Jacqueline Stewart, "Negroes Laughing at Themselves? Black Spectatorship and the Performance of Urban Modernity," *Critical Inquiry* 29, no. 4 (Summer 2003): 655, quoted in Eve Oishi, "Visual Perversions: Race, Sex, and Cinematic Pleasure," *Signs: Journal of Women in Culture and Society* 31, no. 3 (Spring 2006): 643.

48. Kelly Oliver, *Women as Weapons of War* (New York: Columbia University Press, 2007), 106, 107.

49. Kobena Mercer, "Reading Racial Fetishism: The Photographs of Robert Mapplethorpe," in *Welcome to the Jungle: New Positions in Black Cultural Studies* (New York: Routledge, 1994), 189.

50. Oishi, "Visual Perversions," 643–45, 648–50.

11. Beauty between Disability and Gender: Frida Kahlo in Paper Dolls

FEDWA MALTI-DOUGLAS

Beauty, disability, and gender crossing: The first two, though provocative, are not an altogether unexpected pair. Disability can be an object of beauty, as Anita Silvers has shown, just as it can be fetishized.[1] Yet one more often thinks of beauty and disability as opposites. But what is gender crossing doing in this mix? Sometimes, apparently, when beauty is conjugated with disability in an atmosphere of glamour and celebrity, games with gender result. This is certainly the case with the representation of the Mexican female artist Frida Kahlo, especially as seen in a book of paper dolls for children.

Beauty and disability are, in the popular imagination, two concepts that do not normally appear together. Each, however, has produced an enormous scholarly literature. The attraction to beauty is universal, but may obviously be subject to cultural variation.[2] Disability, while it has always existed among world populations, entered the world of cultural scholarship later than beauty.[3]

Frida Kahlo (1907–54) is without doubt one of the most visible woman artists in the centuries-long history of art. We may ask, in the words of Linda Nochlin, "Why have there been no great women artists?"[4] Frida Kahlo is one woman artist who has succeeded in becoming, if not a great artist (I would say she is; others might disagree), an artist whose fame transcends art-critical circles, and whose paintings have become part of our international circulation of images. She did this partly through her life, partly through her art, and partly through the connections between her life and her art.

Married to the Mexican artist and muralist Diego Rivera, Frida led a pain-filled and tumultuous life. She was afflicted with polio in her right leg at age six, and was bedridden for almost a year. The result of this misfortune was an atrophied right leg and a limp. At age eighteen, she was grievously injured in a streetcar accident which almost took her life. The multiple fractures of her spine and other bones left her with chronic severe pain for the rest of her life, adding to her disability. Yet it was a life to which art was vital.

Frida Kahlo has had an uncanny appeal to an enormous international public as well as to art aficionados. Her admirers are insatiable. How else could Frida-inspired objects fill a store in and of themselves? Frida key chains. Frida designer scarves. Frida designer ties. Frida pins. Frida art cubes. Frida T-shirts. Frida pens. Frida wooden boxes. And on and on. Some of these objects can be had from street vendors in Xochimilco, the area of Mexico City where Mexicans gather on weekends and holidays not only to enjoy the stands but to take a ride in colorful and highly decorated barges, *trajineras*, that transport passengers through the canals in the area. But for those who do not wish to chase Frida objects in such a general tourist location, there is always the store attached to La Casa Azul, the Blue House, where Frida lived. Here, one can purchase books on Frida, postcards featuring photos of Frida, and photos of Frida and Diego, as well as copies of her paintings and other memorabilia. Margaret Lindauer in *Devouring Frida* and Bárbara C. Cruz in *Frida Kahlo* present even more types of memorabilia.[5]

Mexicans venerate Frida. On a visit to San Cristóbal de las Casas in the state of Chiapas during the November Day of the Dead celebration, my husband and I found ourselves in a restaurant that was decorated inside with an enormous altar dedicated to Frida, on which a large picture of the artist was surrounded by all the flowers, foods, and decorations associated with that holiday. For those who did not know her, Frida's reputation was sealed with the appearance of the prize-winning Hollywood film *Frida* (dir. Julie Taymor, Miramax Films, 2002), with Salma Hayek in the title role. The film did not shy away from Frida's bisexuality or her general magnetism. It should come as no surprise that Frida's work, including her stunningly visual and verbal diary, has attracted numerous critics and writers.[6]

How does one introduce children to a beautiful and famous female artist who was flamboyant, creative, and extremely passionate? One way to fulfill this task is to take advantage of the varied clothing for which the artist was famous. Among the products directed at children is a fascinating paper-doll book entitled *Aquí cuelgan mis vestidos: Frida Kahlo* (Hang My Clothes [or "Dresses"] Here), published in Mexico (fig. 11.1).[7] As is usual with such booklets (I grew up with them in Lebanon), the book presents a large image of a minimally dressed figure and a series of outfits that can be popped

Figure 11.1. Cover of *Aquí cuelgan mis vestidos: Frida Kahlo,*
by Francisco Estebanez. By permission of Francisco Estebanez.

out and placed over it, thus dressing and redressing the figure as the child wishes. Next to each outfit, Francisco Estebanez, the book's creator, provides a description, both in Spanish and in English, of it and its role in Frida's life. These paper dolls thus significantly differ from the cloth dolls of a variety of sizes sold in museum and gift shops, which generally depict Frida in Mexican peasant dress.

I should like to concentrate my attention on the Mexican booklet, paying particular attention to clothing that directs us to the intersection of beauty and physical disability. I shall then compare the individual outfit with its source, that is, either a painting by Frida or a photograph of her. The confrontation of the clothing intended for children with the photographs and paintings will shed light on the intersections of beauty, disability, and gender.

The book of paper dolls bears the title *Aquí cuelgan mis vestidos*. Those familiar with Frida Kahlo's work will see the title as a reference to her 1933 painting *Mi vestido cuelga ahí* (*Hang My Dress Right There*), which shows a dress hanging amidst a proliferation of New York buildings and objects.[8] The paper-doll book contains a model of the dress, described in this way:

> Diego and Frida remained in the United States until 1933; that same year, she painted this dress hanging from a washing line in a typical "Gringo" urban setting. The painting is entitled *Here Hangs My Dress*, and is currently on show at the Hoover Gallery in San Francisco.

One can see the similarity between the titles of the book and the painting as mere coincidence. Paper dolls always concern dress, and the booklet advertises itself as the first of a series depicting Mexican figures in paper dolls. Yet, as the description of this painting suggests, pictorializing Frida Kahlo's outfits hardly introduces a foreign element into her corpus. A 1937 painting entitled *Memory* plays in a corporally disquieting way (by creating intermediate states between hanging clothing and a human body) with the relations between Frida and sets of her clothing on hangers.[9] The project embodied in the book of paper dolls engages with more than just Frida's oeuvre. Carlos Fuentes notes that for Frida "clothing was something more than a second skin," stressing the purposeful theatricality in her carefully selected and arranged outfits.[10] One might expect, from the "*mis vestidos*" of its title, that the booklet presents only clothing worn by Frida. But no. The last two pages include clothing worn by her husband, Diego Rivera, and a paper doll of him to dress in them.

The cover of the booklet presents a fascinating and ambiguous image of the Frida destined to be popped out and dressed with the clothing inside. The doll's hair is shown as long but pulled back and intertwined with a purple scarf, typical of how Frida often wore it. It is parted in the middle, highlighting the forehead, as it often is in paintings and photographs in which Frida appears. In the paper likeness, golden earrings dangle from her earlobes. Earrings were not foreign to the real Frida, but they do not appear in every rendition of her. More problematic is the pink fingernail polish. While colored nail polish appears in some of the photographs of Frida and some of her self-portraits, it is by no means usual.

Those familiar with Frida's life and iconography recognize immediately that she is wearing a medical corset that she herself richly decorated with flowers and personal and political symbols. In this way her medical problems are visually represented. (These are also evoked in the text at the beginning and end of the book.) A person without such knowledge, however, such as a little girl holding the book in her hands, could see a quite different picture. To the untrained eye, the medical corset looks like a fashion corset: an undergarment, a foundation for other outfits. The lively and colorful decorations reinforce this appearance. Frida decorated other corsets with more intellectual and less decorative iconography.[11] This difference is further accentuated by the fact that on the cover of the paper-doll book, Frida's right hand blocks a medallion on her corset which, by its size and artistic border, would distract from the decorative style of the garment as a whole if it were visible. The paper-doll corset can be read as a medical garment, as sexy lingerie, or fetishistically as both at the same time. Unlike the outfits, this image of Frida's body in a corset is not directly related to, or legitimized by, a reference to a painting or photograph of Frida. Thus readers are neither told that they are looking at a medical corset nor offered any explanation for its presence.

The rest of the image in question reinforces this ambiguity, in that it shows a beautiful and perfect female body. The corset wraps Frida from her underarms to just below the waist. Her right arm is bent, with her hand resting on her upper abdomen (covering the medallion). The left arm is bent as well, but her left hand rests on her waist. Below the corset is a pair of pink underwear, trimmed on the bottom with white lace, that stops at the upper thigh. The silky-looking underwear creases so as to outline the tops of her thighs as they meet her pubic area. To make sure that the viewer does not miss these creases, the lines of the creases are in darker pink. Below these provocative undergarments are Frida's long legs, culminating in her feet slipped into a pair of black stiletto heels that leave the top of her feet visible but for a thin black strap across the ankle.

The paper pose is graceful, the figure elegant: Frida as a fashion model. While one could interpret this pose, with the right leg partly blocked by the left, as a reference to her childhood polio, the total effect is of a beautiful woman on high heels. Injury, paralytic atrophy, disability: all are missing. The stiletto heels are particularly inappropriate for a woman with Frida's physical challenges.

Among the outfits in the paper-doll book is one of a man's suit, complete with vest, tie, and pocket handkerchief in the jacket (fig. 11.2). Frida, in reality, was sometimes photographed in masculine clothing. But the pose of the paper figure references a specific family photograph (fig. 11.3). The children's book explains the outfit: "This is a reference to a famous photograph of Frida with her family taken by her father, Don Guillermo Kahlo. At the time, in 1926, she wore her hair very short and parted in the middle." Frida's father was a photographer, a German who immigrated to Mexico. After the death of his first wife, he married a devout and old-fashioned Catholic woman, and Frida was born nine years later. Guillermo was a professional and extremely talented photographer who was honored by the Mexican dictator Porfirio Diáz by being appointed the first official photographer of Mexican culture and its heritage.[12]

Figure 11.2. Frida Kahlo paper doll outfit: a light tan man's suit. By PERMISSION OF FRANCISCO ESTEBANEZ.

Figure 11.3. Frida Kahlo wearing a man's suit, far left, and
family, including her father, Don Guillermo Kahlo, c. 1924.
PHOTOGRAPH BY GUILLERMO KAHLO. BY PERMISSION OF VINCENTE WOLF.

In this important family picture, Frida catches our attention not only
because of her position in the photograph. Standing on the left edge of the
group, she is the only adult whose body can be seen in its entirety. The three
individuals standing in the back of the group are partly hidden from view by
those sitting in front of them; we only see their heads and some of their upper
bodies. And in front of those three in chairs are two younger Kahlo children
seated on the ground. Frida stands with right hand in her right pants pocket,
while her left rests on the shoulder of a seated individual.

The brilliant French critic Roland Barthes, in his book *La chambre claire: Note sur la photographie*, translated into English as *Camera Lucida*, speaks of the *punctum* in a photograph:

> For *punctum* is also: sting, speck, cut, little hole—and also a cast of the dice. A photograph's *punctum* is that accident which pricks me (but also bruises me, is poignant to me). . . . [A] "detail" attracts me. I feel that its mere presence changes my reading, that I am looking at a new photograph, marked in my eyes with a higher value. This "detail" is the *punctum*.[13]

For me, the *punctum* of the Kahlo family photograph is precisely the cross-dressed Frida herself, with her distinct look, her status as the only character standing, her hand the only one touching a family member. To use Barthes's words, her "mere presence changes my reading" of the visual text, the photograph. She represents an anomaly, a "hole," in the otherwise frozen family photograph.[14]

Looking at the strength of Frida's expression, the way in which she dominates the photograph, one is reminded of Roland Barthes's comment:

> Now, once I feel myself observed by the lens, everything changes: I constitute myself in the process of "posing," I instantaneously make another body for myself, I transform myself in advance into an image. This transformation is an active one.[15]

Most distinctive, of course, is Frida's decision to wear a man's suit. The photo was taken after both her polio and the horrific accident. The long pants serve to hide Frida's disability, just as the pose obscures the uneven length of her legs. It is well known that the most common way Frida obscured her legs was by wearing full-length dresses in the Tehuana style, many examples of which appear in the paper-doll book. Although the masculine clothing crosses genders, it does so only halfway. Closely tailored, it exposes an almost feminine elegance. When combined with Frida's smoldering, almost arrogant expression, it leaves her hovering between a highly effeminate young man and a sassy, erotically cross-ta painting or a photograph.[16] Neuroscientists have stressed the importance of faces in both art and cognition.[17] The paper Frida, facing the viewer's left, inverts the position of Frida's head in the family photograph, in which the face is directed to the viewer's right, toward the assembled family members. While both faces are in a minimal three-quarters profile, the photographed Frida lowers her head in an extremely provocative manner, eyes directed at the camera. The three-quarters profile singularizes Frida's gaze, since the other family members look at the camera directly. If we can infer that Frida's gaze is challenging the camera, the gazes of her family members are submissive and frozen in time. As Susan Sontag says so eloquently of politicians, "The three-quarter gaze is more common: a gaze that soars rather than confronts, suggesting instead of the relation to the viewer, to the present, the more ennobling abstract relation to the future."[18]

This is not the only male outfit offered for the paper doll. Estebanez provides another. Yet when it is compared with its original, in this case a painting by Frida, a different set of gender dynamics emerges. Estebanez explains the outfit by saying, "In 1940, when she was separated from Diego, Frida painted herself with short hair and dressed in a man's suit; she holds a pair of scissors in her hand and her hair clippings may be seen all over the floor."

The "man's suit" that the paper Frida will wear is black, accessorized with a black belt and a purple shirt whose sleeves sneak out ever so little from under the suit sleeves (fig. 11.4). Frida's left hand slips into her left pants pocket while her right hand, positioned palm up near her hip, holds a pair of scissors points downward, away from her body. Clearly visible is the red polish adorning the nails of her right hand. Were we to place this male outfit on the paper Frida doll, the fit would be reasonable. It might make, however, for a rather kinky version of the artist, her breasts emphasized by the close-fitting purple shirt and her stiletto heels appearing below the pant cuffs.

However, discrepancies would arise if we dressed the doll this way. One would be invisible: the substitution of red nail polish for the pink worn by the doll, since the male outfit includes a replacement right hand. More important is the clash between, on one hand, the crown of long hair that Frida wears wrapped around her head and intertwined with a purple scarf, and on the other, the hair of the painting on which the outfit is based. The purple of the scarf uncannily matches the purple of the shirt. But did not the commentary on the outfit point out that Frida "painted herself with short hair?"

The painting that inspired this outfit is *Autorretrato de pelona (Self-Portrait with Cropped Hair)*, a work presently hanging in the Museum of Modern Art in New York (fig. 11.5).[19] An extremely significant self-portrait, this painting is striking within the corpus of Frida's self-portraits. The artist is shown seated in a light-colored chair that highlights the fallen locks of black hair surrounding it like little black snakes. She returns the viewer's look with a three-quarters profile. Her suit, unlike the doll's outfit, is enormous, with the jacket hiding most of the purple shirt. Her shoes have a modest heel, as opposed to the stiletto shoes she wears as the doll. Most significant, perhaps,

Figure 11.4. Frida Kahlo paper doll outfit: a man's black suit with a purple shirt. By PERMISSION OF FRANCISCO ESTEBANEZ.

is the direction in which she holds the scissors. In the painting, both of her hands are on her thighs, with the scissors in her right hand. By their open blades and their proximity to the artist's vulva, they suggest a violent penetration or excision (were we to substitute a male for Frida, castration would come to mind immediately). Frida's head, fully proportional in her other paintings as well as in the paper-doll book, is here reduced in size relative to her body. The smaller head suggests a loss of personality, especially as the figure sits in a space of desolation. The chair that holds her is transformed into an almost live companion sharing her misery. This is a far cry from the crown of decorated hair the paper-doll Frida wears atop her head. That fashionably suited Frida is a proud figure, unlike her seated likeness.

This Frida in a man's suit is also a far cry from that in Guillermo Kahlo's photograph. While Frida in the photo smolders with androgynous eroticism, the painted Frida is aggressively defeminized without being butch. If the short hair in the photo creates ambiguity, the shorn hair in the painting is the removal of an attribute of beauty. The link of long hair to attractiveness is made explicit in the words of a popular song that Frida has penned at the top of the painting: "I see that if I loved you, it was for your

Figure 11.5. Frida Kahlo, *Self-Portrait with Cropped Hair*, 1940. Oil on canvas, 15 ¾ × 11 in. © ARS, N.Y. Gift of Edgar Kaufmann, Jr. Location: The Museum of Modern Art, New York. Photo credit: Digital image © The Museum of Modern Art, licensed by SCALA / Art Resource, N.Y. Image reference: ART165643.

hair, / Now that you are shorn, I no longer love you." The pants, whose original function was to hide disability, have taken on a second function as the negation of feminine beauty.

One could argue that the children's booklet had no other choice but to keep the suited Frida standing, as in all her other paper outfits; that it would have been much too difficult to execute the transfer of a seated subject. But would it not have been feasible to outfit the standing Frida doll in an oversized suit, and to show her shorn hair flowing down in semiliving strands over her suit? And, of course, the booklet could have simply omitted reference to this painful painting. Every image, however, represents a choice. The booklet's illustrations opt not only for a triumphant Frida but also for one that repeats, and perhaps increases, the androgyny that was inherent in the photograph. A painting of desperation becomes a fashion statement. A masochistic renunciation of beauty is transformed into an alternate form of beauty.

It is hardly surprising that a children's book should have prettified its heroine and made her more conventionally feminine. But once it enters the highly charged world of Frida Kahlo's clothing—of Frida's closet, we might say—it cannot escape the tangles and contradictions where beauty, disability, and gender collide.

NOTES

1. Anita Silvers, "From the Crooked Timber of Humanity, Beautiful Things Can Be Made," in *Beauty Matters*, ed. Peg Zeglin Brand (Bloomington: Indiana University Press, 2000), 197–221; and Russell Shuttleworth, "Disability, Fetishization of," in *Encyclopedia of Sex and Gender*, ed. Fedwa Malti-Douglas (Farmington Hills, Mich.: Macmillan Reference, 2007), 397–98.

2. See, for example, Brand, *Beauty Matters*; Francette Pacteau, *The Symptom of Beauty* (London: Reaktion, 1994); Susan Bordo, *The Male Body: A New Look at Men in Public and in Private* (New York: Farrar, Strauss, and Giroux, 1999); Dominique Paquet, *Miroir, mon beau miroir: Une histoire de la beauté* (Paris: Gallimard, 1997); Linda Nochlin, *Bathers, Bodies, Beauty* (Cambridge, Mass.: Harvard University Press, 2006); and Naomi Wolf, *The Beauty Myth: How Images of Beauty Are Used Against Women* (New York: William Morrow, 1991).

3. See, for example, Susan Crutchfield and Marcy Epstein, eds., *Points of Contact: Disability, Art, and Culture* (Ann Arbor: University of Michigan Press, 2000); Leonard J. Davis, ed., *The Disability Studies Reader* (New York: Routledge, 1997); David T. Mitchell and Sharon L. Snyder, eds., *The Body and Physical Difference: Discourses of Disability* (Ann Arbor: University of Michigan Press, 2000); and Fedwa Malti-Douglas, *Blindness and Autobiography: Al-Ayyam of Taha Husayn* (Princeton: Princeton University Press, 1988).

4. Linda Nochlin, "Why Have There Been No Great Women Artists?" in *Art and Sexual Politics: Women's Liberation, Women Artists and Art History,* ed. Thomas B. Hess and Elizabeth C. Baker (London: Collier MacMillan, 1971), 1–39.

5. Margaret Lindauer, *Devouring Frida: The Art History and Popular Celebrity of Frida Kahlo* (Hanover, N.H.: University Press of New England, 1999); and Bárbara C. Cruz, *Frida Kahlo: Portrait of a Mexican Painter* (Springfield, N.J.: Enslow, 1996), 88–93.

6. The literature on Frida is enormous. Among the most important are Hayden Herrera, *Frida: A Biography of Frida Kahlo* (New York: Harper, 2002); Hayden Herrera, *Frida Kahlo: The Paintings* (New York: Harper, 2002); Lindauer, *Devouring Frida*; Araceli Rico, *Frida Kahlo: Fantasía de un cuerpo herido* (Mexico City: Plaza y Valdés, 1990); and, for a recent and highly informative account, Christina Burrus, *Frida Kahlo: "Je peins ma réalité"* (Paris: Gallimard, 2007).

7. Francisco J. Estebanez, *Aquí cuelgan mis vestidos: Frida Kahlo* (Mexico City: Reproducciones Fotomecánicas, 1999), unpaginated. Except for the titles of paintings, all translations from Spanish are my own. For the gendered cultural significance of such playthings see, for example, Beverly Lyon Clark and Margaret Higonnet, eds., *Girls, Boys, Books, Toys: Gender in Children's Literature and Culture* (Baltimore: Johns Hopkins University Press, 1999).

8. The Spanish titles of the paintings are taken from the Spanish translation of Herrera's *The Paintings:* Hayden Herrera, *Frida Kahlo: Las pinturas,* trans. M. J. and R. C. (Mexico City: Editorial Diana, 1994), 98–101.

9. Herrera, *The Paintings,* 112–13.

10. Carlos Fuentes, "Introduction," in *Frida Kahlo, 1907–2007,* English edition (Mexico City: Instituto Nacional de Bellas Artes, 2007), 34–35.

11. See, for example, Marthe Zamora, *Frida Kahlo: The Brush of Anguish,* abridged and trans. Marilyn Sode Smith (San Francisco: Chronicle, 1990), 127; the corset that appears on the doll can be seen on p. 119.

12. Burrus, *Frida Kahlo,* 15.

13. Roland Barthes, *Camera Lucida: Reflections on Photography,* trans. Richard Howard (London: Vintage, 2000), 27, 42 (originally published as *La chambre claire: Note sur la photographie* [Paris: Gallimard Seuil, 1980]).

14. See also Graham Clarke, *The Photograph* (Oxford: Oxford University Press, 1997), 27–29.

15. Barthes, *Camera Lucida,* 10–11.

16. See, for example, Barthes, *Camera Lucida,* 34–38; Susan Sontag, *On Photography* (London: Penguin, 2002), 37–38; and Alexander Sturgis, *Faces* (London: National Gallery Company, 2001).

17. See, for example, Robert L. Solso, *The Psychology of Art and the Evolution of the Conscious Brain* (Cambridge, Mass.: MIT Press, 2003), 133–53.

18. Sontag, *On Photography,* 38.

19. Herrera, *Las pinturas,* 150–52.

PART 3.

THE BODY IN PERFORMANCE

12. Beauty, Youth, and the Balinese *Legong* Dance

STEPHEN DAVIES

Prologue

At about the age of twenty, the renowned *legong*[1] dancer of the village of Peliatan, Cokorda Istri Ratih Iryani (born 1963, and known less formally as Cok Ratih; plate 8), anticipated the imminent end of her performing career. She said,

> When I get older and weaker people will not want to see me. Later when I look older and people do not like to see my face I may dance the dances where you wear masks. Here everyone is an expert and everyone can criticise, and a poor dancer is openly criticised and told to leave. Dancers can be criticised also just for not being beautiful, though it's not their fault and they can dance very well.[2]

In this chapter I discuss beauty and youth in Balinese dance, with special reference to *legong*. *Legong* is the "classic" Balinese dance genre for females and is represented by Balinese to the world as the quintessence of grace, charm, and beauty in their performing arts. The core of the genre comprises about fourteen dances, a third of which are now lost, though new dances are occasionally created. Traditionally, the dances were from thirty to sixty minutes in length, though they are typically cut much shorter for tourist performances. Despite the fact that some dances relate stories, the dancers are always dressed the same, the narrative elements are stylized, and the focus falls on the beauty of form and movement rather than on the dramatic content. In the dances of the basic repertoire, two identically clothed dancers, called *legong*, are elaborately costumed in gold and green or silver and purple. An abstract introduction (which can be dropped) is provided by a third dancer, the *condong*, usually dressed in red and gold. The gamelan orchestra that is most appropriate for the accompaniment of *legong* is of the kind known as *semar pegulingan* or *pelegongan*, though the more common *gong kebyar* ensemble, with its different tuning and weightier tone, is often substituted nowadays. About thirty musicians are involved. Formerly, both the choreographies and the accompaniments differed from region to region, but such distinctions are being eroded and *legong*, like other traditional dance and dramatic forms, is in decline overall.[3]

I take Cok Ratih's remarks, quoted above, as my text. The views she presents might not seem surprising, given that patriarchal societies generally equate female beauty with youth. Before jumping too quickly to conclusions about how Bali conforms to a wider pattern, however, we should note that a prominent *legong* dancer in the early 1980s viewed an age of merely twenty years as the twilight of a *legong* dancer's public career. Apparently, the notion of beauty that is invoked here is not straightforwardly equivalent to heterosexual male norms for female sexual attractiveness, which may favor younger women but don't require them to be under twenty. What then is the connection between beauty and youth in Balinese *legong*?

Youth

Girls usually begin to learn *legong* at about six years of age and, if they are good enough, begin performing publicly at about nine. Balinese experts identify ten as the ideal age for a dancer in this genre.[4] In an earlier period, Cok Ratih would have retired from public dancing well before the age of twenty. In the 1930s and '40s, the age of retirement was twelve to fourteen, though one "superannuated" seventeen-year-old dancer was noted.[5] In 1948, Colin McPhee wrote,

> At the age of ten, with the approach of adolescence, [*legong* dancers] have become "too heavy." Their haunting, sexless charm, their swift, miniature virtuosity suddenly vanishes. The club looks about for new dancers, and as these become expert, the older ones retire. They never appear again, unless as members of the operetta company. But no girl dances after marriage, except perhaps as one of the group of ritual dancers in the temple.[6]

In a similar vein, John Coast, on a visit to the village of Saba in about 1950, records,

> Suddenly a bunch of neatly dressed girls, hand in hand, brushed past us, one of them turning toward us and smiling, for we saw the flash of white teeth. Raka laughed when we asked him who the girl was. "It was Soli, the Legong dancer," he said. "She is nearly a woman now. She goes with older girls these days, seldom any more with the other Legong girls. It is a nuisance, but soon we shall be looking for another Legong dancer." "But Raka—how old is Soli? Eleven? Twelve?" "Maybe. She doesn't know how old she is. But she has a young sister who has already menstruated. Soli will be carried off [that is, married] soon. Tuan has noticed perhaps that when she dances her eyes sometimes glance at a man? That is very bad indeed in a Legong. It is good if she marries."[7]

The *legong* dancers of the past were often married at puberty, frequently to high-caste males.[8]

Several points emerge here. The beauty of *legong* dancers does not consist in their looking or acting in a sexually provocative or inviting manner. In the past, girls stopped dancing about the age of puberty, perhaps because they married almost immediately. More recently, performers have continued to dance into womanhood. Gusti Ayu Wartini, writing in 1978, noted that dancers were replaced at sixteen, and only a few years later Cok Ratih was dancing at twenty.[9]

Because of their youth, it has long been held that *legong* dancers must be virgins. A film shot by Henry de la Falaise in Bali in 1933 is titled *Legong: Dance of the Virgins*.[10] Even Balinese experts have made this claim.[11] But if this was true previously, it is not so now, given the number of *legong* dancers who are also mothers.

Several of the most sacred temple dances, such as *sanghyang dedari* and *topeng sanghyang*, are performed only by prepubescent girls.[12] Menstruating women are regarded as ritually impure (as are people in mourning, among others) and, therefore, do not enter the temple precincts. While some holy dances, in particular *rejang* and *mendet*, are performed by the women of the village in the temple during temple ceremonies, dances central to the ritual that require specialists cannot easily be entrusted to women performers, in case they will be unable to attend.[13]

Such proscriptions do not apply to *legong*, however. Unlike the most sacred (*wali*) dances, such as *sanghyang dedari* and *mendet*, which are reserved for the temple's inner courtyard, and unlike semiceremonial (*bebali*) dances, performed in the temple's middle courtyard, *legong* is secular (*balih-bali-han*).[14] Originally, its function was to entertain the village royalty. It is often performed at temple ceremonies, but the dancing takes place in the performance space immediately outside the temple. So no religious prohibition prevents dancers' extending their careers as far as they (or their audiences) choose.

These observations leave us with two questions: why do the dancers begin at such a young age, and what made it possible for dancers to postpone their retirement as the twentieth century progressed?

The answer to the first query has nothing to do with purity or virginity. Girls traditionally start with *legong* because it is the fundamental and most complete repository of female dance movements and techniques.[15] There are names for at least two hundred *legong* dance positions and attitudes (*agem*); movements that link positions (*abah tangkis*); postures, strides, and foot movements (*tandang*); facial expressions (*tangkep*); movements of the head and neck (*guluwangsul*); and shoulder, hip, hand, finger, and fan movements.[16] The eyes, face, neck, arms, hands, fingers, and fan can be used in dozens of ways. A dancer who has mastered *legong* is prepared to take on any other form of female Balinese dance.

Moreover, the movements and attitudes require such flexibility that the basic techniques must be acquired at a very young age. McPhee recognized this:

> The little girls who learn the difficult *legong* dance work hard. They begin at the age of six or seven, while their fragile bodies are still alert enough for the lightning-swift dartings and turns, the jointless backward bends. Only after a year, when hands and feet, head, shoulders and arms, accents of eyes and innumerable details have been timed to perfection with the music will they be allowed to appear in public.[17]

Dr. Wayan Dibia, professor of choreography at ISI, the college of the arts in Denpasar, said this:

> In the old days everything was tough. They were taught the basic positions first. Now, at ISI, we train dancers who are already adult. It is hard to adjust technique and even mentality—they can get insulted if someone fixes their movement. . . . With older dancers, sometimes it is hard to move the body. In Balinese dance you basically mold your body to very difficult positions. It is better to do this before eight years of age, when the body and bones have elasticity and flexibility. At twenty you can learn, but the kinesthetic awareness is not as good.[18]

The answer to the second question, which asked what changes allowed danc-ers to prolong their careers past the onset of puberty, must be more complex and speculative.

Though many authorities date the appearance of *legong* to the early nineteenth century, I disagree. *Legong* first appeared about 1889 and reached its modern form between 1915 and 1930.[19] It superseded an earlier and related genre, *andir*, which was danced by attractive boys. At this time, there was a close association between prostitution and women dancers, espe-cially in connection with the social dance called *joged*, in which the dancer draws males from the audience to dance with her.[20] A related form, *gan-drung*, involved boy dancers dressed as girls. Though many *legong* dancers graduated to *joged*,[21] the dances of which closely resembled the more formal parts of *legong*, it was not widely regarded as proper for them to do so. And it was not appropriate for those who married to continue dancing in public.

Things began to change in the 1920s and '30s, however. The impe-tus toward female equality initiated at this time came not from Dutch colo-nial rule—the Dutch conquered south Bali in 1908—but rather from within Balinese society. Women replaced men in the traditional opera and drama forms of *arja* and *gambuh* from the late 1920s.[22] They took over the roles of refined male characters as well as those of women. Also, the raunchier forms of *joged* were traded for more decorous versions,[23] which remain pop-ular today. (*Gandrung* has all but disappeared, though.) About the same time, the new musical genre of *gong kebyar* became dominant, and *kebyar* dances created for women became increasingly common, with famous exam-ples including the pieces choreographed by I Nyoman Kaler in the 1940s and "Teruna jaya" and the bumblebee dance "Oleg tamulilingan," both choreo-graphed in 1952.[24] The Indonesian government's attempt to foster national-ism in the 1950s and 1960s led to many new *kebyar* dances showing peasant labor—for example, the fishing dance "Nelayan," the weaving dance "Tenun," and "Tani," which depicts farmers. And in the 1980s, many new dances were derived from the innovative dance-drama genre, *sendratari*, including repre-sentations of deer ("Kicang kencana"), ducks ("Belibis"), and birds of paradise ("Cendrawasih").[25]

The demand for new dances and for the women to dance them came from a number of sources, then. A conscious attempt to develop a national identity provided some impetus, as did the New Order move in the 1970s to devolve more autonomy to regions, including Bali, whose arts are recognized in the country's constitution as "peaks of culture" (*puncak-puncak kebudayaan*). From the 1970s, the regional Balinese government has promoted cultural tourism and linked it to the development and preservation of Balinese culture. The number of tourists rose from 23,000 in 1970 to 133,000 in 1978.[26] By the mid-1990s Bali saw more than a million foreign tourists and a million Indonesian tourists each year, and these figures increased until the Kuta bombing of October 2002. The Balinese marketed their culture to this huge influx and, since the late 1970s, scores of performance groups, the vast majority of which involve many women dancers, have performed nightly in centers such as Sanur, Kuta, Legian, and Ubud. In the 1990s, about thirty-five performance groups performed weekly in the Ubud area, for instance. As might be guessed, the deleterious effects of cultural tourism on the Balinese arts have been much debated, and it is certainly true that many dance forms have been cut or simplified for tourist consumption.[27] Nevertheless, funds from tourism have been used to preserve classical Balinese forms of drama and dance, and there can be no denying the benefits that many dancers and other performers have derived from tourist-related employment.[28]

About the time the Balinese began to showcase their arts to the wider world, they became self-conscious about the study and preservation of their traditions. The college of the Balinese arts (ASTI, later STSI, now ISI) was founded in 1967 and there was a huge increase in Indonesian-language studies of Balinese music and dance written by Balinese scholars. These works discussed the classification of Balinese dance into sacred and profane types, the development and evolution of Balinese dance, and the history and status of *legong*.[29] Efforts culminated with Dr. Madé Bandem's *Ensiklopedi tari Bali* (Encyclopedia of Balinese Dance) of 1982. Meanwhile, attempts were made to record and revive classical dance genres, such as *legong*.[30] In addition, the annual, month-long Bali Arts Festival (Pesta kesenian Bali) was founded in 1979 to feature indigenous performing arts.[31] From its inception, it has attracted huge crowds of Balinese but very few Westerners.

Another consideration may have led to retaining dancers rather than replacing them: each new generation was of lower quality. There are always many Balinese girls keen to learn to dance, but modern life—school, cell phones, video games, extracurricular classes in English and in computer skills, and so on—makes it impossible for them to train as hard and with such single-minded dedication as was usual as recently as thirty years ago. Besides, they do not generally get the individual attention that characterized traditional methods of teaching. As a result, the best of the older dancers are almost always technically superior to those who follow them.[32]

In addition to factors affecting the arts specifically, wider social changes altered the behavior and status of women.[33] Many became educated and left the home, rice fields, and open-air markets to work in offices and shops. The age of marriage rose and the number of children per woman fell. As elsewhere, slowly the range of choices and liberties for women increased.

As these various considerations indicate, not only did it become socially acceptable for female dancers to extend their careers, it also became hugely more practical to do so. They could continue as *legong* dancers or move into *kebyar* or other dance and drama repertoires.[34] Inevitably, the rate at which senior dancers were replaced slowed.

Terminology

Before discussing the topic of beauty in connection with the *legong* dance, it may be useful to describe the vocabulary used to characterize the beauty of the dancers and of the dance.

The Balinese language distinguishes between beauty in females and beauty or attractiveness of appearance in nonhuman items. A beautiful woman is *jegeg* in high Balinese and *ayu* in low, whereas a beautiful thing would be *becik pisan* in high Balinese and, in low Balinese, *luwung sajan* in the south and *melah gati* in the north.[35] A similar distinction is made in Indonesian, with *cantik* referring to a beautiful woman and *indah* to a beautiful view, for example. A beautiful *legong* dancer will be described as *jegeg* or *ayu* (or as *cantik* in Indonesian), whether she is ten or twenty. Depending on the context, these words can be translated as "pretty," "cute," or "nice," as well as "(sexually) attractive or beautiful." The vocabulary for describing attractiveness in particular female (or male) attributes is, of course, much richer than I have so far indicated. For instance, a young woman should be *lansing lanyar*, which means slender, gently rounded, and elegant.

Melah or *luwung* and *becik* mean "good" or "fine," and can be used to describe dancing of high quality. *Bagus* (in both Balinese and Indonesian) is another general term for "good." Terms for praising dancers include *lincah* (in both Balinese and Indonesian, meaning "energetic," "agile"), *dueg* (Balinese, "clever at"), and *luwes* (Indonesian, "elegant," "flexible").[36]

Beauty

If the ideal *legong* dancer is a ten-year-old child with, as McPhee put it, "haunting, sexless charm," it is obvious that the beauty of the dance does not rely on the explicit display of female sexuality. In what, then, does the beauty of *legong* consist? The most obvious objects of admiration are the richly ornate,

gilded, glittering costumes and frangipani-crowned headdresses; the precision
with which the dancers match every note and accent of the music with movements of their bodies, eyes, fingers, or fans; the accuracy with which the two
legong dancers synchronize their dancing; the effortless virtuosity with which
they perform intricate and extremely demanding steps and movements; and,
above all, the controlled energy, grace, suppleness, elegance, and charm of
the dance itself. In other words, the dance has an exquisite formal and aesthetic character. This is not to say that the sex of the dancers is of no moment,
however. Generally, we can tell people's sex from how they move, even in
darkness with their movements visible only as the motion of points of light
attached to the body.[37] And, like the dance of many other cultures, Balinese
dance steps, gestures, and gaits often come in "male" and "female" versions,
so there should be no mistaking the gendered character of the *legong* dance.
Inevitably, then, the formal and aesthetic character that here is so exquisite is
unmistakably that of a dance for girls or young women.[38] In other words, the
dance may be sexless in that it does not make a display of female sexuality, but
it most certainly is not thereby desexed.

When Cok Ratih danced *legong* as a young adult, she did not invest it
with sexual tension or play to the audience. The aesthetic and formal values of the performance remained paramount. So why was she so concerned
with her appearance? She lamented the imminent arrival of the moment
"when I look older and people do not like to see my face." In what way does
female beauty enter into assessing the beauty of the dance? One key lies in
the Balinese religion.

Bali is nominally Hindu, though the religion takes a distinctive form on
the island.[39] The pervasive influence of animism and of ancestor worship is
noticeable, as is the range of spirit forces, both good and bad, that inhabit
the ground and air. To placate and balance these various gods and ancestors,
constant rounds of offerings are made, and this task falls mainly to women.
Many women spend up to a third of their waking time fabricating offerings
from leaves, flowers, fruit, and rice and presenting offerings around the housing compound, at the house temples, at shrines by crossroads and in the rice
fields, at the temples of the village, and at more distant temples with a connection to the village or family. The presentation of offerings at the home
or business place is a daily ritual for almost all women, and they dress for
the task. At the very least they wear a sash (*selempot*), sarong (*kamben*), and
shirt. On more important occasions, they wear a *kebaya*—a lacy, sheer, long-
sleeved shirt with a built-in bodice—and put their hair up.[40] The appearance
of the presenter is part of the offering.

Women have a religious obligation to beautify themselves for religious observances. Nowhere is this more apparent than at the ceremonies (*odalan*) celebrating the anniversaries of temples.[41] These begin with rituals inviting the ancestors to descend and dwell in shrines in the temple for the duration of the ceremony. The ancestors and gods are lovers of beauty in all things, and everything that takes place in the ceremony acknowledges this. There are elaborate tributes and sculptures made of food and flowers, everyone wears their finest clothes, and shadow puppet plays, dramas, and music are offered for the gods' entertainment. Dancing plays a central role. The primary invitation to the gods and ancestors is the women's dance *rejang*.[42] This is often performed by the young girls of the village, but females of all ages may take part. Another, very informal, dance, *mendet*, involves mainly (and often older) women, and takes place on the first night and near the ceremony's close. These are offerings to the ancestors and gods that celebrate female beauty in its many manifestations.

Even secular dances such as *legong* take place during temple ceremonies, immediately outside the temple's entrance. Moreover, all dances, including secular ones, are always offerings to the gods, whether they are performed as part of a temple festival, as an entertainment for the Balinese public, or as part of a tourist show. To class a dance as secular is to say that it cannot be performed within the inner sanctum of the temple and that it may be performed apart from formal religious rituals, but is not to deny that it is presented for the delectation of the gods whenever it occurs.

> Balinese music in its traditional setting is essentially religious. . . . Every performance is an offering to the gods or an attempt to placate evil spirits. . . . Music for entertainment is also religious. Unlike ceremonial music, however, it is a spectator performance. Although the visible audience is composed of Balinese, its primary purpose is to entertain and propitiate an invisible audience: the gods.[43]

Moreover, Balinese seek an aesthetically pleasing balance of factors in ordinary contexts.

> In Bali, beauty within ritual is a basic ingredient of efficacy and, in a sense, of any social activity at all. Not only are the Balinese gods and deities notorious connoisseurs of the arts, appreciating both embellishment and minute aesthetic detail, but also, physical interaction or activity within any environment or space seeks a flow and balanced ordering, an equilibrium that is appreciated as an aesthetic property, sensually, formally, and psychologically.[44]

Now, the Balinese ancestors and gods have all-too-human aesthetic preferences when it comes to estimating the beauty of young women. No one would deny that there is beauty associated with childish innocence and openness, or with the dignity and grace of old age, and there is also beauty of character and spirit, not only of appearance. The Balinese gods respect and acknowledge these kinds of beauty, no doubt. Yet Cok Ratih expects her audience, both living and ancestral, to consider attractiveness of appearance in assessing a young woman's beauty, and that includes her beauty as a *legong* dancer. (Though the costumes are tight around the chest, older *legong* dancers do not bind their breasts or try to pass for thirteen-year-olds.) The fact that it is not appropriate to judge child *legong* dancers in terms of sexual attractiveness does not mean that older *legong* dancers should not be. Indeed, this is to be expected, given that the dance should be beautiful in all the aspects it displays.

These attitudes are predictable if evolutionary psychologists are correct in some of their claims about the biological roots of our aesthetic preferences. For instance, it has been argued that our ancestors sought habitats that offered food, water, shelter, safety, good hunting conditions, and so on. Over time, the preference for such habitats developed as an aesthetic fondness. Without calculating or even understanding why, *Homo sapiens* came to regard habitats with such features not only as desirable but also as beautiful or pleasing.[45] Something similar is proposed as the evolutionary basis of the aesthetic judgments we apply to our fellow humans' physical appearances. Fitness markers for health and potential fecundity, as well as secondary sexual features, were found to be pleasing by heterosexuals of the opposite sex.[46] Eventually, concern with such features took on an aesthetic dimension, so that the relevant characteristics were experienced more widely in terms of what is beautiful or handsome.[47] And just as we find features of landscapes and habitats that were significant to our ancestors' survival to be aesthetically pleasing even when we have no desire to live or hunt there, so we find that the marks of human beauty retain their aesthetic significance even when we are not seeking a mate or assessing a sexual rival.

So here is Cok Ratih's situation: she may perform the *legong* dance, but in doing so she has an obligation to please her audience and the gods. To discharge this duty, she must continue to dance beautifully, of course. In addition, she must meet an ideal of womanly beauty. Why, though, does she fear that she will not be able to do so much beyond the age of twenty? I can think of three possible reasons.

A first and probably the most important consideration is respect for the dance tradition: even if *legong* dancers need not be prepubescent, they should be young and lithe. The age at which it is no longer appropriate for a woman to continue to dance *legong* is established informally by social practice and convention, as was noted previously. As the wider Balinese society and the place of women within it altered, older dancers were progressively accepted, though twenty seemed close to the upper limit by the 1980s. So Cok Ratih's position might be like that of a twenty-year-old actress who takes on the role of a seventeen-year-old in a potentially long-running play. She can pull off the part now, but there is a definite limit to the number of years in which she will be able to do so plausibly, however artistically good she is as a performer. Women do not lose their beauty at twenty-five, but an otherwise beautiful woman would have ceased to be a beautiful *legong* dancer at that age.

A second possibility is that, like many very young people (who cannot seriously imagine that they will ever be thirty), she simply believes that the full flower of womanly beauty is so short-lived that it fades by the mid-twenties. Allowing that there are many kinds of beauty and that beauty is not skin deep, many young men and women still assume that the kind of beauty that characterizes sexual attractiveness in women belongs exclusively to the very youthful. They are wrong. The flame of attraction need not gutter with maturity, unless the individuals involved are ground down by physical labor, childbearing, and the relentless and agonizing task of scratching out a living, which was unavoidable for our ancestors and is the common fate still across much of the globe. The fact that sexual attractiveness need not be compromised by age is not obvious to the young, however. That awareness, which no doubt the Balinese gods possess, is learned later.

Third, though Cok Ratih talks about her appearance, she may have lurking doubts about her capacity to dance beautifully when she has reached her mid-twenties. Note that few female gymnasts can perform at the highest level beyond twenty. Though *legong* is not a competitive sport and is not as demanding as international gymnastics, it is physically challenging. Dancing of the highest quality requires a degree of stamina and suppleness that can be achieved only through dedicated practice and commitment, and both the taste and the capacity for these can be anticipated to wane as other facets of life become more salient.

Putting Biology into Beauty

It might be thought that my earlier invocation of evolutionary biology is crude and unnecessary. This could be the view, for example, of a person who regards gender as socially constructed in all its aspects. Alternatively, another critic might maintain that the biological aspect of womanly beauty must be irrelevant to Cok Ratih's concerns, and that they are prompted mainly by worries over passing the expected age of retirement rather than by fears about the diminution of her attractiveness as a woman.

My first opponent might agree that a concern with the beauty of the dance inevitably implies awareness of the dancer's beauty, but then deny the relevance of the link I posited between biologically conditioned preferences for a sexually beautiful woman and the beauty of the dance. The *legong* dance is culturally contrived and highly artificial, this critic would say. Notions of female gender and beauty are also socially constructed. How we decorate, clothe, and present ourselves is dictated by customs and fashion, not by biology, and the same is true of the shapes into which we sculpt our bodies and of the manners in which we express and realize our sexuality. There may be a connection between the beauty of *legong* and norms for female beauty, but it is not possible to explain this link by reference to evolution by sexual selection, because gender norms transcend and supersede biological sex and animal predilections.

Here is the theme of the argument that resists this first position: as a dance, *legong* is artificial and cultural, but the girls and women dancing it are biological organisms with a long evolutionary history shaped in part by sexual selection. They judge themselves and are judged by others according to the standards of beauty of appearance that are apt for their age, not solely as dancers, and, as was argued previously, there is no easy or fitting way to divorce consideration of the dance's beauty from consideration of the beauty of the dancer who performs it. I maintain that we cannot take the biology out of beauty, though there is more to beauty than is provided by biology, and we cannot take the sex out of gender, though there is more to gender than is contributed by biological sex.

I do not deny the extent to which mutable, variable cultural conventions direct many of the ways we gender and beautify ourselves. And I am no defender of biological essentialism or determinism as regards such matters.[48] As well, I allow that there is much more to sexual attractiveness and beauty than physical appearance, though the emphasis in this paper falls on beauty's outward show. Nevertheless, we should not lose sight of the fact that present-day humans are the product of a long evolutionary history and the descendants of its adaptational successes. Our ancestors sought mates who showed signs of health, immunity from disease, and fertility, and whom they perceived as sexually attractive.[49] This was a mutual process, with each partner not only choosing but also having to be chosen by the other. In consequence, both had to be aware not only of what they found desirable but also of what was fancied by the other, and both aimed, as far as they could, to satisfy the other's preference. Inevitably, both also worried about whether they would measure up to the preferences of those they most desired as mates. And because so much of our self-esteem and social standing is bound up with how we are assessed by our conspecifics, the wish to be admired by members of the other sex (and of one's own) came to persist more generally, even where one was not in the market for a mate.

We can surmise that at twenty Cok Ratih was much like others of her age, both in Bali and abroad. She would judge the desirability and attractiveness of both males and females. She might do so in choosing a preferred mate or assessing potential rivals, but more generally she would include judgments of attractiveness as one among many relevant to predicting and understanding the social behavior and relationships of the members of her community. Of course, many of the norms to which she would appeal in arriving at such judgments are culturally established. For instance, if she were seeking a husband, as a high-caste female she would likely consider her choice to be restricted to high-caste males. Caste is a socially grounded distinction, not a biological one. However, other factors relevant to her judgments might include universally applicable biological features and indicators that have been highlighted by evolution as possessing adaptive value under most social circumstances.

As well as estimating the desirability and attractiveness of others, Cok Ratih would also judge herself. Often such judgments are harsher than others would expect, perhaps because people are inclined to hold themselves to high, even exaggerated, standards and to overemphasize their flaws. Moreover, when standards are thus exaggerated, they are often inappropriately skewed, so that, for instance, the majority of heterosexual males are wrongly assumed to prefer extreme youth and slimness in females. Meanwhile, though Cok Ratih no doubt realizes that there is more to female beauty than physical attractiveness, these other factors are liable to drop out of account when she considers the duties of a dancer. In a highly stylized dance such as *legong*, the dancer is not supposed to imprint her individual personality, character, or feelings on the dance, so she will be assessed mainly on how the dance looks, which will be a function of her skill, technique, presentation, and appearance. As a ten-year-old girl, she will be judged for the beauty appropriate in the appearance of female children, and as a twenty-year-old woman, she will be evaluated for the beauty appropriate to a young woman. She has an obligation to the ancestors, the gods, and her audience to exemplify the kind of beauty that is appropriate, and no doubt this will be important also to her sense of herself and her self-esteem.

These arguments invite a reply from the second of the critics I described above, who argues that it should not be the biological notion of womanly beauty that concerns Cok Ratih. Signs of health, immunity from disease, and fertility, along with other features acknowledged as sexually attractive in women, do not suddenly fade in the mid-twenties. So it should not be physical attractiveness that Cok Ratih had in mind when she said, "When I get older and weaker people will not want to see me."

My view is that, rather than showing the irrelevance of biological considerations, this important observation challenges us to consider how they relate to and are inflected by the cultural context. The judgment of beauty needs to be suitably relativized. As a woman, Cok Ratih would not lose her beauty at, say, twenty-five, but as a *legong* dancer she would appear to her audience to be less beautiful because less suited to dancing, having passed the age at which retirement from public performance is commonly expected.[50] The practices and conventions setting the age at which a dancer should retire are mutable and to some extent arbitrary; they are socially established and, as was noted earlier, have altered over the years. A woman's beauty as a *legong* dancer is judged according to social norms that go beyond the merely biological, beyond physical appearance alone; the judgment takes account of her age in relation to the age expected for retirement. This shows that there is more to the beauty of a twenty-year-old dancer than her looks. It does not demonstrate, however, that her attractiveness as a young woman is irrelevant to the beauty of her dancing provided she is not deemed too old to perform, and it does not indicate that her attractiveness is assessed by reference to norms established arbitrarily by social legislation, as opposed to ones shaped in part by evolution. Culture and evolution are not opposed and incompatible. Rather, they stand to our human way of life as eggs and flour do to the cake in which they are ingredients. I would not oppose calling the relevant norms of womanly beauty socially established, so long as the relevant kind of sociality is also acknowledged as an aspect of our evolved nature. The point is that the norms of physical attractiveness are not completely arbitrary—they could not be set purely at whim—but this is fully consistent with their being subject to cultural structuring.

In the *legong* dance, we cannot be indifferent to the fact that the dancer is a girl, female adolescent, or woman, though the topic of the dance is not femaleness as such. Our awareness of the dancer's gender and age informs and enriches our appreciation of the dance. Where the dancer is a young woman, she brings her sexual attractiveness to the beauty of the dance. In other words, we cannot take the body out of the dancer or the dancer out of the dance, even if the physical appearance of the dancer is not the only aesthetically relevant factor on show. Just as the offerer is part of the offering, so the dancer and how she looks, given her age and provided she is not too old according to the social expectations of the day, is integral to the dance and the beauty it displays.

Epilogue

The famous ensemble Tirta Sari performs weekly in Peliatan for tourists. The show contains two *legong* dances. At the time of writing, one of these is danced by young women. They first performed together at about ten years of age in late 1996. Probably they will stop dancing soon, or graduate to other dances that use slightly older women, and will be replaced by a new group of prepubescent *legongs*. The second *legong* dance in the Tirta Sari show is performed by Cok Ratih, now well into her forties, and by other women of a similar age, including Anak Agung Gek Raka and Anak Agung Alit Serimpi. The dancers, as well as the dance and the dancing, are as beautiful as ever, and the gods and ancestors have not yet been heard to complain.

Notes

I thank Carolyn Korsmeyer, Sherri Irvin, and Laura Noszlopy for their advice and helpful criticism.

1. Note that technical terms for musical types, dances, dance movements, and the like are usually Balinese words, while Indonesian is the language of publication and of the state. I do not usually indicate which language is used. Translations of interviews and publications in Indonesian are my own.

2. Hugh Mabbett, *The Balinese* (Wellington: January, 1985), 134.

3. Stephen Davies, "Balinese *Legong*: Revival or Decline?" *Asian Theatre Journal* 23, no. 2 (Fall 2006): 314–41.

4. Anak Agung Gede Oka Dalem, interviewed in Indonesian, Peliatan, July 6, 2003; Wayan Dibia, interviewed in English, Denpasar, July 12, 2003; and Sang Ayu Ketut Muklin, interviewed in Indonesian, Teges, July 6, 2003. All interviews were conducted by me.

5. Walter Spies and Beryl de Zoete, *Dance and Drama in Bali* (1938; Singapore: Periplus, 2002), 229–30. See also Miguel Covarrubias, *Island of Bali* (1937; Singapore: Periplus, 1999).

6. Colin McPhee, "Dance in Bali," *Dance Index* 7, no. 8 (August 1948): 195.

7. John Coast, *Dancing out of Bali* (1953 as *Dancers of Bali*; Singapore: Periplus, 2004), 47–48.

8. Spies and de Zoete, *Dance and Drama in Bali*, 229.

9. Gusti Ayu Wartini, "Legong keraton Peliatan: Suata tinjuan terhadap style dan fungsinya" [*Legong Keraton* in Peliatan: Certain Observations about Its Style and Function], typescript (Denpasar: Akademi Seni Tari Indonesia, 1978).

10. The filmmakers made up the story and were in Bali for only a short time, though the actors were Balinese. The movie had considerable success in the U.S. In it, Balinese women in casual dress were naked above the waist, as was the custom at that time. No doubt this contributed to the film's exotic appeal.

11. See Madé Bandem and Frederik Eugene deBoer, *Balinese Dance in Transition: Kaja and Kelod*, 2nd ed. (Kuala Lumpur: Oxford University Press, 1995). Madé Bandem, "The Evolution of Legong from Sacred to Secular Dance of Bali," *Dance Research Annual* 14 (1983): 113–19, suggests that virginity is expected in the traditional Balinese context, but is not required for *legong* dancers in tourist concerts.

12. Both dances are older than *legong* and are among its sources, and the former was subsequently influenced by *legong* in its turn. Though *topeng sanghyang*, which belongs to the village of Ketewel, is known also as *topeng legong*, I regard it as a distinct genre (Stephen Davies, "The Origins of Balinese Legong," *Bijdragen tot de taal-, land- en volkenkunde* 164, nos. 2–3 [2008]: 194–211). On the young dancers, see Wayan Dibia, *Pragina: Penari, aktor, dan pelaku seni pertunjukan Bali* [The Balinese Dancer: Dancer, Actor, and Performer in the Balinese Performing Arts] (Malang: Sava Media, 2004), 15. Each of the two *topeng sanghyang* dancers has an attendant who must be both unmarried and a former *topeng sanghyang* dancer, according to I Wayan Sudana, "Tari topeng legong di Ketewel" [The *Legong Topeng* Dance of Ketewel], typescript (Denpasar: Akademi Seni Tari Indonesia, 1977). This is the closest to a requirement for virginity in a dance setting of which I am aware.

13. At least, this is the reason why female mask dancers apparently cannot perform *topeng pajegan*, which brings temple ceremonies to a close. In recent years, some women have taken up *topeng pajegan*, a suite of solo mask dances that was formerly a male preserve, but none that I know of has performed the dances in the temple. My source for this information is Carmencita Palermo.

14. "Proyek pemeliharaan dan pengembangan kebudajaan daerah Bali: Seminar seni sacral dan seni profan bidang tari" [Project for the Preservation and Development of Balinese Culture: Seminar on the Classification of Dance into the Sacred and Profane], anonymous typescript (Denpasar, 1971).

15. See I Nyoman Rembang et al., "Proyek pengembangan sarana wisata budaya Bali: Perkembangan legong sebagai seni pertunjukan" [Project to Develop Facilities, Means, and Instruments for Cultural Tourism in Bali: Promotion of *Legong* as a Performance Art], typescript (Denpasar, 1974–75), 6. Fifty years ago, girls would spend up to a year mastering the basic positions before learning *legong* (Ketut Arini

Alit, interviewed in Indonesian, Denpasar, July 2, 2003). Nowadays, they sometimes bypass *legong* to begin with other, easier dances.

16. For descriptions of some of these, see McPhee, "Dance in Bali"; Madé Bandem, *Ensiklopedi tari Bali* [Encyclopedia of Balinese Dance] (Denpasar: Akademi Seni Tari Indonesia, 1982); and R. M. Moerdowo, *Reflections on Balinese Traditional and Modern Arts* (Jakarta: PN Balai Pustaka, 1983), 87–90.

17. McPhee, "Dance in Bali," 195.

18. Dibia, interview; see also Dibia, *Pragina*, 113.

19. For discussion, see Davies, "The Origins of Balinese Legong."

20. Bandem and deBoer (*Balinese Dance in Transition*, 86–88) spell out the connection with prostitution; see also Covarrubias, *Island of Bali*, 228–29, and Spies and de Zoete, *Dance and Drama in Bali*, 242–44. Covarrubias (*Island of Bali*, 229) describes *gandrung* of the time as decadent and as sometimes having an intoxicating effect on the audience. Spies and de Zoete (*Dance and Drama in Bali*, 244) suggest that the *gandrung* dancer allowed more liberties to the males with whom he danced. Bandem and deBoer write, "According to older Balinese informants, in former times the liberties permitted often went far beyond kisses and caresses. Very often, too, a young boy dressed in a woman's costume, called a *gandrung*, danced the solo and received partners from the audience; apparently, the substitution did not inhibit the enthusiasm of the male audience for fondling the dancer" (*Balinese Dance in Transition*, 87). An observer in the 1880s, Dr. Julius Jacobs, wrote, "You know that they are boys and it disgusts one to see how, at the end, men from all ranks and conditions of Balinese society offer their coins to perform dances in the oddest attitudes with these children, and it disgusts you still the more when you realise that these children, worn out and dead-tired after hours of *perpendicular* exercises, are required yet to perform *horizontal* manoeuvres, first stroked by one, then kissed by another" (John Emigh and James Hunt, "Gender Bending in Javanese Performance," in *Gender in Performance: The Presentation of Difference in the Performing Arts*, ed. L. Senelick [Hanover, N.H.: University Press of New England, 1992], 200, italics in the original). In the past, casual homosexuality was inconsequential to the Balinese (Covarrubias, *Island of Bali*, 145).

21. Bandem and deBoer, *Balinese Dance in Transition*, 89.

22. See Spies and de Zoete, *Dance and Drama in Bali*, 196; Bandem and deBoer, *Balinese Dance in Transition*, 81; and Dibia, *Pragina*, 16–17. Kellar notes, "According to Balinese scholar, I Wayan Dibia, progressive ideas about women's place in society that were circulating in palace circles set the precedent for the shift from an all-male to a female-dominant genre. Specifically it was in the *puri* or palace of Ubud that palace wives were first allowed to participate in *Arja* performances—a trend beginning in the 1920s that gradually saw these women acquire *gengsi* or prestige from the display of their artistic abilities. That it was elite women of Bali, who first took part in *Arja* is consistent with the fact that the promotion of female equality was instigated by educated sectors of Balinese society in the period" (Natalie Kellar, "Beyond New Order Gender Politics: Case Studies of Female Performers of the Classical Balinese Dance-Drama Arja," *Intersections: Gender, History and Culture in the Asian Context*, no. 10 [August 2004], http://intersections.anu.edu.au/issue10/kellar.html, para. 31). Covarrubias, writing in 1937, recorded, "At one time the dramatic

arts were restricted to the men, although older women danced in religious ceremonies. But today girls have successfully invaded the theatrical field. In general the condition of Balinese women is better than in other Eastern countries" (*Island of Bali*, 83).

23. Anak Agung Istri Suryani, "Tari Leko di Sibanggede" [The Leko Dance of Sibanggede], typescript (Denpasar: Akademi Seni Tari Indonesia, 1986).

24. Coast, *Dancing out of Bali*; and Wayan Dibia and Rucina Ballinger, *Balinese Dance, Drama, and Music* (Singapore: Periplus, 2004), 90–94.

25. Bandem and deBoer, *Balinese Dance in Transition*, 133–41.

26. Mabbett, *The Balinese*, 224–25.

27. In traditional centers for *legong*, the goal is to preserve the full-length versions, even if they are not presented to tourists. Despite current moves to preserve *legong*, I judge that the genre is in decline. For detailed discussion, see Davies, "Balinese *Legong*: Revival or Decline?"

28. The verdict of the Balinese tends to be positive on balance. Western anthropologists and ethnographers usually provide a negative assessment—for instances, see Adrian Vickers, *Bali: A Paradise Created* (Ringwood, Victoria: Penguin, 1989); Michel Picard, "Dance and Drama in Bali: The Making of an Indonesian Artform," in *Being Modern in Bali: Image and Change*, ed. A. Vickers, Yale Southeast Asia Studies, Monograph 43 (New Haven: Yale University, Southeast Asia Studies, 1996): 115–57, and Edward M. Bruner, *Culture on Tour: Ethnographies of Travel* (Chicago: Chicago University Press, 2005). For a more relaxed conclusion, see my *Musical Works and Performances: A Philosophical Exploration* (Oxford: Clarendon, 2001), 268–92.

29. "Proyek pemeliharaan dan pengembangan kebudajaan daerah Bali"; "Proyek sasana budaya Bali, denpasar: Perkembangan seni tari di Bali" [Project on the Relationships of Balinese Culture: The Development of Art Dances in Bali], anonymous typescript (Denpasar, 1977–78); "Proyek penggalian/pembinaan seni budaya klasik (tradisional) dan baru; Evolusi tari Bali" [Project of Excavation/Construction of Classic Cultural Art (Traditional) and New: The Evolution of Balinese Dance], anonymous typescript (Denpasar, 1980–81); and Rembang et al., "Proyek pengembangan sarana wisata budaya Bali."

30. Davies, "Balinese *Legong*: Revival or Decline?", 318–24.

31. For detailed social analysis of the current status and function of the Bali Arts Festival, see Laura Noszlopy, "The Bali Arts Festival—Pesta Kesenian Bali: Culture, Politics and the Arts in Contemporary Indonesia" (Ph.D. diss., University of East Anglia, 2000).

32. For accounts of this decline offered by dance teachers and others, see Davies, "Balinese *Legong*: Revival or Decline?", 325–27. For descriptions of the traditional methods of teaching, see Covarrubias, *Island of Bali*, 221–22; McPhee, "Dance in Bali"; Spies and de Zoete, *Dance and Drama in Bali*, 31–32; and I Nyoman Darma Putra, "Duta seni budaya bangsa" [National Art-Cultural Mission], in *Wanita Bali tempo doeloe: Perspektif masa kini* [Balinese Women of the Past: The Perspective from Now] (Gianyar, Bali: Yayasan Bali Jani, 2003), 107–12. For consideration of how these techniques have altered since the 1970s—for example, through the use of mirrors and the positioning of the teacher in front of and facing a large class—see

Rucina Ballinger, "Dance in Bali: The Passing On of a Tradition," *CORD Dance Research Annual* 14 (1983): 172–83; and Dibia and Ballinger, *Balinese Dance, Drama, and Music,* 14–17.

33. For a summary of moves toward gender equality in Indonesia over the past forty years, see Kathryn Robinson, "Gender Equity and the Transition to Democracy in Indonesia," a talk given at the Indonesian–American Society, Washington, D.C., December 7, 2001; and Kathryn Robinson and Sharon Bessell, eds., *Women in Indonesia: Gender, Equity and Development* (Singapore: Institute of Southeast Asian Studies, 2002). For the wider Asian context, see Krishna Sen and Maila Stivens, *Gender and Power in Affluent Asia* (London: Routledge, 1998).

34. For discussion of the roles and status of Balinese women in the contemporary performing arts, see Natalie Kellar, "The Politics of Performance: Gender Identity in Arja and Other Contemporary Balinese Theatre Forms" (Ph.D. diss., Monash University, 2000); and Kellar, "Beyond New Order Gender Politics." For the wider Indonesian context, see Barbara Hatley, "Women in Contemporary Indonesian Theatre: Issues of Representation and Participation," *Bijdragen tot de taal-, land- en volkenkunde* 151, no. 4 (1995): 570–601.

35. Some scholars recognize up to five levels in the Balinese language. The level of language used depends on the caste of the person addressed (or the formality of the occasion). About 10 percent of Balinese belong to the three high castes. The Indonesian language, by contrast, has only one level. Incidentally, "Cokorda," Cok Ratih's full first name, marks her as of the high Satria caste, whose members claim descent from ancient princes and prime ministers.

36. I thank Mark Hobart, Doug Myers, Rucina Ballinger, and Uli Kozok for their advice on these terminological matters.

37. Karl Grammer, Viktoria Keki, Beate Striebel, Michaela Atzmüller, and Bernhard Fink, "Bodies in Motion: A Window to the Soul," in *Evolutionary Aesthetics,* ed. Eckart Voland and Karl Grammer (Berlin: Springer Verlag, 2003), 295–323.

38. Some males have danced *legong,* and some still do, but they do all they can to emulate the appearance and movement of females when they do so. Kellar, "Beyond New Order Gender Politics," describes the current Balinese attitude as hostile to cross-dressing male dancers in what are traditionally female genres.

39. When Islam swept from the west in the fourteenth century, it bypassed Bali. Many of the Majapahit rulers of eastern Java retreated to Bali with their followers to preserve their religion, culture, and way of life. Their descendants now dominate the island and only a few villages preserve intact the culture of the earlier inhabitants, the Bali Aga.

40. Men also dress for temple ceremonies, wearing a cap (*udeng*), a white shirt or jacket, a sash, and a cloth wrapped round the lower body (*saput*) over the sarong.

41. It is said there are as many temples as people in Bali. The anniversary of each temple comes every 210 days, according to the Balinese calendar. The length and scale of the ceremony depends on the anniversary's significance. Ceremonies of two to seven days are common.

42. Describing a version of *rejang* performed in the region of Gianyar, Dibia and Ballinger write, "It takes nearly half an hour to advance 20 metres. The slow

movements and constant shifts of weight give the illusion of a sea of women undulating back and forth" (*Balinese Dance, Drama, and Music*, 56).

43. Ruby Sue Ornstein, "Gamelan Gong Kebyar: The Development of a Balinese Musical Tradition" (Ph.D. diss., University of California, 1971), 8, 65–66, 369–73; and David Harnish, "Balinese Performance as Festival Offerings," *Asian Art* 4 (1991): 9–27.

44. Edward Herbst, *Voices in Bali: Energies and Perceptions in Vocal Music and Dance Theater* (Hanover: Wesleyan University Press, 1997), 122.

45. See Gordon H. Orians and Judith H. Heerwagen, "Evolved Responses to Landscapes," in *The Adapted Mind: Evolutionary Psychology and the Generation of Culture*, ed. Jerome H. Barkow, Leda Cosmides, and John Tooby (New York: Oxford University Press, 1992), 555–79; Stephen Kaplan, "Environmental Preference in a Knowledge-Seeking, Knowledge-Using Organism," in Barkow, Cosmides, and Tooby, *The Adapted Mind*, 581–98; and Bernhart Ruso, Lee Ann Renninger, and Klaus Atzwanger, "Human Habitat Preferences: A Generative Territory for Evolutionary Aesthetics Research," in Voland and Grammer, *Evolutionary Aesthetics*, 279–94.

46. On beauty as honest signaling for fitness, see Amots Zahavi and Avishag Zahavi, *The Handicap Principle: A Missing Piece of Darwin's Puzzle* (New York: Oxford University Press, 1997); Steven Pinker, *How the Mind Works* (New York: W. W. Norton, 1997); Vilayanur Ramachandran and William Hirstein, "The Science of Art: A Neurological Theory of Aesthetic Experience," *Journal of Consciousness Studies* 6, nos. 6–7 (June–July 1999): 15–51; Nancy Etcoff, *Survival of the Prettiest: The Science of Beauty* (New York: Doubleday, 1999); Geoffrey Miller, *The Mating Mind: How Sexual Choice Shaped the Evolution of Human Nature* (London: William Heinemann, 2000); Uta Skamel, "Beauty and Sex Appeal: Sexual Selection of Aesthetic Preferences," in Voland and Grammer, *Evolutionary Aesthetics*, 172–200; and Randy Thornhill, "Darwinian Aesthetics Informs Traditional Aesthetics," in Voland and Grammer, *Evolutionary Aesthetics*, 9–35.

47. The claim is not that everyone's preferences will be identical. The totality of individuals' preferences is likely to spread over the full range of possibly relevant features, though the extremes will appeal to fewer individuals.

48. Few thoughtful evolutionary psychologists support biological essentialism or determinism, even if they think it is possible, indeed crucial, to recognize a human nature and believe also that evolutionary adaptations are no less important in their influence on modern humans than on our late-Pleistocene forebears. For example, see Pinker, *How the Mind Works*; Steven Pinker, *The Blank Slate: The Modern Denial of Human Nature* (Viking Penguin, 2002); and Miller, *The Mating Mind*.

49. Among the honest indicators of health and vitality are symmetry, clear skin, glossy hair, white teeth, appropriate body weight and muscling, and so on. Bodily markers that distinguish human women from the mature females of other primate species, and that therefore probably indicate the operation of selection on the basis of (possibly arbitrary) male heterosexual preferences, include round, plump breasts and buttocks, skin smoothness and hairlessness, and a low waist-to-hip ratio. The characteristics favored by *Homo sapiens* females in the physical appearance of males differ, of course. Also, women seeking long-term partners place more weight on signs of intelligence, humor, status, and wealth than on bodily attractiveness. There is

evidence, though, that when men are looking for long-term breeding partners, as opposed to casual sexual liaisons, they factor in cognitive, social, and other non-physical attributes no less than women do (Douglas T. Kenrick, Edward K. Sadalla, Gary Groth, and Melanie R. Trost, "Evolution, Traits, and the Stages of Human Courtship: Qualifying the Parental Investment Model," *Journal of Personality* 58, no. 1 [March 1990]: 97–116).

50. Notice the ambiguity in "Dancers can be criticised also just for not being beautiful, though it's not their fault." This might mean that they are technically proficient dancers who never meet the expected standards for beauty in girls, adolescents, or young women. But it might also mean that a woman looks less beautiful as a *legong* dancer as a result of passing the age of expected retirement, though her age is not her fault and her appearance is otherwise unchanged.

13. Bollywood and the Feminine: Hinduism and Images of Womanhood

JANE DURAN

A great deal of the impetus for contemporary commentary on Bollywood, its images, and its effects on Indian culture as a whole comes from a pervasive sense that the tropes of the Indian cinema (specifically, the Hindu cinema of the north) tell us much about India's past and future. Indeed, new work on the Hindu cinema appears all the time—much of the more recent work engages the topic from many of the postmodern and poststructuralist points of view available to us, but it is also the case that even this commentary often cites historic images from South Asian art and architecture.[1]

In much recent film from India, Western-clad young women make regular appearances, and the naïve viewer might be forgiven for thinking that the images derived from history, mythology, and sacred literature, such as those based on the figure of Sita, the self-sacrificing ideal heroine of the Ramayana, are now irrelevant and forgotten. But a closer look at Bollywood's products reveals that the aspects of the traditional culture that have often proven most problematic for women—the emphasis on motherhood, purity, and dress—are alive and well. Indeed, it might be argued, Bollywood today is more invested than ever in preserving the traditional views of women's roles and their social place. Those who hope for progressive change will have to be careful viewers of the Bollywood product. It will be the task of this paper to delineate some of these constructs, and to try to untangle them with an eye toward their relevance to India's history. Using approaches from art history, the history of Indian drama and dance, and film studies, I argue that no one reading or take on Bollywood is possible, with the corollary that commercial film production in India will not necessarily promote progressive social change for women. The variegated strand that constitutes the cinema may, however, yield change in some instances and is, in any case, open to multiple interpretations.

Introduction

In *Reading "Bollywood,"* Shakuntala Banaji constructs a lengthy analysis of the various strands of the Indian cinema and investigates its effects on moviegoers in South Asia as well as diaspora sites (that is, sites of emigration from South Asia, such as London and Trinidad). Although "Bollywood" normally means the cinema produced in Bombay (now Mumbai), it has come to stand for almost all Indian commercial film. One of Banaji's larger arguments is that there are very few solid inferences that can be made about the impact of the cinema: some see the films as valorizing tradition, while others see many of them as harbingers of new, more Western, attitudes toward gender relations. Banaji writes,

> For instance, as [another critic] found, many Hindi films are indeed denigrated by some viewers for their lack of realism and their melodramatic tendencies; nevertheless, as I discovered, they are also viewed as sources of knowledge which can have a fairly profound impact on the life choices of young people.[2]

The escapism and the overromanticized versions of the Hindu past that seem to characterize many Bollywood productions might be thought to have little to do with any real-life choices, yet one of Banaji's main conclusions is that diasporic audiences know little about India and Indian traditions, and that viewing Bollywood films in London or Trinidad was a way of learning about South Asia.

Two strands of thought, then, seem to lead contemporary analysis of the Bombay (Mumbai) productions that constitute the genre of popular Indian cinema. One emphasizes the extent to which familial and gender roles are reproduced in the films, even if their reproduction is not always obvious—the recent full-scale version of the Ramayana made for and shown on Indian television is an excellent example. The second underscores the notion that more contemporary (Western) attitudes are being introduced to Indian audiences through the cinema, undercutting tradition; nontraditional clothing, for example, has appeared in Bollywood films at least since the 1970s (*Mera nam Joker*, 1970), and the actress Urmila Matondkar wears it in all her recent films. This subversion of tradition, as Banaji says, is extremely important with respect to dress.

But if it is the case that the films of Bollywood contain multiple messages and a bewildering variety of images, there is a real and genuine sense in which this multiplicity, too, is also a product of India's past. A great deal of the art-historical commentary on the stonework and carvings of the Hindu traditions notes the many variants of female imagery to be found. Although representations of the submissive Sita, devoted to her spouse and, according to some, the prototype for various versions of *sati*, or widow immolation, are ubiquitous in Hindu popular culture, the erotic carvings of Konarak and Khajuraho present another array of images. Admittedly, the latter images have much to do with cosmic notions of union, but they are still a strong part of the history of the subcontinent. Indeed, scholars of the temple work have struggled to find a way to divorce the plasticity and fluidity of the erotic carvings from some blatantly sexual interpretation. Although such an interpretation might seem unsophisticated—the critic Charles Fabri says that the carvings of Khajuraho lack the "cold calculation" of pornography[3]—the fact that the topic continually recurs indicates that the conflict has yet to be resolved.

In short, sexuality, eroticism, and the status of the female are all contested areas in Hinduism, and the products of Bollywood reflect this contestation in their own way. Indeed, it could be argued that the lack of univocality in both the films and their interpretations is simply part and parcel of the very set of familial and gender traditions under examination. As Banaji also says, any one interpretation of the cinema is problematized by the reactions of young filmgoers to the product.[4]

Art History and Indian Visual Constructs

The disparity in the nature of images of women in the world of Hinduism is partly due to the import of myth. Both the Ramayana and the Mahabharata—which includes the Bhagavad Gita, a crucial document in religious history—contain extensive references to idealized, self-sacrificing females. The devoted Hindu wife is not simply a helpmate; she is ready to martyr herself for her husband and family, and this ideal of physical sacrifice is one that, however constructed, has persisted throughout history and made its way, in one form or another, into the twentieth century. The strength of this classic myth at least partially accounts for both the occurrence of, and Western fascination with, the few episodes of *sati* that have occurred recently, mainly in Rajasthan.[5]

At least one or two of the contemporary episodes seem to be related to the new rise of Hindu fundamentalism. Although we cannot examine these episodes here, a notion of the ideal woman as chaste, submissive, faithful, filled with a desire to keep house, and having no desire for a life outside the home permeates the construction of Hindu social life. Many grown women make virtually no decisions on their own; when Western guests are in the home (even in comparatively well-educated families), they stay in other rooms. In his classic and authoritative work on the art of India, Benjamin Rowland notes that the Ramayana has been regarded as "emblematic of the virtues" of higher castes;[6] Banaji states that even televised versions of the Ramayana may rely for their impact on an "'imagined community' of Hindu viewers based on patriarchal authority."[7] But the delineation of women within the culture also includes at least two notions that might be thought to be in conflict with the patriarchal ideal: one is the sheer physical attractiveness of the ideal woman, however faithful, and the other is the potent female force or *shakti*, as articulated in the Vedic worldview.

Rachel Dwyer and Divia Patel note that the Hindi film industry merely recapitulates existing cultural standards for both male and female beauty, many of which involve skin color, facial features, and so forth. In *Cinema India*, Dwyer and Patel assert,

> The operation of a star system was further reinforced by the films' specific requirements for their heroes and heroines to appear as ideals, rather than as natural, psychologically plausible characters. The norm of the film's characters is that of the urban, upper-caste, north Indian Hindu. Characters from other . . . regions . . . are portrayed as "others."[8]

This is true not just of the Hindi film industry, but of non-Hindi films as well. To a surprising extent, the ideals associated with mythology in India, even as depicted in carvings and stonework, portray a physiological type that is somewhat at variance with the actual phenotypical appearance of individuals in the region. This may be true of the artwork of most cultures, wherever they are located, but the ideal in India has always involved lighter skin color—even in the south—and a sort of voluptuous attractiveness that (in Western terms) might be thought to be at variance with the ideals of chastity that seem to be concomitant with the mythological view. Thus Sita is often portrayed in such a way that, except for dress, she little resembles a woman of South Asia.

In addition to this set of constraints, it is also the case that a large variety of tropes and constructs about female power and female energy pervade the Hindu worldview. To be fair, these constructs are today more at work in the Dravidian south than in the north, and that region, in general, contains a larger number of darker-skinned individuals. But the notion of *shakti*— female energy—comes from the Vedas and from a number of alembications of Hindu scripture. It is becoming increasingly popular in India as a way of explaining women's attempts to reappropriate male constructs to gain status. Margaret Egnor says, "The power acquired through suffering and servitude is a special case of the Hindu theory of *tapas*, whereby through certain forms of self-denial (called *tapas*), the individual accumulates a certain internal heat (also called *tapas*). . . . If the accumulated power of suffering is great enough, the rebellion may be successful."[9]

The point is that—like the tropes of the cinema as a whole—cultural metaphors and constructs are sometimes at odds with each other, and defy straightforward categorization. One might, for example, worry that *shakti* will be misused; this anxiety is what the notions of self-denial and self-sacrifice attempt to displace. Thus the virtuous female, at least in most parts of the tradition, is the one who appropriately abnegates herself so that the *shakti* can do its proper duty. In addition, she is curvaceous, light-skinned, and attractive. From the Mughal miniatures of the Islamicized regions of the north to the stonework of Khajuraho, Konarak, and Mahabalipuram, the female is voluptuous but chaste, sexual but submissive, and powerful but with her power held in check.[10]

Much of the imagery of Hindi film recapitulates, in its own way, this important set of constructs from the past. Both Banaji and Dwyer agree that there is no one reading of the Hindi cinema, but they would concur that much of the construction of women in the film industry reinforces their often subjugated status. Dwyer, in particular, has a historical analysis of the industry that helps to clarify various points.

Dance, Drama, and the Importance of Convention

Dwyer and her coauthor, Divia Patel, note that "a new visuality was created in colonial nineteenth-century India, distinct from that seen in traditional art forms such as miniatures and religious sculpture. New forms of painting emerged, including 'bazaar art' [and] the 'Company' style."[11] These new visual constructs ultimately gave rise to Indian film.

Photography and its allied arts arrived in India, thanks to the Europeans, shortly after they took hold in Europe, and this arrival made possible the Indian cinema as it evolved during the twentieth century. Dwyer and Patel emphasize the extent to which the developing cinema relied on modes taken from an amalgam of traditional Sanskrit drama and the imported British theater of the nineteenth century.[12] This amalgam may have relied more on visual effects and dance than did standard European drama of the time; the importance of songs and choreography was derived from traditional Hindu drama, and the advent of sound recording meant that film relied on them still more. Thus the dramatic forms that moved into the film house during the 1930s, 1940s, and 1950s were a mixture of the traditional (such as the choreographic form Bharatnatyam), the new, and a few carryovers from British theater, but most of the films made during this period (and later) promulgated what Dwyer and Patel refer to as the "feudal family romance." It is this romance that gives rise to much that undergirds the traditional images of women: as the authors note, the patriarchal family structure dramatized in even contemporary films is "connected to the . . . part they play in the resurgence of Hindutva politics in the 1980s and '90s."[13] As far back as 1957, the now-classic *Mother India* tells the story of Radha, a young village bride; as Dwyer and Patel comment, over time "she displays her courage, strength and moral resolve. She is an embodiment of the values and codes of behaviour [that form] the very basis of traditional Indian society."[14] What this means in conventional terms is that she will not hesitate to deny herself or engage in acts of self-abnegation (fig. 13.1).

If a number of Indian films can be cited that promote traditional images of women, it is also important that the films that put forward these images are, in general, not considered to represent the height of Indian cinema. Indeed, there has long been a great disparity between the work of internationally acknowledged Indian filmmakers, such as Satyajit Ray, and the Bollywood film industry. But even if it is true that Bollywood products are lacking in the kinds of film studies desiderata that drive the films of Ray and others, it is also true that, for most, Bollywood products stand for the Indian cinema. Their ubiquity and sheer number make it difficult to dismiss them. Moreover, even Ray's work, such as *Pather Panchali*, contains specific references to the broader culture and to some of the same tropes discussed here, especially traditional depictions of women.[15]

As the film industry has developed, the debate about women, their clothes, and their status has continued, with little apparent agreement or result. The more Westernized dress shown in some films has simply led some viewers to reaffirm older, or conservative, values rather than to discard them. Banaji asserts that one of her respondents said that Urmila Matondkar "must hardly be needing any material for her dresses." She adds that her interviewee

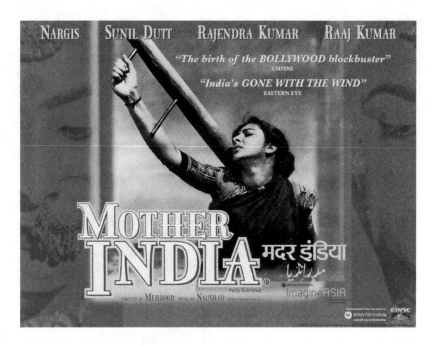

Figure 13.1. Poster for *Mother India*, directed by
Mehboob Khan, 1957.

"worries that after watching performances by Matondkar on screen young
women and girls will feel pressured into wearing things that they neither enjoy
nor feel comfortable in. . . . He poses the issue in terms of younger women
falling prey to male predations."[16] In other words, close to one hundred years
of development of the national Hindi-language cinema has produced an
audience so accustomed to the notion that the film industry replicates the
culture—in the form of drama and song-and-dance productions—that some
viewers may be taking lessons from the cinema at variance with the directors'
intention (if we could be sure that we knew what their intentions were). One
thing is certain—the audiences take the films seriously, in a variety of ways.

Film Studies and Bollywood

Philosophy of film, and film theory in general, intersects with the
Bollywood industry in a number of its facets. Many commentators have
claimed that aspects of film's reproductive and technological status make
it difficult to class film as an art: Murray Smith has noted that, "for Adorno,
the aesthetic potential of film was often corrupted by the mechanical and

Figure 13.2. Actress Urmila Matondkar as a gypsy dancer in
Ram Gopal Varma ki aag, directed by Ram Gopal Varma,
2006.

commercial nature of film-making, this commercial function conflicting with the 'autonomous' development necessary for art, debasing the Kantian 'purposelessness' of art into the barren 'purpose' of commerce."[17] Given this, a double set of difficulties might be thought to beset the Bollywood product.

Another part of this argument is that the technology itself inhibited the construction of an art; as Smith also remarks, film was regarded as an "advanced technolog[y] of recording, and thus unable to effect that transformation of 'material' vital to art."[18] That Bollywood is indisputably commercial we have already seen—indeed, as mentioned above, its products have seldom been felt to really represent the status of film in India, insofar as we might think of film production as an art form. However, although the difficulty with the notion of mechanical reproduction might seem straightforward, it is somewhat more complex in the case of the Indian film. For this particular objection is similar to that lodged, at least initially, against musical recordings in comparison to live performances of music (this is an area of intense debate, as many have countered that recordings are a special type of artifact). In the case of film, the problem is that it is considered a flat reproduction of something rather than an artifact susceptible to interpretation. But because so much of what Bollywood purveys is already based on the mythological, layers of interwoven reproduction and interpretation dog the status of the film itself. In a sense, film suffers from the same sorts of problems that accrue to fundamentalist Hinduism when it tries to make statements about Krishna or Rama. Jesus and Mohammed were actual historical figures whose existence is documented in the records of their time. The same cannot be said of the icons of Hinduism, and thus many Bollywood products—whatever their cinematic qualities—use a mechanical means of reproduction to attempt to capture notions of family and gender (especially concepts of self-abnegation and sacrifice) that are not rooted in actual events.

Thus even the most carefully contrived Bollywood motion picture is already a step removed from most films, simply because those films that are usually discussed in film theory typically employ actors and actresses portraying events that might occur in real human lives. But a Bollywood product loosely based on the Ramayana, with its army of helpful monkeys, attempts to portray something far less realistic. And even when the Bollywood material is only vaguely related to the mythological, the fact that it is constructed in this way renders it less easily analyzed than are most films, of whatever provenance. Thus even in its status as film, the Indian picture industry is already at odds with most film theory, which since before the 1940s has been largely based on discussions of the motion picture as an artistic endeavor.

It may, in fact, be for these reasons that, as Banaji has it, "reading" Bollywood turns out to be so problematic. The combination of fantasy, overt use of mythology and mythological tropes, and lack of sophistication in plot development means that it is simply not possible, in many cases, to address a Bollywood product in standard film theory terms. This is particularly the case when a feminist analysis is attempted. The critic Maggie Humm, in *Feminism and Film*, gives sophisticated analyses of a number of well-known American films, including such Oscar-winning productions as *Klute*. The latter, perhaps one of Jane Fonda's best-known pictures, strikes Humm as being antifeminist in some respects because of the number of scenes in which the murder suspect, in an attempt to recreate moments of sexual stimulation, replays his recording of conversations with Bree (Fonda's character) about the joys of uninhibited sexuality. Although the fact that he is using a recording is perhaps not central to the movie in any way, Humm finds the "disembodied" nature of Fonda's voice in these scenes to be disempowering, and she claims that, on a feminist analysis, Bree is reduced to nothing.[19] Needless to say, although one might be tempted to try to apply such an analysis to some work in the Indian cinema, the cultural assumptions underlying the production of a film like *Klute*—and its promotion—simply do not apply most of the time, and such an interpretation would be strained. One could, of course, give up on Bollywood and claim that many of its products simply are not "readable," but the point is, as Banaji has shown, that viewers in South Asia and throughout the diaspora do respond to these films. It is simply the case that their response may be different from what many of us would expect, or different from what someone with a similar cultural background might expect. Scantily clad heroines may fall prey to various disasters, or they may emerge triumphant—but in any given case, we may not be able to say with any certainty why the outcome is what it is, or how a viewer will respond. Banaji notes that her respondents all wanted to comment on how Urmila Matondkar was dressed, but in varying ways; one interviewee, named Neha, asserted that "girls should avoid very less clothing . . . because it is spoiling the whole of what Indian culture is," while another respondent, Sonali, claimed that "even if you go around totally veiled from top to toe the men will . . . make comments."[20] Urmila's famous lack of attire (in comparison to the culture's general expectations) evokes completely different responses in different viewers.

Smith's commentary, and even to some extent Humm's (with respect to the notions of mechanical reproduction and the arts, and a feminist reading of *Klute*), problematize Hindi-language Bollywood cinema because it does not stand in the same relationship to the other arts as does most film. Thus it is difficult to ask the same questions about mechanics, notions of reproduction, or the status of film as an "art" about it. But, as we have seen, this should not preclude the notion that Bollywood products can be construed artistically, or that there is, indeed, a "reading" of them. It is simply the case that Bollywood films are susceptible to numerous interpretations that vary wildly from viewer to viewer, to a greater extent than are such classic films of Western provenance as *Chinatown* and *Citizen Kane.* As we have also indicated, their importance cannot be underestimated, because they are viewed not only in India but throughout the diaspora. (Indeed, it might well be argued that their effect is greater in the diaspora.) Notions of representation cut in a number of ways in this cinema, because figures such as Rama and Krishna are mythological figures. Bollywood and its entire line of products are themselves both a potent source of mythology and a product of that mythology. Although Rama and Krishna may appear as characters in only a small minority of films, dramatic figures based on them, in whatever way, will immediately be recognizable to most viewers.

Conclusion

I have been arguing throughout this paper that the images available to us through Bollywood recapitulate important parts of Hindi-language myth and drama, and do so in ways that have an extraordinary impact on their viewing audience. As Rowland has told us in his delineation of the importance of certain tropes in the art and architecture of India, various constructs are seen as "emblematic of the virtues" and have a long history of repetition within Hindu culture.[21] Dwyer and Patel have taught us that a good deal of what is now regarded as art-historical in Indian dramatic circles stems from the amalgamation of nineteenth-century British colonialism and traditional Hindu dramatic and narrative forms.[22] As noted earlier, imported theater from the United Kingdom influenced the drama and dance of late nineteenth-century India. But whatever the case, Bollywood has become sufficiently powerful, even as it interacts with and reproduces some of these traditional choreographic notions taken from the arts, that there is now a wealth of commentary on it, and one focal point of much of the commentary is that the contemporary Indian cinema cuts both ways.

This gives rise to the sorts of arguments in which the naïve viewer might want to indulge—does Bollywood reproduce patriarchy and female subjugation? Does it insist on a sort of colorism that has always been prominent in India?—and reinforces the notion that these arguments are indeed naïvely formed, because it is clear that, more than most film, Bollywood is what the viewer chooses to see. Adolescent viewers, in particular, may make what might be regarded as completely nonstandard interpretations. The scantily clad heroine may be breaking new ground; she may be punished. She may be the herald of something coming; she may be a transgressor whose past will overtake her. But each of these interpretations is made by the viewer, and there is no simple formulation that will capture the relationship between the temples at Khajuraho and Konarak, the narrative of the Ramayana, the impact of British colonial literature, and the Hindi-language cinema of today.

It may very well be the case that part of our desire to try to find one "reading" for Bollywood comes from Western film theory. But it is here that we have to move against theory, so to speak, and work with our own anec-dotal and reportage-based information on the films and their promulgation. It is for these reasons that Banaji starts her work by noting that "this book is concerned primarily with the significance for and reception by young audi-ences of contemporary sexual and gender iconography in commercial Hindi films."[23] Banaji's point is that reception varies from community to commu-nity, from viewer to viewer. The youthful viewer may be living in Mumbai, Kathmandu, or London, or perhaps in a small town in the middle of Madhya Pradesh. He or she may have been reared traditionally, in almost completely Western terms, or in that middle style that is now so common in the major cities of India. She or he may appreciate the classical Hindu past, may be a Muslim, a Jain, a Parsi, or Buddhist, or may be someone whose family iden-tifies with one of these traditions, but who has little or no interest in it. This staggering array of possible responses—and, obviously, here allusion has been made only to a few—is one of the reasons that Banaji strives to make the case that any reading is possible.

Globally, images of women continue to reinforce, in large measure, tra-ditional roles. But the actual variability that we have seen in responses to the Hindi-language cinema (and, indeed, in the history of artifacts leading up to it) militates against the notion that progressive change in women's status and gender roles is not possible. The mere presence of such women directors as Mira Nair on the international scene gives room for hope; more complex plots involving women who are autonomous and not subject to retribution seem to be on the horizon. Perhaps, after all, this variegated strand that is the Hindu cinema will be a source for the kind of change that feminists are hop-ing for, will offer a new view that refuses to valorize the past at the expense of women. Whether or not this will take place remains to be seen.

NOTES

1. See, for example, Shakuntala Banaji, *Reading "Bollywood": The Young Audience and Hindi Films* (New York: Palgrave Macmillan, 2006).

2. Ibid., 26.

3. Charles Fabri, "The Fulfillment of the Baroque in Khajuraho," in *Khajuraho*, ed. Mulk Raj Anand (Bombay: Marg, 1968), 12.

4. Banaji, *Reading "Bollywood,"* 48.

5. *Sati* is itself the subject of extensive analysis. Several excellent pieces by South Asian scholars are to be found in Nivedita Menon, ed., *Gender and Politics in India* (New Delhi: Oxford University Press, 1999).

6. Benjamin Rowland, *The Art and Architecture of India: Buddhist, Hindu, Jain*, 3rd. ed. (Baltimore: Penguin, 1967), 130.

7. Banaji, *Reading "Bollywood,"* 29.

8. Rachel Dwyer and Divia Patel, *Cinema India: The Visual Culture of Hindi Film* (New Delhi: Oxford University Press, 2002), 20.

9. Margaret Egnor, "On the Meaning of Sakti to the Women of Tamil Nadu," in *The Powers of Tamil Women*, ed. Susan S. Wadley, Foreign and Comparative Studies 6 (Syracuse, N.Y.: Maxwell School of Citizenship and Public Affairs, Syracuse University, 1980), 16–17.

10. For an analysis of the well-known Rajasthani miniature *The Hour of Cowdust*, see Rowland, *The Art and Architecture of India*, 209–10.

11. Dwyer and Patel, *Cinema India*, 43.

12. Ibid., chapter 1, "Indian Cinema."

13. Ibid., 22.

14. Ibid., 161.

15. Ibid., 21.

16. Banaji, *Reading "Bollywood,"* 91.

17. Murray Smith, "Film," in *The Routledge Companion to Aesthetics*, ed. Berys Gaut and Dominic McIver Lopes (New York: Routledge, 2001), 464.

18. Ibid., 466.

19. Maggie Humm, *Feminism and Film* (Bloomington: Indiana University Press, 1996), 49–50.

20. Banaji, *Reading "Bollywood,"* 92.

21. Rowland, *The Art and Architecture of India*, 130.

22. Dwyer and Patel, *Cinema India*, 43.

23. Banaji, *Reading "Bollywood,"* 1.

14. Seductive Shift: A Review of
The Most Beautiful Woman in Gucha

VALERIE SULLIVAN FUCHS

Breda Beban's stunning two-screen video installation, *The Most Beautiful Woman in Gucha*, documents a mutually seductive encounter between a beautiful belly dancer and an inebriated young man at a Romany brass band festival in Serbia. She edits this encounter in two separate videos, eight and eighteen minutes respectively, and installs them in adjacent galleries. In this configuration, Beban begins to challenge and expose the filmic editing conventions of controlling time, narrative, and sound, but not without first engaging the viewer by those very same conventions. Although the two videos are a combined twenty-six minutes, their slippage between hot sensory overload and cool low-information underload, where viewer participation is necessary to complete the narrative, makes them feel only a few minutes long.

The hot sensory overload begins with a cacophonous barrage of brass horns, drums, and the sexy clarinet melody "Pelno Me Sum" spilling out of the first gallery. The 10 × 13 ft. video projection is edited with real time and actual sounds of the festival and is juxtaposed against slow-motion sections underscored by the seductive clarinet melody. The action takes place in a crowded room of revelers, where a belly dancer, surrounded by a brass band, invites a young man who is sitting with a group to stand up so she can perform for him. After pulling money from his pocket, he moves up next to her and the dance begins. The encounter unfolds in both real time and slow motion as the man, with a banknote now placed between his lips, leans down slowly toward the glittering belly of the dancer as if to place money in her waistband. She moves her head underneath his and leans up toward his lips and they look as if they will kiss, until she tries to snatch the banknote with her teeth. To her surprise, he suddenly pulls back. She laughs. He is teasing her. Their roles are reversed (plate 9).

This is how Beban plays with and repositions the viewer. When viewers have experienced both of the differently edited versions of the same real recorded event, their interpretation of the action destabilizes. Gradually, and only after viewing both projections, they change from passive voyeurs to critical observers. In the first projection, the festival sounds, plus the encounter of the beautiful dancer with the seductive young man and the expressions on the crowd surrounding them, fill the senses and are mesmerizing. The slippage between different time structures invites viewers to further scrutinize the actions and reactions of the couple in detail. In the microscope of slow motion, accentuated by the seductive clarinet melody, the signs of true love or readiness for a partner appear decipherable. The preening of the male when he adjusts his hat, his pouting lips, and the dancer's outreached arms can be interpreted as signs of interest or signals of the intention to touch. Beban's editing of this first projection teases and pulls the viewer into a vortex of wonder that assumes there is a real sexual chemistry between the dancer and the young man.

But is it real?

The second projection, in the adjacent gallery, runs eighteen minutes and provides more information and clues. It is essentially the unedited version of the first projection. The hand-held camera follows the dancer as she and her troupe make their way through the revelers. There are close-ups of her performing for men with outstretched hands, clutching money to stuff down her waistband. This extended version of their encounter records her waking the young man from a drunken stupor, dancing for him, and eventually using a table as a stage, where she takes up a brass instrument and plays with the band while the young man tugs at her for attention. "The way the woman switches from being a dancer to musician to dancer gets people thinking about wiles verses talents," notes Louisville-based artist Chris Radtke, "whether they are one and the same thing."[1] In this second projection, the viewers' position shifts and they begin to understand that it is the dancer who initiates and controls most of the action; she acts as a protagonist, not just passive and female. As film theorist Laura Mulvey has noted, "In a world ordered by sexual imbalance, pleasure in looking has been split between active/male and passive/female. The determining male gaze projects its fantasy onto the female figure. . . . In their traditional exhibitionist role women are simultaneously looked at and displayed. Woman displayed as sexual object . . . plays to and signifies male desire."[2]

Other background action within the videos also resituates and further erodes the viewer's scopophilic pleasure, the pleasure of looking at another person as an erotic object, what Laura Mulvey calls "the look." In the gallery space, the viewer becomes conscious of his own voyeurism as he is engaged by the reactions of the spectators crowding around the couple. As described in Mulvey's analysis of Hitchcock's film *Vertigo*, the viewer's erotic involvement with Beban's work "boomerangs." As Mulvey points out, "The spectator's own fascination is revealed as illicit voyeurism as the narrative content enacts the processes and pleasures that he is himself exercising and enjoying." This pleasure in looking as a voyeur is further unveiled as the viewer's presence seems to complete the circle of voyeurs surrounding the couple. The angle of the camera and framing on the screen positions the viewer, in real space, as part of the crowd. "The spectator [viewer] is absorbed into a voyeuristic situation within the screen scene and diegesis, which parodies his own in the cinema [gallery]." The viewer's awareness of his own presence as voyeur forms another break in the continuity of a narrative and again changes him from passive to active.

Beban's presentation of both edited and unedited versions of the same event makes the editing of the films transparent and visible by bringing the "existence of the materiality of the recording process" to the viewer's attention. From this presentation, the viewer begins to develop a "critical read" or analysis of the events or narrative. This begins the breakdown of "the voyeuristic-scopophilic look that is a crucial part of traditional filmic pleasure. . . . Without these two absences (the material existence of the recording process, the critical read of the spectator), fictional drama cannot achieve reality, obviousness, and truth."

Beban's brilliance lies in her ability to invert obviousness and truth in a recording of reality. By adding the special effect of slow motion and a sexy clarinet to the first projection, and leaving these effects out of the second projection, she exposes the manipulation of time, space, and sound that structure or convey the meaning of narrative or action. Her installation of two different depictions of one real recorded event leads the viewer to analyze or critically read the "truth" of the actions and motivations of the main players. The viewer flips from passive voyeur to active observer while working to construct the narrative or action. Beban makes transparent the powerful traditional editing conventions of film and video while simultaneously using those same conventions to actively engage the viewer. The seductive shift of roles between the belly dancer and the young man, in the first projection, is mesmerizing as it mirrors the viewer's own shifting role in the experience of the projections. With *The Most Beautiful Woman in Gucha*, you can have your cake and eat it too, because this cake has a whole-grain, antioxidant, omega-3 excellence running through it.

NOTES

This story originally appeared in the *Louisville (Kentucky) Eccentric Observer* and was revised for publication here.

1. Telephone interview by author, 2007.

2. This and subsequent quotations are taken from Laura Mulvey, "Visual Pleasure and Narrative Cinema" (1975), in *Visual Culture: The Reader,* ed. Jessica Evans and Stuart Hall (London: SAGE, 1999), 386–88.

15. Feminist Art, Content, and Beauty

KEITH LEHRER

Art reconfigures experience. Art is a mentalized physical object. Danto remarks that art is embodied meaning.[1] Hein says that feminist art chats on the edge.[2] Our mental life is filled with meaning, but art opens the question of the meaning of experience. There is the felt quality of it, which, when it becomes the focus of our attention, allows us the autonomy of reconfiguring how we respond to our sensory encounters with the world. A salient aspect of the art experience, the way in which our attention is directed to the immediate, to the sensory exemplar, in an aesthetic stance, frees us to rethink and re-feel as an act of self-trust. Brand has noted how we toggle back and forth between, on the one hand, the immediate, and on the other, our thoughts and feelings about our world and our place in that world.[3] Art, chatting on the edge of experience, nevertheless invites us to choose our stance in that world. I suggest that that is the beauty, or, at least the value, of art. The art experience presents us with a sensory exemplar that can convey, and exhibits, content. The exhibited content of the mode of presentation of the exemplar suggests a reconfiguration of the content of experience outside of art as well as within. Art, then, is that part of experience that changes us by changing the content of our experience. My claim here is that feminist art provides us with a paradigm of what art does, and that is why I admire it.

Let me begin with my personal experience of feminist art. My first encounter with feminist art was Judy Chicago's *The Dinner Party* in San Francisco.[4] I had no idea what to expect. The lines were long, the wait was excessive, but the experience was exhilarating. The first view was the triangular dinner table. I live in a house in Tucson, Arizona, that Margaret

Sanger had built for herself, and so I sought her place setting. Like most of the pieces, it had an unmistakable relationship to the female sex organ. It was blood-red, and, yes, I remembered that Margaret Sanger had been radicalized by witnessing the butchering of women in illegal abortions. But blood is the material of life, and that was more fundamental. My thoughts raised in the encounter, which spurred me to conceptualize the experience of *The Dinner Party*. Beyond the particular place setting there was the grandeur of the triangle, the strength of the triangle, and the feminine biology of the triangle. The power of the feminine confronted me. And thought raced on. Femininity was on every plate. Georgia O'Keeffe may have denied the often-noted similarity of her flowers to the vaginal opening, claiming it was only an interest in scale that led to the flower paintings, but Chicago, in her place setting, left no ambiguity. It was a new view of the female sex organ as a source of creativity and power. My thought was, "Of course, even Courbet portrayed it as the origin of it all."[5] I made ceramics at the time I saw *The Dinner Party*, and I found it hard to take my eyes from those amazing pieces: subtle, brilliant variations on the grounding of us all, of woman and earth.

The movement to the walls and rooms documenting the role, the contributions, and the experience of women was amazing. It was not so much the detail as the overall impact of the feminine in life. I was left thinking at the time of the paradoxical character that is the art character of the experience. It was a revelation of the concealed, a revelation of what we knew and did not know about the known and unknown world of woman. I walked and gawked with my eyes hanging out. Fortunately, after a disappearance, *The Dinner Party* is back on exhibition in Brooklyn.[6] That venue seems correct to me. Brooklyn is somehow an earthy place, not as pretentious as the Manhattan mainstream. It is the alternative place. Jackie Robinson, with the Brooklyn Dodgers, and Judy Chicago, with *The Dinner Party*, in Brooklyn.

The long disappearance of *The Dinner Party* after its remarkable initial success is an indication of the artworld's discrimination against female artists and feminist artists. The Guerrilla Girl movement was and remains a critique of the art establishment. My sympathies are with them. One reads Pierre Bourdieu and is infuriated by the combined sociological acuteness of his work and the sense that art is not about the exercise of the power and institutions of the commercial artworld establishment.[7] It was rather brilliant of Wartenberg, in his anthology, to place the reading from Bourdieu between pieces on feminist art and on African art.[8] As an artist, I am revolted by the soundness of Bourdieu's analysis. His account and the critique of the Guerrilla Girls tell the same story of the museum object being socially constructed by the power of the wealthy and privileged. People sometimes ask why I do not charge more for my art.[9] Art is about what the art object does, how it changes and reconfigures experience for the viewer, not about the commercial value and artworld status of the work. The Guerrilla Girl movement, however central its feminist motivation, is a protest against the power of the establishment. The central role of art is not the creation of cultural capital for the sophisticated few. It is the transformation of the life of us all.

I love to show my work and watch the response of others. Vik Muniz remarked that he does not make art for himself, he makes it to watch how others respond.[10] However, much feminist art is a protest against established commercial art traditions; art objects that become mainstream retain their feminist power to change consciousness. There is a deeper aspect of feminist art, and I think it is widely recognized among artists even when it goes unexpressed: feminist artists remind us what art is about. Their goal is to change experience, to reconfigure how we think and feel about ourselves, our world, and our relation to each other. There is an external world that is not of our making, and there is our internal world, how we think and feel. Feminist art raises consciousness about feminist issues because it confronts us with questions: What do you think and feel about this? How does this relate to what you and your world are like? Feminist art confronts us as art should. It says something, often very explicitly, but asks something at the same time: What are you going to think, feel, and do about this? What does this mean to you? In bringing that question to consciousness, feminist art shows what art does; it reconfigures experience. Or it fails. If it fails, we can say that it fails to be art or that it is bad art, and that it is nothing. Art makes us want to laugh, cry, think, or feel. So there is a paradox in feminist art. As it succeeds, it raises our consciousness about feminist issues and in so doing shows us what art is and does. Feminist art transcends itself and reconfigures what art is for us. Art, when it succeeds, reconfigures experience; it reconfigures our experience of art. In the dullness of standard artworld absentmindedness, we forget that the point of art is to change our experience, to use experience to change experience. In an aesthetic moment, feminist art reminds us of what art—all art, not just feminist art—does.

After *The Dinner Party*, I retained an interest in feminist art because I knew that it worked to change how I felt and thought; it changed me. Change is uncomfortable, but the alternative to change of consciousness is thinking and feeling the same thing for life. Not for my life, thank you. In Tucson, Arizona, where I live, Bailey Doogan works and shows, so I know about uncomfortable feminist art.[11] And Peg Zeglin Brand has been a friend since she sat in a tightly analytic seminar of mine ages ago thinking god knows what, and I have had the joy of watching her philosophy and art change mine. Her art and her presentation of ORLAN have become part of my philosophy of art course.[12] I show some of ORLAN's work to my philosophy of art classes, usually only a jpeg or three. Their response reveals the success of the art. There is always some very bright male student who associates her performance art with violence, with castration or the production of snuff movies. I first ask why they make this association, since plastic surgery is a run-of-the-mill thing in our lives. Then I tell them they have understood. The performance is, after all, an emotionally profound attack on the dominance of the male conception of female beauty. They are right, not wrong, in feeling it to be an attack. However, once I ask them why they respond this way, they rethink and re-feel, and their experience is reconfigured.

In her series *Picture Yourself Here*, Brand has repainted famous images of women by male artists but left holes where their faces would be, allowing you to put your own face in the hole and be photographed in the role of the artwork's subject.[13] The experience of doing this creates amusement that works in the same way as the anger in response to ORLAN. Brand has a lighter touch. Your take on the traditional art is changed by both. Art changes the content of art as it changes the content of experience. Both ORLAN's and Brand's works take me back to the originals, to the male chauvinist side of the male painters, to their role as *flâneurs* and their sometimes hostile vision of the feminine. I reenter their world with heightened consciousness. Sometimes critical or even hostile and sometimes not. Art, as Tolstoy says, is shared communication of feeling,[14] and to enter a world of reconfigured experience in a chauvinist painting of a woman confronts you, as art does, with the question, the personal question, so what do you make of this? It is like the arches of a chapel that you tie together in the keystone loop at the top of the arch that supports the structure of your life as you experience your autonomy in what you make of the art object.

Some of my students responded similarly to *Interior Scroll* by Carolee Schneemann, a performance art piece in which she—in a birthing squat— extracts a scroll from her vagina.[15] Offense. Outrage. So I ask, "How many of you have never seen a naked woman?" "How many of you do not know that something comes out of the vagina of a naked woman; indeed, how many of you do not know that sometimes a woman extracts something from her vagina?" And finally, "Where do you think you all come from, anyway?" My take is that *Interior Scroll* is about the mystery and sacredness of the biology of life. Sorry, we do not drop from heaven, we drop from a woman. The paradox in this work is that we come to know what we already know, but we know it in a new way, and that matters. It changes us. It changes how we feel and think about our experience, about ourselves, about others, about our world. I wish I had experienced her performance. I think I would have felt something remarkable.

Now here is the point. Feminist art shows us, often by a confrontation we cannot ignore, what art does, not only feminist art. Art changes, reconfigures, experience, including our experience of art. We rethink and we re-feel as a result. In that way, feminist art, however focused on feminism, reminds us what art is all about. ORLAN's surgery can teach you how to look at paintings of martyrs. I do not think I ever understood the Renaissance paintings of martyrs until ORLAN. The martyrs have the courage to confront material harm for their spiritual cause, as she confronts material harm for her feminist art. Of course, that is obvious. The paintings are about the ecstatic in suffering. One student, a male artist, responded to ORLAN's art, "She has balls to do that for her art. I admire her." He was an artist, a film artist. His choice of words was deliberate. It was a capsule of performance art.

So what about the wonderful color and form in those martyr paintings? They are not just about color and form. They are about suffering, cruelty, and spiritual transcendence of the body. You do not have to believe in God to understand. You only need to open yourself to the experience. Let me return to *The Dinner Party* to close the loop and tie in the immediacy of experience of color and form and the value of it. Wollheim called our attention to a kind of double vision in our perception of art.[16] Peg Brand reminded us of it.[17] Let us use her metaphor of a toggle switch. We toggle back and forth between an immediate awareness of color and form and an awareness of meaning we find in the color and form. Every artist, and not only artists, is struck by a special kind of sensory immediacy that becomes the focus of aesthetic attention in aesthetic awareness. Sorry, Dickie; there is a special way of attending to art that is aesthetic and distanced from meaning.[18] Brand suggests we toggle from this immediacy into the complexity of the meaning, and the notion of a toggle suggests we can return to immediacy.

I like the metaphor, but I am not sure the psychology is quite right. Once a certain meaning, a gestalt, for example, is part of our perception, it may not be possible to toggle back to immediacy. One of the most striking painters to exploit the two-stage character of perception is Jack Yeats. Look at his painting *The Gay Moon* and at first you will not see the faces, and then you will.[19] Once you see them, you may not be able to toggle back to your original immediate awareness of color and shape. The point I want to make is that there is an initial perception which may be quite formal and not figurative. Once the initial perception is surpassed, however, you will find it difficult to return. One way to do so may be to turn the painting upside down. However, that may, as in a painting I supply (see plate 10a and b), rapidly produce a new figurative take, a different one, when inverted. I do not want to urge the importance of fixed as opposed to more flexible response.

My point is that you become aware in such processes of your configuration of the experience. In the gestalt response, you might experience the perception as compelled and as one from which you cannot be released. Other ways of configuring an experience, for example, my configuring of *Interior Scroll* as being about birth and the mystery of being, may allow the viewer greater autonomy in the configuration of meaning. It is the special feature of a good deal of feminist art—Brand, ORLAN, and Schneemann provide examples—that you know that it is up to you what you make of it, what meaning you give it. A good deal of Renaissance art seems to close the toggle switch pretty early in the perceptual process, though the viewer's imagination may find some residual opportunity to autonomously assign meaning, some free play of the faculties, as Kant suggested.[20] One great strength of some feminist art—*The Dinner Party*, for example—is that it leaves the toggle switch open. You can put aside your interest in meaning and appreciate the color and form of the plates in *The Dinner Party* as well as the whole scope of the triangular table. Here, of course, there is the opening for beauty. *The Dinner Party* is imbued with beauty. Is the beauty a carryover from the response to immediacy? In part, perhaps, but I find beauty in *The Dinner Party* in the meaning of the sensory components. I suggest that there is a kind of intrinsic value in the way the meaning is exhibited in the sensory materials. I am not sure that this intrinsic value of experience is always beauty or even a source of pleasure. There is a value in the way the message is expressed in the sensory materials. The value is in the experience of what the sensory meaning is like.

I think I shocked Brand once by responding in a positive way to the face ORLAN created. Of course it is artificial, as are many of the faces we see, especially on the silver screen. But there is a value in the sensory experience of that face, in the critique being embodied in the experience. Is it beauty? It is value. What is the value like? You have to experience it to know it. Once you experience the value, you are changed. The way you feel and think and experience is changed. Or put the point more cautiously: there is a suggestion of how you might change. Hilde Hein proposes, as I noted above, that the feminist aesthetic is not theory but chatting on the edge of experience: an important proposal because it is not only feminist art that should be viewed in that way. Art chats on the edge of experience. The sensory materials exhibit meaning, and it is that exhibit of meaning, that embodied meaning, as Arthur Danto puts it, that yields the value. There is beauty in the conversion of matter to meaning. Why? We are, ourselves, mentalized bodies. The work, when it is art, is a mentalized physical object. It lives, full of feeling and thought, as we live full of feeling and thought. The intrinsic value of art is the extension of the intrinsic value of our humanity.

There is a natural connection between the intrinsic value of art and the extension of art to performance art, and feminist art exhibits that connection. The struggle of the artist to mentalize a physical object such as a painting or a sculpture, to fill it with meaning, with thought and feeling, leads naturally to the idea of using a body that is already mentalized as the medium. You are confronted with a reconfiguration of experience in a mentalized body, a person. I do not argue that performance art is superior. I only attempt to explain it. If art chats on the edge of experience, and that activity and mentalization are sources of intrinsic value, the use of the already mentalized body has a power to engage the observer in the chat. Think about the difference between Courbet's *The Origin of the World* and Carolee Schneemann's *Interior Scroll*. The latter, unlike the former, cannot be dismissed as mindless. The mind, the thought and feeling of Schneemann, confront you in the experience. You may not like it. You may think it is tasteless or offensive. But you are confronted with the meaning of the thought and feeling of the act. You have to decide what to make of it. The body you see is a mentalized body asking you what you make of it. The Courbet allows you to make nothing of it easily enough. The Schneemann confronts you more directly.

My conclusion loops back to where I began. Art challenges you to exercise your autonomy, your basic autonomy to remake yourself and your world. When it succeeds, you find value in the art object; indeed, that is part of why you consider it art. Is the value beauty? The experience of reconfiguring yourself and your world incorporates the value of the self and others. It joins personal autonomy with social connectedness in a moment of sensory thought and feeling. There is a pleasure in experiencing the content of your world as your own, in the value of your autonomous reconfiguration of yourself and your world. That is beautiful.

NOTES

For a broader discussion of these topics, see my *Art, Self and Knowledge* (New York: Oxford University Press, 2012).

1. Arthur C. Danto, *Embodied Meanings: Critical Essays and Aesthetic Meditations* (New York: Farrar, Straus and Giroux, 1994).

2. Hilde Hein, "Refining Feminist Theory: Lessons from Aesthetics," in *Aesthetics in Feminist Perspective*, ed. Hilde Hein and Carolyn Korsmeyer (Bloomington: Indiana University Press, 1993), 3–18.

3. Peg Zeglin Brand, "Disinterestedness and Political Art," in *Aesthetics: The Big Questions*, ed. Carolyn Korsmeyer (Malden, Mass.: Blackwell, 1998), 155–71.

4. Created between 1974 and 1979, *The Dinner Party* (http://www.judychicago.com/) is a collaborative, multimedia installation that presents a symbolic history of women in Western civilization through a series of thirty-nine place settings, set on a triangular banquet table forty-eight feet per side. It includes the names of an additional 999 women of achievement whose voices have previously been silenced throughout history. *The Dinner Party* first opened to the public at the San Francisco Museum of Modern Art in March 1979. Five thousand people attended the opening, and during its three months on view approximately one hundred thousand people came to see it. *The Dinner Party* traveled extensively throughout the United States and to five other countries.

5. In 1866, Gustav Courbet (1819–77) painted *The Origin of the World*, oil on canvas, 46 × 55 cm. The painting was acquired by the Musée d'Orsay in Paris in 1995. According to the museum's website, "Courbet regularly painted female nudes, sometimes in a frankly libertine vein. But in *The Origin of the World* he went to lengths of daring and frankness which gave his painting its peculiar fascination. The almost anatomical description of female sex organs is not attenuated by any historical or literary device. Yet thanks to Courbet's great virtuosity and the refinement of his amber colour scheme, the painting escapes pornographic status. This audacious, forthright new language had nonetheless not severed all links with tradition: the ample, sensual brushstrokes and the use of colour recall Venetian painting and Courbet himself claimed descent from Titian and Veronese, Correggio and the tradition of carnal, lyrical painting" (http://www.musee-orsay.fr/index.php?id=851&L=1&tx_commentaire_pi1%5BshowUid%5D=125&no_cache=1).

6. *The Dinner Party* found a permanent home in 2007 at the Elizabeth A. Sackler Center for Feminist Art at the Brooklyn Museum; see http://www.brooklynmuseum.org/eascfa/about/index.php.

7. Pierre Bourdieu, *The Field of Cultural Production* (New York: Columbia University Press, 1993).

8. Thomas E. Wartenberg, *The Nature of Art: An Anthology*, 2nd ed. (Belmont, Calif.: Thomas Wadsworth, 2007).

9. My art can be seen online at http://www.u.arizona.edu/~lehrer/ga.htm.

10. Vik Muniz's website is at http://www.vikmuniz.net/.

11. Julie Sasse, ed., *Bailey Doogan: Selected Works, 1971–2005* (Tucson, Ariz.: Etherton Gallery, 2005). See also http://www.baileydoogan.com.

12. Peg Zeglin Brand, "Bound to Beauty: An Interview with ORLAN," in *Beauty Matters* (Bloomington: Indiana University Press, 2000), 289–313. Some images of ORLAN's series of aesthetic surgeries/art performances entitled *The Reincarnation of St. ORLAN* can be seen at http://www.orlan.net.

13. Examples of these repaintings, i.e., feminist parodies, can be seen at http://www.pegbrand.com. For an essay discussing them, see Peg Brand, "Feminist Art Epistemologies: Understanding Feminist Art," *Hypatia: A Journal of Feminist Philosophy* 21, no. 3 (Summer 2006): 166–89.

14. Leo Tolstoy, *What Is Art?* trans. Richard Pevear and Larissa Volokhonsk (Harmondsworth, Middlesex, England: Penguin Classics, 1995).

15. Carolee Schneemann's performance *Interior Scroll—The Cave* (1993–95) was captured in a twelve-minute video by Maria Beatty and is described on her website as follows: "In a vast underground cave, Carolee Schneemann and seven nude women perform the ritualized actions of 'Interior Scroll'—reading the text as each woman slowly extracts a scroll from her vagina. The scroll embodies the primacy of an extended visual line shaped as both concept and action. The extracted text merges critical theory with the body as a source of knowledge. Beatty's camera moves from the naked group actions into close-ups of the unraveling text" (http://www.caroleeschneemann.com/bio.html, under "Film/Videography").

16. Richard Wollheim, *The Art of Painting* (Princeton: Princeton University Press, 1987).

17. Brand, "Disinterestedness and Political Art," 163ff.

18. George Dickie, *Art and the Aesthetic: An Institutional Analysis* (Ithaca: Cornell University Press, 1974); and George Dickie, *An Introduction to Aesthetics* (New York: Oxford University Press, 1997).

19. Jack Yeats's *The Gay Moon* can be seen in the online collection of the National Gallery of Ireland, at http://onlinecollection.nationalgallery.ie/.

20. Immanuel Kant, *Kant's Critique of Judgement*, trans. J. H. Bernard, 2nd ed. (London: Macmillan, 1914).

16. ORLAN Revisited: Disembodied Virtual Hybrid Beauty

PEG ZEGLIN BRAND

If you are squeamish
Don't prod the
beach rubble
—Sappho, fragment 84

Between 1990 and 1993, the artist ORLAN offered nine surgical performances of Carnal Art in a series entitled *The Reincarnation of St. ORLAN*. In "Bound to Beauty: An Interview with ORLAN," I sought to explain the complexities of these performances, as well as those of her series of large-scale photographs, begun in 1998, called *Self-Hybridizations*.[1] In the *Reincarnation* series, ORLAN's actual body underwent multiple surgeries that permanently altered her physical self, turning it into an imagined self inspired by the forehead of the Mona Lisa plus the eyes, chin, and mouth of other women painted by well-known male artists throughout history, each with his own particular ideal of female beauty.[2] In that essay, I suggested a workable concept of virtual beauty that defined beauty as "being in essence or effect, not in fact; not actual, but equivalent, so far as effect is concerned. Virtual beauty substitutes for, yet is not in fact, real beauty."[3] In a later publication, I further expanded upon the concept of virtual beauty by citing conditions for its uniqueness and difference from real beauty.[4] However, unlike some recent critics who call themselves ORLAN admirers, I did not call ORLAN's performances hideous or her beauty monstrous. In fact, I cited her own report of how people react to her in public: that they might *think* she looks monstrous, although she does not feel that way. I remarked that "one could even say that there is beauty in her eyes, evidence that only *some* of her features have been changed to contrast with today's standards of beauty."[5] I still hold to that description, in spite of the time that has passed since the 1998 interview, and I now marvel that so many contemporary interpreters of her work have cast her as monstrous. My initial reaction is that this reading reduces her to an artworld beauty-basher who sounds more like a seller of shallow shock than a serious artist of feminist intent.[6] Even if ORLAN's goal is to create a substitute for female beauty or to subvert ideals of physical beauty per se, does she warrant the descriptor "monstrous"? Human blood and sutures may indeed be distasteful, abject, or even disgusting, but surely the artist's intent is more complex than what is seen on the surface. Viewers who are squeamish are well advised to step back and refrain from prodding the metaphorical beach rubble of ORLAN's postoperative detritus. But for those of us who cannot help but look—like snatching a glimpse of a horrible car wreck—I offer a more nuanced analysis to give ORLAN her due.

Consider ORLAN's later work *Self-Hybridizations*, which carries her exploration of virtual beauty to new levels and engages in less theatricality involving blood and bandages. In describing how ORLAN was "bound to beauty" with this work, i.e., tied to imitating features of ancient Olmec and Mayan sculpture by means of digitally altered self-portraits—I suggested that these were her most successful realizations of virtual beauty. Unlike the *Reincarnation* series, which utilized a surgeon's scalpel, these on-screen images are the result of digitized, manipulated data. As self-portraits, they are imaginative and art-historically inventive. Moreover, they represent the disembodied ORLAN, based as they are on a computerized composite of features. They have elicited some unexpected criticisms, however, being described as "comical and grotesque," "potentially racist," like "a minstrel's use of blackface," and "carnivalesque, somewhat extraterrestrial, and generally misinterpreted." Cast as "caricatures" and as images of "the offspring of the carnival freak and the humanoid," they have been critiqued as being more about "costume" and digital technology than the physical process of "looking into the opened body," i.e., the actual body of ORLAN under the knife (as in the *Reincarnation* series).[7] Because of this, some judge them inferior to her earlier surgeries.

But they are also about a much broader context of standards of beauty, international in scope, whereas the localized physical changes to ORLAN's own body were based on a masculinist version of European art history. The pre-Columbian images, for instance, incorporate both female and male standards of beauty. ORLAN extracts herself from the narrow confines of

European art history, transporting us back to reexamine an incised stone mask from 900 BCE and a stucco head of Lord Pacal from a seventh-century BCE tomb. The autonomy of the artist is essential to a healthy sense of identity across cultures; what follows in her work is an evident sense of empowerment and control. *Self-Hybridizations* is additionally about *self*-control. Under her own power, ORLAN creates extraordinarily colorful selves. To call her work "potentially racist" or similar to "a minstrel's use of blackface" seems to misconstrue her intentions and to limit her artistic freedom through the censorship of a distorted form of political correctness. (Such a charge also demonstrates a lack of knowledge that African Americans themselves applied blackface, increasing the complexity of meaning of their actions . . . and hers.)[8] Are current interpreters becoming too (in)sensitive? too PC? too dismissive of the artist's intent, preferring their own misreadings instead? Moreover, is the aesthetic value of her work lost in these readings?

I argued in 2000 that ORLAN may have moved away from the *Reincarnation* performances toward *Self-Hybridizations* because she thought that in the latter she would be more transparently obvious in meaning and less frequently misunderstood. I may have overstated the ability of audiences to comprehend, however. I will argue in this essay that the virtual beauty that ORLAN unfolds in her ongoing series *Self-Hybridizations* is not a real or actual beauty but rather a fake beauty, causally disembodied, based on the effects she intends to create from an imaginative use of combined hybrid imagery. Subverting the familiar philosophical notions of aesthetic distance and aesthetic appreciation,[9] hers is not a monstrous beauty unless one redefines the concept "beauty" and couples it with "monstrous" in fairly unprecedented ways. And yet fake beauty still has aesthetic features, ones not routinely discussed in assessing ORLAN's work. Finally, in my attempt to problematize the tendency of current critics to interpret her works as monstrous, I suggest the possibility of generational differences in understandings of the term "feminist," shifts in meaning from early feminist theory of the 1970s to ever-evolving, twenty-first-century notions of the term, all of which add to the confusion. As I negotiate this terrain, I hope to steer both critics and viewers more directly to the words of the artist herself, who seems to plead for clearer understanding and appreciation when she laments, "I have tried to make my *Self-Hybridizations* as 'human' as possible, like mutant beings, but I still did not think that the confusion could be possible."[10]

Entre Deux (1997)

First, a brief word about the precursor to *Self-Hybridizations*: a series which dates from 1997 and is entitled *Entre Deux* or *Between the Two*. These photos are all about ORLAN: a series of eighty-two self-portraits arranged in two horizontal rows, like a diptych, with forty-one digitally altered images of changes to her face on the bottom row based on the five male inspirations of her actual surgeries in the *Reincarnation* series, as described by Kathy Davis.

> She devised a computer-synthesized ideal self-portrait based on features taken from women in famous works of art: the forehead of Da Vinci's *Mona Lisa*, the chin of Botticelli's *Venus*, the nose of Fountainebleau's *Diana*, the eyes of Gérard's *Psyche* and the mouth of Boucher's *Europa*. She did not choose her models for their beauty, but rather for the stories which are associated with them. Mona Lisa represents transsexuality for beneath the woman is—as we now know—the hidden self-portrait of the artist Leonardo Da Vinci; Diana is the aggressive adventuress; Europa gazes with anticipation at an uncertain future on another continent; Psyche incorporates love and spiritual hunger; and Venus represents fertility and creativity.[11]

Her visage is already "morphed with this source material," as Peggy Phelan notes, "creating a photographic hybrid, a half-'natural' and half-constructed image of her face, thus exposing the ways in which the natural is inflected by the constructed and vice versa."[12] The top row consists of forty-one photographs of her face, taken on successive days of her healing from the 1993 surgery entitled *Omnipresence* (with each photograph's date and time noted). A textual banner reading "Between the Two" connects the two rows. ORLAN referred to the top row as produced by a "machine-body" (i.e., her own face) and the bottom row as produced by "the machine-computer."[13]

The lower row presents computer-generated blurred images of her face, with her mouth in muted shades of blue, green, peach, and red on each print. In *Between the Two, no. 15* (1994), she morphs into Botticelli's renowned fifteenth-century *Birth of Venus*, complete with wind-blown hair, as if Zephyros were just off-camera (fig. 16.1).[14] In others, her lips are heavily outlined with dark red, revealing the bloody aftereffects of the surgery. In most she looks calm; in some she looks anguished, with her face twisted and lips askew. Looking saintly, suffering, and stoic—like a goddess in the making—she subtly alludes to Western European ideals of beauty. These images are about ORLAN dealing with what is inside her head prior to launch, before she goes global. She is located between two realms of identity, her former and her future selves: *entre deux*. She is shadowy; contemplating; a chrysalis waiting to open. The repetitive shots of her face, like Andy Warhol's stacking of the image of Marilyn Monroe, show her mulling over her self, her identity: an inner churning with, as yet, no discernible direction. Once we see the work that follows, *Self-Hybridizations*, we can, in retrospect, discern a sense of deliberation: her self-obsessed introspection is about to expand to worldwide scope. She is about to project her self into the entire history of art, across different cultures, over thousands of years and various continents, becoming—herself—the virtual traveler through the interconnected continuum of civilization. The pensive positioning of her head (tilted, like Venus's) and the anticipatory demeanor of her gaze off camera do not prepare us for this explosion of intent, the breaking down of barriers, the breakthrough of subtlety into a deluge of color and form.

Figure 16.1. ORLAN, *Between the Two, no. 15,* 1994. Color photograph in light box, 120 × 160 cm. © ORLAN.

It is important to highlight that strict visual copying or imitation of the original artworks' formal properties is not the artist's intent here; recall ORLAN's own words:

> I do not want to resemble Botticelli's Venus.
> I do not want to resemble the Europa of Gustave Moreau—who is not my favorite painter. I chose the Europa of this painter because she figures in an unfinished painting, just like so many of his paintings!
> I do not want to resemble Gérard's Psyche.
> I don't want to resemble Diana of the Fontainebleau School.
> I don't want to resemble Mona Lisa, although this continues to be said in certain newspapers and on television programs despite what I have said on numerous occasions![15]

This explanation allows us to understand the error of many of the claims made about ORLAN, namely, that she is trying to replicate the physical ideals of female beauty; that she fails; and that (whether intentionally or not) she becomes monstrous. She borrows visual motifs, but she is more interested in the characteristics of these women than the way that male artists portrayed them. She appropriates, but not to replicate. This fact is often lost on viewers. Thus, hers is not an imitative art form; rather, she is concerned with what I would describe as inner beauty: the aggression of an adventuress, the courage of facing an uncertain future, love and spiritual hunger, fertility and creativity. These are qualities derived from the stories or narratives of goddesses, not their visages; they are not visible, but rather lie below the surface. (After all, goddesses *are* mythical and fictional, i.e., nonreal beings, at their outset.)

In 1997, Davis (who has subsequently written extensively on the topic of cosmetic surgery) sought to distinguish ORLAN's surgeries for the sake of art from typical cosmetic surgery utilized by women for the sake of enhancement or beauty:

> Although she draws upon mythical beauties for inspiration, she does not want to resemble them. Nor is she particularly concerned with being beautiful. Her operations have left her considerably less beautiful than she was before.... While ORLAN's face is an ideal one, it deviates radically from the masculinist ideal of feminine perfection. Her ideal is radically nonconformist. It does not make us aware of what we lack. When we look at ORLAN, we are reminded that we can use our imagination to become the persons we want to be.[16]

In assessing *Reincarnations* in 1997, Davis offers the clue to the first works of *Hybridizations*—ORLAN'S ongoing series that is all about imagination and becoming something one is not, something imaginary, something unreal, fictional, and disembodied:

> ORLAN's project explores the problem of identity. Who she is, is in constant flux or, as she puts it, "by wanting to become another, I become myself." "I am a bulldozer: dominant and aggressive . . . but if that becomes fixed it is a handicap. . . . I, therefore, renew myself by becoming timid and tender."[17]

In other words, one can undermine and change one's identity in a variety of ways. From 1987 (the year of the first *Reincarnation* surgery, on ORLAN's fortieth birthday) to 1997, ORLAN used her own body ("My body is my art"). From 1997 on, the alterations are digital; she moves beyond scalpels and blood, unleashed upon multiple traditions of visual representation within the entire history of art. Davis adds,

> Her identity project is radical precisely because she is willing to alter her body surgically in order to experiment with different identities. What happens to the notion of "race," she wonders, if I shed my white skin for a black one? Similarly, she rejects gender as a fixed category when she claims: "I am a woman-to-woman transsexual act." . . . ORLAN's art can be viewed as a contribution to postmodern feminist theory on identity. Her face resembles Haraway's (1991) cyborg—half-human, half-machine—which implodes the notion of the natural body. Her project represents the postmodern celebration of identity as fragmented, multiple and—above all—fluctuating.[18]

Disembodied identity becomes, overwhelmingly, the *modus operandi* that transitions ORLAN from surgical alterations to her visual exploration of pixels printed on paper. She moves from the real to the virtual, and her appropriations of beauty, within her self-described "self-portrait," become virtual as well:

> At the inception of this performance, I constructed my self-portrait by mixing and hybridizing, with the help of a computer, representations of goddesses of Greek mythology—chosen not because of the canons of beauty that they are supposed to represent (seen from afar), but for their histories.[19]

Histories are chosen and illustrated but not, strictly speaking, imitated. ORLAN is up to much more here: I suggest that what she is up to is the creation of virtual beauty. Consider the conditions I placed upon "real" versus "virtual" in 2001:

> X is an instance of *real beauty* in artworks for perceiver P at time *t* if and only if P recognizes and appreciates with (disinterested) pleasure the perfection, or uniformity amidst variety, or smoothness, or smallness, or uniqueness, or symmetry, etc., in X.

Y is an instance of *virtual beauty* created by artist A for perceiver P at time *t* if and only if P recognizes and appreciates with (disinterested) pleasure that

> (i) Y is created by A by means of reconfiguring digital information in cyberspace;
> (ii) the figures and objects represented in Y are disembodied;
> (iii) the digital information reconfigured in Y may be reconfigured by P; and
> (iv) Y is not an instance of real beauty.[20]

ORLAN has subsequently elaborated on the distinction by blurring the boundaries:

> The aim is not to confront what is real with what is virtual—and vice versa—in a sort of endless Manichean and reductive opposition. On the contrary, virtuality mingles with reality as its imaginary part and the reality which I create is not devoid of virtuality. . . .
> All figurative works can be said to be "virtual." The representation of the Virgin and Child by Jean Fouquet [ca. 1450], for instance, is the portrait of Agnès Sorel. Still we do not see Charles VII's mistress, but a painting.
> . . . The virtual and the real elements, when they are used at the same time, become new ways of obliquely questioning art itself and the world around us.[21]

Like numerous artists before her, ORLAN seeks to create and understand a multiplicity of selves through both her own likeness and invented faces; like many women uncomfortable with their own bodies, Davis claims, she first used plastic surgery as "a path towards self-determination—a way for women to regain control over their bodies."[22] As a digital artist, she moves beyond the mere physical. As a feminist, she combines the two goals in order to become empowered: in control. As Davis notes, "ORLAN has to be the creator, not just the creation; the one who decides and not the passive object of another's decisions."[23] *Entre Deux* is just the beginning. There are no limits to the identities ORLAN can imagine. Freed from her body, her new identities are disembodied and hybrid: unreal and virtual. *Entre Deux* lies between the two bodies of work: the earlier *Reincarnations* and the later series of *Self-Hybridizations* to come.

Self-Hybridizations Pre-Columbian (1998–2000)

Just one visit to ORLAN's website (http://www.orlan.net) immediately immerses a viewer in a dizzying array of work: clicking, one moves forward and backward, in and out of time. Gone are the days when to see such works one needed to travel to a museum or gallery, pick up an exhibition catalogue from the library, or purchase an art magazine for glossy reproductions. It's all there on your screen, in living color, bursting with vim and vigor: an instant look at art produced in a studio outside of Paris by a woman whose conceptual reach far exceeds her geographical grasp.

In 1998 ORLAN commented on the scope and intent of *Self-Hybridizations:* "My new work is a global survey of standards of beauty in other civilizations and at different periods in history. I start with the pre-Columbian civilizations and will eventually study Africa and Asia." Like many other artworks currently celebrated in international artworld environs as explorations of cultural, multicultural, and cross-cultural identities, this series was intended to pursue a "range of multiple, evolving, mutating identities" by means of a global travelogue.[24] Having chosen the Olmec colossal heads (weighing five to twenty tons) found on the Gulf Coast of Mexico—male heads that signify respect and honor—she additionally utilized smaller stone masks of rulers that flaunted the proportion and symmetry of the formal incised patterns across the face. Both originals invoke the shamanic or godlike power of the male ruler that ORLAN dons in her self-portraits as she recreates her self as a hybrid of cultures and a virtual beauty with underlying meaning and power: a reference to inner power and beauty. She explained her use of the visage of Lord Pacal similarly: "It wasn't a religious thing; it was an aesthetic thing."[25] In this series she becomes obsessed with the physical ideals of beauty, performance, and royalty that operate within a culture totally outside the paradigm of the white European middle class. She engages in aesthetic play by engaging her imagination in the manipulation of what used to be and what could be, all constructed without the interference of real bodies. Gone are the shadowy references to Botticelli as muse. ORLAN has projected herself back in time with her creativity under complete control; she manipulates her self and her face in virtual sacrifice to the gods of beauty standards past. The updated version of her 1998 face, photographed by Gerard Rancinan in 2001 as *Woman with Self- Hybridized Head*, incorporates the same incised facial marks but is even more powerful, because her head is shown, disembodied, upon a platter.[26] My previous essay explains how the incised lines on ORLAN's face in her *Refiguration, Pre-Columbian Self-Hybridization, no. 1* (1999) replicate those on an Olmec mask made of white and gray jadeite, making her a hybrid that seeks to appropriate the shaman's power to enter the supernatural realm (fig. 16.2).[27] As rephotographed in 2001, ORLAN literally highlights her disembodiment and dismemberment (her head without body); virtuality triumphs.

Figure 16.2. ORLAN, *Refiguration, Pre-Columbian Self-Hybridization, no. 1*, 1999. Digital photograph, 100 × 150 cm. © ORLAN.

In my 2001 attempt to expand (or "explode") the aesthetics of "art" and "beauty" that help us understand such works, I compared ORLAN's photographs to those of the Japanese artist Yasumasa Morimura, who photographed himself as various actresses, both American and Japanese. Whether dressing up as Vivien Leigh or Marilyn Monroe, Morimura took traditional analog photographs of his body; that is, he was never Morimura-as-Marilyn in the disembodied sense of computerized art. Like Cindy Sherman in many of her works, he merely dresses up and poses for the camera. In another series, however, he digitally pictured his face on the body of a nude and pregnant Mona Lisa (*Mona Lisa in Pregnancy*, 1998), and then replaced the belly of the nude Mona Lisa with an internal view of the fetus and organs, reminiscent of da Vinci's sketchbook drawings of the fetus in utero (*Mona Lisa in the Third Place*, 1998).[28] These composite collages span centuries, combine and hybridize body parts (real and fictional), and create virtual beauty of its own sort: the beauty of a "person" who is not real, but only virtual. When Morimura appropriated Sherman's *Untitled #96* (1981) by scanning the original and reconfiguring it with a computer to produce *To My Little Sister (For Cindy Sherman)* (1998), he again created a disembodied hybrid fictional candidate for expanding or exploding the traditional category of beauty into that of virtual. Interestingly, no critic has called either artist's work "monstrous."

In addition to undermining any one philosophical definition of "beauty" that may provide comfort to those of us craving the ideals of Western civilization that we so devotedly learned in art history and aesthetics classes, ORLAN seeks to create new hybrids that exercise the autonomy of the artist and the empowerment that viewers subsequently derive from the image. Her insistent pushing of the boundaries of "multiple, evolving, mutating identities" is a playful but reverential romp; the process is more important than the product, although the product becomes more vivid and intense as the series progresses. She does not set out to portray real beauty, to re-create real beauty, or to imitate it. Rather, as I have been arguing, hers is an intentionally false beauty: fake as can be, yet—and here is where her true genius lies—as seductive as the real thing. Virtual beauty is that of the disembodied object, the fictional ORLAN-as-Mayan or ORLAN-as-Olmec. Why, then, does she elicit the more serious charge of monstrosity, even from her defenders?

Self-Hybridizations African (2000–2003)

The next phase in *Self-Hybridizations* is a series of photos inspired by African natives, photographed as if being discovered for the first time in the nineteenth century by a probing explorer with a new camera (most are in black and white). Consider the image entitled *Ancient Crest of Ejagham Nigeria Dance and Face of Euro-Saint-Etienne Woman* (2000; fig. 16.3). Also included in the African series is a life-size sculpture of a human body (ORLAN's) scarified in decorative patterns. As described by one sympathetic critic, Serge Gruzinski, the photographic images exemplify the "still relatively little explored—and therefore relatively unfamiliar" phenomenon of mélange: "Mixing, mingling, blending, cross-breeding, combining, super-imposing, juxtaposing, interposing, imbricating, fusing and merging are all terms associated with the mestizo process, swamping vague descriptions and fuzzy thinking in a profusion of terms." Considered as a manifestation of

Figure 16.3. ORLAN, *Refiguration, African Self-Hybridization* series, *Ancient Crest of Ejagham Nigeria Dance and Face of Euro-Saint-Etienne Woman*, 2000. Digital photograph, 124 × 155.5 cm. © ORLAN.

the fracturing of modern society, ORLAN becomes a forerunner of a trend whereby "standard frames of reference are being shattered by these surprising and sometimes awkward juxtapositions and presences."[29] Beauty is hardly subject only to subversion, as in the twentieth century. In the new millennium, it is shattered, shocked, and shunted. Prompting more questions than they answer, these are the harbingers of a so-called postmodern, hypernarcissistic, amortal, mutant world.[30] But what, exactly, does this mean?

Consider ORLAN's own words, written expressly for Elisabeth Azoulay and Françoise Gaillard's five-volume collection *100,000 Years of Beauty*:

> Like sex and money, beauty follows the dictates of criteria of recognition, codes and laws in which the artist's job is to divert so as to expose supremacy. In an attempt to thwart the authoritarianism of the perceptions of beauty that prevail in our societies, I had two small lumps implanted on my temples. They are like two erupting volcanoes that threaten the predominant notions governing female beauty, which gives my work a subjective and political meaning.[31]

The artist's feminist intentions are undeniable; she continues to challenge the patriarchal norms that have established the dictates of female beauty over the centuries, continuing into the present day of mass media saturation and consumer culture.[32] She is, herself, the photographic print upon which the battle between actual and virtual body ensues.

> I show that beauty is in no way a natural phenomenon but a cultural construct. I also want to mark the fact that, in an age of globalization, the range of possibilities is simultaneously spreading and shrinking. In one sense, we are witnessing a proliferation of pluralistic expressions and theatrical orchestrations; in another we are using Western criteria as a filter to all of this multiplicity and creativity, in the image of what Impressionism and Cubism in particular did for Oriental and African arts.

In addition to her feminist perspective, ORLAN adopts the Western lens by which most artworld aficionados view the world: us versus them; us versus other. Her goal is to expose the bias we bring to the perception of multiplying "expressions" and "orchestrations" as she projects a utopian possibility that lies beyond the intensifying pressures of today:

> I construct images of mutant beings whose presence may be envisaged in a future civilization not beholden to the same physical pressure as we are. It

might therefore accept their potential for beauty and sexual attractiveness. The *Self-Hybridizations* are created through the hybridization of my face, supposedly corresponding to current codes of beauty, along with works from other civilizations and other timescales that embody standards of beauty different from our own.

The beauty of her future, however, is a virtual beauty of hybrids and mutants. It has little connection with beauty as defined by the power brokers of the multi-million-dollar "beauty industry" today. It is a false, nonreal, made-up beauty of the disembodied; it is a fakery of the original, a deliberate offspring. Note ORLAN's use of the phrase "supposedly corresponding to current codes of beauty." Moreover, it is explicitly constructed, *socially* constructed by the artist, with no tie to a "real" beauty that is considered innate, inherited, or genetic. It is fiction, though based in fact and social standards. She concludes, while simultaneously projecting even further into the future with the introduction of bio-art:

> My work has always been a struggle against all that is innate, inexorable, programmed, against nature and DNA. And also against all the pressure of prevailing ideologies, all bodily formatting procedures. One of my current projects involves the development of an installation called the Harlequin cloak from the culture of my own cells and those of different origins (animal and human). While the body is a language, it is above all a theatre for the staging of alternative, nomadic, mutant and shifting identities. A theatre of pleasure and humour that opens onto the infinite interplay of metamorphosis, marking the global hybridization of beings and cultures.

As if to verify that virtual beauty is causally connected to the diffuse disembodiment of the original physical body, but not an imitation of it, art critic M. Perniola offers the following:

> Virtuality is not a simulation,
> An imitation, a mimicry of reality,
> But an entry into another dimension,
> Ontologically different, as it were.[33]

Ontological difference is essential to understanding the ephemeral, metaphysical selves of ORLAN disembodied. She hybridizes herself into multiple "copies," but not imitations. Attempts to understand her work have not always carefully maintained this distinction. Operating in another dimension lifts her from the physical, even the (traditionally) photographic, into another realm that is tricky to distinguish and even more difficult to discern. How, then, do we put into words her apparent imitation of, for instance, a nineteenth-century painting by George Catlin (plate 11)?

Self-Hybridizations American-Indian (2005–2007)

Numerous life-size photographic prints of ORLAN dressed in Native American garb with rich red backgrounds pulsate while her painted face changes, mutates, and explores. Consider one example, entitled *Painting Portrait of Wash-Ka-Mon-Ya, Fast Dancer, a Warrior, with ORLAN's Photographic Portrait, Refiguration, American-Indian Self-Hybridization, no. 3 (2005)* (plate 12). The theme of a 2010 group show in which she participated entitled "Islands Never Found" is vague and indeterminable, like the seeking of an elusive "place" or perhaps a frame of mind:

> Leading, internationally renowned contemporary artists interpret their very own islands never found through a series of extraordinary works—some never before exhibited. Installations, videos, photographs, sculptures, drawings and paintings take the visitor on a journey, where each island—a metaphor for life and constant exploration—raises questions and doubts about the very meaning of life.
>
> The artists taking part in this project have embarked on a journey through uncharted waters, on a never-ending voyage, continually haunted by the possibility that the destination might in fact be a nonplace, a utopia, a simple territory of desire—and therefore beyond reach.[34]

ORLAN's identity is ever evolving and can adapt to a new swatch of paint worn boldly on her face, an imposing bearclaw necklace hanging defiantly around her neck, or the feathers and beads that sprout from her head and ears. According to one description of these works, the large-scale series was created during ORLAN's New York studio residency at the International Studio and Curatorial Program and was based on the paintings of George Catlin, who documented native tribes before the widespread use of photography.[35] The Indian is romanticized here, beautified perhaps, but ORLAN's goal is not to make herself beautiful in the traditional sense, nor to approximate the real beauty of an Indian that she, as a white European woman, can never attain. Hers is a false beauty, purely virtual, where virtuality is not a simulation, an imitation, a mimicry of reality, but an entry into another, ontologically different dimension.

One way to interpret this distinction is to deem ORLAN's virtual beauty without substance or interiority, as Jill O'Bryan notes: "The *Self-Hybridation* photographs have no interior, no texture, no body."[36] Her claim is similar to an earlier observation by Arthur C. Danto about ORLAN's previous *Reincarnation* series:

> Hegel characterizes Romantic Art as responsive to the demand for making inwardness visible, of showing what a person is so far as that person is coincident with his or her feelings. And that would explain why *The Spear-carrier* is bland: classical art, if Hegel is right, had no concept of inwardness. It explains as well why a contemporary artist, ORLAN, who submits herself to plastic surgery in order to make herself conform to aesthetic prototypes, in fact looks, well, creepy. She shows no inwardness.[37]

Can this description be extended to *Self-Hybridizations* as well? Is O'Bryan, following Danto, on to something here? One of ORLAN's inspirations is Catlin's painting *White Cloud: Head Chief of the Iowas* (1844–45), one of many he created to portray "paradigmatic 'Indianness'"—images that became icons of the "wild" inhabitants of the western United States, as imagined by the more "civilized" immigrants back east who were new to the land, fresh from Europe, or descended from newcomers to America.[38] ORLAN's vacuous look may digitally replicate the way that George Catlin sought to depict Native Americans, but for this reason it lacks the real thing, or, as Danto frames it, a "person coincident with her or her feelings." She uses Catlin's image to replicate the vacuity that Europeans and newly arrived "Americans" perceived in Indians. Her comment upon their colonialist superiority is not racist, but rather points out the narrowness of their encounters with people they condescendingly referred to as "savages."

Consider the contrast between ORLAN's disembodied, virtual, hybrid images, devoid of inwardness and interiority, and contemporary art by Native Americans. When Indians themselves satirize or parody images like Catlin's paintings and Edward Curtis's photographs, their works are considered reclamations and subversive examples of commoditization.[39] When ORLAN does so, according to some critics, the result is potentially racist and "monstrous." Upon what interpretive strategy do such labels depend? It is time to dive into monstrous beauty.

Mistaking Monstrous Beauty: ORLAN's Virtual Beauty

Joanna Frueh originally defined "monster/beauty" in 2001 in a book of the same name, subtitled "Building the Body of Love," locating the concept of monster/beauty within an ideal, prescribed beauty—our current "standard of success," i.e., cultural norms that extol purely visual beauty, equal to perfection, and its attendant sexual charisma that attracts lovers of beauty. In contrast, monster/beauty is self-care and self-development that comes from "aesthetic/erotic attentiveness, . . . self-consciousness, self-pride, self-pleasure, and self-love." "Aesthetic/erotic wit, a decisive way of dressing oneself in the sensuality and beauty of Aphrodite, proceeds from the corporeal subjectivity and agency that define monster/beauty." Moreover, it is not (merely) a visual beauty; Frueh emphasizes "the sensual dimensionality that is a human being's beauty . . . the aesthetic/erotic field that people create for themselves and inhabit, the field that they in fact are. . . . Beauty as only and simply a visual feature—a still picture—is erotically devoid, a failure of love. . . . In contrast, and in eros, monster/beauty is the flawed and touchable, touching and smellable, vocal and mobile body."[40]

Focusing on the agency of the woman whose body might traditionally be culturally seen as lacking, disappointing, or aging, monster/beauty embodies the agency of action and not just her passive reception of the gaze of others; it also includes discomfort with her physical body that is never perfect. Thus it offers the (still) taboo personal voice, i.e., the body that speaks (up for itself). It is "an aesthetic/erotic aptitude, fleshed out and inspirited with the essence of Aphrodite."[41] This aptitude is a form of sexual allure, and monster/beauty is a "monster" only insofar as the woman embodies the allure of pleasure and satisfaction with(in) her own body, in spite of cultural norms, resulting in the true enjoyment of her own body and the authentic valuing of her beauty. As such, the "monster" learns to "build the body of love" whereby the aesthetic (the seen) and erotic (the sensed) are inseparable.[42]

Frueh is focused primarily on American culture and her role as a middle-aged woman within prescribed beauty norms not of her own creation. The monster who builds the body of love is engaged in the positive and constructive task of making herself more comfortable in her own skin, not in the negative and destructive critique of cultural norms or her own physicality. This so-called monster learns to accept her body while bypassing cosmetic surgery for the purpose of enhancement; self-empowerment comes from self-love and strength. In contrast, ORLAN challenges and undercuts the ideal beauty norms that exist to be challenged. Her work, *Reincarnation* or *Self-Hybridizations*, is not about love or the seeking of love or self-love. Thus Frueh's concept of monster/beauty—as innovative and insightful as it is—offers little in the way of helpful interpretation of ORLAN's performance art. In fact, Frueh offers explicit evidence that it is inadvisable to apply monster/beauty either to the documentations of ORLAN's surgeries or to certain photos by Cindy Sherman, Jo Spence, and Hannah Wilke; she calls their work "the modern erotics of damage." As an aberration from the socially accepted ideal of physical perfection, the monster/beauty of the bodybuilder, for instance, may be considered grotesque, abject, bizarre, incongruous, eccentric, strange, and ridiculous. For Frueh, it is separate from violence, disease, breakdown, mutilation, or the hospital. Hence it is not, Frueh adds, the "Sadeian or Battailean erotics of horror based in an aesthetics of disgust," i.e., an erotics of damage, nor is it attached to the Western tradition of shame and transgressiveness outlined by Freud.[43] Yet, as we will see shortly, Frueh's concept of monster/beauty has been inappropriately applied to ORLAN's work by at least three recent authors.

But first, let us look briefly at the comments of Tanya Augsberg, another feminist who, like Frueh, focuses on woman's subjectivity and agency by citing the history of philosophy's male-dominated construction of woman as an inferior, irrational being who is merely passive and inactive. Writing in 1998, she suggests ORLAN's surgical performances constitute an antidote to this tradition, calling them "performative transformations of feminist medical subjectivity" which "cannot simply be reduced to extreme acts of self-mutilation in the guise of art."

> ORLAN's multimedia surgical theatre is meant to be *transformative* as well as risky; by undergoing a planned series of cosmetic surgeries, ORLAN is self-consciously exploring a means of identity transformation. . . . [She] undergoes a particular beauty ritual—cosmetic surgery—in order to expose and question those techniques of gender that simultaneously construct and discipline "beauty-conscious" female identity.[44]

Like Frueh, Augsberg highlights the proactive agency and subjectivity of ORLAN's work, but refrains from calling it monstrous. Citing criticisms of her as "hysteric, a narcissist, a fetishist, a scalpel slave (or polysurgical addict), and even a sufferer of Body Dysmorphic Disorder," she defends (but does not necessarily condone) her body art as an act of social resistance (one of many forms since 1990) that results in an uglification of self within our rapidly evolving age of technologized beauty.[45]

Only when Augsberg is explaining ORLAN's "complicity in, and dependence on, these institutions [of medicine, science, and art] in order to stage the resistance she enacts"—what she calls ORLAN's "Staging the Medical Subject"—does she invoke the concept of the "bloody, slimy, ghastly, yet also celebratory carnivalesque scene reminiscent of Gargantua's birth in the writings of Rabelais." But she takes this characterization of the carnivalesque (professed by ORLAN herself, as mentioned earlier) no further; rather, she highlights the uniquely created subject of ORLAN who orchestrates the live surgical scene, in which she is awake and gazes back at the camera filming her:

> ORLAN may allow her body to be cut, stretched, and resculpted, but her persistent gaze signals not only her resistance to becoming the completely docile body that medicine requires but also her insistence on being recognized at all times as *more than just a body*. Her art demands of her audience that we witness her self-awareness not only of her surgery but of *us* looking at her. In other words, ORLAN not only returns the viewer's gaze, but expects—if not demands—that her recognition of us be in turn recognized by each individual.[46]

Augsberg is comfortable calling ORLAN's exposure of her body's living tissues mesmerizing and revolting. Moreover, she interprets ORLAN's challenge to us as one of "highlighting the body's grotesque abjection in surgery and in recovery" without reducing it to "visceral performance." "To put it bluntly, ORLAN's art does a lot more than just gross all of us out: she provokes us to become more self-reflexive in our roles as spectators."[47] Augsberg's cogent analysis of ORLAN as a medical subject who creates and controls a self-conscious subjectivity in her performances neither suggests nor lends credence to the charge of monstrosity, perversion, or mental imbalance. There seems no reason to presume that "grotesque abjection" is equivalent to or implies monstrosity. Moreover, sometimes ORLAN is playful and perversely provocative, as in *Kiss on Tracing Paper, The Fourth Surgery-Performance Titled Successful Operation* (1991), a photograph in the *Reincarnation of Saint ORLAN* or *Picture New Pictures* series (fig. 16.4). Yet at multiple points, Augsberg cites the tendency for viewers and critics to misinterpret ORLAN and to cast her as mad and irrational. This analysis presents a stark contrast to the critics who follow—writing in 2005, 2007, and 2009 respectively—who mistake ORLAN's intent or misconstrue her meaning. Question: What has happened to such criticism in the twenty-first century? ORLAN, it appears, becomes monstrous.

Figure 16.4. ORLAN, *The Reincarnation of Saint ORLAN
or Pictures New Pictures* series, *Kiss on Tracing Paper, The
Fourth Surgery-Performance Titled Successful Operation,*
1991. Photograph, 165 × 110 cm. © ORLAN.

Three significant critics currently invoke either Joanna Frueh's mon-
ster/beauty or Sigmund Freud's theory of the terrifying castrated woman as
their inspiration for misinterpreting ORLAN as monstrous.

First, C. Jill O'Bryan (2005), already cited earlier, does not directly ref-
erence Frueh's concept of monster/beauty in her *Carnal Art: ORLAN's
Refacing*, although she includes a chapter entitled "Beauty/The Monstrous
Feminine."[48] Rather, in this chapter, O'Bryan calls ORLAN's work "the
monstrous feminine" in an attempt to locate ORLAN within the binary tradition of beauty and the monstrous, personified by the gorgon Medusa. When
Medusa's beauty "prompts" Neptune to rape her in the temple of Minerva,
Minerva's revenge for this transgression turns her into a snake-haired monster who, in turn, transforms—into stone—all who gaze upon her. According
to Ovid's *Metamorphosis*, her serpent-hair frightens evil-doers.[49] This myth
prompted both Freud and Jacques Lacan to link Medusa's head to male fear
of castration; to quote Freud,

> To decapitate = to castrate. The terror of Medusa is thus a terror of castra-
> tion that is linked to the sight of something. Numerous analyses have made

us familiar with the occasion of this: it occurs when a boy who has hith-erto been unwilling to believe the threat of castration, catches a sight of the female genitals, probably those of an adult, surrounded by hair, and essen-tially those of his mother.

Lacan describes Medusa's head as

this something, which properly speaking is unnamable, the back of this throat, the complex, unlocatable form, which also makes it into the prim-itive object *par excellence*, the abyss of the feminine organ from which all life emerges, this gulf of the mouth, in which everything is swallowed up.[50]

O'Bryan utilizes these descriptions of "an anxiety of sexual difference that traverses the centuries" to analyze a 1978 performance piece by ORLAN entitled *Documentary Study: The Head of Medusa* in which she allowed viewers to view her sex through a large magnifying glass while simultane-ously showing the heads of persons arriving, viewing, and leaving on video monitors. Exiting visitors were handed a copy of Freud's text on Medusa, including the words "At the sight of the vulva even the devil runs away. "[51] I have no quarrel with O'Bryan's contention that ORLAN is exploiting the "monstrousness" of her sex in this early performance work, but when she extends the accusation of monstrousness to the skin lifted from ORLAN's face in her surgery in *Omnipresence*, she holds that viewers (like the devil) will similarly run away from such monstrousness, leading her to conclude that "like those who gazed upon Medusa, we respond to ORLAN's mon-strousness." Our gaze upon ORLAN's flayed face, or, as she calls it, her ani-mal nonface, directly refers to the gaze that alternatively turns the body to stone, the gaze that instills fear in the male who sees the castrated female. O'Bryan realizes the need to explain how ORLAN's subsequent work, how-ever, transcends this binary entrapment in the monstrous; she points out that "the myth of Medusa and Freud's analysis exhibit a male understand-ing of female genitalia that culminates in horror—the monstrous femi-nine" and that ORLAN's subsequent work "points toward overcoming the male economy of viewing described by Freud, to the degree that ORLAN's images begin to redirect the relationship of the female body to language and to representation."[52]

Along those lines, in a later chapter of *Carnal Art*, O'Bryan extends the explanation of the digital images of *Self-Hybridizations* by mentioning an occasion in 1999 when she presented the work of ORLAN to a group of feminist art historians who strongly objected, denouncing ORLAN's future humanoid hybrids—her fantasy aliens and fictional beings—with "accusations of ORLAN's overwhelming pretence and racism," likening them to "a minstrel's use of blackface," and saying that they exhibited "a carnivalesque otherness that serves to exacerbate the gap between the normative and the grotesque (the self and the other)." Apart from the art historians' reactions, O'Bryan herself believed that ORLAN's images were "comical and grotesque," and appeared "carnivalesque, somewhat extraterrestrial, and generally misinterpreted." But she succumbs to calling ORLAN's faces "offspring of the carnival freak and the humanoid" and critiques them as being more "about digital technology or, at best, costume" than the physical process of our "looking into the opened body," i.e., the actual body of ORLAN under the knife (in the *Reincarnation* series).[53] These are the images O'Bryan previously described as having no interior, no texture, no body, compared to the images of ORLAN's actual surgeries.

When O'Bryan moves on to discuss ORLAN's *Self-Hybridizations*, she initially defends ORLAN's use of both the carnivalesque and the grotesque but equates the female grotesque with going beyond sexualization, an odd sense of the term indeed; she even calls some of ORLAN's images "really quite sexy."[54] (It is important to note here that ORLAN herself suggests that different styles were used in her operations, ranging from the carnivalesque and the parodic to the grotesque and the ironic, and since *Self-Hybridizations* is a continuation of the *Reincarnation* series, these styles persist.)[55] O'Bryan's deeper analysis of ORLAN's mutating and mutant photographic identities undergirds her preferred sense of "grotesque," borrowed from Bakhtin, in which the grotesque body is "in the act of becoming. It is never finished, never completed: it is continually built, created, and builds and creates another body."[56] Thus, ORLAN does not mock other cultures but rather "plays with our own prejudices and the often absurd perceptions that Western culture projects onto other cultures." Her images "appear more sci-fi than cross-cultural."[57]

ORLAN herself, quoted in O'Bryan's chapter on *Self-Hybridizations*, reports on people's reaction to the images, just as she reported on their reactions to the bumps on her forehead: "People talking about these photographs have a tendency to describe me as a 'monster' with a strange face, a distorted face; still these two pigeon eggs do not seem to produce the same effect when I am seen in reality."[58] This is the second instance of ORLAN rejecting the terms "monster" and "monstrous." To use these words to describe her face as well as digital images of her face seems misguided at best and dismissive of the artist's intentions at worst.

Our second author, Elizabeth C. Mansfield, does not cite Frueh on monster/beauty but builds upon references to Freud in her 2007 book *Too Beautiful to Picture: Zeuxis, Myth, and Mimesis.* The first objection to Mansfield's approach is her insistence that ORLAN's performances and imagery are instances of imitation, strictly speaking. Her book is about Zeuxis and the copying of formal features, i.e., mimesis. The story of the painter Zeuxis dates back to Cicero and Pliny; he set out to paint the portrait of Helen of Troy only to realize that a single model would not suffice. Helen's beauty could only be realized by combining the best features of five different models. Mansfield touts this story as a lesson in imitation and in the triumph of ideal beauty over natural beauty. Much of the text focuses on various depictions of the legend, both artistic and literary, as well as the possibility of a female Zeuxis, e.g., someone like Angelica Kauffman (1741–1807): child prodigy, recognized portraitist by age fifteen, and the first female artist to depict Zeuxis selecting his models.[59] The inclusion of her own self-portrait in the scene significantly alters the meaning of the painting and subverts the traditional discourse of the male artist depicting female beauty. Kauffman deliberately challenges the hitherto uncontested authority of the male artist, the artistic conventions of the genre, and the social norms of gender hierarchy. Mansfield also cites Mary Shelley, author of the 1818 novel *Frankenstein,* as a challenge to the Zeuxis myth by attributing to her its recasting as a tale of monstrosity. Like Kauffman, Shelley assumes a critical position, taking "aim at both academic and romantic theories of creativity"; the monster's creator, Victor Frankenstein (whom Shelley called "the artist" in the introduction to her 1831 revised edition of the novel), is a symbol—verging on a parody—of Enlightenment faith in human knowledge (science) and his creation is formed with "a discriminating approach. . . . 'His limbs were in proportion, and I had selected his features as beautiful.'"[60] Mansfield concludes, "Both Frankenstein and Zeuxis seek perfect form through a composite of well-chosen parts."[61]

Mansfield sees ORLAN as a third in this series of pioneering women creatively recapturing artistic agency by undermining repressive patriarchal norms, and she devotes an entire chapter to her work, entitling it "Zeuxis in the Operating Room: ORLAN's Carnal Art." She sees ORLAN's borrowing from the faces of five different painted women for her *Reincarnation* series as a perfect match to Zeuxis, except that she reminds us that ORLAN is quoting the goddesses' stories, not strictly copying their physical features. But her explanation is brief and unclear, linking mimesis to DNA. More to the point, she offers a lengthier analysis that likens ORLAN to Mary Shelley, drawing "an explicit comparison between the artist's studio and the operating room. . . . ORLAN's theatricalization of the operating room through the use of props, costumes, and recitations echoes Hollywood's treatment of Frankenstein's laboratory as a carnivalesque chamber of horrors."[62]

This connection between ORLAN's art performances and Hollywood horror movies relies upon the presumption that both serve to expose and disguise enacted trauma by a fetishistic means, where "fetishism [according to Freud] is a consequence of an unresolved castration complex"; recall the boy witnessing his mother's genitals (her lack of a penis) and his subsequent anxiety and castration complex. Freudians also assume that that anxiety can be assuaged by means of a fetish, usually a body part. Through the less traumatic, and perhaps even comforting, vehicle of the fetish, "the moment of originary trauma is revisited and the scene is unconsciously reenacted under controlled and reassuring circumstances." Mansfield interprets ORLAN as an explorer of fetishism; explicit photos of her surgeries—complete with distracting designer couture worn by the physician and ORLAN's reading of French philosophical texts: visual props and theatricality—serve as fetishes "through which her performances might be psychically reenacted or authenticated" and by which we watch with horror.[63] Mansfield believes that horror is the specific emotion ORLAN seeks to arouse in viewers, yet she argues that fetishism transforms trauma to reassuring spectacle. As in Hollywood's campy versions of *Frankenstein*, the horror is both preserved and disguised. Like Kauffman and Shelley, ORLAN orchestrates the Zeuxis myth on her own terms, viz., those of a woman with a point of view unavailable to men.

The comparison of ORLAN to both Kauffman and Shelley seems forced, however. First, Kauffman repeats the Zeuxis myth in order to inject female agency into a genre of painting and to counter a long-standing attitude that denied any identity and activity to beautiful models. By injecting herself into the scene, she replaces Zeuxis, taking control and coordinating the action. Moreover, she does not create anything like a monster, or provide any sort of fetishistic displacement of Freudian castration anxiety to her viewers. Shelley does create a monstrous literary invention, but her artistic intent seems quite unlike that of ORLAN, who repeatedly and undeniably states that she does not seek to make herself beautiful (as cosmetic surgery typically intends) nor to make herself monstrous (in spite of how viewers might initially see her, i.e., before they understand her artistic intent). Furthermore, if we invoke any standard definition of horror or the monstrous—for instance, that of Noël Carroll—horror (as often embodied in a monster) is the antithesis of beauty both visually and ethically.[64] In other words, someone of horror, like Frankenstein, is also morally depraved. Where does Mansfield see the analogy between ORLAN's fetishistic self-portraits and the evil of Frankenstein and his monster creation? ORLAN's intent to subvert, not imitate, beauty ideals and her feminist agenda to create shifting, disembodied, hybrid identities is neither immoral nor ethically suspect. In fact, she optimistically aims for multiplicity, possibility, and virtuality. As far back as 1988, in a series of painted posters prior to her transformative surgeries, such as one entitled *Imaginery crédits for ORLAN before Saint ORLAN* (fig. 16.5), she playfully parodied Bernini's sculptural tribute to the ecstatic Saint Teresa of Avila, dressing up as the devotee but with breasts exposed and body on display.[65] Mansfield's harsh comparison and unfair characterization seems mistaken in that it denies a fair and plausible interpretation of ORLAN's oeuvre. Her misunderstanding of ORLAN's work also serves to influence the third author I discuss, Danielle Knafo.

Danielle Knafo's 2009 essay "ORLAN: Monster Beauty" praises ORLAN for the rebelliousness of her work—its deviance, its challenge to the social order, and its intention to change the world—by citing Frueh's concept of monster beauty and by adding her own reference to "the terrifying aspects of femininity . . . that simultaneously embrace and challenge Freud's notions of the castrated woman." She quotes Frueh:

> Monstrousness is an unnamed and implicit feminine condition. . . . The Western tradition is populated by terrifically exciting female monsters, whose threat to men or male dominance is so great that they must be killed; Tiamat, the Sphinx, Medusa. Woman has been constructed as a hormonal and sexual monster whose physical attractions lure man into the *vagina dentata*, where he will be emasculated; whose femininity must be controlled through the administration of estrogen and progesterone and through dieting, the constriction of appetite. Female monsters in film can be monsters whose protectiveness of their spawn and whose procreative powers are both deadly to the human species—witness female villainy in the *Alien* films.

Frueh speaks of monstrousness as an implicit feminine condition that threatens men and makes them fear castration, recalling Freud. But she also points out how these assessments of women are male fantasies, or male projections, as Knafo readily admits. Frueh's goal is to suggest a productive way to build the body of (self-)love, not to create a monster to fulfill male fantasies. How, exactly, does Knafo argue that ORLAN actually seeks to be monstrous? Knafo goes on,

Figure 16.5. ORLAN, *Painted Posters* series, *Imaginery crédits for ORLAN before Saint ORLAN*, 1988. Acrylic on stretched canvas, painted by Publidécor, 300 × 200 cm. © ORLAN.

Indeed, it can be said that ORLAN's reincarnation gives birth to a type of she-monster. She has explicitly compared her artistic aim with the creation of a monster; and even had herself photographed as the Bride of Frankenstein in 1990. The difference between the two "monsters" is that she is the creator as well as the final product: the sacré monstre.[66]

Here Knafo is replicating an argument (without citation) that appears in Manfield's chapter on ORLAN, where Mansfield provides pictures of ORLAN's 1990 photograph *Self-Portrait with a Bride of Frankenstein Wig* next to a publicity photo of actress Elsa Lanchester from the 1935 Universal Studios film *The Bride of Frankenstein*.[67] At the outset, it should be noted that ORLAN has never compared her artistic aim with the creation of a monster; recall her comments specifically refuting this interpretation. Knafo is simply wrong on this issue.

Next, in the original comparison, Mansfield describes the filmic bride of Frankenstein as a being who is created (i.e., reanimated as a human being) "to mollify the monster's loneliness and violent hatred of humanity." Several observations come to mind. First, this hardly seems to be the stuff—evil, horror, castration-anxiety-inducing she-monster—of which a monster, male or female, is made. Yet Mansfield insists that ORLAN's imitation of the bride of Frankenstein is her creation of a new identity, "an unstable icon of femininity": "At once reassuring in its mimicry of Hollywood glamour shots or glossy advertisements and threatening in its evocation of monstrosity, violence, and death, the figure in 'Self-Portrait with a Bride of Frankenstein Wig' vacillates between two subject positions: phallic mother and castrated and therefore threatening other."[68]

Second, being neither monster nor mother, the bride of Frankenstein was intended (we presume) to be the helpmate of the male monster, the Eve to his Adam. To attribute monstrosity as well as "erotic potential" to her is to present a caricature of the bride (who is already a parodic figure herself) as erotically charged and alluring monster. It is doubtful that Frueh would agree that the bride of Frankenstein, even as a mythic creation, could possess the allure of which she speaks so highly, the self-possessed, agentic sexuality of beauty and self-love.

Third, ORLAN's self-portrait as the Bride of Frankenstein was created in 1990, quite early in her artistic output: before *Entre Deux*, before *The Reincarnation of St. ORLAN*, and even before *Self-Hybridizations*. The photo of her with wig and dramatic pose is not the outgrowth of her surgeries and imaginative photographic plays on hybrid identity; rather, it is the precursor. To ascribe monstrosity to it as if it is tied to the bloody surgeries of her performances is to misconstrue its role within the evolution of her total artistic output and to inject a 1990 photo into 2009 critical discourse without acknowledging its date of production. Knafo goes on to briefly discuss *Self-Hybridizations*, and although she does not call these photographs monstrous (she sees them, in part, as ORLAN's refusal "to accept her body's limitations—its difference and/or lack—which place her in a state of castration"), she lumps them together with the previous examples, as if they too might be monstrous:

> Thus, whether we gaze at Medusa's head, the head of Frankenstein's Bride, or the composite images of ORLAN's face with those of pre-Columbian, African, or Native American origin, we come tête-à-tête with the artist's hybrid images in an intimate yet bizarre reciprocal mirroring of her own devising.[69]

Fourth, to link the supposed horror of the photo, i.e., the fact that ORLAN chose to picture herself as the Bride of Frankenstein, to the horror of Hollywood movies seems superficial. It leads Knafo down the path of ascribing horror to ORLAN herself (birthing herself as a she-monster), ending with the "virtual disappearance of the female as the subject of beauty in the art of recent decades." Nothing could be further from the truth; nearly every artwork and performance by ORLAN deals with beauty. Knafo is incorrect to claim ORLAN leaves it behind, just as she is wrong to attribute to her a preoccupation with monster beauty concurrent with her dismissal of real beauty. Her final assessment of ORLAN's monstrosity reveals something even more important, however: "When classical traces of beauty appear in the works of artists like Hannah Wilke, Cindy Sherman, or ORLAN, it speaks as social commentary, rather than bristling with its own aesthetic energy."[70]

This leads to a final criticism of all three authors, and in fact, many feminist critics to date: they dismiss aesthetic concerns by attending primarily and solely to the nonaesthetic. Of course ORLAN, like many other artists with feminist intentions and effective strategies to construct critical discourse and viewer reactions, is explicitly concerned with social commentary. But that is not her only concern. Her choices of form, color, expression, medium, size, and technology all attest to her aesthetic decision-making priorities. It is not inconsequential that her photographs, whether of real or virtual beauty, are in themselves often both stunning and beautiful. Artistic choices are dictated by aesthetic concerns; to deny her that agency is to relegate the aesthetic import of her work to the trash heap. ORLAN expects her critics, particularly her supporters, to understand and appreciate the combination of both social commentary and artistic value.[71] Viewers need to multitask! It is undeniable that ORLAN demands a lot of her audience, but then again, she spares us nothing. She gives her all.

Changes in Feminist Discourse

Perhaps, not surprisingly, there is a significant yet subtle change in the term "feminist" in evidence here, visible over time from 1998 to 2010. Tanya Augsberg, at one point in her 1998 essay, compares ORLAN's negative views of her mother with those of Simone de Beauvoir, who unabashedly denounced the bourgeois housewife of twentieth-century France as too self-sacrificing (for the sake of family) and obsessed with an overly clean house and its sterile objects within. Augsberg is not alone in seeing similarities between generations of women, noting how both ORLAN and Beauvoir—in attacking idle housewives, i.e., their mothers—"can be viewed as the succeeding generation's rebellion against its predecessors."[72] The history of feminism, like that of philosophy, includes self-criticism and self-correction, so we should not expect this rebellion against one's predecessors to be unnatural or unwelcome. I only mention it here in order to make sense of why certain critics of ORLAN, namely Augsberg and still others too numerous to mention (including myself), have never attributed the descriptor "monster" to her work, and yet it has been applied three times (by O'Bryan, Mansfield, and Knafo) in only the first decade of the twenty-first century. Perhaps it is the psychoanalytic turn in the assessment of her work that invites the term. My suggestion is that a careful analysis of ORLAN's work with a focus on her artistic intent shows that it does not warrant the charge of monstrousness.[73]

Conclusion: The Future of Virtual Beauty

Sorry, Kant and Kantians near and far, but virtual beauty is the wave of the future, and ORLAN is not the only one leading the charge. Elisabeth Azoulay and Françoise Gaillard, editors of the outsized project *100,000 Years of Beauty*, consider the many variations of "Mona Lisa and me" in an introductory essay to the fifth and final volume of the series, *Future/Projections*. Although Yasumasa Morimura's versions are not mentioned, they could easily have been included, since his virtual self-portraits as the Mona Lisa qualify as much as those they discuss, by Bani Thani, Dominic Philibert, Paul M. Constantin Boym/ELIKA, and an anonymous artist, all of whom hybridize the body and face to make it more diversified in its expansion to the five themes of the volume: cosmopoliteness, hypernarcissus, the third sex, amortality, and cyber sapiens. "Each one represents a window open onto a future whose mysteries stir our collective imagination," they write as they predict a future world that borrows from the imaginations of decades of science fiction writers and unlimited artistic visions.[74] They base their prediction on demographics, emphasizing that by the year 2050, 70 percent of the world's nine billion people will live in cities, all mixing together—majorities with cultural minorities—in melting pots of globalization, hybridization, new canons of beauty, and cosmopoliteness, where individuals will seek unique ways to distinguish themselves from others by beautifying in unimaginable ways, asking themselves "How many am I?" rather than "Who am I?" In light of this projection, ORLAN's deliberate exploration of self-hybridization is revered as a highly personal form of beauty and technoscience. Artificial wombs, cloning (of a third sex?), and the blurring of traditional age categories will lead to people living much longer lives, creating a new norm of elderly beauty for the species, a hybrid of postmortality, i.e., a form of amortality. Moreover, technoscience will bring us far beyond the advances in self-invention offered by technologies like Photoshop, doubtless soon to be outdated.

> The digital revolution has explored only a fraction of the full potential of virtual reality. The virtual realm will develop into a flood of ideas, images and sounds beyond our control, accessible instantaneously and simultaneously in all four corners of the globe.[75]

These are lofty predictions with scary implications, particularly one's sense of loss of control, given the rather unfathomable number of nine billion people all being sustained by Planet Earth.

In an introductory essay, the philosopher Gaillard imagines persons of the future to be "nomads of identity," free from the delusion of "purity" because we have all come from various strains of lineage and we are "the fruit of inter-ethnical and inter-cultural mélanges. . . . We are all hybrid children of history." The nomad of identity will be at home anywhere, accepted and encouraged, resulting in a hybrid humanity. Most importantly, we will have overcome the resistance to change, the new, the alien, and the hybrid: "Deep-rooted prejudices had to be overcome as the hybrid figure had long borne the brunt of archaic fears. It was seen as an anomaly of nature, a monster that menaced a group's homogeneity by undermining its purity."[76] But those days are over, replaced by an open, optimistic, and welcoming view of the future:

> The world has never before experienced such human migration through interposed images. From the East, South, Middle East or Far West, representations of oneself and others are diffused, exchanged and interpenetrated, along with one's cultural practices, beginning with those relating to beauty. An unprecedented kind of cosmopolitism is being engendered before our eyes, at the junction of the real and the virtual. . . . What outcome will it have for the people of tomorrow? Two ways take shape: the fusion and confusion of aesthetic models and norms or their juxtaposition and cohabitation.[77]

Acknowledgment and welcome of aesthetic change will follow nomadic identity, and this vision of the future is replete with considerations of new aesthetic norms, particularly for virtual beauty. There will be an aesthetic of "shock" that includes collages and juxtapositions (already very much in vogue), hybridizations of genes, cultures, and images from all over the planet, and the unlikely mix of both real and virtual whereby beauty will often be defined as ugliness transcended. "The dictators of beauty will be disorientated, as instead of leading the ball they will be the ones who have to follow the movements of the street's orchestration."[78] In this unprecedented world, seeing ORLAN on the street will seem as ordinary as encountering her disembodied virtual hybrid beauty in large-scale, colorful, aesthetically pleasing photographs.

Notes

My thanks to art historian Jean Robertson for comments on an earlier draft of this essay, as well as to the participants at the "Bodies of Art Conference" held at Florida Atlantic University, December 2, 2010, organized by Richard Shusterman. We were graced with the presence of ORLAN at this conference; she did not fail to impress.

The epigraph is fragment 84 from *Sappho: A New Translation*, by Mary Barnard (Berkeley: University of California Press, 1958). Sappho wrote poems from approximately the seventh to sixth centuries BCE on the Greek island of Lesbos. Many survive only as fragments.

1. Peg Zeglin Brand, "Bound to Beauty: An Interview with ORLAN," in *Beauty Matters*, ed. Peg Zeglin Brand (Bloomington: Indiana University Press, 2000), 289–313. On ORLAN's website and in most writings about her work, the spelling used is "Self-Hybridations." In two essays (one written by ORLAN herself) in Elisabeth Azoulay and Françoise Gaillard, eds., *100,000 Years of Beauty* (Paris: Gallimard, 2009), vol. 5, *Future/Projections*, the spelling used is "Self-Hybridisations." In *ORLAN: Le récit* [ORLAN: The Narrative] (Milan: Edizioni Charta, 2007), two spellings are used: "Self-Hybridation" and "Self-Hybridization." This essay will use "Self-Hybridization." Also, the artist now spells her name ORLAN, in capitals. All of her artworks can be found at http://www.orlan.net.

2. ORLAN's *Imaginary Generic no. 31: Successful Operation(s)* (1990) was a view of her posing in front of a schematic poster of her visual inspirations.

3. Brand, "Bound to Beauty," 290.

4. Peg Brand, "Virtual Beauty: Orlan and Morimura," in *Exploding Aesthetics*, ed. Annette W. Balkema and Henk Slager, Lier en Boog Series of Philosophy of Art and Art Theory 16 (Amsterdam: Editions Rodopi B.V., 2001), 92–104.

5. Brand, "Bound to Beauty," 295.

6. In "Bound to Beauty," I noted that ORLAN's work "elicits shock and disgust" (289), particularly at the beginning of the *Reincarnation* series when audiences were unaccustomed to her graphic performance practices and their underlying meanings. At their most outraged, critics called her insane and deranged; at the very least, she was condemned as medically unethical, given her use of actual physicians to accomplish her surgical goals for the sake of art. A careful reading of my essay and its attempt to undergird her performances with philosophical, art-historical, and religious meaning yielded, at most, a description of her face as that of "an attractive woman" who had become "an odd combination" of superimposed features, most prominently the bumps on her forehead (295). Author Elizabeth C. Mansfield criticizes me for writing

one of many "ostensibly scholarly essays on her work [that] begin with statements like 'ORLAN is a French performance artist whose work on beauty elicits shock and disgust,'" thereby implying that I was highlighting viewers' response of shock and disgust and that I had somehow trivialized or denigrated ORLAN's work. Nothing could be further from the truth, as my personal encounter with ORLAN only heightened my sense of curiosity and respect for her work. Interestingly, Mansfield herself describes ORLAN's performances as "horrifying," "grisly," eliciting "outright disgust," "dread," and "horror" (Elizabeth C. Mansfield, *Too Beautiful to Picture: Zeuxis, Myth, and Mimesis* [Minneapolis: University of Minnesota Press, 2007], 140–47 passim).

7. Jill C. O'Bryan, *Carnal Art: ORLAN's Refacing* (Minneapolis: University of Minnesota Press, 2005), 135, 134, 136, 134, 135.

8. See John Strausbaugh, *Black like You: Blackface, Whiteface, Insult and Imitation in American Popular Culture* (New York: Jeremy P. Tarcher/Penguin, 2006).

9. Brand, "Bound to Beauty," 293.

10. Quoted in O'Bryan, *Carnal Art*, 140, from "Body and Action," in *ORLAN: 1964–2001*, ed. Maria Jose Kerejeta, trans. Brian Webster and Careen Irwin (Vitoria-Gasteiz: Artium; Salamanca: Ediciones Universidad de Salamanca, 2002), 228.

11. Kathy Davis, "'My Body Is My Art': Cosmetic Surgery as Feminist Utopia?" *The European Journal of Women's Studies* 4, no. 1 (February 1997): 26.

12. Peggy Phelan, "Cinematic Skin," in *ORLAN: Le récit*, 73.

13. Ibid.

14. According to Wikipedia, a 1488 poem by Demetrios Chalcondyles described Venus as "blown by the moist breath of Zephyros" and was one source of the painting (http://en.wikipedia.org/wiki/The_Birth_of_Venus_(Botticelli)).

15. ORLAN, "Intervention," in *The Ends of Performance*, ed. Peggy Phelan and Jill Lane (New York: New York University Press, 1998), 320.

16. Davis, "'My Body Is My Art,'" 29. Davis also authored *Dubious Equalities and Embodied Differences: Cultural Studies on Cosmetic Surgery* (Lanham, Md.: Rowman & Littlefield, 2003).

17. Ibid., 29–30. The quotation is from *Actuel* (January 1991), 78.

18. Ibid., 30.

19. ORLAN, "Intervention," 319.

20. Brand, "Virtual Beauty," 94. Condition (iii) was prompted by an exhibition in which ORLAN invited viewers to participate by transforming and altering her digital images on computers she made available in the gallery.

21. O'Bryan, *Carnal Art*, 148, quoting ORLAN, "Body and Action," in *ORLAN, 1964–2001*, 227, 229.

22. Davis, "'My Body Is My Art,'" 30.

23. Ibid.

24. Brand, "Bound to Beauty," 305.

25. Ibid., 310.

26. The photograph can be seen on the website of the French Institute Alliance Française, on a page advertising a 2010 event celebrating the publication of Azoulay and Gaillard, *100,000 Years of Beauty*, http://www.fiaf.org/events/winter2010/2010 -02-02-loreal-beauty.shtml.

27. Brand, "Bound to Beauty," 306.

28. Brand, "Virtual Beauty," 97. For images, see the Luhring Augustine Gallery's website at http://www.luhringaugustine.com/artists/yasumasa-morimura.

29. Serge Gruzinski is a historian from France, author of *The Mestizo Mind*, trans. Deke Dusinberre (New York: Routledge, 2002); his remark is quoted in Azoulay and Gaillard, *100,000 Years of Beauty*, 5:30.

30. Volume 5 of Azoulay and Gaillard, *100,000 Years of Beauty*, includes discussions of these issues and more, such as cosmopoliteness, new genders (a third sex), and cyber sapiens (mutants, posthumans, and cyborgs that bid "farewell to bodies," 166). I return to these topics later in the essay.

31. This and the following quotations are from ORLAN, untitled essay in Azoulay and Gaillard, *100,000 Years of Beauty*, 33.

32. See, for instance, *Killing Us Softly: Advertising's Image of Women 4*, the most recent version of a DVD examining hundreds of images from advertising and popular media, narrated by Jean Kilbourne (Media Education Foundation, dir. Sut Jhally, 2010, http://www.mediaed.org/cgi-bin/commerce.cgi?preadd=action&key=241).

33. M. Pernioa, *Il sex appeal dell'inorganico* (Turin: Einaudi, 1994), 38, quoted in Eugenio Viola, "Le récit," in *ORLAN: Le récit*, 45.

34. "Isole mai trovate—Islands Never Found," Palazzo Ducale Fondazione per la Cultura, Genoa, http://www.palazzoducale.genova.it/isole/index.html, describing a group show at the Palazzo Ducale, Genoa, Italy, March 13–June 13, 2010.

35. ORLAN's newsletter for July 22, 2006, http://www.orlan.net/download/newsletter22jui106_bis.pdf, p. 2.

36. O'Bryan, *Carnal Art*, 134.

37. Arthur C. Danto, *The Abuse of Beauty: Aesthetics and the Concept of Art* (Chicago, Ill.: Open Court, 2003), 75.

38. Janet C. Berlo and Ruth B. Phillips, *Native North American Art* (Oxford: Oxford University Press, 1998), 30. See also Gregory y Trianosky's essay in this volume.

39. Berlo and Phillips, *Native North American Art*, 212. For instance, portraits by Fritz Scholder (1937–2005, Luiseño) depict the "psychic cost of the gap between romantic and backward-looking popular stereotypes of Indians and the actualities of their daily lives" (224–25) while Carl Beam (born 1943, Ojibwa) has juxtaposed images from Western and Native history in his *Columbus Chronicles* (232).

40. Joanna Frueh, *Monster/Beauty: Building the Body of Love* (Berkeley: University of California Press, 2001), 5, 2.

41. Ibid., 8.

42. Ibid., 11.

43. Ibid., 19–20, 289–92. Frueh cites Sherman's *Disasters and Fairy Tales* series, Jo Spence's breast surgery images, and Hannah Wilke's cancer treatment photographs.

44. Tanya Augsberg, "ORLAN's Performative Transformations of Subjectivity," in Phelan and Lane, *The Ends of Performance*, 288–89.

45. Ibid., 291. Here Augsberg invokes Philip Auslander's interpretation of ORLAN's uglification in "Orlan's Theatre of Operations," in *Theatre Forum*, no. 7 (Summer–Fall 1995): 26, as well as Kathryn Pauly Morgan's call for a reassessment of "the domain of the ugly" in "Women and the Knife: Cosmetic Surgery and the Colonization of Women's Bodies," *Hypatia* 6, no. 3 (Fall 1991): 45–46.

46. Augsberg, "ORLAN's Performative Transformations of Subjectivity," 305.

47. Ibid., 306.

48. O'Bryan, *Carnal Art*, chapter 5, 107–22.

49. Ibid., 107.

50. Ibid., 110, 111, quoting Sigmund Freud, "Medusa's Head" (1922), in *The Standard Edition of the Complete Psychological Works of Sigmund Freud*, trans. and ed. James Strachey (London: Hogarth, 1953–74), 18:273, and Jacques Lacan, *The Second Seminar: The Ego in Freud's Theory and in the Technique of Psychoanalysis, 1954–1955*, ed. Jacques-Alain Miller, trans Sylvana Tomaselli (New York: Norton, 1991), 164.

51. O'Bryan, *Carnal Art*, 112.

52. Ibid., 113.

53. Ibid., 134–36.

54. Ibid., 137.

55. ORLAN, "Intervention," 321.

56. O'Bryan, *Carnal Art*, 137, quoting Mikhail Bakhtin, *Rabelais and His World*, trans. Hélène Iswolsky (Bloomington: Indiana University Press, 1984), 317.

57. O'Bryan, *Carnal Art*, 137, 136. Indeed, O'Bryan compares the hybrids to Diane Arbus's photos of circus freaks (139).

58. Ibid., 135, quoting ORLAN, "Body and Action," 228.

59. Mansfield, *Too Beautiful to Picture*, chapter 5, "Women Artists and the Zeuxis Myth," 75–102.

60. Mansfield, *Too Beautiful to Picture*, 96, quoting Mary Shelley, *Frankenstein*, ed. Johanna M. Smith (Boston: Bedford Books/St. Martin's Press, 1992), 55, 57, 58.

61. Mansfield, *Too Beautiful to Picture*, 97.

62. Ibid., 144.

63. Ibid., 144–45, 146.

64. See, for instance, Noël Carroll, "Ethnicity, Race, and Monstrosity: The Rhetorics of Horror and Humor," in Brand, *Beauty Matters*, 37–56, as well as Noël Carroll, *The Philosophy of Horror* (New York: Routledge, 1990).

65. Bernini's *Ecstasy of Saint Teresa* can be seen on Wikipedia: http://en.wikipedia.org/wiki/Teresa_of_%C3%81vila.

66. Danielle Knafo, "ORLAN: Monster Beauty," in *In Her Own Image: Women's Self-Representation in Twentieth-Century Art* (Madison, N.J.: Fairleigh Dickinson University Press, 2009), 162.

67. Mansfield, *Too Beautiful to Picture*, 149.

68. Ibid, 150.

69. Knafo, "ORLAN: Monster Beauty," 163, 166.

70. Ibid., 162. As in her treatment of the *Reincarnation* series, she ignores the aesthetic properties and value of the *Self-Hybridization* images as well.

71. In her manifesto on Carnal Art, ORLAN expressed her assumption of aesthetic priorities: "My work is not feminist in its artistic dimension alone; I have also worked a lot in the political arena" (Brand, "Bound to Beauty," 303).

72. Augsberg, "ORLAN's Performative Transformations of Subjectivity," 293.

73. Given the limits of this essay, I leave the important and detailed task of assessing the differences in rhetoric between generations of feminist art criticism to others,

and I encourage all art lovers to pay more attention to the terminology we choose, particularly in light of ORLAN's repeated plea for more understanding and appreciation of her work.

74. Elisabeth Azoulay and Françoise Gaillard, "Mona Lisa and Me," in Azoulay and Gaillard, *100,000 Years of Beauty*, 7.

75. Ibid.

76. Françoise Gaillard, "Nomads of Identity," in Azoulay and Gaillard, *100,000 Years of Beauty*, 15.

77. Ibid., 18, 14.

78. Ibid., 18.

PART 4.

BEAUTY AND
THE STATE

17. Beauty Wars: The Struggle over Female Modesty in the Contemporary Middle East and North Africa

ALLEN DOUGLAS AND FEDWA MALTI-DOUGLAS

In the past forty years, the Muslim Middle East and North Africa have been the scene of a struggle over fashion, clothing, and makeup—over beauty. This struggle is most often seen as being about the veil or as a process of reveiling. It is actually a battle between competing visions of female display. Often presented as a contest between Western modernity, on the one hand, and Islamic traditionalism, on the other, the struggle is actually between two competing forms of modernity. One favors a more open society with a greater public female presence as well as a greater acceptance of female display and more open forms of courtship. The other, which we can call neopatriarchal, fears the chaos of unregulated sexuality and leans toward greater social control, segregation of the sexes, and female public modesty.

The high point in the region of the open, more secular social vision was marked by the debut of the most popular Egyptian film up to that time, *Khally ballak men ZouZou* (Watch Out for Zouzou), in 1972. This musical, with screenplay by the Nasserite Salah Jahine, recounts a romance between Zouzou, a lower-class University of Cairo coed, and her wealthy professor. The film ridicules the traditionalist who accuses the heroine of immodesty and immorality. In the happy ending, male and female college students dance in blue jeans. No one is veiled. In a concession to nationalism, the beautiful, black-haired, modern Egyptian heroine is contrasted with a Doris Day clone, an evil relative of the upper-class male heart-throb. Zouzou's main challenge is overcoming her background as a belly dancer from a family of dancers and popular entertainers. The film takes a middle view of the problem of display implicit in Zouzou's profession. On the one hand, it argues, she should not be held down by old-fashioned notions of shame. On the other, dancing in night clubs can easily lead to sexual perdition. And of course, viewers are treated to Zouzou's dark-eyed, full-figured beauty in a variety of dance scenes. Such a film could not be made in Egypt today.

Veiling, which marks the movement of a woman from private to public space, exists on a continuum. At one end is the hijab, which covers most or all of the hair, and often much of the neck and shoulders as well. At the other extreme lies the niqab (and, further east, the chador and the burqa), which envelop the entire body, including the face and hands. Thirty years ago, the veil was relatively rare among middle- and upper-class women in the streets of Arab cities like Cairo and Tunis. The niqab was an oddity. Today it is the unveiled woman who is the exception, and niqabs, while not the dominant form of dress, are as common as hijabs were a quarter century ago, having replaced them as public markers of piety.

In some Western countries, like France, veiling can function as a form of political protest, and this has also sometimes been the case in Turkey and Iran, whose earlier, militantly secularizing governments sought to ban the veil. In Iran today the position is reversed—a visible lock of hair is a sign of revolt.

In Arab countries, veiling represents not rebellion against Westernization but knuckling under to local social pressure. Pressure ranges from the indirect (husbands of office workers may be advised that their women should not come to work bareheaded) to the forceful (inappropriately dressed women may be admonished or harassed in the street). In regions like formerly French North Africa, where the most daring European fashions came into collision with rising Islamist movements, miniskirted young women have been attacked in the streets by young men with belts. In public universities like the University of Cairo a tipping point was reached when a third of the coeds were veiled. A bareheaded young woman came to be seen as labeling herself unrespectable. Makeup, too, became suspect. The Muslim-revivalist writer Ni'mat Sidqi recounts a much-quoted story of a woman whose dental abscess leads to severe facial inflammation. She is only cured when she realizes that her afflictions are divine punishment for her having smeared makeup on that part of her face. In the early 1990s, a controversy developed when a number of well-known actresses declared they were adopting the veil. Traditionalists hailed this triumph of religion. Secularists blamed Saudi bribery. Cynics noted that the stars were already beyond their prime.

No such pressure is applied to the males of the species, who are generally free—at least outside Taliban-controlled Afghanistan—to wear jeans and Western shirts without fear of harassment. The full beard, especially

Figure 17.1. Kariman
Hamza, pictured on
the cover of *Elegance
and Modesty.*

when accompanied by a white skullcap, did emerge as a political uniform
associated with the Muslim Brotherhood. In Tunisia, such a beard could
bring negative attention from the police.

Neither vanity, fashion consciousness, nor the desire to singularize oneself were eliminated by the shift to Islamic dress. And this despite the claims
of its defenders that Islamic dress eliminates class distinctions. In major
cities, shops opened dedicated to fashions for the veiled woman. Color-
coordinated hijabs were puffed into virtual crowns, sometimes even decorated with rhinestones.

Kariman Hamza, a leading Egyptian religious television personality,
sought to combine the clothing of obedience, as she called it (that is, the
hijab), with a sense of color and play. Her own outfits featured color-coordi-
nated, highly ornamented hijab and dress ensembles (figs. 17.1, 17.2). Her
fashion magazine, *Elegance and Modesty,* interspersed minimally translated
Western cosmetics advertisements with her own images of Islamic tennis and
bathing costumes. None of this stopped Islamic traditionalists from attacking

Figure 17.2. Kariman
Hamza, in Islamic tennis
costume, pictured in
Elegance and Modesty.

Kariman, reminding her that the whole purpose of Islamic modesty was to avoid attracting attention.

In Turkey, a shift to headscarves accompanied the rise of Islamic political parties. The newly veiled women immediately began buying the brilliantly colored scarves that the local silk industry makes available at reasonable prices. Stores specializing in such scarves sprang up in Islamist-dominated neighborhoods on the Asian side of the Bosphorus. In the Western-style malls of Kuwait, fashionable young women now parade in stiletto heels and Versace accessories. Their hair is fully hidden under long, tight-fitting black scarves. Jeans and colorful tops hug their contours as closely as if they were painted on their bodies.

Despite such forms of veiled display, the pressure toward modesty in dress and comportment, and with it the segregation of the sexes in public places, continues to increase. The only partial exception is Iran, where the revolutionary government seeks to reimpose strictures that urban middle-class youth continually try to evade.

18. Orientalism Inside/Out:
The Art of Soody Sharifi

CYNTHIA FREELAND

"Orientalism" is a term made prominent by critic Edward Said in his 1978 book of that title. It is often used now in a loose way to denote an attitude of scornful superiority toward anything "Eastern" (including both the Middle and the Far East), with this "Other" seen as exotic and alluring but also barbaric and strange. In fact, Said specifically used the term to designate a field of self-constituted experts who proposed to explain the Orient to the West. Among its other features, he explains, Orientalism was a system of expertise in which,

> standing before a distant, barely intelligible civilization or cultural monument, the Orientalist scholar reduced the obscurity by translating, sympathetically portraying, inwardly grasping the hard-to-reach object. Yet the Orientalist remained outside the Orient, which, however much it was made to appear intelligible, remained beyond the Occident. This cultural, temporal, and geographical distance was expressed in metaphors of depth, secrecy, and sexual promise: phrases like "the veils of an Eastern bride" or "the inscrutable Orient" passed into the common language.[1]

If anything, it has become even more critical for us to understand the "mysterious East" since the events of 9/11 and the war in Iraq, events which have led to increased suspicion, misunderstanding, paranoia, media misrepresentation, and in some cases, outright persecution of a variety of people ranging from foreign students to Muslim Americans and ranging far afield to target Sikhs, Armenians, and others who dare to look different from "us." Thirty years after the publication of Said's groundbreaking book, the cultures of Islam and the East still await representation in ways that depict an insider's view rather than that of the self-taught expert from outside.

One such insider is the artist and photographer Soody Sharifi, an Iranian who has lived and worked in Houston, Texas, since 1974. Born in Tehran, Sharifi came to the United States in the early 1970s to pursue a degree in industrial engineering. Although she worked in that field for a time, she never felt she belonged there. This was partly because she had other interests, and partly because of resistance she met as a petite foreign woman working in a mostly male field. Sharifi began to explore her interests in the humanities and arts, where she felt more at home. She spent time in a doctoral program in Spanish literature and took a course in London on women in art. That course led to her eventually applying to the University of Houston's School of Art, where she earned an MFA in studio photography in 2004. Sharifi's exhibition record since then has included various series in which she addresses the representation of Muslims in general and of Muslim women in particular. This work has been shown in exhibitions such as "Women of Cover" (2002), "Simply Girls" and "Veiled/Unveiled" (2004), "Teenagers and Maxiatures" (2006), and "Garden of Persian Delight" (2007). Sharifi collaborated with her adult son, Payam Sharifi, an artist now living in Moscow, on the show "Proud and Sad/Wrong and Strong" for the Women and Their Work Gallery in Austin in 2006. She is also engaging in a long-term project to document the lives and activities of Muslim Americans, especially young people.

As a naturalized U.S. citizen, Sharifi feels strongly that she has a foot in the culture of both West and East. The problem of representing Islam has a long history. As Said wrote, "even the simplest perception of the Arabs and Islam [is] a highly politicized, almost raucous matter." He deplored the "almost total absence of any cultural position making it possible either to identify with or dispassionately to discuss the Arabs or Islam."[2] Sharifi's work takes a step toward filling these gaps in a quiet, often witty way.

Sharifi left Iran before the Islamic Revolution of 1979, and after observing the changes introduced by the new rulers she decided not to return. When she was able to go back for visits, she found the country much transformed, in particular in its treatment and situation of women. Having grown up during the liberal, Westernizing Pahlavi reign, when women did not wear the veil, Sharifi found herself wearing a hijab for the first time as a mature adult. This strange and disorienting experience prompted much self-reflection. After a trip back to Iran in 1999, she began a self-portrait series exploring how she felt about being a Muslim woman in a hijab for the first time.

Of course, the typical Western view is that veiling is a form of oppression of women, masking their individuality and limiting their freedom. In an article on Arab feminism, Susan Muaddi Darraj describes a basic conflict that "obstructed the recognition of my feminist identity: America's exoticism of Arab women. Although we were considered veiled and meek, we were simultaneously and ironically considered sultry, sexual, and 'different.'" This modern young woman sounds much like Said when she recounts the basic ingredients of Orientalism:

> Orientalism itself . . . was an exclusively male province; like so many professional guilds during the modern period, it viewed itself and its subject matter with sexist blinders. This is especially evident in the writing of travelers and novelists: women are usually the creatures of a male power-fantasy. They express unlimited sensuality, they are more or less stupid, and above all they are willing.[3]

Sharifi wants to construct a more truthful and balanced picture of the veiled woman. Despite her own ambivalence about veiling, she seeks to show Western viewers that wearing a veil does not reduce women's capabilities or their desire to take part in the world around them. Despite the country's changes, the women Sharifi saw in Iran were often independent and self-confident. Persian women were still unique individuals, ambitious, and convinced they could do anything. Her *Women of Cover* series shows aspects of Muslim culture, both in the U.S. and in Iran, that a Western visitor is unlikely to see. Iran had had fifty years of modernization, enabling its residents to become familiar with Western ideas, art, popular culture, and fashion, and people were not going to forget all that simply because of an oppressive regime. Sharifi found that Iranian women resisted the strict rules of covering and managed to be expressive and even chic with their headscarves. On her trips back home, Sharifi was amazed to see subversive fashions developing: during one visit, pink was the in color, the next year red, then green, and so on. Even beyond this, younger women were expressing resistance to the regime through their public compliance with its standards:

> Ironically, Hijab has actually provided women in Iran with the tool of resistance. They have learned to work for progressive change through the symbol of patriarchal control, and this is what inspired my "Teenager" series. Young women are using the veil to signal propriety, to signal acquiescence with patriarchal ideals of female modesty, and at the same time insisting, since they are observing the code of modesty, that they should be allowed to participate

more fully in contemporary public life. After the revolution in Iran, there are more women college graduates than ever before and you see women in areas of employment and public life that would have been unheard of during the ostensibly more progressive days prior to the revolution.[4]

These expressive declarations of fashion independence are visible in some of her portraits in the *Women of Cover* series. For example, in *Raha* (fig. 18.1), the subject wears a patterned gold-and-brown scarf wrapped across her forehead and tied on top of her head to create a unique fashion statement. She gazes back at the photographer with a bemused expression.

Individuality includes more than fashion, of course. Other portraits from this series depict women going about the business of daily life: marketing, chatting on cell phones, and, in one bizarre and fascinating image, carrying a small dummy as if it were a child (fig. 18.2). The humor of this image is also evident in some of the photographs in which Sharifi pokes fun at gender stereotypes, as when she shows (in *Honeymooners*) a beefy man in swim trunks and his completely covered bride, seen from behind as they sit on the beach, companionably staring out at the blue water (plate 13).

Figure 18.1. Soody Sharifi, *Raha*, 2008. Fine art inkjet print, 16 × 20 in. COURTESY OF SOODY SHARIFI AND THE ANYA TISH GALLERY.

Figure 18.2. Soody Sharifi, *Woman with Her Doll*, 2008.
Fine art inkjet print, 16 × 16 in. Courtesy of Soody Sharifi
and the Anya Tish Gallery.

    The *Women of Cover* series comprised fairly traditional documentary por-
traits from real life, but in *Teenagers* Sharifi asked her models to enact pseudo-
documentary images. These pictures featured young women who were
self-consciously carrying out specific activities or playing specific roles before
Sharifi's camera. In *Neda* (fig. 18.3), for instance, we see a young woman clad
in gorgeous gauzy pink. She grasps a railing that might seem to restrain her,
but she seems thoughtful, as if she might just decide to vault over it.

    This expressive scene was one of a series Sharifi shot at the ancient site
of Persepolis in Shiraz. Persepolis was the capital and center of the great
Persian Achaemenid Empire (sixth–fourth centuries BCE), under the wise
and powerful rulers Cyrus, Darius, and Xerxes.[5] Sharifi's teenage models
spontaneously arranged themselves amidst the grand ruins of ancient grey
marble. They evoke the unexpectedly lush and colorful cactus blossoms that
spring to bloom in the desert when the time is right. Surely a culture with
so rich and ancient a lineage, Sharifi suggests, will not be suppressed by any
regime of the present moment.

Figure 18.3. Soody Sharifi, *Neda*, 2005. Fine art inkjet print,
11 × 14 in. Courtesy of Soody Sharifi and the Anya Tish Gallery.

On the whole, the *Teenagers* series shows young Muslim women to be just typical girls who are involved with popular culture. They engage in beauty rituals, flirt with members of the opposite sex, smoke cigarettes, sunbathe, enjoy hula-hooping, pore over movie magazines, and so on. *Three on a Match II* (fig. 18.4) shows three young women in black headscarves leaning in conspiratorially to light their cigarettes from the central match while sharing glasses of tea. In *Hair* (fig. 18.5), one girl fixes another's ponytail while her veil comically blows down over her face. Sharifi comments, "Teenagers as a group are constantly aware of themselves, especially as individuals caught between cultures. In Iran in particular, these teens exist in and partake of the larger adult culture that surrounds them while participating in another culture exclusive to teens."[6]

Sometimes Sharifi's subtle gender commentary encompasses the strange ironies of the fact that in Iran, unlike other Muslim countries, it has become the practice to use a head covering even for quite young girls. *First Love* and *Mr. and Mrs.* (figs. 18.6, 18.7) explore how this custom reinforces gender roles from an early age. Both depict young girls of perhaps four or five years old wearing veils. In *First Love*, the little girl stands slightly behind,

Figure 18.4. Soody Sharifi, *Three on a Match II*, 2004. Fine art inkjet print, 29 × 36 in. COURTESY OF SOODY SHARIFI AND THE ANYA TISH GALLERY.

Figure 18.5. Soody Sharifi, *Hair*, 2007. Fine art inkjet print, 16 × 20 in. COURTESY OF SOODY SHARIFI AND THE ANYA TISH GALLERY.

Figure 18.6. Soody Sharifi, *First Love*, 2007. Fine art inkjet print,
16 × 20 in. Courtesy of Soody Sharifi and the Anya Tish Gallery.

Figure 18.7. Soody Sharifi, *Mr. and Mrs.*, 2007. Fine art inkjet print,
29 × 36 in. Courtesy of Soody Sharifi and the Anya Tish Gallery.

and rapturously gazes up at, a bigger boy whose entire attention seems to be absorbed in his book. In *Mr. and Mrs.*, the young girl sits primly while the gawky little boy stands shyly posed in his little suit and vest.

Because she grew up in a Westernizing Iran that turned to Europe and America for artistic inspiration, Sharifi had little awareness of her own cultural heritage. This changed when, on one of her trips back to her home country, she saw the book *Gardens of Imagination* at a friend's home. She became fascinated by the colorful exoticism of Persian miniature painting—she became almost an Orientalist in her own land. As she strolled the streets of contemporary Tehran, Sharifi wondered how the miniature painters might depict it now. She observed a sharp contrast between their colorful world and the stark black, white, and gray imagery of the Islamic Republic of Iran. Public space in Tehran is full of images of male martyrs, both recent and ancient (the martyrs of Shia Islam, that is, as well as men who died during the Iran-Iraq War). Large murals offer a sort of Socialist Realist imagery: portraits of the country's imams wearing their black turbans.

Against this drab and austere backdrop of public space in modern Iran, women still exist. Sharifi highlights their position by capturing, in a photograph entitled *Pallestine Square*, a striking image of a woman absorbed in her cell phone conversation while large hands on a mural behind her seem to reach out threateningly, as if to punish her for ignoring the martyrs and turbaned leaders featured at gigantic height behind her (fig. 18.8).

Iranian women seem more free to be themselves in the interior spaces of homes and courtyards. Sharifi relishes these spaces, which remain colorful and vibrant, filled with elegant details like beaded curtains, etched tea glasses, and rich carpets. And these interiors are not as closed against Western influences as the Republic's leaders might suppose—witness the numerous satellite dishes atop buildings all over the city. A similar contrast between interior rich individuality and exterior conformity in Iran is drawn by the scholar Azar Nafisi in her popular book *Reading Lolita in Tehran*.[7] Nafisi, an English literature professor, invited young female university students to join a secret reading group. They met weekly for years to discuss works by Henry James, Jane Austen, Vladimir Nabokov, and others. Nafisi narrates how the young women would arrive in full cover and take off their jackets and veils to reveal their body shapes and choices of hairstyle and clothing. In fact, she opens the book by discussing two photographs in which each young woman can be identified and described.

The works that evolved from Sharifi's love for the Persian paintings in classic books were titled "maxiatures." Sharifi shot 4 × 5 in. negatives either

Figure 18.8. Soody Sharifi, *Pallestine Square,* 2007. Fine art inkjet print, 20 × 24 in. COURTESY OF SOODY SHARIFI AND THE ANYA TISH GALLERY.

from original books (if she could find them) or from reproductions, then painstakingly created digital collages by integrating into them elements from her own photographs of contemporary life. She concentrated on fifteenth-century miniatures, a highly developed form of secular art illustrating stories by such classic poets as Rumi, Hafez, and Saadi, which would be well known to an Iranian audience. The miniatures show scenes of courtly life, hunting, garden seductions, musical entertainments, feasts, and more. Sharifi points to the painting *Courtly Love* (fig. 18.9) to show how some of them also display contrasts between exterior landscapes, often a monotonous dry beige, and ornate interior courtyards and homes, rich with flowers, gardens, terraces, windows, patios, and stairways. The flatness of traditional Persian miniature paintings posed certain challenges as she tried to make her digital collages seamless. For example, the miniature painters did not use shadows; thus, to make her own images work well in their new contexts, she had to shoot only at certain times of the day, when she could avoid shadows.

Her collages, often printed at sizes as large as 36 × 40 in., are glossy and colorful; seen from a distance, they are dominated by the alluring overall patterns of color and texture. Examined up close, they are full of wit and humor, so that the viewer must look twice to get all the jokes. Their name,

Figure 18.9. Soody Sharifi, *Courtly Love*, 2007. Fine art inkjet print,
32 × 40 in. COURTESY OF SOODY SHARIFI AND THE ANYA TISH GALLERY.

"maxiatures," alludes to the idea of both physical and intellectual or emotional "enlargements" upon themes in the earlier works. Their size both brings out the originals' colorful beauty in a newer, glossy format and enables the audience to find and enjoy all of their witty details. Western viewers can come to appreciate the particular allure of this historical art form, with its brilliant range of jewel-like colors and exquisite details, while at the same time noticing the subtle social commentary that Sharifi offers through clever juxtapositions.

In *The Feast of Id Begins*, for example (fig. 18.10), a line of dancers and musicians enter from a central arched doorway to celebrate the feast marking the end of Ramadan. This line cleverly alternates new and old: a contemporary young woman with a tambourine stands behind a fifteenth-century woman dancer whose arms are raised in celebration, and the alternation between ancient and modern continues up to the front. At both the middle and the upper levels of the picture archways offer views into yet further interior spaces; such archways are typical of the miniatures. In each case the figure at the left of the arch belongs to the original painting, but the other, at the right, is integrated from Sharifi's own work. The picture as a whole is full of motion and fun, a rich feast of color, pattern, and texture.

Frolicking Women in the Pool is one of the funnier and more pointed entries in the *Maxiatures* series (plate 14). It reverses some aspects of the original image, which is taken from a 1494 edition of the *Khamsa of Nizami*, a tale of legendary love affairs. In the original, *Bahram Gur Observing Frolicking Women*, Bahram Gur peeps through shutters at the naked young women who play in the pool below him.[8] These women have black hair and Chinese-looking features, presumably reflecting the painter's ideals of beauty.[9] In Sharifi's *Frolicking Women in the Pool*, we first notice, at the front of the image, the garments the naked swimmers have removed, neatly piled in a row indicated by small dollops of lovely citrus colors. Meanwhile, across the pool lounge three of Sharifi's modern young women, "sunbathing" despite being wrapped in cloaks. One of them wears a brilliant red jacket with a yellow headscarf, echoing the lovely colors of the original costumes. The pale, naked beauties in the pool are joined by two contemporary women, who swim and seek to "tan" despite being fully covered. One of them lounges happily on an inner tube brandishing a cold drink. To both left and right are young modern couples sneaking off for private time in the garden. Though the original voyeur, Bahram Gur, is still visible here, he is outnumbered, significantly, by two modern women whom Sharifi has added. One of these young women looks out

Figure 18.10. Soody Sharifi, *The Feast of Id Begins* (detail), 2007. Fine art inkjet print, COURTESY OF SOODY SHARIFI AND THE ANYA TISH GALLERY.

from behind a curtain in an upper window, while another spies openly upon everyone from the roof.

Space in the fifteenth-century miniatures is shown entirely differently from how it was beginning to be depicted around the same time in Italy. Rather than using Western one-point perspective, with lines receding to a vanishing point to conjure an illusion of three-dimensional space, and thus unifying the image so as to foreground a central event or figure, the Persian paintings employ an "all-over" flattened style in which every detail attracts the eye. Indeed, the miniatures employ an amazing array of architectural details. They are replete with towers, rooftops, balconies, gardens, windows, fences, gates, courtyards, arches, windows, doorways, lattices, entryways,

French doors, and angled stairways. And every inch of the space is covered with texture and pattern, from geometrical tile-work to floral carpets to cross-hatched lattices to arabesque trellises to swirling wallpaper.

An intriguing explanation for this Persian fondness for patterns is offered by the ethnomusicologist Bruno Nettl, who spent some time studying the Persian radif, a repertory of short musical pieces whose rhythms and structures form the basis for improvisatory music in Iran. Nettl compares the resulting complex internal interrelationships to ones found in Iranian carpets and poems.

> I came to realize . . . that similar patterns in music and social life could be identified. Without going into detail, I'll just say that Persians think of society on the one hand as a set of hierarchies; on the other a group of cells in which a group of people look to a single leader for authority and guidance; and in the third place, a group of equals, all humans being equal before God in Islamic theology. Also, Iranians think of themselves as individualistic, like to surprise each other, and relish the unexpected.[10]

The complex maxiatures, like the originals from which they derive, resemble the famous tales of Scheherazade in the *Arabian Nights*. The entrancing tale-spinner created stories within stories, so that the process of telling them became the point, rather than reaching the end of one. No tale in the *Arabian Nights* concludes without first detouring into several others, each with its own intricate byways and passages. Thus they arouse listeners' curiosity, enticing them to enter and remain within the story spaces. Gazing at the maxiatures is a similar experience, because the more you look, the more pathways you observe. A viewer may wish she could go into the rooms whose doorways are shrouded by beaded curtains. Intriguingly, on occasion a person seems trapped within the space, looking outward as though to seek escape, if only in fantasy. For instance, the woman at the center of *Seduction (Leila and Majnoon)* (fig. 18.11) gazes longingly out through open French doors at a lush pink flowering tree outside. Its blossoms match her pink headscarf and are echoed by the delicately etched frame around the windows. Her dreamy isolation is reinforced by its contrast with the other figures shown in the picture. At the left is a young couple who look very emotionally engaged despite their respectful physical distance from each other, while another young woman lounges on the ancient stairs, chatting on her cell phone, no doubt sharing stories of love and adventure with her best friend.

Figure 18.11. Soody Sharifi, *Seduction (Leila and Majnoon)*, 2010.
Fine art inkjet print, 32 × 40 in. Courtesy of Soody Sharifi and the
Anya Tish Gallery.

The image derives from a painting by Bihzad called *Joseph Escaping from Zuleykha* in a 1488 copy of *Bustan of Saadi*. This painting depicts a married woman's efforts to seduce the young, handsome Joseph. In the maxiature version women are still engaged in seduction, but they are now more nearly the equals of the men. Sharifi explains that seductions still occur among young people despite official bans on their interaction.

> I believe that in most Islamic countries, whether it is Afghanistan, Iran or Saudi Arabia, the government aggressively attempts to keep males and females separate. But despite restrictions, young people still manage to talk with their boy- or girlfriend by e-mail and cell phone, or meet in secluded places where adults are not watching. The title of this piece is *seduction*, and I believe young men and women alike seduce one another with the looks they exchange. And that this gaze is not so one sided and aggressive because it's about mutual attraction, and not social control.[11]

Similarly, in *Movie Set* (fig. 18.12) the women in cover or black chadors are actively engaged with the cameras or the scripts, while a turban-clad figure

Figure 18.12. Soody Sharifi, *Movie Set* (detail), 2007. Fine art inkjet print.
COURTESY OF SOODY SHARIFI AND THE ANYA TISH GALLERY.

from the old illustration patiently waits with the action clapboard. He wears a brilliant scarlet outfit with indigo sleeves. His parrot-bright hues are echoed in the attire of the modern woman in the background, who wears a red jacket with a blue headscarf.

Sharifi says that when she undertook the collage process she was surprised to find so many color correspondences between the old and the new images. Time and again she would observe that the colors from the original interiors wound up matching colors in her new imagery. She points, for example, to how a modern woman's rich aqua-blue headscarf exactly corresponds to a man's robe in the original painting. Other small surprises lurk in these images, such as the inclusion of several gay male couples in *Lovers Picnicking*. One young man casually drapes an arm over the other to signify they are a couple despite the patrolling gaze at work in contemporary Iranian public space. Physical expressions of friendship among men have always been more accepted in Middle Eastern cultures than in the West, but Sharifi recognized these men as gay couples and asked permission before taking their pictures. One couple is shown only from behind.

Another set of works is gathered together under the title *The Garden of Persian Delights*. In this series she adopts the opposite of the maximalism of her previous large-format digital collage work. Again she combines imagery from the old paintings and the new world, but this time in a very spare, pared-down way. The images involve a simple juxtaposition of two elements on a 12 × 12 in. canvas, both rather small in proportion to the brilliant flat wash of color that fills the rest of the frame. The background looks almost like it has been covered with a flat latex paint, and these images read much more like paintings than her previous work. Exuberance still shows here in their wit as well as in their color. For example, in *Prince and the Balloon* (fig 18.13), a courting pair is centered at the bottom edge of the square against a brilliant lemon-yellow background. The prince who pauses before the woman sits atop an elegant slim horse. He raises his hand in a gesture of—what—appeal? greeting? amazement? He appears entranced by the vision before him of a pretty young dancing girl who at first matches our Orientalist imagining of an exotic Middle Eastern belly dancer. On closer scrutiny we can see she is wearing colorfully patched and fringed jeans with a white T-shirt and flip-flops. She is concealed by an odd, gauzy balloon that precisely covers her upper body. She pushes against it, but her gesture is also ambiguous—does she hold it up in a kind of tease, or attempt to break through a veil to touch her prince?

My favorite in this series is *Heaven Can't Wait* (fig. 18.14). Here a young man gazes dreamily up toward a wonderfully puffy white cloud. Both

Figure 18.13. Soody Sharifi, *Prince and the Balloon*, 2007. Fine art inkjet print, 12 × 12 in. Courtesy of Soody Sharifi and the Anya Tish Gallery.

he and the cloud appear like cut-outs against a flat, sky-blue background. Within the cloud appear various lovely young things—some from miniature paintings and some contemporary. All of them are adorned with wispy wings and clothed in cotton-candy colors of purple, pink, and light blue. The title alludes to the promise that, in the gardens of heaven, seventy-two virgins await the martyrs of jihad. In her ironic image, which hints that perhaps heaven *can* wait, Sharifi cautiously warns against this kind of unfortunate enthusiasm. She may also be alluding to Western forms of romantic myth-making, since there are two Hollywood movies entitled *Heaven Can Wait*—the old Ernst Lubitsch one from 1943, starring Don Ameche and Gene Tierney, and the remake by Warren Beatty in 1978. Each film paints its own, typically American picture of one man's adventures in heaven, hell, and the afterlife in the context of romantic comedy.

Figure 18.14. Soody Sharifi, *Heaven Can't Wait*, 2010. Fine art inkjet print, 20 × 22 in. COURTESY OF SOODY SHARIFI AND THE ANYA TISH GALLERY.

Sharifi's newest work continues her effort to represent the outside from within, but now she is focusing on Muslim life in the United States. Aware that there are many aspects of such life with which non-Muslims are not familiar, at one level she simply revels in the diversity of American Muslims, especially highlighting young people. Sharifi enjoys their exuberance and humor, the ways they mug and play to the camera. Their energetic innocence in many of these images is charming and works to help defuse negative stereotypes that have become associated with Islam in the United States since 9/11.

There are images in this ongoing documentary project that exhibit a more political edge. Sharifi wants to emphasize that there are Muslims who are loyal U.S. citizens. She does this in part through her long-standing interest in U.S. flag imagery, which also figured into some of her previous work.

Figure 18.15. Soody Sharifi, *American Gothic*, 2008. Fine art inkjet print, 32 × 40 in. COURTESY OF SOODY SHARIFI AND THE ANYA TISH GALLERY.

Posing a "Middle-Eastern-looking person" with a flag-decorated soccer ball in *Nation of Heros*, for example, can be politically challenging, as is her stark depiction of a woman standing in a black chador with the only visible portions of her face painted in a mask-like Stars and Stripes in *In God We Trust*. At other times the photographs are more broadly satirical. For example, in *American Gothic* a young couple duplicate the poses of the figures in Grant Wood's well-known painting (fig. 18.15). The serious young wife holds a beautifully bound Koran and turns her eyes respectfully toward her husband, who stares out at the viewer while holding a pitchfork, its tines decorated in red, white, and blue. Some of this work implicitly asks whether the rest of the United States will ever be willing to recognize that these people can join with others under the flag that supposedly unites us all, despite our differences.

Sharifi's work has been exhibited and sought by collectors both in the United States and overseas in Finland, Germany, and Slovakia. She is now also planning a show for Dubai. But she can't show her work in her home country, where for the time being she must remain content with being, ironically enough, the outsider looking in.

NOTES

1. Edward Said, Orientalism (New York: Vintage, 1978), 222.

2. Ibid., 26–27.

3. Susan Muaddi Darraj, "It's Not an Oxymoron: The Search for an Arab Feminism," in Colonize This! ed. Daisy Hernandez and Bushra Rehman (Emeryville, Calif.: Seal Press, 2002), 304, 207.

4. Soody Sharifi, "From Miniatures to Mixiatures [sic]: An Interview with Soody Sharifi," by Pamela Karimi, ArteNews, July 2006, http://www.arteeast.org/artenews/artenews-articles2006/political-art/artenews-karimi.html.

5. Marjane Satrapi used the city's name as the title of her autobiographical graphic novel, Persepolis: The Story of a Childhood (New York: Pantheon, 2004), which was filmed as Persepolis (dir. Vincent Paronnaud and Marjane Satrapi, 2007).

6. Personal communication, June 1, 2008.

7. Azar Nafisi, Reading Lolita in Tehran: A Memoir in Books (New York: Random House, 2003).

8. Sharifi, "From Miniatures to Mixiatures."

9. The master painter who figures as one of the main characters of Orhan Pamuk's brilliant novel My Name Is Red (trans. Erdag Goknar [New York: Vintage, 2002]) suggests that a miniaturist, "to emphasize [his subject's] flawless beauty, whitened her face as the Chinese do and painted her with slanted eyes" (328). Other painters in the novel note that such things as trees, clouds, and horses are also depicted in a Chinese style.

10. Bruno Nettl, "'Musical Thinking' and 'Thinking about Music' in Ethnomusicology," in Aesthetics: The Big Questions, ed. Carolyn Korsmeyer (Malden, Mass.: Blackwell, 1998), 349.

11. Sharifi, "From Miniatures to Mixiatures."

19. Beauty and the State: Female Bodies as State Apparatus and Recent Beauty Discourses in China

EVA KIT WAH MAN

The global economy has an impact on female beauty today, regardless of the multicultural and historical factors in its formation and construction, resulting in monolithic crazes in women's fashion and appearance. But female beauty in China has been greatly contested within China's turbulent modern history, and this contestation deserves serious consideration, together with the policies by which the Chinese state apparatus has promoted and regulated female beauty.

I argue that certain factors have been constant in contemporary discourses of female beauty. Ideal bodies, in all their specifics, are defined by physical standards very few women can attain. These standards are accompanied by demeaning characterizations of women who fail to achieve them, and who are therefore destined to be discontent. It is now necessary for feminist theorists to examine the social and cultural roles of the body in terms of gender, power, the established patriarchy, and its oppression of women.[1]

This oppression has been complex and multifaceted in China as well as in the West. In recent Chinese history, beauty standards were tied up with the political necessities of the state, injecting another patriarchal feature into the discourse. Western beauty ideals and practices are associated with sexism and hostility toward women. In modern China, however, beauty ideals and practices have been more fluid, heterogeneous, and practical, working for the country's benefit. A review of them will contribute to a deeper understanding of China's reception and adaptation of Western standards.[2]

Socially pervasive ideals of femininity are in dialectical relations with women's lived experiences. It is important to review the interaction between images of beauty and the actual living conditions of Chinese women in the country's recent discourses. We must also consider the implications of self-enhancement and self-fulfillment, and women's emotional and mental states. Ideals of women's bodies are circulated through fervently political and nationalist media and propaganda. Contemporary portraits of female beauty are consistent in their depictions of ideal physical features, irrespective of race and class, and those in contemporary China focus on young women and link images of them to images of the future of the state. Theories of social cognition emphasize the effects of the prevalence of such images and of the incentives offered by the media and social propaganda, consistent with the way ideal female bodies were promoted by the national government as an important part of building the nation at the turn of the twentieth century. The impact of this dialectical development over time on Chinese ideals of female beauty is visible in the country today.

Historians have divided the discourses of female beauty in twentieth-century China into three phases.[3] These are the "enlightening period," from 1919 to 1949; the "degradation period," from 1949 to 1978; and the "awakening period," from 1978 to 2000. All had built-in political burdens and social implications. These discourses, created by male Chinese intellectuals, shaped and constructed the bodies and minds of the so-called "new women" (*xin nuxian*), and women themselves developed through related cultural, political, and economic discourses.

National Discourses of Feminine Beauty in Recent China: The Movement of *Jianmei*

During the "enlightening period," immediately after the May Fourth Movement in 1919, women's liberation became a part of the new cultural movement. Western science and democracy, imported into China, brought new ways of thinking that promoted gender equality in order to build up images of new women, images that implied a revolt against tradition and a pursuit of freedom. These images of new women contributed to the new images of feminine beauty. In contrast to the traditional fashion, new women wore less jewelry and their clothes were more tightly cut, emphasizing feminine body curves. Women sometimes wore men's suits, and girls' school uniforms usually consisted of white socks and shirts and black skirts and shoes; such outfits presented a carefree and reformative style which matched well with the revolutionary cultural slogans of the May Fourth Movement. The *qibao*, the long, one-piece dress of Manchu origin that was popular among

Figure 19.1. A Shanghai beauty in a long *qibao*.

Chinese women at the time, was shortened or "moderated." (Long, elaborate, sexy *qibao* were still popular in celebrity circles in Shanghai.) This new look, together with short hair and the release of young women's bound feet from their tight wrappings, were the main signifiers of women's liberation at the time (fig. 19.1).

A study by Gao Haiwen on the *jianmei* movement demonstrates how female bodies had long signified competing nationalist and feminist discourses of womanhood in modern China.[4] The 1931 Mukden Incident launched a series of Japanese aggressive military maneuvers in northeast

China, which continued until Japan was defeated in 1945. During that time Chinese nationalists encouraged Chinese men and women to become physically strong in order to build up the overall strength of the nation. The government required women to develop strong physiques and participate in *tiyu* (sports, physical education, physical culture) as a civic obligation. When Chiang Kai-shek and his wife Song Meiling launched the New Life Movement in the 1930s to instill ideas of self-discipline and moral regulation, the female body was taken as embodying the unchanging essence and moral purity of the Chinese nation.[5]

Women trained in gymnastics and dance, and promoted hygiene through open-air exercise, diet, clothing reform, and natural therapies. Gao points out that women advocates of the movement built a cult of health and beauty called *jianmei*, which was backed by a populist feminist agenda for popular culture. This promotion of women's bodies simply presented, without makeup and with bare legs and feet (but never going so far as nudity, which was viewed as harmful to public morals), echoed the liberation fervor of the May Fourth Movement of the 1920s (fig. 19.2). The promotion of *jianmei* by the national party produced a female space that interacted with the nationalist agenda in complex ways, as *jianmei* and *tiyu* became prevalent in fashion and mass media, especially in highly successful pictorial magazines across major cities in China. Gao particularly mentions the literary and visual influence of the magazine *Linglong*, which repeatedly called on women to make sacrifices for the nation, to educate themselves in politics, to be brave and strong, and to develop their bodies in order to make nationalist concerns a priority, Women's liberation was to be sought through national liberation.[6]

Gao's visual analysis of *jianmei* reveals that the movement presented examples of modern Western women's bodies in the early 1930s. Chinese magazines featured photographs of white women in miniskirts, bathing suits, and gym shorts, ice skating, doing gymnastics, standing on their heads, and dancing, in order to show that "Western women have gained *jianmei* physiques through athletic exercise."[7] Camera angles frequently accentuated strong bare legs, and magazines used paintings and photographs of nude Western women with "healthy curves" and robust physiques. In an effort to move away from traditional conservative attitudes, admiration of these physiques was elevated to the level of pure, spiritual, reverential contemplation of nature. Images of glamorous Hollywood stars reinforced *jianmei* as an aspect of fashionable Western aesthetics.[8] Dancing, as a significant form of *tiyu*, linked *jianmei* with fashion, and Chinese magazines carried pictures

Figure 19.2. The *jianmei* movement of the 1930s.

of Chinese dancers wearing short dresses, sleeveless shirts, and gym shorts, showing *jianmei* legs and arms.[9]

In this way, national ideals of health and beauty during the Sino-Japanese war were set. Women's strength was promoted, and body standards were also discussed in terms of health and beauty. The science of physiology offered disciplined workout routines in conformity with specific measurements. It was suggested that Chinese women should be five feet tall and weigh 130 pounds, with a "wide chest," "large and erect breasts," "high nipples," an "ample behind," a "slender waist," an "even-proportioned figure," and "strong legs." Most attention was drawn to women's breasts and legs, which had never before been considered important aspects of Chinese feminine beauty.

This national emphasis on young female bodies in the 1930s reminds one of the national body movement in Germany in the same era. Both countries hopefully promoted national pride through healthy bodies, plain faces, fit physiques, healthy skin color, and lively gestures. The display of the female body became part of a new public discourse of modernity in everyday life which ushered in a war in the ideological sense. A 1929 *tiyu* law addressed the need to fight against traditional conservative attitudes toward female bodies that would hamper a successful *tiyu* program for women. It also condemned the modern girl's extravagant clothes and permed hair. In June 1936, Chiang Kai-shek instructed officers on the streets to enforce the law by accompanying violators to their homes to change their clothes, and by jailing and fining those who resisted.[10]

Gao shows that Chinese modernity was built via the *jianmei* movement on Western ideas and motifs in a discursive way. Through an emphasis on clean, strong female physiques and simple, practical clothing, beauty ideals were interpreted as indigenous, culturally authentic, and moral, engendering new national strength and pride. The movement clearly demonstrates that female bodies were a site of national contestation.

Female Bodies and State Control: The Notion of *Funu* and the "Iron Girls"

Historical records routinely connected women to the state, as in the image of the *femme fatale*: "a woman's beauty can subvert a city and a country" has become a common saying. For instance, until the twentieth century there were only the words *fu* and *nu* to designate women's inferior labor and status. The combined term *funu* appeared after the May Fourth Movement, when the discourse promoted individualism and gender equality. The New China, founded in 1949, brought strong Communist fervor in which women were called *funu* as an indication of respect. The term glorifies women; like the words "proletariats" and "laborers," it designates a group often suppressed in classed societies, and at the same time it indicates approval of women's self-actualization and liberation. It also conveys ideas of chastity, sexual loyalty, and purity, and has moral and political implications in the context of the state.

In contrast to the cult of health and beauty of *jianmei*, the new feminine beauty emphasized toughness and iron-like strength. The New Chinese women were also sexually neutral; they were not sexy and romantic, but devoted all their sexual and emotional energy to loving their nation. This devotion was represented by unattractive looks: short hair and loose

Figure 19.3. A Chinese woman smiling, seated. Courtesy of CORBIS.

revolutionary outfits of workers' green, gray, and blue (fig. 19.3). Political discourse dominated, and individual eros was replaced by nation building and reform. Historians call this the "degradation period" because the earlier ideals of female beauty were degraded into genderless norms of a working-class ethic. While new terms for women commonly used in later eras, like *nulang* (sexy girls) and *nuseng* (girl students), connote sexiness and innocence and imply superficial values, customary terms for female beauty imply inner qualities and have evolved together with the state.

In the 1950s, ideals of female beauty were combined with political purity. Women's inner qualities were more important than their appearance.

The propaganda about the "iron girls" is an outstanding example. At the end of the 1950s, under the Chinese Communist Party's radical policy of rapid industrialization, women became the first reserved labor force and peasants the second. Urban women entered heavy industry, construction, and mining.[11] The term "iron girls" originated in 1963 with the Dazhai Iron Girl brigade, who could bear hardship with iron-like shoulders.

These female labor forces also participated in the revolutionary agenda and embodied liberated ideals of gender equality.[12] They worked more efficiently than mixed-gender groups. But when only healthy young women with solid political consciousness could be admitted to the Communist society, masculine women like the Iron Girls eventually received harsh aesthetic criticism in comparison to traditional forms of femininity. Yet the movement, with its praise of female strength, had become a dynamic political force, and the image of the working-class Iron Girl, created by the state, had become an inspirational role model (fig. 19.4).

Figure 19.4. Women working in a factory. COURTESY OF CORBIS.

In the 1960s, women's class consciousness and participation in class struggles were more important than their physical features. Beauty figures in political propaganda dramas, like the female characters in *The White-Haired Girl* and *The Red Detachment of Women*, are straightforward in their political orientations and revolutionary attitudes.[13] Again, the traditional charms of tenderness and modesty gave way to heroic images of toughness, enhancing the revolutionary situation. Women's loyalties, in the patriarchal sense, were extended to the new country, for which they were presumed to sacrifice and fight. Toughness and tolerance were combined after the Cultural Revolution of the 1970s, befitting survivors of the political disaster. Such female characters are common in "scar" literature and paintings, which depict the sufferings and tragic stories of the victims of the Cultural Revolution, who were accused, beaten, and cursed because of their landlord and bourgeois backgrounds. It was not until the 1980s that female sexual bodies were depicted with a new, liberating fervor, and bodily sexual beauty—together with a lively personality—became the qualities of the main female characters in novels and films. Young women finally replaced sophisticated and loyal women fighters and intellectuals, and in response to the growing foreign investment in the beauty industry, female bodies were elaborated and physical appearance prioritized.

Female Body Entities in China and Contemporary Discourses

The "awakening period" began in the late 1970s, following the fall of the Gang of Four in 1976. Women characters in the "scar" literature that followed were liberated figures who emerged as individual, sexually awakened spirits in search of the real meanings of life, love, and gendered being. Yet the effect on the market economy of the economic reform promoted by Deng Xiaoping in the 1990s reenhanced and relegitimated the male gaze on and desire for women's bodies. The global trend was toward bodies and the homogenization of standards of female beauty, so that developing countries competed with the West by duplicating the process of modernization, confirming that they are the big consumers of technological devices, fashions, and cosmetics. Female bodies became the contested sites and symbols of modernization, economic growth, and national pride. Standard female faces and bodies were stamped on pictures at beauty parlors and magazine covers all over the country. Women's sexual awakening was clearly tied to the dynamics of the state and the world beyond.

People began to discuss "cosmopolitanism with Chinese characteristics." The term is used here in a broad sense and includes meanings promoted by Deng's economic reform of 1979, namely, that China was open to international investments and trade and involved itself vigorously in a global economy. China has slowly extended its influence beyond its geographical borders and into the international arena. The 2008 Olympics, held in Beijing, were one of the most significant ways in which the country has gained cosmopolitan glory. In Lisa Rofel's reading, "cosmopolitanism" serves as one of the key nodes through which Chinese contemporary sexual, material, and affective desires bind citizen-subjects to state and transnational neoliberal policies. The cosmopolitan discourses of feminine beauty in China mesh with Rofel's suggested tension between two desires: on one hand, the desire to self-consciously transcend locality by developing a consumer identity; and on the other, a the desire to domesticate cosmopolitan cultures by renegotiating China's place in the world (fig. 19.5).[14]

Figure 19.5. A model presents Jean-Paul Gaultier's collection at Shanghai Fashion Week. COURTESY OF CORBIS.

By a process of structured losses of memory that reinvent the past—that is, in the case of China, by a process of forgetting the Cultural Revolution and the many wars before it—young women are pulled into the negotiation. Women's fashion definitely has the power to remind and to cause to forget, and with young women as the ultimate consumers, fashion is all about how to embody a new self.[15] Rofel casts women as desiring subjects in this context, including their desires for sex and for consumption of various sorts. The elaborate efforts to build up a unique form of sexiness, and other bodily practices that try to capture the desire to be a cosmopolitan state, are also a national discourse about normality and about the kinds of citizens representing China to the world, and this discourse is tied up with representations of women.[16] This ideal is caught up in the tension caused by China's "self-conscious transcendence of locality, [which is] posited as a universal transcendence, accomplished through the formation of a consumer identity."[17]

The contemporary dichotomous discourses of the private and the public are also operating in China, with the result that political domination and traditional ethics are giving way, in the regulation of social bodies, to the choices increasingly made by individuals. People's bodies are situated in tensions and contestations among ages, genders, ethnicities, regions, and cultures, which are all striving for identities and uniqueness. There are new Chinese faces and bodies in the media representing and legitimating a wide variety of classes, sexualities, and ethnicities. These media products, which are representing bodies in ways that are enhancing the related desires of the male gaze, are inevitably affected by political and economic factors. The desires that are excited through body performance and visual pleasures negotiate with the traditional discourses of the epistemologies and ethics of the body. This process works more vigorously in places with a repressive past like China, which is catching up with the modernization and international progress of the Western world through its search for new identities and images.

One reading of consumer society is that the value of objects produced in these societies is determined by more than their use; additionally, the fashion represented in them is determined by more than their beauty. Value and fashion have social meanings as signs and symbols; they may act as social or even national identities providing comforts and gratifications. This reading offers a good description of the pictures in China in which bodies have already become the finest consumer objects, as both capital and fetish. Fashionable female bodies are marketed as more than just objects of desire; they are also functional entities in various senses. Jean Baudrillard, for example, points out that woman's sensible, expressive body in the culture of sensibility is disciplinary rather than pleasurable.[18] Media representations and advertisements of ideal female bodies are demonstrating secular and mundane pleasures—beauty and happiness on the surface—but, at the same time, they are reconstructing the social and cultural, psychological and sensational paradigms of the state at the cost of female physical and mental constraints. The rapid changes in female body aesthetics that followed China's economic reforms of the late 1970s are thus both surprising and predictable.

Social scientists researching female self-image, especially perceptions of obese bodies and their relation to social comparison and social support, demonstrate similar findings among countries whose national economies are integrated into the international economy through trade, foreign direct investment, capital flows, and migration. In 2001, half the commercials for health products in China were for weight-reducing products, which have a culture of slimness, leading to the disciplinary bodies that Baudrillard mentions. Research shows that such commercials in Beijing, Shanghai, and Guangzhou target young and middle-aged women, promote a slim figure with sex appeal, and foster a morbid culture of slimness. Although men's and women's obesity rates are equal, and older women are more obese than younger women, advertisements for weight-reducing products target younger females who have a high regard for slimness. The names of these products are Chinese adjectives describing slimness, and their users are female celebrities who are symbols of beauty and success. Moreover, slimness enhances rather than reduces sexiness; it is regarded as equivalent to health, normality, and emotional achievement. When the slimness of female bodies gains love, public praise, and admiration, it is said that the ideal body is easy to attain through product consumption rather than disciplinary measures taken upon oneself, as Baudrillard stated.[19]

Women's magazines make up at least half of the magazine market in China. The Chinese versions of international fashion magazines like *Vogue*, *Elle*, and *Marie Claire* are no doubt shaping the country's standards of female beauty. They are directing Chinese women to dress and carry themselves in internationally fashionable ways. At the same time, they are increasing readers' sexual, emotional, and materialistic desires. Even scholars in the People's Republic realize that the study of women's bodies has become a specialized area, professionally and economically, and women are no longer autonomous subjects themselves. Representations of conservative and contemporary women appear simultaneously in various media, including the Internet, and these representations are fulfilling various imaginary desires and purposes.

Desirable female bodies and characters have also become popular in recent literary work and films. Chinese critiques point out their double functions: to provide imaginary pleasures that will meet the male desires that turned into forms of national pride, and to shoulder moral judgments and comments. In the dialectical movement from revolutionary women in the 1950s to individual women in the 1970s to sexy or "bad" women in the 1990s, the notion of female purity has become ambiguous. In a political context, it has swung from the extreme left to the global capitalist economy, in which female body ideals appear on the public stage. The body has always been the site of identity tactics, and socialist female bodies have been replaced by desirable, fashionable ones, with no regard for class, religious, political, and social backgrounds, and with ideological judgments diminished. Female bodies and feminine ideals remain important signifiers of the modernized country, and the related discourses are also the languages of national strengths and resources.

Changes in the Representation of Female Bodies in Consumer China

In meeting fashion's and consumers' desires, female bodies in the global economy have become superficial and flattened. Their images in media and advertising deprive them of aesthetic depths and a genuineness that was so richly depicted in classical Chinese literature and arts. A study of contrasts reveals that women's portraits created by traditional Chinese literati were resources of imagination and interpretation, operating within the spiritual domains of ethics and aesthetics. They were more than representations; they held meanings and expressed aesthetic qualities waiting to be appreciated and contemplated.

The famous ancient literary work *The Book of Songs*, for example, collects more than three hundred musical pieces and poems by nobles and laymen from the Western Zhou period (eleventh century BCE) through the late Warring States period (sixth century BCE). The work is a significant creative record of male and female images of the time, and a large portion of it focuses on various kinds of women. Besides the mother goddesses of the myths and legends of the predynastic Zhou and Shang-Yin periods mentioned in the collection's subsections *The Major Odes* and *The Hymns*, there are the young ladies vividly portrayed in *The Airs of the States* and *The Minor Odes*. They come from different regions and various customs and traditions, manifesting a range of temperaments, physical attributes, and manners. They are also members of different classes and of different ages, including nobility, courtesans, young brides-to-be, middle-aged women, fisherwomen, laborers, silk workers, weavers, and farmers. These women probably sang and danced well, and their excellent performances contributed to a country of songs and poetry. The works they performed were cultivated products of Zhou's civilization, promoting the cultural quality and standard of the time, and the female bodies discussed or described in them functioned as a contrast to the dark age of the Shang-Yin period.

A wide range of adjectives relating to beauty and femininity are used to described the female characters of the songs. Examples include the famous phrase "the modest, retiring, virtuous young lady," in "The Ospreys Cry" ("Guan Sui") of the *South of Zhou,* which describes queens and court ladies whom men seek and think about while awake and asleep. Some metaphors for feminine beauty have meaning beyond mere physical appeal, indicating cleanliness, tidiness, health, and inner beauty as well. But morality is a less important source for the discussion of Chinese female ideals than are daring emotional and erotic expressions. The songs recorded vitality, intuitiveness, spontaneity, joy, passion, and variety. They form the map of a lost female world of both the body and the mind. It is said that the dichotomy of subject and object that is structured in the Western notion of the male gaze is absent in Chinese aesthetics, as is the dichotomy of the mind and the body. A more appropriate representation is that of a female as a whole in her appearance, as illustrated in the *Book of Songs.*

Women were described as "holding up half the sky," in praise of their labor, during the economic campaigns of the Mao regime, and after that came the discourse of female beauty under the political promotion of virtuous wives and good mothers. Rofel suggests that the post-Mao economic reform legitimates its specific imaginary of the modern body politic as it revolves around the natures of women, while the naturalization of womanhood promoted in post-Mao politics has shown that women in China lead an uneasy and provisional existence as subjects of the nation.[20] When the state's economic reforms failed, it asked women to perform domestic roles as wives, daughters-in-law, and mothers, so as to leave paid jobs to men. This suggests that female ideals are nationally constructed for the social and political benefit of the state. But the objectification of female beauties in the current commoditization process is a departure from the past, and it might have led to the dissolution of personalities that past Chinese arts used to glorify. There are no subjects here; one has no more knowledge of the particular females being represented, when they are all shown in the monotonous language of globalized cosmetic products and fashion.

It is well known that the government of the People's Republic has incorporated a capitalist economy in what the government usually calls "socialism with Chinese characteristics" in its public statements. Rofel argues that although "socialism with Chinese characteristics" is quite distinct from Maoist socialism, its manner of attempting to fasten together economic policies, moral evaluations of social life, and the emergence of new kinds of persons closely resembles the earlier socialist articulations of power, knowledge, and subjectivity.[21] Yet my study of the *Book of Songs* shows that the modern representations of the female body differ from the subjectivity of the earlier forms. At the very least, genuine vividness and individualistic identities are all lost or become pretentious in the discourses of female beauty. They are sacrificed in the quest for a combination of national economic pride and cosmopolitanism.

The hoopla surrounding the 2008 Beijing Olympics produced new forms of female beauty. Some young female university students dreamed of being Olympic volunteers, and therefore frequented English training centers, gyms, and beauty parlors. The touching story of a young female boxer tells all: in order to meet the body and posture requirements of the volunteer training center, she twisted her muscular body to tenderness, aiming to become soft-looking, an ideal reception model. Her training in becoming a lady included walking in steady, light steps, holding her torso upright, and practicing strict smiling exercises that required mirror training three hours per day. She was required to hold her head and eyes straight and control the number of teeth she exposed (fig. 19.6). Tough stories of this kind, reported in the media, show the embodiment of a new self, which is not only historically and culturally specific, but also tailor-made as national pride.

Figure 19.6. Women training to be Olympic stewardesses and ushers, Beijing 2008. COURTESY OF CORBIS.

While the making of the image of the "Olympic girl" is another process of normalization in the history of China, one may query the origins of these ideals and the reasons they have become the standards of female beauty representing today's China. It is obvious that certain bodily appearances represented in the traditions are appropriated and incorporated into the present (like the *qibao*, which originated in the Ching dynasty, and the body postures of courtesans of the past), yet they have also been seriously reduced to and designed for the international and global imaginations of "Chinese beauties." The Olympic girl can also be read as an updated "domestication of cosmopolitanism," with the implications just stated.[22] Through deliberate construction of female bodies, this new development is negotiating for a place in the world, and the move is loaded with desires for a global recognition of the state's wealth, resources, and pride.

Notes

1. Gordon B. Forbes, Linda L. Collinsworth, Rebecca L. Jobe, Kristen D. Braun, and Leslie M. Wise, "Sexism, Hostility toward Women, and Endorsement of Beauty Ideals and Practices: Are Beauty Ideals Associated with Oppressive Beliefs?" *Sex Roles* 56, nos. 5–6 (March 2007): 265–66.

2. Ibid., 273.

3. Haiwen Guo, "Er shi shi ji zhong guo nv xing mei de yan hua wen hua chan shi" [The cultural explanation on evolution of Chinese women's beauty in the 20th century," *Zhonghua nuzi xueyuan xubao* [*Journal of Chinese Women's University*], China Academic Journal Electronic Publishing House, 1 (2008): 107–11.

4. Yunxiang Gao, "Nationalist and Feminist Discourses on *Jianmei* (Robust Beauty) during China's 'National Crisis' in the 1930s," in *Translating Feminisms in China*, ed. Dorothy Ko and Wang Zheng, trans. Kimberley Manning and Lianyun Chu (Oxford: Blackwell, 2007), 104–30.

5. Ibid., 104.

6. Ibid., 106–108.

7. Ibid., 108.

8. Ibid., 111.

9. Ibid., 115.

10. Gao quotes a regulation issued by the national government stating, "All customs that hinder the regular physical growth of young men and young women should be strictly prohibited by the countries, municipalities, villages and hamlets; and their programmes should be fixed by the Department of Education and the Training Commissioner's Department" (ibid., 117–18). Although this clause was primarily directed at the prevalent rural customs of breast and foot binding, it was put into practice in quite other ways.

11. Jin Yihong, "Rethinking the 'Iron Girls': Gender and Labour during the Chinese Cultural Revolution," in Ko and Zheng, *Translating Feminisms in China*, 188–214.

12. Ibid., 194.

13. Both *The White-Haired Girl* (*Bai maonu*, 1965) and *The Red Detachment of Women* (*Hongse niangzi jun*, 1964) were standard elements in the national ballet repertoire after the founding of the PRC in 1949. Both have successfully promoted the socialist agenda of class struggles and political correctness. *The White-Haired Girl* was premiered by the Shanghai Dance Academy in 1965; the eight-act ballet is an adaptation of the Chinese opera of the same name that premiered in 1945. It tells of a peasant girl, Xi'er, whose father is beaten to death by the local despotic landlord because he is unable to pay his debts. She is taken by force to work in the landlord's home, but escapes into the mountain forest. Her fiancé joins the Eighth Route Army and returns three years later to liberate the village and rescue her. By then, Xi'er has endured such suffering that her long black hair has turned white. *The Red Detachment of Women* was produced by the Central Ballet of China in 1964. The six-act ballet deals with a Communist-led company of women on Hainan Island during the civil war in the early 1930s. It shows the liberation of a peasant slave girl, who becomes a member of the Communist Party and finally the leader of the company.

14. Lisa Rofel, *Desiring China: Experiments in Neoliberalism, Sexuality, and Public Culture* (Durham, N.C.: Duke University Press, 2007), 111.

15. Ibid., 118.

16. Ibid., 121.

17. Ibid., 111.

18. Jean Baudrillard, *The Consumer Society: Myths and Structures* (London: Sage, 1998).

19. Xu Min and Qian Xiao-feng, "Jian fei guang gao yu bing tai de miao tiao wen hua—Guan yu da zhong chuan bo dui nv xing shen ti de wen hua kong zhi" [Weight-reducing advertising and morbid slim culture—On mass media's cultural control of women's bodies," *Fu nu yinjiu lunchong* [*Collection of Women's Studies*] 3, no. 46 (May 2002): 22–29. The journal is published in China by Hangzhou.

20. Rofel, *Desiring China*, 57.

21. Ibid., 111.

22. Ibid.

20. Gendered Bodies in Contemporary Chinese Art

MARY BITTNER WISEMAN

The idea of beauty in the West has often been connected with the idea of woman, whose beauty has been celebrated in sculptures of the nude since classical Greece and in paintings since the sixteenth century. The nude is not a genre in either traditional or contemporary Chinese art, however, and although there has been nakedness in the representations of the body in the contemporary art of China, its presence is marked by two characteristics that distance the Chinese naked body from the Western nude. One is that gender boundaries are not drawn in the same way in China as they are in the West. In China they are not based on oppositions: to be a woman is not, for example, simply to lack the traits that make someone a man. Gender difference does not, therefore, make so deep a cut in the conceptual schemes in Chinese thought as it does in those in the West.

The other is that the female body is identified or valued not as an object of male desire but as the site and possibility of its flowering, while the male body is typically presented as marked in some unusual way or performing some unusual action. Neither is identified as an object worthy of respect or interest for its own sake. Nor does the idea of beauty take refuge elsewhere in Chinese art. Beauty was not a value articulated or striven for by the artists of China, governed as they were by the six principles of painting articulated by Hsieth Ho in the late fifth century. In his book *Criticism of Painting*, he listed six technical factors of painting and said that few artists mastered them all. "The first is: Spirit Resonance (or Vibration of Vitality) and Life Movement. The second is: Bone Manner (structural) Use of the Brush. The third is: Conform with the Objects (to obtain) Likeness. The fourth is: Apply the Colors according to the Characteristics. The fifth is: Plan and Design, Place and Position (i.e. composition). The sixth is: To Transmit Models by Drawing," that is, to copy the master. He then ranked twenty-seven artists into six grades, depending on which of these techniques they had mastered and how well.[1]

Under the reign of Mao, from 1949 to 1976, the sexes were also treated with relative indifference to gender and to the body as such. But gone are the dark blue genderless suits of those days, and the body itself is on show in the art of the Chinese avant-garde. What exactly is on show? The brute presence, the there-ness and materiality of the body, its persistence despite the fragility of the memory of traditions, the instability of what count as social virtues and vices, and the uneven power of language to capture what is happening at the level wherein lies the possibility of what can be thought, felt, and said. And what might we learn from avant-garde art's foregrounding the materiality and persistence of the body? That art—born as it is of intuition and imagination—can express this fragility of memory, instability of values, and fallibility of language and enable its viewers to reconfigure their sightlines and their habits of thinking, feeling, and saying.

In the opening decades of the twenty-first century Chinese artists are asking what art is in the China made new by Deng Xiaoping's 1979 invitation to the West to invest in its natural and human resources. They might also ask about the Chinese-ness of the current art, given that what is local in the new China is compromised by the country's now housing the formerly opposed factions of the Cold War, communism and capitalism. While communism and capitalism do not exhaust the political and economic systems of the nations across the globe, they come near to doing so. There is, then, this simple sense in which the global has insinuated itself into the Chinese local. There is also a less simple sense: the traits encouraged by capitalism sit uneasily next to those encouraged by the Cultural Revolution. The aim of this revolution was to further erase the memory of imperial China and to abolish differences between city and country, intellectual and peasant, one individual and another. Under capitalism, however, difference reigns, and the individual is increasingly on his or her own as the expansion of capitalism erodes "the idealism and altruism that once guided the Chinese conscience."[2]

China's artists are asking not only what art is, but also what it is to be Chinese in these times. And one way in which they are working out answers about art and Chinese-ness is through artworks, including installations and performances, that represent or use the body. This art is perforce an art of the avant-garde, because the continuity of the development of Chinese art was interrupted by Mao and because the West's innovations and revisions of its own art history have happened so rapidly that they have not had time to settle in and be naturalized by artists in China. It is an art that has lost its moorings in its own history and in modern Western art. Functioning below the level of discourse, where the murmurings of classical China and the modern West can be heard along with the gradually fading voice of Mao, it is the laboratory in which criteria for something's being art and someone's being Chinese are being forged. It can, then, be called experimental, which is what art of the avant-garde is.

Such connection as contemporary Chinese art has with the art of the West is superficial, because the art being made by Chinese artists incorporates neither the problems Western artists have tried to solve nor the questions they have used their art to answer. The problems, questions, and tensions that drive the art of the Chinese avant-garde can be addressed at the level of the body, at a level more or less immune to the ideologies of communism and capitalism, to the distance between the classical past and the aftermath of the Cultural Revolution, and to the overlap between the local and the global.

The body in avant-garde art can be put into two frameworks: one, that of the absence of the nude in the art of China, and the other, that of the failure of communication between Chinese and Western feminisms that became clear in the course of an art journey made in 2002 along the route of Mao's Long March. Lu Jie, the convener of the Long March Project, sought to explain the failure as follows: "We are interested in feminist art in China, which has a very different genealogy and timetable from feminist art in the West, and particularly in America. Even though Chinese 'feminist art' started to develop more recently than in the West, it grows out of a different context. In fact, part of the communist revolution was about feminism, and through the People's Republic there have been certain official manifestations of feminism quite different from what you see in the West, and which came before the women's movements of the 1970s."[3]

One reason for the failure of communication between feminist artists in contemporary China and in the West is that representations of women in the work of the Chinese artists tend to be about the women themselves rather than, as in the work of Western artists, how they are regarded by men. Before we look at the mode of presence of male and female bodies in contemporary Chinese art, however, let us consider the absence of the nude in this art.

The Absent Nude

The making, not the made, has traditionally been valued in the art of China, as it has been in its thought. Process, not product, and energy, not form, underlie and constitute the real. This is why the path of the flow of energy through the body, rather than anatomy, has been the lode-star of Chinese medicine, and why the human form does not have the role in Chinese art that it has in the art of the West.[4] The gestures of the ink-drawn or clay-modeled human figures, the folds and curves of their robes and sleeves, represent the path of the energy, the life force, the breath — what the God of Genesis breathed into the figure of clay that became Adam — and capture what is important to the Chinese about the human figure.

In the Guimet Museum of Asian Art in Paris are a pair of terracotta female dancers from the Tang Dynasty (618–907 CE) (fig. 20.1). The women bend toward each other, each with one knee on the ground, spine, neck, and piled-high hair in a continuous curve, arms outstretched with one bent and one straight, their deep sleeves in motion. They gaze at the ground from which the rhythm of their bodies seems to rise: the space around them, the earth under them, and the gowns covering them are one. The body's form, as such, does not stand out. Put a polo stick in the hand of the dancing woman, put her astride a horse in the company of like-outfitted women, and let the game of polo that China inherited from Sassanidean Persia begin. A num-ber of such figures sport on a wall in the Guimet. Motion is everywhere: the horses run, the women lean with arms outstretched, and women and horses are one. These are funerary figures destined to play forever in the tombs of the privileged.

Move now from the Tang Dynasty to the turn of the twenty-first cen-tury, from women to men, motion to stasis, and free-flowing to constrained energy. In a performance called *Breathing* (1996), the artist Song Dong lay face down for about forty minutes at night in Tiananmen Square, where the temperature was -9°C and, again, for about forty minutes during the day on the Back Sea, a frozen lake in the old quarter of Beijing whose temperature was -8°C. In Tiananmen Square, a thin layer of ice formed on the cement surface where Song breathed; the ice onto which he breathed on the Back Sea was unchanged.

Song Dong's breath, like the dancers' energy, is what Hsieth Ho's first principle of painting would have the artist express: "Spirit Resonance (or Vibration of Vitality) and Life Movement." Song's body was joined with the surfaces on which he lay as intimately as were the dancers with the space

Figure 20.1. Two dancers, Tang Dynasty, mid-seventh century. Ceramic with lead glaze, h. 17 cm. Musée des Arts Asiatiques-Guimet, Paris. Photograph by Robert Asselberghs. Photo credit: Réunion des Musées Nationaux/Art Resource, N.Y.

within which they moved. Between the times and places on which he lay and breathed were these differences: night and day; a cultural and a natural site; earth covered with cement and water with ice; Song's breath making a difference on the Square and not on the Sea. Whatever moral one might be tempted to draw from the result of his experiment, it was through his breathing on the surfaces to which he gave himself up that Song expressed the spirit, vitality, and life that Hsieth Ho would have an artist express in the act of making art. Song Dong, in his performance, showed himself to be one with the life that flows through all there is: heaven, earth, and human being, as the artist who made the Tang figures showed them to be one with the rhythm of the world.

In *Printing on Water* (1996), Song Dong took a wooden block on which the character for water was carved and tried to print it on the water in a sacred river in Lhasa, bringing the block down onto the water again and again. In each case it was the gesture and the place in which the gesture was made that mattered, not whether it produced something lasting. In *Breathing*, Song did what one does to breathe life into someone, and in *Printing on Water*, he did what one does to print a character by hand. *Breathing* occurred in places on which the history of China has been written: a massacre had occurred in Tiananmen Square (on June 4, 1989) and ancient buildings are being demolished in the neighborhood of the Back Sea to make way for the new. *Printing on Water* was not performed on just any water, but on water in a river deemed holy by the people of Buddhism-rich Tibet.

The sustained (breathing on the ground for forty minutes) and repeated (bringing down the block again and again) activity, not any resulting product, is what constitutes the art in these two works. In classical Chinese aesthetic theories, art is created when an artist captures the spirit, vitality, or life movement of some object or activity through the use of the brush (of a traditional artist) or the body (of a performance artist), giving herself up to the vital movement so that she transfers its resonance in her to the medium in which she is working. Song Dong did what one does when one breathes and when one prints: he attended to his breathing by attending to nothing else, and he repeatedly brought the character block down even though his repeated motions did not "take"—he was just doing what one does when one prints.[5]

The sculpted bodies dance and play polo, the performing bodies breathe and print. In neither case, not in the time of the Tang dynasty and not now, is the body any more than a vehicle for the vitality of the universe, the site of the energies passing through it and keeping it in existence, whereas in Western poststructuralism it is the site of the languages passing through and identifying it. The artist as described in the Chinese treatises on painting is a person who can look at a mountain long enough for it to reverberate in him so that when, having cleared his mind and quieted his spirit, he picks up the brush, the brush, ink, hand, and wrist move in such harmony with the mountain that it reappears on the paper.

If the body as such is not of moment in Chinese art, then the nude is not going to be. In particular, it is not going to define a genre whose members portray the ideal human body, stripped bare, with nothing hidden and nothing to hide. The West's nude has no past and no future, because it is an ideal. There is, for it, no becoming and no passing away; it exists only in the present and is fully present, as only Being is. Not only do representations of the unclothed human body not define a genre in the art of China, but the job for which the nude is conscripted in the West is not one the Chinese would undertake. For in the Chinese view of the world, there is only what is not quite yet and what is already starting to leave: there is no pure presence. There is, that is to say, only coming to be and passing away. Unlike depictions of the nude in Western art, representations of the body in Chinese art do not stop the flow of the world and the passage of time. Nor is the body, as Courbet's *Origin of the World* implies, the source of the world itself.[6]

The Present Body

Nevertheless, bodies are represented in paintings, photographs, and videos and presented in performances in contemporary Chinese art, even though they call attention not to themselves but to what they are doing or are being used to do. Experimental artists use the image or the presence of the body to do what they have also used calligraphy to do, namely, divest the subject of their art of its received meaning.

Chinese characters are lines and shapes that have meaning, and calligraphy can be looked at either for the vitality and grace of its brushstrokes or for what the strokes convey: signifier or signified can occupy center stage. The marriage of the *prima facie* incompatible theories of communism and capitalism and the relation of the present power brokers in the People's Republic of China to its recent and distant past have unsettled China's relation to language. Signifiers slip and slide over what they are supposed to signify, as stable meaning is all but lost. Contemporary China seems not to be intelligible at the level of discourse, and artists declare this by making works that enact the divorce of signs from their meanings.

What is it, however, to divest the human body of meaning? Or what is the analogue, with respect to the body, of stripping language of its meaning? Since Chinese thought does not distinguish mind from body, which it holds to be as inspirited as mind is embodied, to divest the body of meaning is not to divest it of spirit or mind nor to treat it as an empty shell, the corpse-like thing that Descartes holds body to be. Not only is mind not distinct from body in Chinese worldviews, but also a person is not distinct from his or her social environment. Indeed, under Mao each person's *raison d'être* was to serve the social collective. The idea that this is what gives individuals their meaning and purpose is being rethought in much of the art of the Chinese avant-garde. The question of what the purpose and source of meaning for a human life can be is what occupies and shapes much of the work of the avant-garde. The idea that a person exists for the state has not simply been replaced with the Western Enlightenment notion of men and women as rational, self-interested individuals who exist for themselves alone, however. The matter is more complicated, and more interesting.

The hard fact of the body, dependent as it is on food, water, air, and shelter, but not on a ready-made world, is one locus of artists' asking about where and how individuals can fit into a post-Mao China. What is on show now that the collective character of the body has been dealt a blow by the removal of the genderless Mao suit and the individual body has come into view? The body is being reworked through its representations in avant-garde art in much the same way as is the Chinese language. For example, in Xu Bing's *Book of the Sky* (1987–91), open, hand-printed books on wooden mounts are installed in rows on the floor and scrolls hang from ceiling and walls. All are printed from four thousand hand-carved blocks of characters, and the materials and techniques used in their production are true to the prescriptions of classical Chinese printing, scroll design, and bookbinding. However, Xu Bing invented the characters, and they are indecipherable. The *Book from the Sky* cannot be read.

Avant-garde artists are treating the body in the uncommon way that Xu Bing treats the Chinese language. Look first at two works whose subject is language—Xu Bing's *Square Words—New English Calligraphy* (1994–96) and Wenda Gu's *United Nations: Babel of the Millennium* (1999)—and then at two that use the body to question the relation of language to the human subject.

In Xu Bing's square word calligraphy, altered English letters are combined in squares to form words that are then combined in rows and columns to form sentences. The installation is a classroom with a video monitor that shows the artist demonstrating calligraphy, and material with which the audience/students can practice. One example is a rectangle with a black ground and white letters arranged in three columns and four rows. Reading the left-hand column from top to bottom, we find "Little Bo Peep Little / Bo Peep Has Lost / Her Sheep And Can . . ." and the story continues. This is not, however, just a fusion of the two languages; it "draws upon principles of calligraphy to make the Chinese legible to an English-speaking audience, while insisting upon a formal structure that remains Chinese."[7] The calligraphy is neither Chinese nor English, but both. The forms of the letters and sentences are Chinese; the meanings of the words they make are not.

In 1993 Wenda Gu started using hair collected from around the world to make installations that constitute the *United Nations* series; some of the installations involve language. *United Nations: The Babel of the Millennium* (1999) was commissioned for the atrium of the San Francisco Museum of Modern Art: it consists of 116 sheer vertical panels of woven hair on which are written pseudo-characters in English, Chinese, Hindi, and Arabic—one Western and three Eastern languages—as well as a fusion of English and Chinese.[8] The words may lack meaning, but the geography—China,

India, and the oil-rich countries of the Middle East, with English fusing with Chinese—does not, nor does the fact that the unreadable words are written on panels of hair. People use their voices to speak, ears to hear, hands to write, and eyes to read, and while spoken words do not last (unless captured and stored electronically), written ones typically do. They linger on papyrus, on clay, on stone, on paper, and, now, on something made not from plant or earth but from the human body—or on the body itself.

There is a way to put language to an unusual use that connects it intimately with the body: by writing on it. A Westerner might be inclined to interpret an artist's writing on his body—as Zhang Huan wrote the names of his ancestors on his face for the series of nine chromogenic prints in *Family Tree* (2001)—as his showing the primacy of the materiality of the signifier. But this hardly need be shown to a Chinese audience: calligraphy is as valued for the quality and rhythm of its lines as for the meanings of the characters. It is a close cousin to painting in that both are produced by the movement of the artist's wrist and hand with its ink-filled brush, a movement whose curves reproduce those of the Tang dancers and polo players. Calligraphy, painting, and dancer figurines are movement captured by ink, paper, and clay.[9]

In the nine photographs that make up *Family Tree*, the frame shows only Zhang Huan's neck and the top of his dark-clad shoulders. In the first image, about half of his face is character-free, while the other half bears names of his ancestors, a fraction of whose genes are his. Their genetic code is encoded in his genes as their names are written on his face, and since approximately half of the traits handed down by his ancestors are expressed in him, we "see" his forebears in him as clearly as we see their names on his face. The point might be that so much of a person is composed of his genetic past that it is as though his lineage were written on his face. But it need not be precisely this, because the ancestors are already there in his genes. As the series progresses, his face is increasingly covered with names, so that by the last one, only his eyes show through the black ink that blankets his face.

This can be read as a demystification of ancestor veneration, saying that the individuality of anyone whose filial piety leads him to submit himself to and identify himself by his lineage will be erased. However, the ancestors' names themselves become unreadable as the man's face becomes unrecognizable. Is the last photograph in the series an argument for the primacy of the genetic over the linguistic? That is, perhaps it says that the unreadability of the ancestors' names does not matter because the forebears persist in the genes of their progeny: one's genetic inheritance is what it is, independent of one's acknowledgment of or respect for those through whom it came. That the individual becomes unrecognizable does not matter, because the individual offspring is important only for the genes he can pass on. Or the series could be a light-hearted *reductio ad absurdum* of the practice of identifying oneself by reciting from whom one comes: "I am the son of A who is the son of B," and so on. The subject in the photographs tries to write (identify) who he is on himself, and the effort self-destructs.

In Qiu Zhijie's *Tattoo II* (1997) the separateness of a body, not of an individual from his family tree or a name from a gene, is sacrificed to the word, and the word is "no" or "not." The photograph is of the artist, who is shown standing shirtless in front of a plain off-white ground. His body is shown cropped at the waist, and he stares straight ahead. The body is painted with a large red character whose horizontal covers the artist's mouth, silencing him, and reaches almost to the edges of the picture plane. Its vertical and diagonal lines reach down and across his chest. Most of the paint is on his body, but some is on the off-white wall behind him, with the result that the character signifies "no" or "not" only so long as the man's body is not taken away from its background, the wall.

So long as the character has meaning and is taken to obliterate the space between it and the wall, the man is not some significant thing independent of the sign and the wall. He cannot claim the impossible space between the sign and the wall. If, however, the sign is read as what it is, an optical trick, then were the man to move away from the wall, the red brushstrokes would cease to form the sign for "no," and the man would be some thing apart from his background or context. Just as a person cannot say "I am not," so no one can pin a sign on another that says "[he is] not." The other has to be present to be so signed. Either the man is a real and separate entity (and the character does not mean "not") or the brushstrokes have meaning (and the man is a phantasm). Either "not" makes impossible the existence of the individual, or it ceases to have meaning.

What is on show in these photographs of a man's head and a man's body? Language. There are pictures aplenty of bodies, but not written-on bodies. People use language. Here artists are using their bodies to protest the power of language, to protest the supposition that if the human body were not specified, singularized, reified by language, it would meld into the earth and sky of which it is a part, just another vehicle for the life movement that courses through everything. The words in *Family Tree* merge the individual with his ancestors, blacking him out. The word in *Tattoo II* does something more complicated by setting up an existential contradiction: the sign has meaning if and only if the body does not exist (as a thing extended in three dimensions).

If signs keep their familiar meanings, the individual is blacked out. In each of these two artworks, the body is assaulted by language in what amounts to an assertion that the identity of contemporary Chinese men and women is threatened by the weight of their lineage and the received meanings of the mélange of discourses—political, economic, and social—now in place in China.

Chinese Landscape—Tattoo (1999) by Huang Yan is another photograph in which the body is the ground, not for language, as in *Family Tree* and *Tattoo II*, but for landscapes (plate 15). The artist covered a model's chest and arms with white powder and painted on the body in the manner of the Chinese scholar-artists. Huang said, as the scholar-artist might have,

> Mountains and rivers are my way of reasoning; . . . mountains and rivers are where my heart and soul find peace; mountains and rivers are where my physical body belongs; . . . I am an avant-garde ink painter who paints mountains and rivers on my body; . . . I believe in instinct, I believe in mountains and rivers, I kill time in mountains and rivers.[10]

And again: "Landscape is an abode in which my mortal body can reside, landscape is my rejection of worldly wrangling, landscape is a release for my Buddhist ideas."[11]

The photograph can be interpreted as saying either that so deep is the connection of the Chinese people to nature that rivers and mountains are metaphorically inscribed on their bodies or that the world is now upside down: the physical body is not in nature but nature is (represented) on the body. There is, however, a reading that eschews talk of metaphor and representation and takes the photograph to speak to the identification of human beings with nature. Rivers and mountains, their water and stone, and human beings are physical things. How can human beings identify with these elements of their land? Rivers and mountains are in the body as blood and bone, and in *Chinese Landscape—Tattoo* they are on the body as a drawing. The artist makes the past present by painting as the scholar-artists did and by declaring his fealty to the mountains to which it is increasingly hard to surrender oneself—by surrendering his body, his skin, to them.

Ancestors, Chinese calligraphy, scholar-artists, the mountains and rivers that define the landscape of China are all, lest they be forgotten, both acknowledged and put into question by the bodies in the photographs called *Family Tree, Tattoo II,* and *Chinese Landscape—Tattoo.* In these works, bodies are the site of artists' questioning, quarreling with, reconfiguring, and, finally, preserving their tradition, their language, and their land. What is passing through the body-representations by these avant-garde artists is not exactly the "Spirit Resonance (or Vibration of Vitality) and Life Movement" of all there is. Rather, the body-representations are the site of the artists' working through questions brought to the fore by the split in the social fabric caused by the political and economic changes of the last three decades, working them through at the level of instinct and matter, below the level of language. The energy released in the artists and their work by this rupture is a version of the "vibration of vitality" classical artists sought to express in their work. A robust materialism is at work at the level at which art is currently being made: it is a level at which bodies are the most real things.

The works discussed so far have been by men. Song Dong used his body in *Breathing* to mark with his breath, which is his life, two historically significant sites in Beijing lest their past be forgotten, and in *Printing on Water* to demonstrate the failure of coition between word and thing. In each case the body did something, In *Family Tree, Tattoo II,* and *Chinese Landscape—Tattoo,* the bodies do not do anything, but are the passive subjects of their artists' ideas. They are, nonetheless, resolutely present in the artworks, and resolutely male.

The Female Body

The materialism strikes a different chord when the material bodies are female. In works of art, they are not apt to serve as vehicles through which to rethink the contemporary Chinese person's relation to her language or tradition or as objects for the male gaze, as they often are in Western art. It is natural to ask what the presence of bodies, naked or clad, in works of Chinese avant-garde art can tell us about current perceptions of the feminine and of gender difference. It is appropriate, as well as natural, to look for answers in works by women. The first reason to do this is that ideas about women and the feminine have typically been articulated by men and have tended, therefore, to ignore the experiences of women. To insist on the importance of women's experiences does not commit one to claiming that women experience things differently from men. It is sufficient that in many circumstances women are regarded and treated differently from men and that the experience of their own bodies belongs to them alone.

The second reason is reflected in something said by Chen Lingyang in an interview with Melissa Chiu:

MC: Feminism has had an entirely different history here in China and I think there would probably be a tendency to see your works in the light of Chinese feminism. How do you feel about this, and what do you think about this identification? CL: I don't care if people think I'm a feminist. I have had a hard time with people. The first time I heard this term, it was used sarcastically by a professor of mine to describe a social phenomenon. . . . China is still very much a patriarchal society. MC: Wouldn't you say your works represent a feminist perspective? CL: Maybe a better way to say it would be that my works have to do with myself, and I am a woman."[12]

The force of Chen's words is heightened by her response to being asked if feminist artists working in the United States in the 1970s were role models; she asserts she starts from her own feelings rather than from art history or someone else's work.[13]

Chen Lingyang is not alone in resisting the description of herself and her work as feminist. Lin Tianmiao said in an interview with *New York Times* art critic Holland Cotter that although women are treated like "inactive thinkers" in China, she was not a feminist because the concept "is too Western. It is too vague. China is not ready for feminism. China has its own brand of feminism." Ms. Lin, born in 1961, lived in New York in the late 1980s and, therefore, was exposed to Western feminism, as the twenty-years-younger Li Shurui has not been. Li said that although male chauvinism is a force in the artworld, "she is still too young, too much in the stage of discovering herself, to figure out whether she considers herself a feminist or not." Yet when asked by Cotter to name a cultural role model, Li Shurui named "the seventh-century ruler Wu Zetian, who through a combination of brains, beauty, unsparing ambition, and tenacious hard work, became China's first and only empress."[14]

Chen was talking about *Twelve Flower Months* (1999–2000), her series of twelve photographs of her menstruating body, each combined with the flower associated with the month. Every photograph has the shape of a garden pavilion window, each of which is different, and each of the body images is seen in a differently shaped mirror. The background of all but three is black, and all are quiet and elegant. The wonder of them is that instead of the mirror's reflecting a flower or the face of a beautiful woman, it reflects the possibility of her flowering. There is no narrative arc here, only repetition. A woman's periods follow the rhythm of nature and mark the movement of life through the species. The photographed streams of blood are a material analogue of what Hsieth Ho's first principle of Chinese painting would have each artwork capture and express.

The mirrors, window shapes, and month-associated flowers are from the dynastic tradition, whereas the subject matter of the photographs is not. But in its sheer materiality, the subject attests to the primacy in avant-garde art of the fundamental workings of the body: Song Dong breathes and Chen Lingyang bleeds. Bodies breathe and menstruate without the cooperation of the agents whose bodies they are and despite the sociopolitical context in which these actions occur. Where Western abstract expressionists sought to give free rein to the instincts of the unconscious, and surrealists celebrated the fabricating talents of the unconscious in giving them rein, artists of the Chinese avant-garde go into the body, not the mind, to tap into something primitive that can break through the scrim of all that communist-capitalist culture has constructed.

Born with the Cultural Revolution (1995), a triptych of chromogenic prints by Xing Danwen, uses the naked body of a pregnant woman to tell a story of the changing influence of Mao (fig. 20.2). The middle photo is thirty inches wide, more than twice as wide as the two side ones, giving the work the shape of a scroll. The pregnant woman is a friend of the artist, and the title refers to her birth in 1966, the first year of the Cultural Revolution. In the large middle panel, shot from below—so the viewer looks up to her—the woman's torso and the lower part of her face, obscured by her hair, occupy the right half of the picture plane. The upper left-hand corner of the plane has a picture of Mao, about half the size of the woman's torso. Behind it and the woman one and a half of the four small stars on the Chinese Communist flag appear, the whole star touching her shoulder. The small stars stand for the people of the People's Republic of China—peasants, workers, bourgeoisie, and capitalists. The woman, pregnant, is equivalent to one and a half.

In each of the side panels, the woman looks out at the viewer. In the right-hand panel, shot from above—so the viewer looks down on her—the flag falls gracefully from the frame of a painting of a reclining woman, clothed, to serve as a backdrop for the naked pregnant woman, who lies on her side in the opposite direction from the woman in the picture. The same picture of Mao as was in the middle panel, now much smaller, is poised above the pregnant woman's head, as the body of the woman in the painting is above her body. (Mao has authority over her mind as the figure in the painting has over her body.) The painting, the folds of the fabric linking it with the pregnant woman, her relaxed pose, all connect this with the Western tradition of putting sensuous women's bodies on display. In the left-hand panel, on the other hand, all is business. The woman is standing with head turned as though just interrupted, and we see in another room a table on which a machine, perhaps

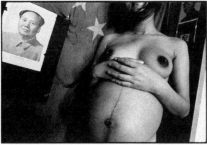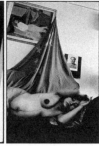

Figure 20.2. Xing Danwen, *Born with the Cultural Revolution*, 1995. Three
black-and-white photographs, each 24 × 20 in. Collection of the artist.
COURTESY OF XING DANWEN.

a printer, sits. On a narrow strip of wall behind the woman is a reproduction
of a painting of a young, feminized Mao from Li Shan's *Rouge* series (1990),
with two standard pictures of Mao under it. Her body is shown cropped mid-
torso, her pregnant belly no longer the subject of the work.

Reading the scroll-like triptych from right to left, we see, first, woman
voluptuous and sensual; then, woman whose body is given up to her pregnancy, to Mao, and to the People's Republic; and, finally, woman as matter
of fact, one who happens to be pregnant, standing under a picture of Mao
as a young woman. The swelling breasts and stomach of the female, echoed
by the supple folds of the draped flag in the right-hand panel, portray a figure men would desire. Move from how woman looks to what her biological
function is: the focus of the woman-body in the large middle panel is what
is inside. She is pregnant, and that is wherein her woman-ness lies. Move to
the left-hand panel, which portrays a scene where gender matters little. The
triptych ends with a picture of a young woman looking out at the viewer and
standing under a picture of Mao seen no longer as a commanding figure but
as a young woman. That the subject of the photograph is naked shows only
that she needs no disguise. This is nakedness as a material, not a social, fact,
and not a lure: it says "this is my body"; that's all.

Clothes are needed in social space and time, but not by the woman
whose image is the subject of Chen Lingyang's large nighttime photograph
(22 × 68 in.) called *25:00, no. 2* (2002) (of course, there is no "twenty-five
o'clock"). Here the real world is resolutely urban. The photograph depicts a
cityscape with vertical skyscrapers in the middle ground and horizontal five-
or six-story buildings in the foreground. Little traffic is on the streets, and
the only lights are a few illuminated signs and lit windows. The building

in the center of the middle ground is perpendicular to the picture plane, while the parallel buildings slant toward it and a far distant vanishing point.

Along the length of the roof of the middle building lies a naked woman, as tall as the building is long. Face down, arms at her side, head and long black hair hanging over the building's side, she is a study in stillness. Her body captures the enormity and power of the sleeping city to which she submits yet over which she has sway. Her body is pale, and the sky, a horizontal band taking up less than the top quarter of the picture plane, is a middling blue. Buildings and streets are various shades of blue-gray, none so pale as her body or so blue as the sky. Together the two reign over the city. In the night sky the moon appears, its cycle the cycle of blood photographed in the artist's *Twelve Flower Months*. It is fitting, then, that the artist has the female join with the night sky to rein in the male world that, she says, often gets mixed up in her mind with the real world.

> They both come from outside me; they both exist very forcefully, with initiative, power, and aggression. Facing these two worlds, I often feel that I am weak and helpless, and don't know what to do. . . . I wish that every day there could be a certain time like 25:00, when I could become as large as I like, and do whatever I want.[15]

The picture is a wish fulfillment, and the first wish is that her body should be as large as she would like it to be.

In *Twelve Flower Months* and *Born with the Cultural Revolution*, the female body is expressed in its closeness to nature through menstruation and gestation, and in *25:00, no. 2*, in a fancied complicity with the night sky, as both female body and sky hover over the dense city rather like Gerard Manley Hopkins's Holy Ghost hovers over the world.[16] In none of the works is movement or gesture in view. The female reproductive system does what it does independently of the movements of the woman whose system it is, and *25:00, no. 2* pictures a sleeping dreamer. No motion there.

Look now at a work in which gesture predominates and the body speaks through its posture rather than its form. *Sanjie* (2003), by Cui Xiuwen, is a video shown on thirteen screens in which a little girl assumes the positions of the twelve apostles and Jesus in Leonardo da Vinci's *Last Supper* (plate 16). Before going into each, she stands up straight in front of the camera, and then, "exceedingly slowly, takes up a pose, like an actress, with an astonishing intensity and verity. And when she has taken up the exact position of the model," she straightens up and bursts out laughing, a little girl again.[17] The clothes she wears are as significant as her gestures: they bespeak the time of the Cultural Revolution, as the gestures bespeak the moment of a grand betrayal that set in motion the revolution effected by Christendom, largely in the Western world.

The girl wears a white shirt with a red scarf under its collar and a pleated blue-checked skirt. The red scarf is the symbol of the Young Pioneer Group, and the artist said that it "represents a period in my memory, a mark of belonging to a certain generation, the desire to gain honor, the exciting and yet unsettling sentiment of being urged on by the martyrs who created the People's Republic, and even more so, the doubt and the quest of identifying the relationship between the individual and the group." And the white shirt "was always so white, white even in dreams, and yet it also created an image that was not exactly so white and pure." That image could be of things not so pure done in the name of the People's Republic, or it could indicate that "the color of history is fading, . . . memory becomes vague and unreliable."[18] The clothes and their color evoke a mood and a memory that make vivid the glory and burden of the People's Republic.

The memories are uneasy because the years from 1966 to 1976 are put into as deep a shadow by China's embrace of capitalism as the shadow into which the Cultural Revolution put imperial China. The turn to capitalism was driven less by contradictions inherent in the world spirit's march toward self-consciousness or workers' growing resistance to exploitation by capital than by the electronic revolution. Therefore those trying to understand and adjust to the changes occurring in China in the early twenty-first century are denied the comfort of familiar explanatory theories grounded in historical determinism.

Under the sway of memories of the last heady decade of high Maoism and the sentiments they evoke, Cui Xiuwen goes not to a place below the level of language to that of instinct and matter, as do many avant-garde artists, but to a time before the individual gets caught in the web of language. Once the individual is immersed in language, she is at risk of losing touch with what is on language's other side—the stillness that can put one in touch with "the deep heart's core" of things.[19] She goes to the innocence of childhood: "I erase the whole process of growing up and let this girl bear the consequence of history. I let her balance herself in the process of breaking up, converging, evolving, and duplicating."[20] For this is what happens to the consequences of history when the present seeks to undo some of what the past has wrought: the historical past breaks up into shards that then either converge with elements in the present, evolve into something new, or blindly repeat.

The artist goes to the innocence not only of childhood, but also of gesture. The body speaks true in a way that words do not. Gestures, like words, can lie and be ambiguous or vague, but the gesturing body's physiological responses can be tamed only with an enormous amount of training and discipline. Fear, worry, embarrassment, shame, and much more write themselves on the bodies of those experiencing them. The body tells tales just as words do.

In the subject of *Sanjie*, there is this trio: the truth of the expression of the girl's body, the memory of the fifties through the seventies in her clothes, and the figures in da Vinci's *Last Supper* whose gestures she copies. In the media in which the subject is presented, there is another trio: an oil painting that was finished first, a photograph, and the video. It has been called "a composite artwork created with three methods," bringing to mind the triple accomplishments of the scholar artists who often put poetry, calligraphy, and painting into one work. In 2005 *Sanjie* was sold at auction in New York City as *The Three Realms (Sanjie)*. Were a fourth realm to be added and terracotta statues made of the girl in each of the poses, the statues could take their place alongside the Tang dancers and polo players in Paris's Guimet Museum.

The robust materialism in play in many avant-garde representations of male bodies has been said to strike a different chord when the bodies represented are female. The chord sounded in *Twelve Flower Months* and *Born with the Cultural Revolution* is of the body's flowering, and in *25:00, no. 2* it is of a dream of the woman-body. In each work the woman-body itself is the subject—for what it does perforce or for its dream of itself. The bodies are not like those in *Family Tree*, *Tattoo II*, and *Chinese Landscape—Tattoo*, surfaces on which puzzles about language and nature are displayed, to be trumped by the bodies that "wear" them. Although puzzles are typically worked out in the mind, avant-garde artists put them on bodies to show that mind is not always capable of them.

These male bodies are not necessary for the jobs they are represented as doing, however, whereas the female bodies are: even the body dreaming of its complicity with the moon and its rhythms. Their sex is what is necessary. But sex is not gender. While many male artists use their representations of bodies to raise questions in a highly conceptual art, many female artists go to a place deeper than reason to discover their woman-ness in a highly expressive art. They go to what goes on in their bodies and to what their bodies can be used to express, which is what *Sanjie* and the Tang dancers do.

Sex is not in play in *Sanjie*, but gender is. The little girl is the only one in the works discussed in these two sections who is clothed, and her clothes signify, as the curves of the robes of figures in classical art contribute to the expression of the vital rhythm of the earth and the sky. Here the clothes signify not the rhythm of the world but a set of desires and aspirations, a movement of the spirit of a time. Hers is also the only body that moves or gestures. Through her movements she is in harmony with the play of the world and of the human heart, with the faith and doubt, the love and fear that coursed through the men at the Last Supper, the men whose body language the little girl's body speaks.

Gender is in play in *Sanjie* because its artist is a woman. In her words, she has erased the whole process of growing up by making a little girl the subject of her art, as though by identifying with the girl she can escape the strictures of being a woman in what Chen Lingyang called "still very much a patriarchal society."[21] To see how gender difference is being defined in twenty-first-century China, look at representations of women in contemporary art and at who is making them. Women are. By way of their art, they are thinking and feeling their way through what it is to be a woman in China now, and the art they make has to do with them rather than, as in the West, with how they are regarded by men.

Chen Lingyang spoke for them all when she said, "My works have to do with myself and I am a woman."[22] She is a material woman, where matter is what composes earth and sky, woman and man, and all are subject to generation and decay. The all-composing matter speaks through water and stone, blood and bone, through its motions and its stillness, its music and its silences. We are here deeper than reason and below the level of language. Words come later.

Coda

In the West, beauty has been a member of the triumvirate of intrinsic values: beauty, goodness, and truth. Its appearances or instantiations have been characterized variously as copies of an ideal that exists in a realm untouched by time; manifestations of the mathematically balanced and harmonious relation of the parts of an object or event to the whole; and those things the mere perception of which delights. If there is a value in Chinese aesthetics that plays the role beauty plays in the art and aesthetics of the West, it will be as different from beauty as the conceptual frameworks within which Chinese thought and feeling operate are different from those within which Western thoughts and feelings work themselves out. There is no Platonic bifurcation of worlds into the unchanging and the changing; form, in its essence mathematical, is changeless and so is not a channel through which the world's breath flows. The vital spirit of a thing, rather than its appearance, is of value. And for artist and audience, what is of value is their capacity for the stillness and the silence in which the pulse of all things can be taken.

NOTES

1. Hsieh Ho, "The Six Techniques of Painting," in *The Chinese Theory of Art: Translations from the Masters of Chinese Art*, ed. and trans. Lin Yutang (New York: G. F. Putnam's Sons, 1967). The importance of this passage cannot be underestimated. Lin Yutang called it the most influential paragraph ever written on Chinese art and identified the first technique as "the sole, undisputed goal of art in China" (35).

2. "At the moment, China is witnessing a rapid growth in the economy, and with it comes unbridled greed and materialism. The idealism and altruism that once guided the Chinese conscience are gradually eroding. Like what the Cultural Revolution did, the money-centered mentality of today has threatened to destroy the Chinese character" (from a project proposal by New York–based artist Zhang Jianjun that is quoted in Wu Hung, *Transience: Chinese Experimental Art at the End of the Twentieth Century* [Chicago: University of Chicago Press, 2005], 206).

3. "A Conversation with Lu Jie, Chongqing, August 18, 2002," Long March Project, http://www.longmarchproject.com/english/e-discourse1.htm. While studying curating in London, Lu Jie examined the memory of his "individual experience in China, in connection with collective memory and consciousness of the quest for revolution." He was struck by the "romantic clash between idealism and pragmatism" in the Long March, during which the beleaguered Communist Army was on the run and yet the marchers were "constantly thinking the unthinkable, trying to imagine a new society." He found "what we now call the 'Long March Methodology'" at work in the production of the many "non-binary meanings" in the course of the current "transformation of the Chinese system—the translations, the different ideologies, locations, and geographies."

4. An elegant explanation of the absence is to be found in François Jullien, *The Impossible Nude: Chinese Art and Western Aesthetics*, trans. Maev de la Guardia (Chicago: University of Chicago Press, 2007).

5. This has a parallel in Immanuel Kant's analysis of the judgment of the beautiful: an object is judged beautiful when the understanding and imagination of the object's perceiver are working harmoniously as they would be if the perceiver were—as he is not—bringing the object under a concept (Immanuel Kant, *The Critique of Judgment*, trans. James Creed Meredith [New York: Oxford University Press, 1952], 50).

6. Gustave Courbet, *The Origin of the World*, 1866, oil on canvas, 46 × 55 cm, D'Orsay Museum, Paris. A naked female figure—cropped mid-thigh and below the shoulders—lies on the diagonal on a rumpled white sheet. Black background is visible at the upper left corner of the picture plane. It and the woman's pubic hair are the only dark things. The title alludes to the figure's anatomically detailed vulva, the origin of the world. The painting is visible at http://www.musee-orsay.fr/index.php?id=851&L=1&tx_commentaire_pi1[showUid]=125.

7. Melissa Chiu, *Breakout: Chinese Art outside China* (Milan: Charta Art Books, 2006), 92.

8. For the importance in contemporary Chinese art of the particular material used in a work, see my "Subversive Strategies in Chinese Avant-Garde Art," *Journal of Aesthetics and Art Criticism* 65, no. 1 (Winter 2007): 109–21, and "Water and Stone: On the Role of Expression in Chinese Art," in *Subversive Strategies in Contemporary Chinese Art*, ed. Mary Bittner Wiseman and Liu Yuedi (Leiden: Brill, 2011), 213–47.

9. Legend has it that Wang Xizhi, whose style of calligraphy shaped much later Chinese art, was influenced in the development of his style by watching geese fly, observing the bending of their wings and the curve of their necks.

10. Huang Yan, artist statement, in Wu Hung and Christopher Phillips, *Between Past and Future: New Photography and Video from China* (Gottingen, Germany: Steidl, 2004), 206. Published in conjunction with the exhibition "New Photography from Chicago" at the Smart Museum of Art, University of Chicago.

11. This quotation was included in a page about the artist at http://www.vam. ac.uk/vasatic/microsites/1369_between_past_future/exhibition.php, the website for "Between Past and Future: New Photography and Video from China," an exhibition at the Victoria and Albert Museum, London, in 2005–2006. The website for the exhibition is now defunct.

12. Chen Lingyang, interview by Melissa Chiu, in Hung and Phillips, *Between Past and Future*, 177.

13. Holland Cotter, "China's Female Artists Quietly Emerge," *New York Times*, July 30, 2008.

14. Ibid.

15. http://www.praguebiennale.org/artists/cina/chenglingyang.php

16. "And though the last lights off the black West went / Oh, morning, at the brown brink eastward springs— / Because the Holy Ghost over the bent / World broods with warm breast and with ah! bright wings" ("God's Grandeur," in *Gerard Manley Hopkins: A Selection of His Poems and Prose*, ed. W. H. Gardner (Baltimore: Penguin, 1953], 27).

17. Michel Nuridsany, *China Art Now* (Paris: Editions Flammarion, 2004), 238.

18. "One Day in 2004—Cui Xiuwen," *NY Arts Magazine* 12, nos. 9–10 (September–October 2007), http://www.nyartsmagazine.com/china-today/one-day-in-2004 -cui-xiuwen.

19. The phrase is from the last verse of William Butler Yeats's "The Lake Isle of Innisfree": "I will arise and go now, for always night and day / I hear lake water lapping with low sounds by the shore, / While I stand on the roadway, or on the pavements grey, / I hear it in the deep heart's core" (*The Collected Poems of W. B. Yeats: Definitive Edition, with the Author's Final Revisions* [New York: Macmillan, 1959], 39).

20. "One Day in 2004—Cui Xiuwen."

21. Lingyang, interview by Chiu, in Hung and Phillips, *Between Past and Future*, 177.

22. Ibid.

Contributors

Peg Zeglin Brand is an artist, Adjunct Associate Professor of Philosophy at IUPUI (Indiana University–Purdue University Indianapolis), and Adjunct Instructor in the University of Oregon School of Law Appropriate Dispute Resolution Center and the UO Robert D. Clark Honors College. She is the author of numerous articles in feminist philosophy and aesthetics as well as the editor of *Beauty Matters* (IUP, 2000) and coeditor with Carolyn Korsmeyer of *Feminism and Tradition in Aesthetics*.

Noël Carroll is a Distinguished Professor in the Philosophy Program at the Graduate Center of the City University of New York. His most recent books are *On Criticism* and *Art in Three Dimensions*. In a former life he was a journalist and the author of five documentaries.

Karina L. Céspedes-Cortes was born in Havana, Cuba, and migrated with her family to the U.S. in 1980. She is Assistant Professor of Ethnic Studies at Colorado State University. Her research and writing is dedicated to the study of Cuban tourism sex work and U.S. Latina/women of color feminist praxis. Her work has been published in the anthologies *Technofuturos: Critical Interventions in Latina/o Studies, This Bridge We Call Home: Radical Visions for Transformation,* and *Tortilleras: Hispanic and U.S. Latina Lesbian Expression,* and in the journal *Callaloo: A Journal of African Diasporic Arts and Letters*.

Stephen Davies is Professor of Philosophy at the University of Auckland. He is a former president of the American Society of Aesthetics. His books include *Musical Works and Performances, Themes in the Philosophy of Music, Philosophical Perspectives on Art,* and *The Philosophy of Art*. He is coeditor of the second edition of *A Companion to Aesthetics*.

Whitney Davis is Professor of History and Theory of Ancient and Modern Art at the University of California, Berkeley, where he has also directed the

Film Studies Program and the Arts Research Center. Most recently he is the author of *A General Theory of Visual Culture* and *Queer Beauty: Sexuality and Aesthetics from Winckelmann to Freud and Beyond.*

Mary Devereaux is a philosopher in the Research Ethics Program at the University of California, San Diego. Her current interests focus on ethics and the arts in medicine. She has published widely in aesthetics and feminist theory, including essays on ethics and the arts, cosmetic surgery, beauty and evil, artistic autonomy and freedom of expression, and the moral evaluation of narrative art. She currently teaches bioethics and provides ethics training to graduate students in the biological sciences in the School of Medicine. She also holds an adjunct appointment at California Western School of Law, where she teaches in the Health Law Program.

Allen Douglas is Professor of History and West European Studies at Indiana University, Bloomington. His most recent book is *War, Memory, and the Politics of Humor: The Canard Enchaîné and World War I.*

Jane Duran is Lecturer in Black Studies at the Gevirtz Graduate School of Education at the University of California, Santa Barbara, where she has also been a Fellow of the Department of Philosophy. She is the author of numerous articles on epistemology, aesthetics, and feminist theory. Her recent books include *Worlds of Knowing: Global Feminist Epistemologies, Eight Women Philosophers: Theory, Politics, and Feminism,* and *Women, Philosophy and Literature.*

Phoebe M. Farris (Powhatan Renape) is Professor Emerita of Art and Design and Women's Studies at Purdue University, and also the arts editor for *Cultural Survival Quarterly.* As an independent curator, photographer, author, and art therapist, Dr. Farris explores issues involving race, gender, indigenous sovereignty, Native American Studies, and peace and social justice. Her books, *Voices of Color: Art and Society in the Americas* and *Women Artists of Color: A Bio-Critical Sourcebook to 20th-Century Artists in the Americas,* create a dialogue about the intersections of social activism and the arts. She is a contributor to *IndiVisible: African–Native American Lives in the Americas.*

Cynthia Freeland is department chair and Professor of Philosophy at the University of Houston. She has published on topics in aesthetics, feminism, film theory, and ancient philosophy. Her books include *Feminist Interpretations of Aristotle, Philosophy and Film,* and *The Naked and the Undead: Evil and the Appeal of Horror.* Her book *But Is It Art?* has been translated into more than a dozen languages. Her most recent book is *Portraits and Persons.*

Valerie Sullivan Fuchs (valeriefuchs.com) is a new media artist. Her exhibitions include "Transparencies and Trans-formations in Contemporary American Art," U.S. Embassy, Stockholm, Sweden (2010–11); "Prospects," Sun Valley Center for the Arts, Sun Valley, Idaho (2009); "H20: Film on Water," Great Rivers Arts, Bellows Falls, Vermont (2009); "KY to CA," Contemporary Arts Forum, Santa Barbara, California (2004); Non Grata Film and Video Festival, Pärnu, Estonia (2005); Galerie Eugene Lendl, Graz, Austria (2005); BELEF Art Festival, Belgrade, Serbia; and "Presence," Speed Art Museum, Louisville, Kentucky (2005). Reviews have appeared in *Art Papers, Dialogue,* and *American Theatre,* among others. Fuchs is a lecturer at the University of Kentucky and a Kentucky Arts Council Al Smith Individual Artist Fellow.

Eleanor Heartney is Contributing Editor of *Art in America* and *Art press* and author of numerous books and articles on contemporary art, including *Critical Condition: American Culture at the Crossroads, Postmodernism, Postmodern Heretics: The Catholic Imagination in Contemporary Art,* and *Art and Today.* She is coauthor, with Helaine Posner, Nancy Princenthal, and Sue Scott, of *After the Revolution: Women Who Transformed Contemporary Art.* She received the College Art Association's Frank Jewett Mather Award for distinction in art criticism in 1992 and was honored by the French government as a Chevalier dans l'Ordre des Arts et des Lettres in 2008.

Jo Ellen Jacobs, who held the Griswold Distinguished Professorship of Philosophy at Millikin University, has two main research interests: Harriet Taylor Mill and aesthetics. Jacobs coedited *The Complete Works of Harriet Taylor Mill* (IUP, 1998) and wrote *The Voice of Harriet Taylor Mill* (IUP, 2002), as well as several articles on Mill. She has also written papers on the aesthetics of kissing, snow, shadows, and music, and edited dictionaries, journals, and a book series in aesthetics.

Carolyn Korsmeyer is Professor of Philosophy at the University at Buffalo. Her chief areas of research concern aesthetics and emotion theory. She has published a number of articles and books, among them *Savoring Disgust: The Foul and the Fair in Aesthetics* and *Gender and Aesthetics: An Introduction.* She is a past president of the American Society for Aesthetics.

Keith Lehrer is a philosopher who has written books on such diverse topics as autonomy, epistemology, consensus, Thomas Reid, and self-trust. His most recent book is *Art, Self and Knowledge.* He is also an artist, a painter, who has become involved with choreography, influenced by feminist performance art, using art to interpret art. His goal is to create a new unity of art and philosophy, "artosophy," an exhibition of the aesthetic value of philosophy in art. He has received many honors, most recently election as a Fellow of the American Academy of Arts and Sciences (2005), and has taught in the last decade at many universities: Arizona, Miami, Santa Clara, Stanford, and Graz. His greatest satisfaction, however, is the privilege he has had for fifty years now of contributing something of value to the lives of his students and colleagues.

Fedwa Malti-Douglas is the Martha C. Kraft Professor in the College of Arts and Sciences at Indiana University, Bloomington, where she is also Professor of Gender Studies and Comparative Literature and Adjunct Professor of Law in the Indiana University Maurer School of Law. Her most recent books are *Partisan Sex: Bodies, Politics, and the Law in the Clinton Era* and *The Bush-Saddam Tapes: From the Secret Iraq War Archives.*

Eva Kit Wah Man is Professor of Humanities at Hong Kong Baptist University. She has published numerous articles in refereed journals, creative prose, and academic books in philosophy and aesthetics. She was a Fulbright Scholar at the University of California, Berkeley, and the 2009–2010 Women's Chair in Humanistic Studies of the Association of Marquette University Women, Marquette University, Wisconsin.

Diana Tietjens Meyers is Ignacio Ellacuría SJ Chair of Social Ethics and Professor of Philosophy at Loyola University, Chicago. In Spring 2003, she held the Laurie Chair in Women's and Gender Studies at Rutgers University. She works in three main areas of philosophy: philosophy of action, feminist ethics, and human rights theory. Her monographs are *Inalienable Rights: A Defense, Self, Society, and Personal Choice, Subjection and Subjectivity: Psychoanalytic Feminism and Moral Philosophy,* and *Gender in the Mirror: Cultural Imagery and Women's Agency. Being Yourself: Essays on Identity,*

Action, and Social Life is a collection of her (mostly) previously published essays. She has edited seven collections and published many journal articles and book chapters. She is currently writing on three topics: victims' stories and human rights, art and politics, and psychocorporeal identity and agency.

Monique Roelofs is Associate Professor of Philosophy at Hampshire College. Her articles have appeared in journals, including *differences*, and in anthologies such as *Constructing the Nation* and *White on White/Black on Black*. She is guest editor of *Aesthetics and Race: New Philosophical Perspectives*, a special volume of *Contemporary Aesthetics*. Currently, she is at work on a manuscript entitled "The Cultural Promise of the Aesthetic" and coauthoring "Reclaiming the Aesthetic in Latin America" with Norman Holland.

Paul C. Taylor is Associate Professor of Philosophy at Pennsylvania State University, where he also serves as the founding director of the Philosophy after Apartheid program at the Rock Ethics Institute. He writes on aesthetics, race theory, Africana philosophy, pragmatism, and social philosophy, and is the author of *Race: A Philosophical Introduction*. He is currently at work on a book called *Black Is Beautiful: A Philosophy of Black Aesthetics*.

Gregory Velazco y Trianosky is Professor and former Chair of Philosophy at California State University, Northridge (CSUN). His work on moral character has been internationally published, reprinted, and discussed; and his more recent work on the history and philosophy of race has begun to receive national attention. His current research focuses on identity, race, and mestizaje, on the one hand, and a study of the altruistic virtues, on the other. Prior to becoming Chair of Philosophy, he held a joint appointment at CSUN in Philosophy and Chicano/a Studies.

Mary Bittner Wiseman is Professor Emerita of Philosophy and Comparative Literature at Brooklyn College and the Graduate Center of the City University of New York. Author of *The Ecstasies of Roland Barthes* and editor with Liu Yuedi of *Subversive Strategies in Contemporary Chinese Art*, she has also published articles in aesthetics, feminism, and ethics.

Index

Note: Black and white illustrations are marked with page numbers in italics (366). Works included in the gallery of color plates are marked with a *cp* and the number of the plate (*cp6*).

Abdul, Lida, 2–3, 10–11, 12, 23n3
Abuse of Beauty: Aesthetics and the Concept of Art (Danto), 8–9, 29, 32, 38, 41
acne, 198
Adorante or Adoring Youth (sculpture), 97, 98, 99, 100–101
advertising, 205, 208–10, 211, *212*, 216n71, 379
aesthetics: Chinese, 404–405; and economics, 82–84; and the erotic, 322; evolutionary basis of, 222, 268, 270–73; and feminist perspectives, 7–8, 144–45; idealization in, 96, 102–104, 110–16, 118; medical, 175–91; philosophical, 14; of race and gender, 9, 85–90; relationality in, 72–75, 89–90; vs. sensuality, xiv; of shock, 335–36; as social, 89–90
After the End of Art (Danto), 33–34
Agard, Nadema, 168, *169*
age, women's, 170, 174, 201, 259–65, 268–73, 322, 372–73
agency: of the body, 10, 12, 15, 138–39, 142–43; Danto on, 29–35; and empowerment, 14–15; and the gaze, 14, 322; women's, 322–23

Albani, Alessandro, 101–102, 109
Alexander Romance, 52
"All of the things I know but of which I am not at the moment thinking—1:36PM, June 15, 1969" (Barry), 30
Amer, Ghada, 133
American Gothic (Sharifi), 366–67, 366
American Headache Society, 178–79
ancestor veneration, 393–94
Ancient Crest of Ejagham Nigeria Dance and Face of Euro-Saint-Etienne Woman (ORLAN), 317–18, 317
androgyny, 254
Ang Lee, 38
anorexia, 209
Antinous (lover of Hadrian), 100, 101, 109, 119
Anzaldúa, Gloria, 230–32, 235–36
Aquí cuelgan mis vestidos: Frida Kahlo (Estebanez), 244–55, 245, 248, 252
Arabian Nights, 360
architectura, De (Vitruvius), 42
Aristophanes, 112–13
Army of Me (Cutler), 130
art: and beauty, 12–13; Chinese, 21, 385–405; concept of, 40–41; content in, 30–31, 40–42, 297–305; and disability, 6–7, 243–54; experience of, 297–305; Greek, 96–105, 111–14; homoerotic, 96–125; ideality in, 106–14; Indian, 282–84; moral order in, 77–82; Olmec, 314, 315; Phidian, 104–106;

art: *(continued)*
   philosophy of, 3, 8–10; visual, xiv;
      women making, 10–14, 137–57,
      162–74, 293–96, 297–305, 306–36,
      347–67, 398–404; works of, 31–35
art history: and male beauty, 96–125;
      and objectification of female bod-
      ies, 148, 149, 157n18; ORLAN
      and, 310–11, 326–27; and philo-
      sophical tradition, 8–10; and stan-
      dards of beauty, 6–8, 42
artworld, the, 12–13, 29, 298–99, 318
Ashery, Oreet, 129
Athleta paradoxos (Zeibich), 104, 112
athletes as models of beauty, 103–104,
      111–14
Atwood, Margaret, 137–38, 141
Augsberg, Tanya, on ORLAN, 323–24
Augustine, Saint, 62
Aurora Leigh (Browning), 197
Autrretrato de pelona (Kahlo), 251–52,
      253
Azouley, Elisabeth, 318, 334–36

Baartman, Sara, 16, 225–28
Bacon, Francis, 144
*Bahram Gur Observing Frolicking
      Women*, 358
Baker, Josephine, 197, 203–204, 233
Bali, dance in, 17, 259–79
Bali Arts Festival, 264
Banaji, Shakuntala, 281–82, 284, 285–
      86, 289
Bandem, Mandé, 264
Barbed Hula (Landau), 131
Barry, Robert, 30
Barthes, Roland, 250
Baudrillard, Jean, on bodies, 378–79
beauty: and age, 170, 174, 201, 259–
      65, 268–73, 322, 372–73; black
      and brown, 229–30; as concept,
      xiii–xiv, 8–10, 19; and disability,

243–54; as discernible property, 33,
      34; as disciplinary practice, 206–
      207, 210; as embodiment, 35–37;
      feminist revaluation of, xv, 7–8;
      and health, 175, 181–82, 188n7; as
      ideal, 6–7, 96–125, 306–308, 371–
      73; internal, 37–38, 40, 41; kin-
      esthetic, 212–13; and light, 201–
      202, 211; male, 96–97, 100; and
      meaning, 302; monstrous, 322–
      40; and moral order, 76–82; move-
      ment of, 259–60; norms/canons
      of, 3–4, 149; and the perfect, 42;
      and the political, 12–13, 19–21;
      as problem, 7, 8–9, 29–44; prom-
      ise of, 22; queer, 10, 96–125; and
      race, 45–64, 218–39; recent litera-
      ture on, 4–6; and relational labor,
      72–95; scholarship on, 1–25; and
      sexual attraction, 265, 270–73;
      standards of, xiv–xv, 14–17, 314–
      34; and the state, 368–83, 385–
      403; as value, xiii, 403–404; vir-
      tual, 313–14, 316, 319–21, 334–36;
      visual representations of, 3–4; of
      youth, 259–65
Beauty, xiii–xiv, 80–81
beauty pageants, 201
"Beauty Surrounds Us" (National
      Museum of the American Indian),
      162–74
Beauvoir, Simone de, 19, 333–34
Beban, Breda, 18, 293–96
Belmore, Rebecca, 132
Berg, Friedrich von, 109
Between the Two, no. 15 (ORLAN),
      309–11, *310*
Bhagavad Gita, the, 282
Binding Ritual, Daily Routine (Coble),
      129–30
biological basis of attraction, 222, 268,
      270–73

biotechnology, 187, 188n5, 190n26
Bird, Cass, 129
Birth of Venus (Botticelli), 309–11
Black Men (magazine), 218
Black Skin, White Masks (Fanon), 230
blackface, 308
blackness, 85–86
body, the: and agency, 10, 12, 15, 138;
    alteration of, 177–78, 225, 322–34;
    control of, 206–207; cultural views
    of, 220–39, 284, 342–46, 365–68,
    385–404; and disability, 243–54;
    enjoyment of, 322; and the femi-
    nine, 81, 138–39; gesturing, 400–
    403; idealized, 112–13, 210; image
    vs. schema of, 138–61; and mean-
    ing, 391–92; mentalized, 302; and
    mind, 88, 208; of movement, 259–
    60, 400–403; and nationalism, 131,
    132, 343–44, 369–82, 398–403;
    objectification of, 142, 148, 149;
    and performance, 10–12, 17–18,
    306–308, 389–90; pregnant, 398–
    99; regulation of, 378–80; reposi-
    tioning, 10–14; and the state, 372–
    76, 398–403; as starting point of
    beauty, xiii–xv; theories of, 139–41;
    types of, xv; victimized, 73; virtual,
    318; visual, 200–201; in visual art,
    xiv, 15, 138–57, 306–36, 385–403;
    young, 372–73
Body Project, The (Brumberg), 198–99
Bollywood films: and cultural history of
    India, 281–86; and difference, 17;
    and film studies, 286–91; gender
    roles in, 281–82; and Hinduism,
    280–81
Book of Songs, The, 380–82
Book of the Sky (Xu Bing), 392
borderlands idea, 231
Born with the Cultural Revolution (Xing
    Danwen), 398–403, 399

Boston, Keziah, 165, *167*, 168
Boston, Thelma, 168, *168*
Botox, 177, 178–79, 187, 188n5, 201
Botticelli, Sandro, 309–11
Bouabdellah, Zoulika, 132
Bourdieu, Pierre, 298–99
Brand, Peg Zeglin, 1–25, 300–302,
    306–40, 407
breasts, female: eroticization of, 223;
    evolution of, 222; implants in, 182,
    185; standard for, 372
Breathing (Song Dong), 388–90, 396
Bride of Frankenstein (film), 331–32
Brideshead Revisited (Waugh), 22
Brillo Box (Warhol), 33, 34
Briscoe, Carl, Jr., 168, *169*
Briscoe, Lorraine Nunn, 165, *166*
Brokeback Mountain (Ang Lee), 38
Brooklyn Museum, 10, 13, 126–34
Brown, Cecily, 144
Browning, Elizabeth Barrett, 197
Brumberg, Joan Jacobs, 198–99
Burke, Edmund: on black woman's
    body, 9, 85–86, 94nn56–57; on
    gendering of the beautiful, 76, 81,
    85–88
buttocks, female, cultural views of, 220–
    39, 278n49

Caliban, 64
Callipygian Venus (statue), 223, *224*
Camera Lucida (Barthes), 250
camp, 96
capitalism, 378–83, 391, 401
Carnal Art (O'Bryan), 326–27
Carroll, Noël, 8–9, 29–44, 407
Carta marìtima (Vespucci), 48, 50, 51
caste, 271, 277n35
castrato, Il (Kozyra), 130
Catlin, George, 320–21
Céspedes-Cortes, Karina L., 16, 218–
    42, 407

Chacon, Iris, 230

Chanel, Coco, 197–99, 203–204, 215n29

Chen Lingyang, 396–98

Chen Qigang, 21

Chiang Kai-shek, 371, 373

Chicago, Judy, 18, 126, 133, 134, 297–98, 304n4

China: classical art of, 21, 380–82, 385–86; Communist era in, 373–76, 386, 397–403; contemporary art in, 385–404; Olympics of 2008 in, 21, 25n39, 382; standards of beauty in, 368–82

Chinese Landscape--Tattoo (Huang Yan), 395–96, 402, *cp15*

Chronica majora (Matthew of Paris), 55

Cinema India (Dwyer/Patel), 283–85

Cixous, Hélène, 9, 72

class: and attraction, 271, 278n49; and beauty, 88–89; and body types, 234; in feminist art, 133; and sun tanning, 196–97; and veiling, Islamic, 344, 345

Clouds, The (Aristophanes), 112–13

Coast, John, 261

Coble, Mary, 129–30

Cok Ratih (Cokorda Isteri Ratih Iryani), 259, 260, 261, 266, 268–73, *cp8*

Colebrook, Claire, on politics of beauty, 7–8

colonialism, 229, 236, 290

colonization, 58, 60–61

Columbus, Christopher, 47, 49, 51, 57, 68n35

Conceptual Art, 8, 34

consumerism, 378–83

content, 30–31, 40–42

cosmetic/aesthetic surgery: as art, 306–308; history of, 176–77; legitimacy of, 178–85; limits of, 185–87; and medical ethics, 15–16, 180, 184–85, 190n29, 336n6; as modern, 14–15; as nonmedical, 175–77; ORLAN and, 180, 306–308, 323–24; vs. reconstructive surgery, 176–77

cosmopolitanism, 377–78, 383

Cotter, Holland, 397

Courbet, Gustav, 298, 304n5

Courtly Love (Sharifi), 356, 357

Criticism of Painting (Hsieh Ho), 385–86, 388–89, 396, 404n1

Critique of the Power of Judgment (Kant), 108–14

cross-dressing, 129, 250–55, 263, 275n20

Crossing Surda (Jacir), 131

Cruz, Bárbara C., 244

Cui Xiuwen, 400–403

"culocentrism," 220–21, 228–32

Cultural Revolution, 376, 378, 386, 398, 400–401

culture: and attraction, 270–73, 284, 322; and film, 289; and standards of beauty, 314–21; and views of the body, 220–39, 284, 342–46, 365–68, 385–403

Cutler, Amy, 130

cynocephali, the, 48, 49, 51–52, 62

Da Vinci, Leonardo, 400, 402

Dadaism, 8, 34

dance: African, 229–30; Balinese, 259–79; belly, 293–96; and the body, 17–18, 132; in Bollywood films, 285, 290; and the gaze, 294–96; in modernizing China, 371–72

Danto, Arthur: on beauty, 8, 29, 37–38, 40, 41; on ORLAN, 321; theory of art, 29–35, 41–43, 44n6

David, Jacques-Louis, 106–107

Davies, Stephen, 17, 259–79, 407

Davis, Kathy, 16, 177, 180, 188n3, 309, 311–12

Davis, Whitney, 9–10, 96–125, 407
Dazhai Iron Girl brigade, 374
de Bry, Theodor, 46–47
décor theory, 42
Delacroix, Eugène, 203
democracy, Athenian, 104–105
Deng Xiaoping, 376–77, 386
Derrida, Jacques, on Kant, 115–18
desire: and flesh, xi; as ideal, 102–104;
    subjugation of, 88
Devereaux, Mary, 15–16, 175–91, 408
Devouring Frida (Lindaue), 244
Diana, Princess of Wales, 202
Diáz, Porfirio, 248
Dibia, Wayan, 262
difference, ontological, 319–20
Dinner Party, The (Chicago), 126, 133,
    134, 297–98, 302, 304n4
disability: in art, 6–7; representation of,
    243–54
Disabled Body in Contemporary Art,
    The (Millett-Gallant), 6–7
Documentary Study: The Head of
    Medusa (ORLAN), 326
Don't Play in the Sun (Golden), 203
Doogan, Bailey, 299–300
Doric order, 42
Douglas, Allen, 19, 343–46, 408
Douglas, Susan, 209–10
Dove soap, 208, 216n71
Duchamp, Marcel, 33
Duffy, Mary, 6–7
Duran, Jane, 17, 280–92, 408
Dwyer, Rachel, 283–85
Dyer, Richard, 201–202

"East," the, 52–57, 66n22, 67n28
Echakhch, Latifa, 129
Eco, Umberto, 201–202
economy, beauty in, 82–84
écriture feminine, 9, 72
Elegance and Modesty magazine,
    345–46

embodiment: and art, 30; and identity,
    10, 12, 212–13, 312–13, 315; of
    meaning, 35–37
Emin, Tracey, 131
Enlightenment philosophy, 72–73
Enough (film), 233
Ensiklopedi tari Bali (Bandem), 264
erotic, the: and the aesthetic, 322; and
    beauty, xiii–xv, 115–16; comic,
    113; heteromasculine, 237; in
    Hinduism, 282; and homosexual-
    ity, 10, 102–103, 110–18; and the
    monstrous, 323–33
erotica, 116–18, 218, 237
Estebanez, Francisco, 246, 251
ethical, the, 77–81, 83–84, 120–21, 220,
    237–39
Euphranor (sculptor), 100
evolutionary basis of aesthetic judg-
    ments, 222, 268, 270–73
experience: of art, 297–305; of femi-
    ninity, 368–69; women's, 128–29,
    138–39, 150, 153–55, 157n1

face, the: cognition of, 250–51; and the
    gaze, 326
Fair Women, Dark Men: The Forgotten
    Roots of Color Prejudice (Frost),
    192
Falaise, Henry de la, 261
Faludi, Susan, 211
Family Tree (Zhang Huan), 393–96, 402
Farris, Phoebe Mills, 15, 162–74, 408,
    *cp*7
Farris, Sienna Capitola, 170, *172*
fashion: and aesthetics, 3; in Islamic
    world, 343–45; in modernizing
    China, 368–73; as political tool,
    19–20, 369–73; and tanning, 192–
    93, 197–99, 207
Feast of Id Begins, The (Sharifi), 358, 359
Felski, Rita, on feminist perspectives,
    7–8

femininity: and the body, 81, 138–39; and disempowerment, 75; effect on women, 6; and experience, 368–69; and modesty, 142–43, 343–46; standards of, 3–4; white, 86; in writing, 9, 72–75

feminism: and cosmetic surgery, 180, 182; and film, 289–91; multiple versions of, 10, 127–28, 308; and nationalism, 369–73; and ORLAN, 307, 308, 333–34; revaluation of beauty in, xv, 7–8; and subjectivity, 6; as Western, 10, 387–88, 397

Feminism and Film (Humm), 289

feminist art: and the body, 10–14; in China, 387–88, 397; confrontation in, 18; exhibitions of, 126–34; experience of, 297–305; ORLAN's work and, 307, 308, 326–27, 333–34

Feminist Theory, 7–8

fetishism, as enacted trauma, 329

FHM (magazine), 218, 227

film: afterlife in, 364; ethnicity in, 231–34; Hindi-language, 280–91; Hollywood, 329, 364, 371; monsters in, 329–33; theory of, 286–87, 291

First Love (Sharifi), 352, 355, 354

Fitzgerald, F. Scott, 196–97

flesh: and desire, xiv; in painting, 156–57

Fluxus, 34

Foley, Fiona, 131

Forberg, Friedrich Karl, 116–17

Forouhar, Parastou, 132

Foucault, Michel: on beauty as disciplinary practice, 206–207, 209; on queer ethics, 120–21

Frankenstein (Shelley), 53, 328–30

Frankenstein movies, 329–33

Frederick II of Prussia, 97

Freeland, Cynthia, 20, 347–67, 408

Freeman, Temeca, 235, 236

Freud, Lucien, 144

Freud, Sigmund: on castration, 325–26, 329, 330; on narcissism, 119; on sexuality, 117; on shame, 323

Frida (film), 244

Frida Kahlo (Cruz), 244

Frolicking Women in the Pool (Sharifi), 358, *cp14*

Froschauer, Johann, 50

Frost, Peter, 192

Frueh, Joanna, on ORLAN, 322–26, 328

Fuchs, Valerie Sullivan, 18, 293–96, 409

Fuentes, Carlos, 246

Fulcrum (Saville), 154–55, *cp6*

funu notion, 373–76

Gaillard, Françoise, 318, 334–36

Gaitskill, Mary, 137–38, 141

Gallagher, Shaun, on body schema, 138–39

gamelan music, 260

gandrung dance, Balinese, 263, 275n20

Gang of Four, the, 376

Ganymede (bedfellow of Zeus), 100

Gao Haiwen, 369–73

Garden of Earthly Delights, The, series (Sharifi), 363–65, 364

Gaskell, Anna, 129

Gay Moon, The (Yeats), 301–302

gaze: hegemonic, 237–38; male, 13, 150, 293–96

Geerlinks, Margi, 128

gender: of the beautiful, 85–87; vs. biological sex, 270–73, 402–403; and body image, 148; crossing, 243; "deep," 13; and disability, 246; and ethics, 79–82; norms of, xv, 157–58; and tanning, 197–99; transformations in, 129–30

German Expressionism, 8, 34

Gesner, Johann, 104
gesture, 401–403
Gibbon, Edward, 101
Gilman, Sander, 16, 176, 181
Girodet, Anne-Louis, 106–107
"Global Feminisms: New Directions in Contemporary Art" (Brooklyn Museum), 10, 11, 13, 24n16, 126–34
globalization, 334, 368, 376–77
Goethe, Wolfgang von, on Winckelmann, 107, 109
Golden, Marita, 203
Grable, Betty, 235
Greek classical period: ideals of beauty in, 3, 103–104, 108; pederastic imagery in, 96–105, 111–14
grotesque, the, 323–27
Guerilla Girls, 20, 298–99
Guerra, Vida, 16, 219; and beauty, 221–22; body of, 223, 227–29; as cultural figure, 233–34, 238–39; popularity of, 218–20

Haberl, Horst Gerhard, 12
Hadrian, Emperor, 100, 119
Hair (Sharifi), 352, 353
hairiness, 47–48, 53
hajib, the. *See* veiling by Muslim women
Hamza, Kariman, 19–20, 345–46, *345*
happiness, 181–82, 190n30
Harris, Ann Sutherland, 127
Hastanan, Skowmon, 132
Hausswolff, Annika von, 128–29
Hayck, Salma, 244
health, 175, 181–82, 188n7, 270, 271, 370–73
Heartney, Eleanor, 3, 10, 12–13, 126–34, 409
Heaven Can Wait films, 364
Heaven Can't Wait (Sharifi), 363–64, *365*

Hegel, G. W. F.: on art, 42, 44n13; on Olympia, 103; and Winckelmann, 107–108
Helen of Troy, 14, 328
Hem (Saville), 145, 150–54, *151*, 156, 160n34, 160n38
Henry the Fourth Part Two (Shakespeare), 99, 120
Hereford *Mappa Mundi*, 49
Herodotus, 49
heterocentrism, 226
HHH #4 (Foley), 131
Hinduism: and Bollywood, 280–91; role of women in, 266–67, 280, 282–86, 291
hiphop, 230, 234
Hippias major (Socrates), 30–31, 41
Historia naturalis (Pliny the Elder), 49, 103
History of the Art of Antiquity (Winckelmann), 103, 104–106
Hitchcock, Alfred, 295
homoeroticism, 9–10, 38, 96–125, 238
Honeymooners (Sharifi), *cp13*
hooks, bell, 13, 242n46
Horizon (Lehrer), *cp10*
Hottentot Venus. *See* Baartman, Sara
Hour of the Star (Lispector), 9, 72–75
Hsieh Ho, 385–86, 388–89, 397, 404n1
Huang Yan, 395–96, cp15
Hume, David: on the beautiful, 76, 89, 90; on taste, 82, 93n36
Humm, Maggie, 289
Hunter, Margaret, 206–207
Hustanan, Skowman, 132
Hutcheson, Francis, on moral order, 76, 80–81, 88, 89, 90, 91n14
hybridity, 203–204, 211, 334

ideal: in art, 106–10, 116; of beauty, 6–7, 96–125, 306–308, 371–73; Classical, 108; of erotic desire,

ideal: *(continued)*
102–104, 106–107; of health,
371–73
identity: and ancestry, 393–94; embodiment and, 10, 12, 212–13, 312–13, 315, 393; moral, 115; Native American, 163; nomadic, 335–36; and photography, 11–13, 14, 128–31, 309–21, 327; racial construction of, 130
images: of athletes, 103–104, 111–14; of death, 128–29; of martyrs, 355; in the media, 209–10; of Native Americans, 45–52, 69n39; pederastic, 96–97; racist, 133; sexually explicit, 13, 118, 133; and the state, 369–82; of war, 1–3
Interior Scroll (Schneeman), 301–302, 305n15
Interview, The (Emin), 131
Irigary, Luce, and Plato, 81
"iron girls," 373–76
Iryani, Cokorda Isteri Ratih. *See* Cok Ratih
Islamic traditions, 343–46, 347–67

Jacir, Emily, 131
Jackson, Michael, 203
Jacobs, Jo Ellen, 16, 192–217, 409
Jeffreys, Sheila, on cosmetic surgery, 15
Jessup, Georgia Mills Boston, 168, *169*
jianmei movement, 369–73
joged dance, Balinese, 263
judgments: of female attractiveness, 222; homosexual, 119; Kant on, 108–14; of taste, 101, 121; of white men, 88

Kahlo, Frida, *248*; disability of, 243, 247, 248; life of, 243–44, 248–50; paintings by, 246, 251–52, *253*; paper dolls of, 16–17, *245*, 246–54, *248, 252*; visibility of, 243

Kahlo, Guillermo, 248, 253
Kaler, I Nyoman, 263
kalliphobia, 34–35
kalon, the, 30–31, 43n2
Kamber, Michael, photograph by, 2, *cp2*
Kanon (Polykleitos of Argos), 111–13
Kant, Immanuel: on art, 44n13; on beauty, 101, 106, 123n18, 124n23, 404n5; Derrida on, 115–18; and Forberg, 116–17; and visual beauty, 334–35; and Winckelmann, 9–10, 108–14, 119, 120
Katte, Hans Hermann von, 97
Kauffman, Angelica, 328, 329
kebyar dance, Balinese, 263
Khally ballak men ZouZou (film), 343–44
Khoisan bodily modification, 225
kinesthetic meaning, 207–13, 212–13
King (magazine), 218, 235
Kiss on Tracing Paper, The Fourth Surgery-Performance Titled Successful Operation (ORLAN), 324, *325*
Klute (film), 289
Knafo, Danielle, 330–33
Korsmeyer, Carolyn, xiii–xv, 13, 409–10
Kozyra, Katarzyna, 130
Kristeva, Julia, and Plato, 81

labor: cultural, 73; and economics, 82–84; relational, 72–95
Lacan, Jacques, on Medusa, 325–26
"laddie" magazines, 218–19, 234
Landau, Sigalit, 131
landscape, 2–3
Lappe, Marc, 193
Last Supper (Da Vinci), 400, 402
legong dance, Balinese, 259–79
Legong: Dance of the Virgins (de la Falaise), 261

Lehrer, Keith, 18, 297–305, 410
Let's Dance (Bouabdellah), 132
Leveson-Gower, Ronald Sutherland, 97, 100, 120
Levezow, Conrad von, 100–101, 119
Li Shurui, 397
liberalism, 104–105, 226
Lin Tianmiao, 397
Lindaue, Margaret, 244
Linglong magazine, 371
liposuction, 187
Lispector, Clarice, 9, 72–75, 90
Livin' the Low Life, 233–34, 241n39
Loktev, Julia, 132–33
Long March Project, 387
looking, ways of, 220–21
Lopez, Jennifer, 227, 228, 231–34
love: homoerotic, 110; as male, 84–85
Love (Moffatt), 132
Lu Jie, 387, 404n3
Lyles, Phoebe Mills, 170, *173*

Magema, Michèle, 132
Mahabarata, the, 282
Maid in Manhattan (film), 232
makeup, 193, 202, 210, 344
males: as artists, 306, 328; beauty of, 9–10; conceptions of beauty of, 300; gaze of, 13, 150, 293–96, 326; judgments of female attractiveness by, 222, 260, 278n49; love and, 84–85; as martyrs, 355; as nudes, 238; pleasure of, 6
Malti-Douglas, Fedwa, 16–17, 19–20, 343–46, 410
Man, Eva Kit Wah, 21, 368–83, 410
Mandeville, Bernard, on the beautiful, 76, 90
Manet, Edouard, 13–15, 142–43, 148, 157n18
MangwiHutter, IngridRobert, 11–13, 14, 20

mannerism, 46
Mansfield, Elizabeth C.: on ORLAN, 328–33, 336n6; on Zeuxis, 14
Manual of Classical Erotology (Forberg), 116–17, 118
Mao, 386, 387, 398–99
Mapplethorpe, Robert, 238
Mariam (Sharifi), 1, *cp1*
markets, beauty in, 82–84
Mashantucket Pequot tribe, 164
Matondkar, Urmila, 281–82, 285–86, 287, 289
Matthew of Paris, 55
Maxiatures series (Sharifi), 356–63
Maxim (magazine), 218, 227, 232
May Fourth Movement, 369, 373
McPhee, Colin, 260–61, 262
Me--Without Mirrors (Semmel), 143
meaning: in art, 35–38, 40–41; and beauty, 302; and the body, 391–92; kinesthetic, 207–13; and perception, 301–302; visual, 200–201
Medusa, 325–26
Memory (Kahlo), 246
menstruation, 397, 400
Mercer, Kobena, 238
Meyers, Diana Tietjens, 15, 137–61, 410–11
Meurent, Victorine, 13–15, 142–43, 157n18
Mi vestido cuelga ahí (Kahlo), 246
Miaoke, Lynn, 21
Miles, Susie Boston, 165, *167*, 168
Millett-Gallant, Ann, 6–7
mimesis, 328, 329
modesty, 19–20, 142, 343–46
Moffatt, Tracey, 132
Mona Lisa, the, 306, 334
Monge, Priscilla, 133
Mongol invasion of Europe, 54–55
Monster/Beauty: Building the Body of Love (Frueh), 322–26, 328

monstrous, the, 9, 36; and moral order, 77; in movies, 329–33; ORLAN and, 18, 322–33; in painting, 144; and race, 49–54, 62–63; and the savage, 48, 63
moral, the, 7, 9, 104, 115, 118
moral order, 76–84
Morimura, Yasumasa, 316
Most Beautiful Woman in Gucha, The (Beban), 18, 293–96, *cp9*
Mother India (film), 285, 286
Movie Set (Sharifi), 362–63, *362*
Mr. and Mrs. (Sharifi), 352, 354, 355
Ms. Foggo (Bermudan Pequot), Pequot Powwow (Farris), 164, *164*
Ms. Foggo and Family Members (Farris), 165, *165*
mulataje, enactments of, 231–32
Mulvey, Laura, on male gaze, 13, 294–95
Muniz, Vik, 299
Muslim concepts of beauty, 19–20, 343–46, 347–67
Mutu, Wangechi, 130

Nachahmung (institution of pederasty), 100–10, 113–15
Nafisi, Azar, 355
Nair, Mira, 291
Named and the Unnamed, The (Belmore), 132
narcissism, 210
National Museum of the American Indian, 162–63
nationalism, 131, 132, 343–44, 369–82, 398–403
Native Americans: beauty and, 15, 162–74; European images of, 45–54, 69n39, 320–21; as "savages," 59–64
Nead, Lynda, on the nude, 139, 142–43
Neda (Sharifi), 351, 352
Neel, Alice, 143–44

neo-classicism, modern, 106–107
Neo-Platonists, 89–90
New Life Movement, 371
Njami, Simon, 11
Noachic legends, 9, 45
Nochlin, Linda, 10, 126–27, 243
norms: of art, 111–12; of beauty, 3–4, 6–7, 181–88; of gender, xv, 157–58; of medical profession, 177, 179–80, 185; queering of, 117–21; of sociality, 87
novo mundo, De (Vespucci), 53
nude, the: absence from Chinese art, 385, 387, 391; feminist remaking of, 137–57; male, 238; and male gaze, 13–15; as object of pleasure, 20–21; in pop culture, 218; queering of, 117–18; as Western, 21

objectification, 142, 148, 149, 238
O'Bryan, Jill, on ORLAN, 321, 325–27
Okada, Hiroko, 128
O'Keeffe, Georgia, 298
Olmec art, 314, 315
Olympia (Manet) 13, 15, 142–43, 148, 157n16, 157n18
"Olympic girl" image, 382, 383
"On the Ability to Perceive the Beautiful in Art" (Winckelmann), 109
One and the Many, problem of, xiii–xv
100,000 Years of Beauty (Azouley/Gaillard), 318, 334–36
Open Your Eyes (OYE) (magazine), 218–20
Opie, Catherine, 128
orientalism: and the "East," 52–57, 66n22, 67n28; and "monstrous" races, 52–57; Said on, 20, 347–48; and skin color, 203–204
Origin of the World (Courbet), 298, 304n5

ORLAN: aesthetic surgeries of, 18, 180, 306–308, 311–14, 323–24; Brand on, 300, 306–40; critical views of, 322–34; and feminist discourse, 307, 333–34; and identity, 309–21; as monstrous, 323–33; performance art of, 306–308, 324, 326; photographic work of, 309–10, 314–24, 331–33; public responses to, 300–302, 306–307, 316; and self-hybridization, 314, 334–36; and skin, 199; and virtual beauty, 313–14, 316, 319–21, 334–36

"ORLAN: Monster Beauty" (Knafo), 330–33

Ostojic, Tanja, 129

Othello, 78

other/Others: and beauty, 22; and dual belonging, 11–12; Europeans and, 61, 318; and Orientalism, 347; and technology, 1; and the viewer, 18, 20

Ottoman Turks, the, 54–56, 67n29

Out of Sight (film), 233

painting: beauty in, 38; Chinese, 385–86, 388–89, 397; feminist, 137, 143–61; idealization in, 111–12; mimesis in, 328, 329; and perception, 301–302; Persian miniature tradition in, 355–63

Painting Portrait of Wash-Ka-Mon-Ya, Fast Dancer, a Warrior, with ORLAN's Photographic Portrait, Refiguration, American-Indian Self-Hybridization, no. 3 (ORLAN), cp12

palaestra (wrestling grounds), 103–104, 113

Pallestine Square (Sharifi), 355, 356

"Parergon" (Derrida), 115–16

Patel, Divia, 283–85

Pather Panchali (Ray), 285

patriarchy, 204–207

pederasty, institution of, 100–10, 113–15

"Pelo Me Sum" melody, 293

Pequot Powow, 165, *166, 170, 171, 172, cp7*

perception, 301–302

perfect, the, 42, 104

performance art, 6–7, 10–12, 17–18, 143, 306–308, 389–90

Phenomenology of the Spirit (Hegel), 107–108

Phidian art, 104–106

Phidias (sculptor), 101, 113

photography: in art history, 33–34; in contemporary China, 393–403; feminist, 128; and identity, 11–13, 14, 309–21, 327; and Native American women, 162–74, 238, 250; ORLAN's, 347–67

physical culture, 371–72

Piccinini, Patricia, 128

Picture of Dorian Gray, The (Wilde), 120

Picture Yourself Here (Brand), 300

piercing, 193, 207

Pindar's odes, 105–106

Pin-Up (Self Portrait) (Echakhch), 129

Plato: and aesthetic relationality, 72–73, 89–90; and the body, 222; idea of beauty, xiii, xv, 80–82; on the ideal, 102; on subjugation of desire, 88, 93n36

Playboy: aesthetic of, 223; centerfolds in, 210; as mainstream, 232

pleasure: aesthetic, xiv, 133; and art, 7, 13–14, 30–31, 41; male, 6; and virtue, 88

Pliny the Elder, 49, 103

politeness, 76, 79

Polykleitos of Argos, 111–14

Poovey, Mary, on Wollstonecraft, 87–88
Pop Art, 34
pornography, 118, 125n24, 150, 201, 234, 282
poverty, aestheticization of, 73–76
Powhatan heritage, 164, 168
pregnancy, 398–99
Prince and the Balloon (Sharifi), 363, 364
Prince Hal figure, 97, 99, 100, 120
Prince of the World (statue), 36–37, 42
Printing on Water (Song Dong), 388–90, 396
Prop (Saville), 145, *146*, 148–50, 156
Propped (Saville), 145, 148–50, *cp5*
prostitution, 263, 275n20
psychocorporeal experience of women, 138–39, 150, 153–55, 157n1
punctum of a photograph, 250
purity, 262–63

qibao dress, 369–70
Qiu Zhijie, 394, 395–96
queer beauty, 96–125

race: and aesthetics, 86–89; and bodies, 16, 220–39; and destiny, 225–27; gendering of, 85–87; and hybridity, 203–204, 211; modern conceptions of, 9, 45; and the monstrous, 49–53; and moral order, 77–80; and the savage, 60–64; and skin color, 192–96, 206–207, 230, 232; as term, 63–64
Race, Gender, and the Politics of Skin Tone (Hunter), 206–207
Raha (Sharifi), *350*
Raka, Anak Agung Gek, 273
Ramayana, the, 280, 282, 283
Raphael (Raffaelo Sanzio), 38
Ray, Satyajit, 285
Reading "Bollywood" (Banaji), 281–82

Reading Lolita in Tehran (Nafisi), 355
Red Detachment of Women, 376, 384n13
Refiguration, Pre-Columbian Self-Hybridization, no. 1 (ORLAN), 315, *315*, 317
Reilly, Moira, 10, 127–28, 129, 133
Reincarnation of St. ORLAN, The (ORLAN), 306, 325, 328, 332
Reinhardt, Claudia, 128–29
relational, the: as labor, 71–90; as psychocorporeity, 153–55
"Rire de la Meduse, Le" (Cixous), 9
Rivera, Diego, 243, 246
Roelofs, Monique, 9, 72–95, 411
Rofel, Lisa, 377–78, 380, 381
Rogaine, 187
Room for Isolation and Restraint (Monge), 133
Rose, Tracey, 130
Rowland, Benjamin, 283, 290
Rudelius, Julicka, 130

Sackler Center for Feminist Art, Brooklyn Museum, 126, 127
Said, Edward, on orientalism, 20, 347–48
sandunguera tradition, 233
Sanger, Margaret, 297–98
Sanjie (Cui Xiuwen), 400–403, *cp16*
Sanssouci Palace, 96–97, 102
sati, widow immolation, 283
"savage," the, concept of, 9, 45–49, 57–64
Saville, Jenny: and autonomy of bodies, 15; and body schema, 149–54; feminist aesthetic of, 144–45; paintings by, 130, 145–54; on the nude, 141–42; reflexive practice of, 155–57
Savulescu, Julian, 184, 190n29
Sawada, Tomoko, 130

scar, 177
schema vs. image in the body, 138–61
Schjeldahl, Peter, 133
Schneemann, Carolee, 18, 300–301, 305n15
Schopenhauer, Arthur, on aesthetic idealization, 110
Scottish Enlightenment, 9, 76–82, 89
Seduction (Leila and Majnoon) (Sharifi), 360, *361*
Selena (film), 231, 232
self, visual vs. kinesthetic, 200–201, 207–209
self-esteem, 181–82
Self-Hybridizations (ORLAN), 306, 307, 314–21, *315, 317*, 326–27, 332, 334–36
self-image, 379
Self-Portrait as Marcus Fisher I (Ashery), 129
Self-Portrait with a Bride of Frankenstein Wig (ORLAN), 331–32
Semmel, Joan, 143, 159n23
sensuality, xiv, 207–208, 211
Serimpi, Anak Agung Alit, 273
sex workers, 132
sexual signals, 194, 206, 209, 234–35, 278n49
sexuality: and attraction, 270–73, 322; vs. beauty, 265; hidden issues of, 10; and the nude, 142–43, 150; queer, 91–125; unregulated, 343
Shaftesbury: on moral order, 76–81, 88, 89, 90, 91n14; on race, 87
Shah, Terjal, 129
Shakespeare, William, 97, 99
shakti, female force, 283, 284
Sharifi, Soody: background of, 348; and orientalism, 20, 347–48; works by, 349–55, 363–65, *cp 1, cp13, cp 14*
Shelley, Mary, 53, 328–30
Sherman, Cindy, 316, 323

Show (magazine), 235
Sidqi, Ni'mar, 344
Sikander, Shahzia, 133
Singh, Dayanita, 130
Sita figure, 280, 282, 283
skin: care of, 198–99; color of, 16, 71n59, 192–96, 203–207, 230, 232; literature on surveyed, 195; meaning of, 199–200
Sleep of Endymion (Girodet), 106–107
Sleigh, Sylvia, 143–44
Smith, Adam, on beauty and the economy, 76, 82–84; and social differentiation, 89, 90
Smith, Roberta, 133
social constructionist approach, xiv–xv, 9
sociality: of aesthetics, 89–90; and attraction, 271–73; of the ideal, 110; normative, 87; and taste, 101, 114
Socrates: on beauty, 80–81; David painting of, 107; on the ideal, 102; on *kalon*, 30–31, 41, 42, 43n2; on pederasty, 104, 115
Socrates sanctus paederasta (Gesner), 104
Song Dong, 388–90, 396
Song Meiling, 371
SPEED-TV, 233–34
Spence, Jo, 323
Square Words (Xu Bing), 392
Staden, Hans von, 50
standards of beauty, xiv–xv, 14–17, 314–34, 368–82
state, the, 19–21, 368–83, 385–403
Static Drift (MangwiHutter), 11–13, 14, 20, *cp4*
Stoics, the, 41
subjectivity, 6
sublime, the, as masculine, 85–86
symmetry, 43n5, 223
Symposium (Plato), xiii, 80–81

Tagged (Rudelius), 130
Taino, the, 51
Taliban, the, 2
tanning: aesthetics of, 16, 207–13; and
    endorphin production, 193, 211;
    future of, 211–13; and gender,
    197–99; meaning of, 199–200; and
    patriarchy, 204–207; and skin color,
    192–96; and social class, 196–97
Tarta Sari ensemble, 273
taste: Burke on, 86; Hume on, 82,
    93n36; judgments of, 101, 102,
    108–14
Tatars, the, 52, 54–56
Tattoo II (Qiu Zhijie), 394, 395–96, 402
tattooing, 193, 207, 394–96
Taylor, Paul C., 16, 218–42, 411
Teenagers series (Sharifi), 352
teeth whitening, 185
Tender Is the Night (Fitzgerald), 196–
    97, 207
terror, war on, 1
Theory of Moral Sentiments, The
    (Smith), 82–83
Thevet, André, 47
Three on a Match II (Sharifi), 352, 353
To My Little Sister (For Cindy Sherman)
    (Morimura), 316
Tomica, Milica, 131
Tongolele (actress), 233
*Too Beautiful to Picture: Zeuxis, Myth,
    and Mimesis* (Mansfield), 14,
    328–33
Transfiguration, The (Raphael), 38, 39
transsexuals, 130, 199
Travels of Sir John Mandeville, 49, 65n10
Troyano, Alina, 233
Tupinambá, the, 50
Twelve Flower Months (Chen
    Lingyang), 397–98, 400, 402
25:00, no. 2 (Chen Lingyang), 399–
    400, 402

Twilight Zone, The, 192

ugliness: in art, 36–37; and black
    women, 229; and economics, 84;
    and poverty, 72–75
United Nations series (Wenda Gu),
    392–93
Untitled (Saville), 145, 147, 148–50
Untitled #35 (hide) (Gaskell), 129
Untitled #96 (Sherman), 316

vagina, the, 298, 300–301, 326
value: aesthetic, 7; beauty as, xiii, 403–
    404; political, 83–84
veiling by Muslim women, 19–20, 344,
    348–49
Velazco y Trianosky, Gregory, 9–10,
    45–75, 411
Venus (goddess), 6–7, 42
Venus Baartman (Rose), 130
Venus de Milo (statue), 6–7
Veronica (Gaitskill), 137–38, 141
Vertigo (Hitchcock), 295
Vespucci, Amerigo, 47, 48, 50, 51, 53
Viagra, 187
video art, 2–3, 18, 129–33, 293–96
Villa Albani, 101–102, 109
virtual beauty, 313–14, 316, 319–21,
    334–36
Vitruvius, 42
Vogtherr, Cristoph, 97, 102
voyeurism, 293–96, 358–59

"Wack! Art and the Feminist
    Revolution" (Museum of
    Contemporary Art, Los Angeles),
    126
Walker, Kara, 133
war, 1–3
Warhol, Andy, 33, 34, 310
Wartenberg. Thomas E., 298
Watteau, Antoine, 97

Waugh, Evelyn, 22
waxing, 194
wealth, 83
Weitz, Rose, 207
Wenda Gu, 392–93
Western civilization/culture: and black bodies, 229; in Bollywood films, 281–82; canons of beauty in, 3–4; in China, 369–70, 387; feminism in, 10, 387–88, 397; nude in, 21; and race, 45–71; shame in, 323
Where the Girls Are (Douglas), 209–10
White Cloud: Head Chief of the Iowas (Catlin), 320–21, *cp11*
White-Haired Girl, The, 376, 384n13
White House (Abdul), 2–3, *cp3*
white privilege, 15, 236
whiteness, 85–87, 202–204, 211
"Why Have There Been No Great Women Artists?" (Nochlin), 126–27
Wild Man figure, 9, 45, 48, 53–54, 57, 59–60, 67n26
Wilde, Oscar, 120
Wilke, Hannah, 323
Williams, Sue, 143–44, 159n24
Winckelmann, Johann Joachim: and art history, 95; as guide, 102; and idealization, 103–105; and Kant, 9–10, 108–14, 119, 120, 123n18; on *Nachahmung* (institution of pederasty), 100–10, 113–15; paradox and, 9–10; on styles of Greek art, 100, 106; on taste, 108–109
Winckelmann und sein Jahrhundert (Goethe), 109
Wiseman, Mary Bittner, 21, 385–405, 411
Wolf, Naomi, on cosmetic surgery, 15
Wollstonecraft, Mary: on the beautiful, 76, 87–90; on the body, 9
woman repairing beadwork, Pequot powwow, *cp7*

Woman with Her Doll (Sharifi), 350, *351*
women: African, 16, 130, 225–28; age of, 170, 174, 201, 259–65, 268–73, 322, 372–73; agency of, 322–23; as artists, 10–14, 137–57, 162–74, 293–96, 297–305, 306–36, 347–67, 398–404; Balinese, 259–79; Chinese, 368–83, 398–403; devaluation of, 6; display of, 201; experience of, 128–29, 138–39, 150, 153–55, 157n1; health of, 176, 177, 371–73; Hindu, 266–67; Hispanic, 218–39; Muslim, 19–20, 343–46, 347–67; Native American, 162–74; and nature, 400, 403; objectification of, 142, 148, 149, 238; oppression of, 368–69; and power, 14, 201, 204, 209, 308; and sports, 198, 371–73
"Women Artists 1550–1950" (Los Angeles County Museum of Art), 127
"Women of Algiers (in their Apartment)" (Delacroix), 203–204
Women of Cover series (Sharifi), 20, 349–52
women's magazines, 379–80
works of art: defined, 31–35; meanings of, 35–37, 40–41

Xing Danwen, 398–403
Xu Bing, 392

Yanagi, Miwa, 129
Yang Peiyi, 21
Yeats, Jack, 301–302
youth, 259–65
Yuskavage, Lisa, 133, 144

Zeibich, Gottlob, 104, 112
Zeuxis (painter), 14, 111–12, 328–29
Zhang Huan, 393–96